COLLECTOR'S
VALUE GUIDE™

HALLMARK

Keepsake Ornaments

also featuring
Merry Miniatures
Kiddie Car Classics

Foreword by
Clara Johnson Scroggins

Secondary Market Price Guide
and Collector Handbook

Santa's Motorcar (1979)
1st in the *Here Comes Santa* series
Market Value: $650

A Cool Yule (1980)
1st in the *Frosty Friends* series
Market Value: $575

Rocking Horse (1981)
1st in the *Rocking Horse* series
Market Value: $580

Three of the most valuable ornaments in the Hallmark ornament collection:
the first editions of the **Here Comes Santa**, **Frosty Friends** *and* **Rocking Horse** *series.*

HALLMARK
Keepsake Ornaments

This publication is *not* affiliated with Hallmark Cards, Inc. or any of its affiliates, subsidiaries, distributors or representatives. Any opinions expressed are solely those of the authors, and do not necessarily reflect those of Hallmark Cards, Inc. Product names and product designs are the property of Hallmark Cards, Inc., Kansas City, MO.

Front cover (left to right): "Rocking Horse" (1st edition in *Rocking Horse* Keepsake series, 1981); "The Clauses on Vacation" (1st edition in *The Clauses on Vacation* Keepsake series, 1997); "Frosty Friends" (14th edition in *Frosty Friends* Keepsake series, 1993).

Back cover (top to bottom): "Starship Enterprise™" (Magic, 1991); "Betsey Clark" (1st edition in *Betsey Clark* Keepsake series, 1973); "1955 Murray® Champion" (Kiddie Car Classics, 1992), "HERSHEY'S™" (Merry Miniatures, set/2, 1st edition in *HERSHEY'S™* series, 1997); "Pansy" (1st edition in *Language of Flowers* Keepsake series, 1996); "Kringle Koach" (10th edition in *Here Comes Santa* Keepsake series, 1988).

Managing Editor:	Jeff Mahony	Art Director:	Joe T. Nguyen
Associate Editor:	Mike Micciulla	Staff Artists:	Scott Sierakowski
Editorial Assistants:	Gia C. Manalio		David Ten Eyck
	Katie M. Adams	Contributing Artists:	Lance Doyle
			Daryl Thompson

ISBN 1-888914-06-8

Collectors' Publishing Co., Inc.
598 Pomeroy Avenue
Meriden, CT 06450
http://www.collectorspub.com

CONTENTS

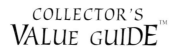

COLLECTOR'S
VALUE GUIDE™

CONTENTS

COLLECTOR'S
VALUE GUIDE™

Foreword by Clara Johnson Scroggins

Noted Hallmark expert Clara Johnson Scroggins is the author of six editions of the Hallmark Keepsake Ornaments Collector's Guide, along with several other books and a wide array of articles about ornament collecting. She counts over 500,000 ornaments as part of her ever-growing personal collection.

As most of you probably know, Hallmark is approaching its 25th anniversary of Keepsake ornaments in 1998 and so many people are asking me my impression of the first quarter-century of Keepsake ornament delights. This makes me feel nostalgic these days.

One of the things I enjoy about Hallmark ornaments is that you don't necessarily have to look back to the early days to feel this wonderful sense of nostalgia. Little treasures within each year's new assortment of ornaments always bring back fond memories of things I've enjoyed or people I've known. The 1997 Hallmark line has really captured many great nostalgic themes.

One of my personal favorites with a nostalgic touch from the 1997 collection is "The Lone Ranger™" tin lunch box that actually opens and closes! Other special nostalgic pieces from 1997 are "Howdy Doody™" celebrating the 50th anniversary of the popular television program, the "Tonka® Mighty Front Loader" and "The Incredible Hulk®." All of the STAR WARS™ ornaments this year will be a delight for many people, especially the superb "Darth Vader™" Magic ornament.

One thing that continually impresses me about Hallmark artists is that they can really do the human face and body. Movie buffs can turn to the 1997 collection for fabulously-detailed ornaments based on "Marilyn Monroe," "Luke Skywalker™" and "Scarlett O'Hara™" from *Gone With The Wind*. Even the casual sports fan can appreciate the wonderful memories of "Jackie Robinson" breaking baseball's color barrier – a definite favorite of mine – and "Joe Namath" leading his team to the Super Bowl.

So when people ask me about the "early days" of Hallmark, I look back with fondness, but really I tell them that for nostalgia, the 1997 collection is far superior to anything that's been done!

Happy Collecting and Happy Holidays!

Clara Johnson Scroggins

5

Publisher's Dedication

To Clara Johnson Scroggins . . .

On behalf of Hallmark collectors everywhere, we dedicate our first edition Collector's Value Guide for Hallmark Keepsake Ornaments to you.

Dear Clara,

> Your knowledge of Hallmark is endless,
> > *you are the true historian . . . .*

> Your glee at each new favorite is a joy to share,
> > *you are the true collector . . . .*

> Your warmth and care towards each and every collector you greet is special to us all,
> > *you are a true friend . . . .*

Collecting Hallmark is a fun-filled and exciting pastime for many of us. And as exciting as our collecting passions are, you, Clara, add so much more.

> To Hallmark collecting, dear Clara,
> > *you are the crowning touch . . . .*

Thank you,

L, L.L., Publisher

Clara Johnson Scroggins

COLLECTOR'S
VALUE GUIDE™

Introducing The Collector's Value Guide™

Welcome to the first edition of the Hallmark Keepsake Ornaments Collector's Value Guide! When the first 18 Hallmark Ornaments were introduced in 1973, the Christmas tree ornament began its transformation from just a pretty decoration into a creative and fun "collectible." Twenty-four years later, the Hallmark Ornament collection has become one of the largest and best-known collectible lines around. For many families, exchanging and collecting ornaments has become a beloved holiday tradition. With well over 3,000 ornaments in all, there are a lot of pieces to keep track of for devoted Hallmark collectors. And there will always be questions such as:

- What are the new ornaments this year?

- Which ornaments do I have in my collection?

- How can I find ornaments that I missed from previous years?

- How much is my collection really worth?

The Collector's Value Guide is an excellent source for answers to these questions, and many more. Inside these pages, you will find full-color pictures and information about every Hallmark Ornament issued since 1973. Collectors seeking those hard-to-find ornaments can learn how to look for them on the secondary market and those interested in protecting their collections will learn the basics of insuring collectibles. You'll also find an overview of the new collectible series, profiles of Hallmark artists, a list of the top ten most valuable ornaments and more!

Collectors interested in the value of their collections will love the full-color value guide section, which lists secondary market prices for every ornament. These values have been gathered from a wide range of sources from all over the country, and are a benchmark that collectors can use to price their pieces for resale, insurance purposes or just for fun. The value guide is designed as a worksheet so you can record the market prices of your pieces and find the value of your collection. A treasured companion for Hallmark Ornament collectors, the easy-to-use Collector's Value Guide makes collecting more fun than ever!

COLLECTOR'S
VALUE GUIDE™

Hallmark Overview

One of the reasons that so many people collect Hallmark Ornaments is the incredible variety of ornaments to choose from. Among the major classifications of Hallmark Ornaments through the years have been the original Keepsake ornaments, as well as Magic, Showcase and Miniature ornaments. This section provides a historical perspective of Hallmark's ornaments, as well as other popular Hallmark collectible lines including Spring Ornaments, Merry Miniatures and Kiddie Car Classics.

KEEPSAKE ORNAMENTS

The world of Christmas tree ornaments was changed forever with the arrival of Hallmark Keepsake Ornaments in 1973. Originally known under several names ("Tree Trimmers," "Christmas Tree Trimmers" and "The Tree Trimmer Collection") before being identified as the Keepsake Collection in 1980, this grouping has become the foundation of the Hallmark Ornaments collection with over 2,500 Keepsake designs.

From the simple yet innovative handcrafted ornaments of 1975 . . .

If it seems that nearly everyone owns a Hallmark Keepsake ornament, that's because it might be true! Because Hallmark typically releases ornaments for one year only, collectors have looked forward to new creative designs every year. The very first Keepsake issues in 1973 were yarn and glass ball ornaments, but within a short time, collectors could also choose from satin, cloth and metal ornaments as well as those made of materials such as wood and porcelain. Probably the most significant innovation in the Keepsake line was the introduction of hand-crafted ornaments in 1975. Designed to capture the "realistic" shapes of figures and structures, handcrafted ornaments were a big departure from traditional ball ornaments. Since then, production techniques have developed to the point that today's handcrafted ornaments feature superb detail and sharp, vibrant color. So, while it's strange to think of the hand-painted "Drummer Boy" ornament from 1975 as the great-grandfather of the 1997 "Mr. Potato Head®" ornament, there is some truth to it!

. . . to the colorful and detailed handcrafted designs of 1997

Hallmark Overview

The creative talents of the Hallmark artists (see *All About The Artists* section) is reflected in the many different styles, inspirations and themes of the ornaments. After releasing fewer than 20 ornaments in 1973, Hallmark has expanded to offer over 100 new Keepsake designs every year since 1982. There are religious ornaments, Santa ornaments, ornaments celebrating special events like a baby's first Christmas, ornaments based on cartoon characters, pop culture icons, BARBIE™ dolls, "Old World" art, sports, animals, historic events – you name the subject and there's a matching Keepsake ornament out there! Licensed ornaments – such as those depicting characters and designs from Disney, PEANUTS®, the Flintstones, Hershey's, etc. – bring familiar and popular themes into people's homes during the holiday season.

Some of the many different Keepsake styles and designs . . .

| Soldier | Classic Cross | SNOOPY® and | Holly and Poinsettia | Cheery Cyclists |
| (1973) | (1997) | Woodstock (1992) | Ball (1978) | (1994) |

Among the many new pieces introduced each year are the ornaments belonging to "collectible series." United by theme or design, the ornaments in the collectible series are a fun way to build a tradition of ornament collecting, whether it's the power and style of the *Classic American Cars* series or the elegance of the *Holiday Barbie*™ series. Each series has a new release every year, which is referred to as an *edition* ("1st edition," "2nd edition," etc.). One of the reasons that Hallmark's series are so "collectible" is the fact that each series has thus far been guaranteed at least three editions, meaning there are future releases to look forward to each year. When Hallmark decides to "retire" a particular series, it lets collectors know by designating the last piece as the "final" edition. Beginning with the *Betsey Clark* series in 1973, there have been a total of 75 Keepsake collectible series, with 41 current and 12 that are brand new for 1997.

COLLECTOR'S
VALUE GUIDE™

Hallmark Overview

Some Keepsake collectible series have existed for almost two decades, with *Here Comes Santa* running continuously since 1979 and *Frosty Friends* since 1980. There are several reasons why series are brought to a close, including soft retail sales, the natural conclusion of a theme (for example, after the 12th edition of *The Twelve Days of Christmas* series) or simply to make room for more exciting new series. Collectible series are also a popular feature of the Magic and Miniature ornament collections. For highlights of the many series debuting in 1997, see the *New Series Spotlight* beginning on page 15.

MAGIC ORNAMENTS

Known as the Lighted Ornament collection when it debuted in 1984, these were the first Hallmark ornaments to feature glowing lights. A real thrill was to come in 1986, when a special motion feature was added to the ornaments, making the entire collection come alive with moving Santas, revolving carousels and dancing animals. The lively collection was given its current name, the Keepsake Magic Collection, in 1987. Sound was added to some ornaments by 1989. The Magic ornament collection has offered some of the most creative and fun designs in the Keepsake line, and many of these have been special issues commemorating notable people or events (such as "The Lincoln Memorial" from the 1997 collection or "Space Shuttle" from the 1995 collection).

The Lincoln Memorial
(1997)

Like the Keepsake ornaments, the Magic collection also has had several collectible series. There have been a total of eight Magic collectible series, with three series ongoing in 1997. "Chris Mouse," the very first Magic series introduced, will come to a close after the final edition in 1997. Each year, Hallmark introduces approximately 20-25 Magic designs. Notably in 1997, Magic ornaments were mixed in with the general Keepsake line in both the Hallmark Dream Book and in retail store displays.

Space Shuttle (1995)

COLLECTOR'S
VALUE GUIDE™

Hallmark Overview

SHOWCASE ORNAMENTS

The Showcase ornaments made their debut as a separate collection within Keepsake ornaments in 1993. These creative ornaments were distinct for their exquisite designs and materials (such as porcelain, die-cast metal and gold accents) and were available only at Gold Crown stores. Nature scenes, traditional folk art and religious themes were featured prominently in the collection. No new Showcase ornaments were introduced in 1997, but several ornaments reflecting the styles and themes of this category were incorporated into the general Keepsake line. Two current Keepsake series were originally issued as Showcase collectible series, *Turn-of-the-Century Parade* and *Language of Flowers*.

Polar Bear Adventure (1993)

MINIATURE ORNAMENTS

The Keepsake Miniature Ornaments, which range between 1/2" and 1-3/4" in size, caused a not-so-miniature stir when they first appeared in Hallmark Gold Crown stores in 1988. These ornaments are somewhat harder for collectors to find (no, not because they're small!) due to their more limited distribution than their larger Keepsake counterparts. Many of the same wonderful features of the Keepsake line have been captured in the Miniature collection, including family themes and commemoratives, the use of materials like porcelain and glass and collectible series.

There have been 25 Miniature collectible series since 1988 and 16 are ongoing, including the four new series beginning in 1997. In addition to the series, a six-piece set of mice engaged in activities such as baking cookies or sewing, has been issued every year since 1991. In a typical year, there are around 30-40 new Miniature designs introduced.

Snowboard Bunny (1997)

Hallmark Overview

OTHER ORNAMENTS

During most years, collectors can find other ornament treats available beyond the regular assortment of Hallmark ornaments. Listed here are several of the most common additional categories of ornaments.

Collector's Club Ornaments

The Hallmark Keepsake Ornament Collector's Club was established in 1987 by Hallmark to accommodate the ever-increasing number of Hallmark Ornaments collectors. For a membership fee, club members enjoy invitations to special events, a subscription to the club newsletter and, best of all, a selection of exclusive gift ornaments and the opportunity to purchase Club edition ornaments each year. Serious Hallmark collectors have had more reasons than ever to join the club in recent years as several pieces complementing popular series have been available only to club members, including *BARBIE*™ and *Kiddie Car Classics* ornaments. (For more information on the 1997 Collector's Club, see the *Collectors' Corner* section).

Premiere Ornaments

As the name indicates, National Keepsake Ornament Premiere events mark the unveiling of the year's Keepsake collection in retail stores. Only Hallmark Gold Crown stores can host these events and there usually are special ornaments offered only at the Premiere. The fifth annual National Keepsake Ornament Premiere events were held on July 19-20, 1997 and two exclusive pieces were available: "The Perfect Tree, Tender Touches," an ornament which features a mommy and son mouse stringing a tree with holly berries, and a three-piece set of Merry Miniatures, "Snowbear Season," which depicts two tiny bears making a snowbear.

COLLECTOR'S
VALUE GUIDE™

Hallmark Overview

REACH Ornaments

The REACH program, which ran from 1989 to 1995, consisted of exclusive pieces that could be purchased for a special price with a minimum Hallmark purchase. The individual pieces making up the themed sets, including ornaments such as PEANUTS® characters (1995) or Santa and his reindeer (1992), were offered over a several week period in November and December from selected Gold Crown dealers.

Artists On Tour Ornaments

Each year since 1993, Hallmark has introduced a special artist signing piece available at national Artists On Tour and Expo events. These events are a real treat for Hallmark Ornaments collectors, who can meet with Hallmark artists, win prizes and purchase exclusive ornaments. Along with other surprises, there are two exclusive Artists On Tour ornaments for 1997: the latest artist signing piece, "Trimming Santa's Tree" (set/2), which is a collaboration of 19 Hallmark artists and bears the pre-printed signatures of every contributing artist, and "Mrs. Claus's Story," a companion piece depicting Mrs. Claus enjoying a good read in a comfy chair. There will be 10 Artists On Tour events held in 1997 from July 26 to November 1 in selected U.S. cities.

Personalized Ornaments

Offered between 1993 and 1995, Hallmark Personalized ornaments gave collectors a unique way to convey a personal message to someone they loved. The ornaments came in a variety of themes and styles and were available through Gold Crown dealers. Collectors could select an ornament, write their message on a form and file it with their retailer, who then ordered the ornament directly from Hallmark imprinted with the personal message.

COLLECTOR'S
VALUE GUIDE™

Hallmark Overview

SPRING ORNAMENTS

Hallmark started a new ornament tradition in 1991 with the issue of the first Keepsake Spring Ornaments (originally called "Easter Ornaments"). Including the 19 new releases for 1997, there have been a total of 120 Spring Ornaments. The collection is built on springtime themes with no shortage of bunnies, geese and ducks. Like the Christmas Keepsake ornament collections, the Spring Ornaments have their own collectible series as well as designs featuring BARBIE™, Kiddie Car Classics and PEANUTS® characters.

MERRY MINIATURES

Another popular Hallmark collectible that has been around almost as long as the Keepsake Ornaments is the Merry Miniatures line, which features tiny figurines of clowns, bears, dogs, cats, bunnies and lots of other critters having a *little* fun. First issued in 1974, the Merry Miniatures are generally grouped according to seasons and also have collectible series. Recent trends for the diminutive figurines include more multiple-piece sets in boxes as well as the individual Hallmark artists being credited for their creations, as they are for their Keepsake ornament work.

KIDDIE CAR CLASSICS

One of Hallmark's most successful non-ornament collectibles, the Kiddie Car Classics line consists of die-cast metal versions of the old pedal cars popular from the 1930s to the 1960s. These miniature cars, first issued by Hallmark in 1992, feature bright colors, amazing detail, moving pedals and real rubber tires. In addition to general releases, there also are limited editions of 29,500 and "Luxury Editions," which are more elaborate in design and are limited to 24,500 pieces. Several of the early releases had even smaller edition sizes of 14,500 and 19,500. Like the ornament series based on Kiddie Cars, this collection brings a sense of nostalgia to collectors who may have had pedal cars growing up, and introduces younger collectors to a new world of fun.

New Series Spotlight

There's an old saying that goes "The best time to plant a tree is 20 years ago, and the second best time is now." These words are especially true when you're talking about the Hallmark Ornament collectible series. Think of how great it would be to have collected the *Here Comes Santa* series right from the first edition in 1979. While many series have come and gone in the course of 24 years of Hallmark ornaments, collectors can always look forward to the start of exciting new series every year. In 1997, 12 new series debut in the Keepsake line (3 of which are Disney-related!), one in the Magic line and four in the Miniature line. So if any of the following first editions catch your eye, now is the time to sow the seed of your own Hallmark tree!

NEW KEEPSAKE SERIES

The Clauses on Vacation – Making toys, taking care of all those little elves and spreading holiday cheer all over the world in one night is no small job, and the Clauses deserve a vacation just like everyone else! In the first edition of *The Clauses on Vacation* series, Santa has talked Mrs. Claus into going fishing and if it weren't for that fluffy white beard, one might not even recognize this disguised St. Nick, dressed in his rustic denim overalls and fisherman's cap. But Mrs. Claus is a good sport (she's even carrying their catch), but maybe that's because he promised that she gets to pick the vacation spot next year.

The Clauses on Vacation
(1st edition)

Disney – For years, Hallmark ornaments have featured classic Disney scenes and characters. Now Hallmark introduces the first edition in the new *Disney* series: "Cinderella" brings the magic of Disney alive, standing on a platform in front of an ornate golden mirror reflecting a castle and chariot. Posed in a graceful curtsy, this fair-haired beauty is sure to grant the wishes of many ornament collectors.

Cinderella
(1st edition)

New Series Spotlight

Hallmark Archives – This new series kicks off in 1997 with a real furor, as the first edition depicts a harried Donald Duck who's wrapped himself up in a Christmas present! This delightful new edition also comes with a collector's card, making the ornament a can't miss for ornament collectors and Disney enthusiasts alike.

Donald's Surprising Gift
(1st edition)

Hockey Greats – Wayne Gretzky shoots and scores as the first edition in the *Hockey Greats* series. With stick raised high enough to have just taken the winning shot, "The Great One" will be the Stanley Cup of ornaments in 1997. And there's not just one but two ways to collect this series as the ornament comes with an exclusive trading card which features Gretzky's photograph and career statistics.

Wayne Gretzky
(1st edition)

Majestic Wilderness – The beauty of nature is celebrated in the new *Majestic Wilderness* series with the first edition, "Snowshoe Rabbits in Winter." The depiction of three white rabbits enjoying the shelter of a snow-capped log will warm the hearts of collectors at Christmastime.

Snowshoe Rabbits in Winter,
Mark Newman
(1st edition)

Marilyn Monroe – Stepping right out of "Diamonds Are A Girl's Best Friend," Marilyn Monroe is immortalized in this new Keepsake series. Wearing a pink gown, complete with large bow on the back, matching gloves, and of course, a brilliant array of diamonds on her necklace and bracelets, the legendary blonde bombshell poses her way into the hearts of Hallmark ornament collectors.

Marilyn Monroe
(1st edition)

COLLECTOR'S
VALUE GUIDE™

Mickey's Holiday Parade – This new series marches into the Keepsake collection with "Bandleader Mickey," a first edition featuring everyone's favorite mouse beating a big bass drum. Dressed in a drum major's uniform and hat, Mickey makes a striking first issue in a series that promises many delightful releases in the future.

Bandleader Mickey
(1st edition)

Scarlett O'Hara™ – Collectors won't be saying, "Frankly, Scarlett, I don't give a . . . " when they see the first release in this new series. Dressed in her scarlet gown, with ornate sleeves and matching trim on the skirt and sequins aligning the neck, long gloves and net veil, this heroine proudly awaits the return of her beloved Rhet from the Civil War. Collectors should act fast to get this classic piece before it is *gone with the wind*!

Scarlett O'Hara™
(1st edition)

Sky's the Limit – This new series celebrates the wonders of air flight with the first edition, "The Flight at Kitty Hawk." This piece immortalizes the Wright brothers' first successful venture into the realm of flight. The fine details of the wings and tail will make this ornament a soaring success with collectors and history buffs alike.

The Flight at Kitty Hawk
(1st edition)

STAR WARS™ – With the recent revival of the STAR WARS™ trilogy on the big screen, it is quite appropriate that Hallmark unveils its own line of space age ornaments with the first release in the series, "Luke Skywalker™." This future Jedi Knight holds his light saber at the ready; with a blaster strapped to his side, Luke looks prepared to take on The Empire's worst.

Luke Skywalker™
(1st edition)

COLLECTOR'S
VALUE GUIDE™

New Series Spotlight

Stock Car Champions – "Jeff Gordon®" is ahead of the pack as the first to race in the *Stock Car Champions* series. A Winston Cup champion, Gordon made his sponsors proud, and collectors will be just as proud to have this new ornament hanging on their trees (as well as in their sports card albums, as this ornament comes with its very own exclusive trading card).

Jeff Gordon®
(1st edition)

Thomas Kinkade – The work of the "Painter of Light" shines into the Keepsake collection with the first edition in the *Thomas Kinkade* series. In "Victorian Christmas," the sunset illuminates a classic Victorian home as light shines outward from the house's windows. Pedestrians pass by, sharing the road with a horse drawn buggy. The oval gold frame is the perfect complement to the golden hue of the skyline.

Victorian Christmas Thomas
Kinkade, Painter of Light™
(1st edition)

NEW MAGIC SERIES

Lighthouse Greetings – Mr. and Mrs. Claus string lights on a tree while a penguin holds a mallet, ready to ring the bell of Christmas cheer in the first edition of the *Lighthouse Greetings* series. High overhead in a festively painted lighthouse, a beacon flashes messages across the land to weary travelers that there is always plenty of warmth at the Claus house.

Lighthouse Greetings
(1st edition)

NEW MINIATURE SERIES

Antique Tractors – A shiny red tractor is the first edition in the *Antique Tractors* series. With wheels that really turn and a pivoting cross bar, collectors will feel like they are down on the farm with this series of ornaments.

Antique Tractors
(1st edition)

Snowflake Ballet – The first star of the *Snowflake Ballet* pirouettes into the Miniature collection. The ice-blue body of her tutu is accentuated with a skirt and collar made from snowflakes. With eyes closed, this beauty will dance her way into the hearts of ornament collectors.

Snowflake Ballet
(1st edition)

Teddy-Bear Style – This dapper little bear is quite the fashion plate in the world Keepsake Miniature Ornaments. The golden teddy's dress is perfectly coordinated, as his green vest matches his hat, his red tie matches the hat band and his white collar matches the handkerchief peeking out of his vest pocket. Future editions in this brand new series will add a small bit of style to collectors' Christmas trees!

Teddy-Bear Style
(1st edition)

Welcome Friends – The warmth of friendship is celebrating *Welcome Friends*, a new Miniature series depicting woodland animals gathering together. In the first edition, a squirrel, two bluebirds and a cardinal share a drink of water from half an acorn. Three tiny gold-colored chains will let you suspend these little critters from your Christmas tree.

Welcome Friends
(1st edition)

Collections & "Unannounced" Series

COLLECTIONS

Unlike the collectible series, which are issued one ornament per year over a period of time, collections are a group of ornaments with a common theme which are all released the same year and sometimes are followed by new additions in later years. The collections are a fun way for collectors to add a "ready made" ornament group to their Christmas trees. The following section features several (but not all!) of the most popular Hallmark ornament collections.

LOONEY TUNES™

Straight out of a Saturday morning cartoon come Bugs Bunny and his pals in this collection that has proven to be a big hit with kids and adults alike! This wacky collection has featured 14 Keepsake ornaments and two Magic ornaments since its inception in 1993.

Top Row (left to right): Bugs Bunny (1993), Porky Pig (1993), Road Runner and Wile E. Coyote (magic, 1993), Sylvester and Tweety (1993), Elmer Fudd (1993), Road Runner and Wile E. Coyote (1994) **Middle Row:** Speedy Gonzales (1994), Tasmanian Devil (1994), Yosemite Sam (1994), Daffy Duck (1994), Sylvester and Tweety (set/2, 1995) **Bottom Row:** Bugs Bunny (1995), Marvin the Martian (1996), Foghorn Leghorn and Henery Hawk (set/2, 1996), Decorator Taz (magic, 1997), Michigan J. Frog (1997)

COLLECTOR'S
VALUE GUIDE™

Collections & "Unannounced" Series

Mickey & Co.

An exciting new collection for 1997 is this six-piece group that captures favorite Disney characters with their classic 1930s look. Mickey is the "main mouse" of the collection, but Goofy, Donald and the beloved Minnie get into the winter fun as well.

Top Row (left to right): Mickey's Long Shot (1997), Goofy's Ski Adventure (1997),
New Pair of Skates (1997)
Bottom Row: Bandleader Mickey (1997), Donald's Surprising Gift (1997),
Mickey's Snow Angel (1997)

Noah's Ark (Miniature)

In 1994, a three-piece Miniature set, "Noah's Ark," set sail to collectors' delight. The display ark, featuring a removable deck and a poseable ladder, provided collectors with many display options. A pair of seals and a pair of bears were the first animals to join the adventure. Four more pairs of animals have been released in subsequent years.

Left to right: Noah's Ark (set/3, 1994), Merry Walruses (1995), Playful Penguins (1995), African
Elephants (1996), Gentle Giraffes (1997)

Collections & "Unannounced" Series

Star Trek

Hallmark takes collectors where no Christmas ornament has gone before with this collection based on the science fiction phenomenon, *Star Trek*. Every year since 1991, Hallmark has introduced at least one Magic ornament featuring a *Star Trek* spaceship. In 1995, Hallmark began introducing ornaments featuring many popular crew members from both the old and new incarnations of the show. Thus far there have been eight Magic ornaments released, as well as six Keepsake ornaments and one Miniature set.

Top Row (left to right): Starship Enterprise™ (magic, 1991), Shuttlecraft Galileo™ From the Starship Enterprise™ (magic, 1992), U.S.S. Enterprise™ THE NEXT GENERATION™ (magic, 1993), Klingon Bird of Prey™ (magic, 1994)

Middle Row: The Ships of STAR TREK® (miniature, set/3, 1995), Romulan Warbird™ (magic, 1995), Captain James T. Kirk (1995), Captain Jean-Luc Picard (1995), Commander William T. Riker™ (1996)

Bottom Row: Mr. Spock (1996), STAR TREK®, 30 Years (magic, set/2, 1996), U.S.S. Voyager™ (magic, 1996), U.S.S. Defiant™ (magic, 1997), Commander Data™ (1997), Dr. Leonard H. McCoy™ (1997)

Collections & "Unannounced" Series

Winnie-the-Pooh

Straight from the Hundred Acre Wood comes Winnie-the-Pooh and all his friends in this delightful and prolific collection, which debuted in 1991. In addition to the 17 Keepsake ornaments, there have been four Magic and two Miniature releases featuring this "hunny" of a bear.

Top Row (left to right): Kanga and Roo (1991), Christopher Robin (1991), Rabbit (1991), Winnie-the-Pooh (1991), Piglet and Eeyore (1991), Tigger (1991) **2nd Row:** Owl (1992), Rabbit (1993), Winnie the Pooh (1993), Kanga and Roo (1993), Eeyore (1993), Owl (1993) **3rd Row:** Tigger and Piglet (1993), Winnie the Pooh (magic, 1993), Winnie the Pooh and Tigger (1994), Winnie the Pooh Parade (magic, 1994), Winnie the Pooh and Tigger (1995), Winnie the Pooh Too Much Hunny (magic, 1995) **Bottom Row:** Slippery Day (magic, 1996), Winnie the Pooh and Tigger (miniature, 1996), Winnie the Pooh and Piglet (1996), Honey of a Gift (miniature, 1997), Waitin' on Santa (1997)

COLLECTOR'S
VALUE GUIDE™

Collections & "Unannounced" Series

The WIZARD OF OZ™

If we're not in Kansas anymore, we must be pretty close! This enchanting collection based on the classic film began in 1994 and now consists of eight Keepsake ornaments, one Magic ornament and a new Miniature set.

Top Row (left to right): The Cowardly Lion (1994), Dorothy and Toto (1994), The Scarecrow (1994), The Tin Man (1994)
Middle Row: Glinda, Witch of the North (1995), Emerald City (magic, 1996), Witch of the West (1996), The Wizard of Oz™ (club edition, 1996)
Bottom Row: Miss Gulch (1997), King of the Forest (miniature, set/4, 1997)

"UNANNOUNCED" SERIES

In addition to collectible series and collections, there are several groupings of Keepsake ornaments that are strongly connected by theme and are issued from year to year. While not official series, these ornaments can be considered "unannounced series" in that they offer collectors a chance to build a collection based on a favorite style or theme. One of the exciting features of an unannounced series is that it's only after the first one "got away" that we realize it's part of an unannounced series. The following is a listing of several unannounced series.

Coca-Cola® Santa

An ornament featuring Santa Claus enjoying a Coca-Cola® appeared in both the Keepsake and Miniature collections in 1992. Each year since, a new addition to the "unannounced" series has been released, making a grand total of six ornaments in each category.

Top Row (left to right): Please Pause Here (1992), Playful Pals (1993), Relaxing Moment (1994), Refreshing Gift (1995), Welcome Guest (1996), Taking a Break (1997)
Bottom Row: "Coca-Cola" Santa (miniature, 1992), Refreshing Flight (miniature, 1993), Pour Some More (miniature, 1994), Cool Santa (miniature, club edition, 1995), Cool Delivery Coca-Cola® (miniature, 1996), Ice Cold Coca-Cola® (miniature, 1997)

COLLECTOR'S
VALUE GUIDE™

Collections & "Unannounced" Series

HERSHEY'S™

The most famous name in chocolate has been the subject of a hand-crafted ornament every year beginning in 1993. Each of the five delicious ornaments depicts a pair of mice enjoying one of HERSHEY'S™ sweet treats.

Left to right: Warm and Special Friends (1993), Friendship Sundae (1994), Delivering Kisses (1995), Time for a Treat (1996), Sweet Discovery (1997)

Norman Rockwell Ball Ornaments

The designs of legendary Americana artist Norman Rockwell have been captured in many ornament designs over the years (including a collectible series devoted to his work). However, most of these heartwarming designs are in an unannounced series of ball ornaments issued from 1984-1992 and then 1994-1995 for a total of 11 pieces.

Top Row (left to right): Norman Rockwell (1984) Middle Row: Norman Rockwell (1985), Norman Rockwell (1986), Norman Rockwell: Christmas Scenes (1987), Norman Rockwell: Christmas Scenes (1988), Norman Rockwell (1989), Norman Rockwell Art (1990)
Bottom Row: Norman Rockwell Art (1991), Norman Rockwell Art (1992), Norman Rockwell Art (1994), Santa's Visitors (1995)

COLLECTOR'S
VALUE GUIDE™

Collections & "Unannounced" Series

Superheroes

Straight from the pages of the most popular comic books comes this grouping of handcrafted ornaments depicting some of the best-loved superheroes of all time. So far, this "unannounced" series has included six Keepsake ornaments and one Magic ornament. Which superhero will fly, leap or swim into this collection next?

Top Row (left to right): Superman (1993), Batman (1994), Superman™ (magic, 1995)
Bottom Row: Batmobile (1995), SPIDER-MAN™ (1996), WONDER WOMAN™ (1996), The Incredible Hulk® (1997)

COLLECTOR'S
VALUE GUIDE™

Hallmark Top Ten

This section highlights the ten most valuable Hallmark Keepsake ornaments as determined by their secondary market value. Not surprisingly most of these are ornaments in collectible series, usually a first edition (the notable exception being the 5th edition in the Betsey Clark series, which is number five in the top ten).

#1 **SANTA'S MOTORCAR (1979)**
1st in the *Here Comes Santa* Series
#900QX1559
Original Price: $9
Market Value: $650

#2 **ROCKING HORSE (1981)**
1st in the *Rocking Horse* series
#900QX4222
Original Price: $9
Market Value: $580

#3 **A COOL YULE (1980)**
1st in the *Frosty Friends* series
#650QX1374
Original Price: $6.50
Market Value: $575

#4 **TIN LOCOMOTIVE (1982)**
1st in the *Tin Locomotive* series
#1300QX4603
Original Price: $13
Market Value: $560

#5 **TRUEST JOYS OF CHRISTMAS (1977)**
5th in the *Betsey Clark* series
#350QX2642
Original Price: $3.50
Market Value: $450

COLLECTOR'S
VALUE GUIDE™

#6   ANTIQUE TOYS (1978)
1st in the *Carrousel Series*
#600QX1463
Original Price: $6
Market Value: $400

#7   CARDINALIS (1982)
1st in the *Holiday Wildlife* series
#700QX3133
Original Price: $7
Market Value: $400

#8   FROSTY FRIENDS (1981)
2nd in the *Frosty Friends* series
#800QX4335
Original Price: $8
Market Value: $360

#9   ROCKING HORSE (1982)
2nd in the *Rocking Horse* series
#1000QX5023
Original Price: $10
Market Value: $350

#10   STARSHIP ENTERPRISE™ (1991)
Magic Ornament
#2000QLX7199
Original Price: $20
Market Value: $350

Value Guide Instructions

How To Use Your Value Guide

The value guide section begins with Hallmark Keepsake Ornaments, which is split into two sections. The first section features all of the collectible series listed in alphabetical order by series name. Keepsake series are first, followed by Magic and Miniature series. The second section is a year-by-year alphabetical listing of the general ornament collections beginning with 1997 and following reverse chronological order back to 1973. Within each year, the order is as follows (when applicable): Keepsake, Magic, Showcase, Miniature, Collector's Club, Premiere, REACH, followed by miscellaneous ornaments. Separate sections devoted to Spring Ornaments, Merry Miniatures and Kiddie Car Classics follow the Hallmark Keepsake Ornaments section. An index starting on page 291 will make it easy for you to find your pieces within the value guide section.

Within each box, you will find a wealth of information about each piece including the material, artist abbreviation (see artist key below), item number and secondary market value. While most Hallmark ornaments are available for one year only, some pieces have been reissued in subsequent years and are marked accordingly. All secondary market prices in this guide refer to "mint in box" (MIB) ornaments, meaning both the ornament and its original box are in perfect condition. If your ornament has no box (NB), a damaged box (DB) or no original price tag (NT), the value will generally be reduced by 10%, 20% or even up to 40%, particularly for ornaments without the original box.

How To Total The Value Of Your Collection

The value guide is a great way to keep track of the value of your collection. In the "Price Paid" column, fill in the price you originally paid for your figurine. You can use the first 3 or 4 digits of the Hallmark stock number to figure out the original retail price of your ornament (for example, a piece with the stock number "1395QX5527" originally retailed for $13.95). To fill out the "Value of My Collection" column, use the value amount listed next to the item number and record it in the space provided. You can then total the columns at the bottom of the page (use a pencil so you can change totals as your collection grows) and transfer each subtotal to the summary pages at the end of the section to find the total value of your collection.

Hallmark Artist Key

ANDR	Patricia Andrews	FRAN	John "Collin" Francis	PIKE	Sharon Pike
AUBE	Nina Aubé	HAMI	Mary Hamilton	PYDA	Michele Pyda-Sevcik
BAUR	Tim Bauer	JLEE	Julia Lee	RGRS	Anita Marra Rogers
BISH	Ron Bishop	JOHN	Cathy Johnson	RHOD	Dill Rhodus
BLAC	Thomas Blackshear	KLIN	Kristina Kline	SCHU	Lee Schuler
BRIC	Katrina Bricker	LARS	Tracy Larsen	SEAL	Ed Seale
BRWN	Andrew Brownsword	LYLE	Joyce Lyle	SICK	Linda Sickman
CHAD	Robert Chad	MAHO	Jim Mahon	SIED	Bob Siedler
CROW	Ken Crow	MCGE	Diana McGehee	TAGU	Sue Tague
DLEE	Donna Lee	N/A	not available	UNRU	Duane Unruh
DUTK	Peter Dutkin	NORT	Lynn Norton	VARI	various artists
ESCH	Joanne Eschrich	PALM	Don Palmiter	VOTR	LaDene Votruba
FRAL	Tobin Fraley	PATT	Joyce Pattee	WILL	Nello Williams

Keepsake Series

Since Hallmark Ornaments were introduced in 1973, there have been 75 Keepsake collectible series, including 41 which are ongoing. An impressive total of 12 Keepsake series are making their debut in 1997, while 4 series are concluding in 1997. Among the notable new series for 1997 are 3 which feature popular Disney characters.

1

**1956 Ford Truck
(1st, 1995)**
Handcrafted • PALM
1395QX5527 • Value $30

2

**1955 Chevrolet Cameo
(2nd, 1996)**
Handcrafted • PALM
1395QX5241 • Value $24

3 NEW!

1953 GMC (3rd, 1997)
Handcrafted • PALM
1395QX6105 • Value $13.95

4

**Christy – All God's
Children® (1st, 1996)**
Handcrafted • N/A
1295QX5564 • Value $17

5 NEW!

**Nikki – All God's
Children®
(2nd, set/2, 1997)**
Handcrafted • N/A
1295QX6142 • Value $12.95

6

**Madonna and Child and
St. John (1st, 1984)**
Bezeled Satin • MCGE
650QX3494 • Value $19

7

**Madonna of the
Pomegranate (2nd, 1985)**
Bezeled Satin • MCGE
675QX3772 • Value $18

8

**Madonna and Child
with the Infant St. John
(3rd & final, 1986)**
Bezeled Satin • MCGE
675QX3506 • Value $27

9

Nolan Ryan (1st, 1996)
Handcrafted • RHOD
1495QXI5711 • Value $35

10 NEW!

Hank Aaron (2nd, 1997)
Handcrafted • RHOD
1495QX6152 • Value $14.95

11

BARBIE™ (1st, 1994)
Handcrafted • ANDR
1495QX5006 • Value $40

12

**Solo in the Spotlight
(2nd, 1995)**
Handcrafted • ANDR
1495QXI5049 • Value $28

13

**Brunette Debut – 1959
(club edition, 1995)**
Handcrafted • ANDR
1495QXC5397 • Value $55

14

**Featuring the
Enchanted Evening
BARBIE® Doll (3rd, 1996)**
Handcrafted • ANDR
1495QXI6541 • Value $25

15 NEW!

**Wedding Day 1959-1962
(4th, 1997)**
Handcrafted • ANDR
1595QXI6812 • Value $15.95

16 NEW!

**BARBIE™ and KEN™
Wedding Day (set/2, com-
plements the series, 1997)**
Handcrafted • ANDR/PALM
3500QXI6815 • Value $35

	Price Paid	Value of My Collection
ALL-AMERICAN TRUCKS		
1.		
2.		
3.		
ALL GOD'S CHILDREN®		
4.		
5.		
ART MASTERPIECE		
6.		
7.		
8.		
AT THE BALLPARK		
9.		
10.		
BARBIE™		
11.		
12.		
13.		
14.		
15.		
16.		
PENCIL TOTALS		

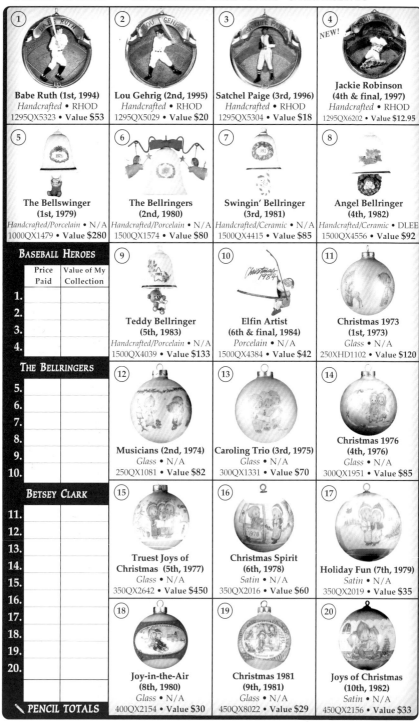

(1)
Babe Ruth (1st, 1994)
Handcrafted • RHOD
1295QX5323 • **Value $53**

(2)
Lou Gehrig (2nd, 1995)
Handcrafted • RHOD
1295QX5029 • **Value $20**

(3)
Satchel Paige (3rd, 1996)
Handcrafted • RHOD
1295QX5304 • **Value $18**

(4) NEW!
Jackie Robinson (4th & final, 1997)
Handcrafted • RHOD
1295QX6202 • **Value $12.95**

(5)
The Bellswinger (1st, 1979)
Handcrafted/Porcelain • N/A
1000QX1479 • **Value $280**

(6)
The Bellringers (2nd, 1980)
Handcrafted/Porcelain • N/A
1500QX1574 • **Value $80**

(7)
Swingin' Bellringer (3rd, 1981)
Handcrafted/Ceramic • N/A
1500QX4415 • **Value $85**

(8)
Angel Bellringer (4th, 1982)
Handcrafted/Ceramic • DLEE
1500QX4556 • **Value $92**

BASEBALL HEROES

	Price Paid	Value of My Collection
1.		
2.		
3.		
4.		

(9)
Teddy Bellringer (5th, 1983)
Handcrafted/Porcelain • N/A
1500QX4039 • **Value $133**

(10)
Elfin Artist (6th & final, 1984)
Porcelain • N/A
1500QX4384 • **Value $42**

(11)
Christmas 1973 (1st, 1973)
Glass • N/A
250XHD1102 • **Value $120**

THE BELLRINGERS

5.		
6.		
7.		
8.		
9.		
10.		

(12)
Musicians (2nd, 1974)
Glass • N/A
250QX1081 • **Value $82**

(13)
Caroling Trio (3rd, 1975)
Glass • N/A
300QX1331 • **Value $70**

(14)
Christmas 1976 (4th, 1976)
Glass • N/A
300QX1951 • **Value $85**

BETSEY CLARK

11.		
12.		
13.		
14.		
15.		
16.		
17.		
18.		
19.		
20.		

(15)
Truest Joys of Christmas (5th, 1977)
Glass • N/A
350QX2642 • **Value $450**

(16)
Christmas Spirit (6th, 1978)
Satin • N/A
350QX2016 • **Value $60**

(17)
Holiday Fun (7th, 1979)
Satin • N/A
350QX2019 • **Value $35**

(18)
Joy-in-the-Air (8th, 1980)
Glass • N/A
400QX2154 • **Value $30**

(19)
Christmas 1981 (9th, 1981)
Glass • N/A
450QX8022 • **Value $29**

(20)
Joys of Christmas (10th, 1982)
Satin • N/A
450QX2156 • **Value $33**

PENCIL TOTALS

Value Guide — Hallmark Keepsake Ornaments

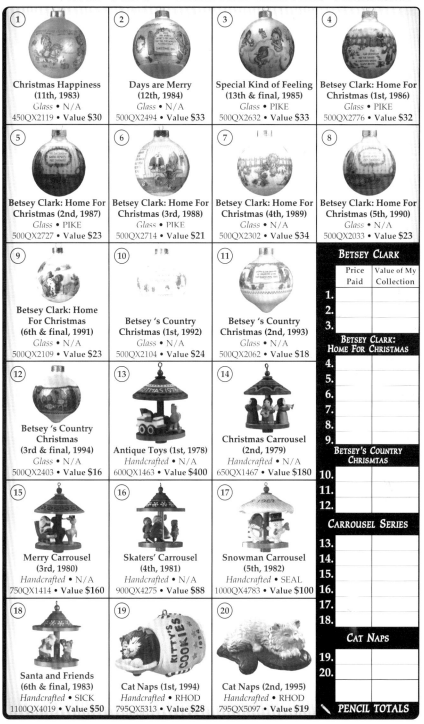

KEEPSAKE SERIES

(1) Christmas Happiness
(11th, 1983)
Glass • N/A
450QX2119 • **Value $30**

(2) Days are Merry
(12th, 1984)
Glass • N/A
500QX2494 • **Value $33**

(3) Special Kind of Feeling
(13th & final, 1985)
Glass • PIKE
500QX2632 • **Value $33**

(4) Betsey Clark: Home For
Christmas (1st, 1986)
Glass • PIKE
500QX2776 • **Value $32**

(5) Betsey Clark: Home For
Christmas (2nd, 1987)
Glass • PIKE
500QX2727 • **Value $23**

(6) Betsey Clark: Home For
Christmas (3rd, 1988)
Glass • PIKE
500QX2714 • **Value $21**

(7) Betsey Clark: Home For
Christmas (4th, 1989)
Glass • N/A
500QX2302 • **Value $34**

(8) Betsey Clark: Home For
Christmas (5th, 1990)
Glass • N/A
500QX2033 • **Value $23**

(9) Betsey Clark: Home
For Christmas
(6th & final, 1991)
Glass • N/A
500QX2109 • **Value $23**

(10) Betsey 's Country
Christmas (1st, 1992)
Glass • N/A
500QX2104 • **Value $24**

(11) Betsey 's Country
Christmas (2nd, 1993)
Glass • N/A
500QX2062 • **Value $18**

(12) Betsey 's Country
Christmas
(3rd & final, 1994)
Glass • N/A
500QX2403 • **Value $16**

(13) Antique Toys (1st, 1978)
Handcrafted • N/A
600QX1463 • **Value $400**

(14) Christmas Carrousel
(2nd, 1979)
Handcrafted • N/A
650QX1467 • **Value $180**

(15) Merry Carrousel
(3rd, 1980)
Handcrafted • N/A
750QX1414 • **Value $160**

(16) Skaters' Carrousel
(4th, 1981)
Handcrafted • N/A
900QX4275 • **Value $88**

(17) Snowman Carrousel
(5th, 1982)
Handcrafted • SEAL
1000QX4783 • **Value $100**

(18) Santa and Friends
(6th & final, 1983)
Handcrafted • SICK
1100QX4019 • **Value $50**

(19) Cat Naps (1st, 1994)
Handcrafted • RHOD
795QX5313 • **Value $28**

(20) Cat Naps (2nd, 1995)
Handcrafted • RHOD
795QX5097 • **Value $19**

BETSEY CLARK		
	Price Paid	Value of My Collection
1.		
2.		
3.		
BETSEY CLARK: HOME FOR CHRISTMAS		
4.		
5.		
6.		
7.		
8.		
9.		
BETSEY'S COUNTRY CHRISMTAS		
10.		
11.		
12.		
CARROUSEL SERIES		
13.		
14.		
15.		
16.		
17.		
18.		
CAT NAPS		
19.		
20.		
PENCIL TOTALS		

Collectible Series – Keepsake

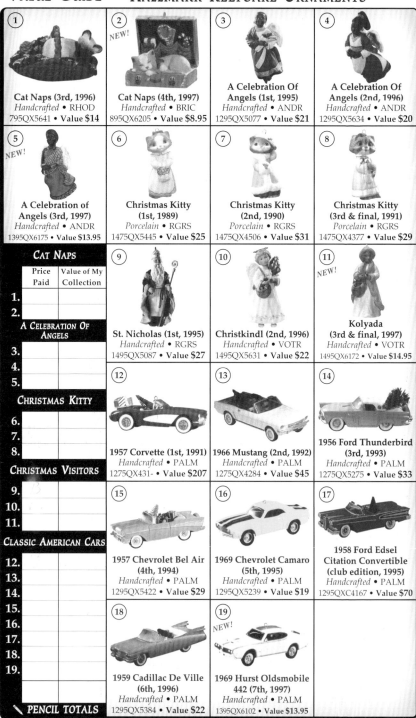

(1) Cat Naps (3rd, 1996)
Handcrafted • RHOD
795QX5641 • **Value $14**

(2) NEW! Cat Naps (4th, 1997)
Handcrafted • BRIC
895QX6205 • **Value $8.95**

(3) A Celebration Of
Angels (1st, 1995)
Handcrafted • ANDR
1295QX5077 • **Value $21**

(4) A Celebration Of
Angels (2nd, 1996)
Handcrafted • ANDR
1295QX5634 • **Value $20**

(5) NEW! A Celebration of
Angels (3rd, 1997)
Handcrafted • ANDR
1395QX6175 • **Value $13.95**

(6) Christmas Kitty
(1st, 1989)
Porcelain • RGRS
1475QX5445 • **Value $25**

(7) Christmas Kitty
(2nd, 1990)
Porcelain • RGRS
1475QX4506 • **Value $31**

(8) Christmas Kitty
(3rd & final, 1991)
Porcelain • RGRS
1475QX4377 • **Value $29**

	Price Paid	Value of My Collection
Cat Naps		
1.		
2.		
A Celebration Of Angels		
3.		
4.		
5.		
Christmas Kitty		
6.		
7.		
8.		
Christmas Visitors		
9.		
10.		
11.		
Classic American Cars		
12.		
13.		
14.		
15.		
16.		
17.		
18.		
19.		
PENCIL TOTALS		

(9) St. Nicholas (1st, 1995)
Handcrafted • RGRS
1495QX5087 • **Value $27**

(10) Christkindl (2nd, 1996)
Handcrafted • VOTR
1495QX5631 • **Value $22**

(11) NEW! Kolyada
(3rd & final, 1997)
Handcrafted • VOTR
1495QX6172 • **Value $14.95**

(12) 1957 Corvette (1st, 1991)
Handcrafted • PALM
1275QX431- • **Value $207**

(13) 1966 Mustang (2nd, 1992)
Handcrafted • PALM
1275QX4284 • **Value $45**

(14) 1956 Ford Thunderbird
(3rd, 1993)
Handcrafted • PALM
1275QX5275 • **Value $33**

(15) 1957 Chevrolet Bel Air
(4th, 1994)
Handcrafted • PALM
1295QX5422 • **Value $29**

(16) 1969 Chevrolet Camaro
(5th, 1995)
Handcrafted • PALM
1295QX5239 • **Value $19**

(17) 1958 Ford Edsel
Citation Convertible
(club edition, 1995)
Handcrafted • PALM
1295QXC4167 • **Value $70**

(18) 1959 Cadillac De Ville
(6th, 1996)
Handcrafted • PALM
1295QX5384 • **Value $22**

(19) NEW! 1969 Hurst Oldsmobile
442 (7th, 1997)
Handcrafted • PALM
1395QX6102 • **Value $13.95**

VALUE GUIDE — HALLMARK KEEPSAKE ORNAMENTS

(1) NEW!
The Clauses on Vacation (1st, 1997)
Handcrafted • SIED
1495QX6112 • **Value $14.95**

(2)
British (1st, 1982)
Handcrafted • SICK
500QX4583 • **Value $127**

(3)
Early American (2nd, 1983)
Handcrafted • SICK
500QX4029 • **Value $43**

(4)
Canadian Mountie (3rd, 1984)
Handcrafted • SICK
500QX4471 • **Value $27**

(5)
Scottish Highlander (4th, 1985)
Handcrafted • SICK
550QX4715 • **Value $24**

(6)
French Officer (5th, 1986)
Handcrafted • SICK
550QX4063 • **Value $24**

(7)
Sailor (6th & final, 1987)
Handcrafted • SICK
550QX4807 • **Value $22**

(8)
Light Shines at Christmas (1st, 1987)
Porcelain • VOTR
800QX4817 • **Value $62**

(9)
Waiting for Santa (2nd, 1988)
Porcelain • VOTR
800QX4061 • **Value $41**

(10)
Morning of Wonder (3rd, 1989)
Porcelain • VOTR
825QX4612 • **Value $23**

(11)
Cookies for Santa (4th, 1990)
Porcelain • VOTR
875QX4436 • **Value $24**

(12)
Let It Snow! (5th, 1991)
Porcelain • VOTR
875QX4369 • **Value $25**

(13)
Sweet Holiday Harmony (6th & final, 1992)
Porcelain • VOTR
875QX4461 • **Value $21**

(14)
Bright Journey (1st, 1989)
Handcrafted • SICK
875QX4352 • **Value $50**

(15)
Bright Moving Colors (2nd, 1990)
Handcrafted • CROW
875QX4586 • **Value $42**

(16)
Bright Vibrant Carols (3rd, 1991)
Handcrafted • CROW
975QX4219 • **Value $32**

(17)
Bright Blazing Colors (4th, 1992)
Handcrafted • CROW
975QX4264 • **Value $32**

(18)
Bright Shining Castle (5th, 1993)
Handcrafted • CROW
1075QX4422 • **Value $26**

(19)
Bright Playful Colors (6th, 1994)
Handcrafted • CROW
1095QX5273 • **Value $22**

(20)
Bright 'n' Sunny Tepee (7th, 1995)
Handcrafted • ANDR
1095QX5247 • **Value $21**

THE CLAUSES ON VACATION		
	Price Paid	Value of My Collection
1.		
CLOTHESPIN SOLDIER		
2.		
3.		
4.		
5.		
6.		
7.		
COLLECTOR'S PLATE		
8.		
9.		
10.		
11.		
12.		
13.		
CRAYOLA® CRAYON		
14.		
15.		
16.		
17.		
18.		
19.		
20.		
PENCIL TOTALS		

VALUE GUIDE — HALLMARK KEEPSAKE ORNAMENTS

(1)
Bright Flying Colors
(8th, 1996)
Handcrafted • CROW
1095QX5391 • **Value $21**

(2) NEW!
Bright Rocking Colors
(9th, 1997)
Handcrafted • TAGU
1295QX6235 • **Value $12.95**

(3) NEW!
Cinderella (1st, 1997)
Handcrafted • CROW
1495QXD4045 • **Value $14.95**

(4)
Native American
BARBIE™ (1st, 1996)
Handcrafted • ANDR
1495QX5561 • **Value $25**

(5) NEW!
Chinese BARBIE™
(2nd, 1997)
Handcrafted • RGRS
1495QX6162 • **Value $14.95**

(6)
Fabulous Decade
(1st, 1990)
Handcrafted/Brass • SEAL
775QX4466 • **Value $35**

(7)
Fabulous Decade
(2nd, 1991)
Handcrafted/Brass • SEAL
775QX4119 • **Value $35**

(8)
Fabulous Decade
(3rd, 1992)
Handcrafted/Brass • SEAL
775QX4244 • **Value $47**

(9)
Fabulous Decade
(4th, 1993)
Handcrafted/Brass • PIKE
775QX4475 • **Value $16**

(10)
Fabulous Decade
(5th, 1994)
Handcrafted/Brass • SEAL
795QX5263 • **Value $19**

(11)
Fabulous Decade
(6th, 1995)
Handcrafted/Brass • SEAL
795QX5147 • **Value $18**

(12)
Fabulous Decade
(7th, 1996)
Handcrafted/Brass • SEAL
795QX5661 • **Value $26**

(13) NEW!
Fabulous Decade
(8th, 1997)
Handcrafted/Brass • PIKE
795QX6232 • **Value $7.95**

(14)
Joe Montana (1st, 1995)
Handcrafted • RHOD
1495QXI5759 • **Value $48**

(15)
Joe Montana
(Kansas City, 1995)
Handcrafted • RHOD
1495QXI6207 • **Value $97**

(16)
Troy Aikman (2nd, 1996)
Handcrafted • RHOD
1495QXI5021 • **Value $26**

(17) NEW!
Joe Namath (3rd, 1997)
Handcrafted • RHOD
1495QXI6182 • **Value $14.95**

(18)
A Cool Yule (1st, 1980)
Handcrafted • BLAC
650QX1374 • **Value $575**

(19)
Frosty Friends (2nd, 1981)
Handcrafted • N/A
800QX4335 • **Value $360**

CRAYOLA® CRAYON	Price Paid	Value of My Collection
1.		
2.		
DISNEY		
3.		
DOLLS OF THE WORLD		
4.		
5.		
FABULOUS DECADE		
6.		
7.		
8.		
9.		
10.		
11.		
12.		
13.		
FOOTBALL LEGENDS		
14.		
15.		
16.		
17.		
FROSTY FRIENDS		
18.		
19.		
PENCIL TOTALS		

Value Guide – Hallmark Keepsake Ornaments

KEEPSAKE SERIES

1
Frosty Friends (3rd, 1982)
Handcrafted • SEAL
800QX4523 • **Value $275**

2
Frosty Friends (4th, 1983)
Handcrafted • SEAL
800QX4007 • **Value $285**

3
Frosty Friends (5th, 1984)
Handcrafted • SEAL
800QX4371 • **Value $85**

4
Frosty Friends (6th, 1985)
Handcrafted • SEAL
850QX4822 • **Value $65**

5
Frosty Friends (7th, 1986)
Handcrafted • SIED
850QX4053 • **Value $68**

6
Frosty Friends (8th, 1987)
Handcrafted • SEAL
850QX4409 • **Value $59**

7
Frosty Friends (9th, 1988)
Handcrafted • SEAL
875QX4031 • **Value $65**

8
Frosty Friends
(10th, 1989)
Handcrafted • SEAL
925QX4572 • **Value $45**

9
Frosty Friends
(11th, 1990)
Handcrafted • SEAL
975QX4396 • **Value $28**

10
Frosty Friends
(12th, 1991)
Handcrafted • PIKE
975QX4327 • **Value $40**

11
Frosty Friends
(13th, 1992)
Handcrafted • JLEE
975QX4291 • **Value $25**

12
Frosty Friends
(14th, 1993)
Handcrafted • JLEE
975QX4142 • **Value $25**

13
Frosty Friends (comple-
ment to series, 1993)
Handcrafted • SEAL
2000QX5682 • **Value $45**

14
Frosty Friends
(15th, 1994)
Handcrafted • SEAL
995QX5293 • **Value $24**

15
Frosty Friends
(16th, 1995)
Handcrafted • SEAL
1095QX5169 • **Value $25**

16
Frosty Friends
(17th, 1996)
Handcrafted • SEAL
1095QX5681 • **Value $20**

17
NEW!
Frosty Friends
(18th, 1997)
Handcrafted • SEAL
1095QX6255 • **Value $10.95**

18
St. Nicholas (1st, 1989)
Glass • VOTR
500QX2795 • **Value $19**

19
St. Lucia (2nd, 1990)
Glass • VOTR
500QX2803 • **Value $19**

20
Christkindl (3rd, 1991)
Glass • VOTR
500QX2117 • **Value $18**

FROSTY FRIENDS	Price Paid	Value of My Collection
1.		
2.		
3.		
4.		
5.		
6.		
7.		
8.		
9.		
10.		
11.		
12.		
13.		
14.		
15.		
16.		
17.		
THE GIFT BRINGERS		
18.		
19.		
20.		
PENCIL TOTALS		

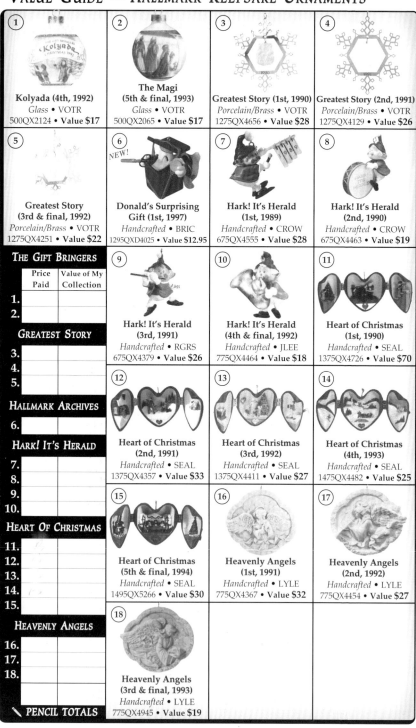

1
Kolyada (4th, 1992)
Glass • VOTR
500QX2124 • **Value $17**

2
The Magi
(5th & final, 1993)
Glass • VOTR
500QX2065 • **Value $17**

3
Greatest Story (1st, 1990)
Porcelain/Brass • VOTR
1275QX4656 • **Value $28**

4
Greatest Story (2nd, 1991)
Porcelain/Brass • VOTR
1275QX4129 • **Value $26**

5
Greatest Story
(3rd & final, 1992)
Porcelain/Brass • VOTR
1275QX4251 • **Value $22**

6
NEW!
Donald's Surprising
Gift (1st, 1997)
Handcrafted • BRIC
1295QXD4025 • **Value $12.95**

7
Hark! It's Herald
(1st, 1989)
Handcrafted • CROW
675QX4555 • **Value $28**

8
Hark! It's Herald
(2nd, 1990)
Handcrafted • CROW
675QX4463 • **Value $19**

9
Hark! It's Herald
(3rd, 1991)
Handcrafted • RGRS
675QX4379 • **Value $26**

10
Hark! It's Herald
(4th & final, 1992)
Handcrafted • JLEE
775QX4464 • **Value $18**

11
Heart of Christmas
(1st, 1990)
Handcrafted • SEAL
1375QX4726 • **Value $70**

12
Heart of Christmas
(2nd, 1991)
Handcrafted • SEAL
1375QX4357 • **Value $33**

13
Heart of Christmas
(3rd, 1992)
Handcrafted • SEAL
1375QX4411 • **Value $27**

14
Heart of Christmas
(4th, 1993)
Handcrafted • SEAL
1475QX4482 • **Value $25**

15
Heart of Christmas
(5th & final, 1994)
Handcrafted • SEAL
1495QX5266 • **Value $30**

16
Heavenly Angels
(1st, 1991)
Handcrafted • LYLE
775QX4367 • **Value $32**

17
Heavenly Angels
(2nd, 1992)
Handcrafted • LYLE
775QX4454 • **Value $27**

18
Heavenly Angels
(3rd & final, 1993)
Handcrafted • LYLE
775QX4945 • **Value $19**

THE GIFT BRINGERS

	Price Paid	Value of My Collection
1.		
2.		

GREATEST STORY

3.		
4.		
5.		

HALLMARK ARCHIVES

6.		

HARK! IT'S HERALD

7.		
8.		
9.		
10.		

HEART OF CHRISTMAS

11.		
12.		
13.		
14.		
15.		

HEAVENLY ANGELS

16.		
17.		
18.		

PENCIL TOTALS

VALUE GUIDE — HALLMARK KEEPSAKE ORNAMENTS

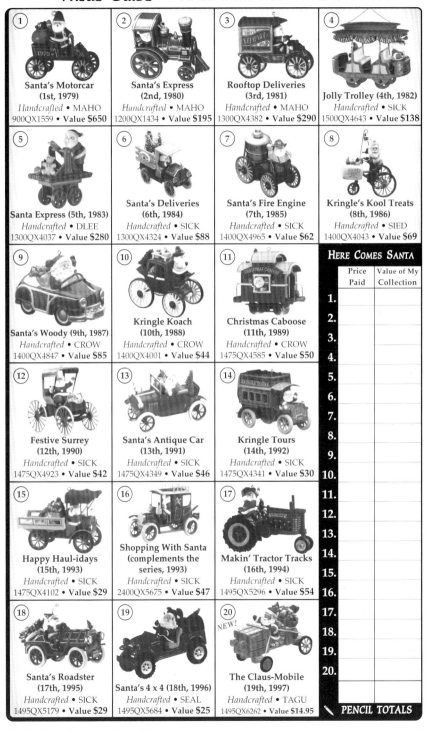

①
Santa's Motorcar
(1st, 1979)
Handcrafted • MAHO
900QX1559 • **Value $650**

②
Santa's Express
(2nd, 1980)
Handcrafted • MAHO
1200QX1434 • **Value $195**

③
Rooftop Deliveries
(3rd, 1981)
Handcrafted • MAHO
1300QX4382 • **Value $290**

④
Jolly Trolley (4th, 1982)
Handcrafted • SICK
1500QX4643 • **Value $138**

⑤
Santa Express (5th, 1983)
Handcrafted • DLEE
1300QX4037 • **Value $280**

⑥
Santa's Deliveries
(6th, 1984)
Handcrafted • SICK
1300QX4324 • **Value $88**

⑦
Santa's Fire Engine
(7th, 1985)
Handcrafted • SICK
1400QX4965 • **Value $62**

⑧
Kringle's Kool Treats
(8th, 1986)
Handcrafted • SIED
1400QX4043 • **Value $69**

⑨
Santa's Woody (9th, 1987)
Handcrafted • CROW
1400QX4847 • **Value $85**

⑩
Kringle Koach
(10th, 1988)
Handcrafted • CROW
1400QX4001 • **Value $44**

⑪
Christmas Caboose
(11th, 1989)
Handcrafted • CROW
1475QX4585 • **Value $50**

⑫
Festive Surrey
(12th, 1990)
Handcrafted • SICK
1475QX4923 • **Value $42**

⑬
Santa's Antique Car
(13th, 1991)
Handcrafted • SICK
1475QX4349 • **Value $46**

⑭
Kringle Tours
(14th, 1992)
Handcrafted • SICK
1475QX4341 • **Value $30**

⑮
Happy Haul-idays
(15th, 1993)
Handcrafted • SICK
1475QX4102 • **Value $29**

⑯
Shopping With Santa
(complements the
series, 1993)
Handcrafted • SICK
2400QX5675 • **Value $47**

⑰
Makin' Tractor Tracks
(16th, 1994)
Handcrafted • SICK
1495QX5296 • **Value $54**

⑱
Santa's Roadster
(17th, 1995)
Handcrafted • SICK
1495QX5179 • **Value $29**

⑲
Santa's 4 x 4 (18th, 1996)
Handcrafted • SEAL
1495QX5684 • **Value $25**

⑳
NEW!
The Claus-Mobile
(19th, 1997)
Handcrafted • TAGU
1495QX6262 • **Value $14.95**

HERE COMES SANTA

	Price Paid	Value of My Collection
1.		
2.		
3.		
4.		
5.		
6.		
7.		
8.		
9.		
10.		
11.		
12.		
13.		
14.		
15.		
16.		
17.		
18.		
19.		
20.		
PENCIL TOTALS		

① Wayne Gretzky (1st, 1997)	*Handcrafted* • UNRU
	1595QXI6275 • **Value $15.95**
② Holiday BARBIE™ (1st, 1993)	*Handcrafted* • ANDR
	1475QX5725 • **Value $150**
③ Holiday BARBIE™ (2nd, 1994)	*Handcrafted* • ANDR
	1495QX5216 • **Value $50**
④ Holiday BARBIE™ (3rd, 1995)	*Handcrafted* • ANDR
	1495QXI5057 • **Value $38**

⑤ Holiday BARBIE™ (4th, 1996)
Handcrafted • ANDR
1495QXI5371 • **Value $24**

⑥ Holiday BARBIE™ (5th, 1997)
Handcrafted • ANDR
1595QXI6212 • **Value $15.95**

⑦ 1988 Happy Holidays® BARBIE™ (1st, club edition, 1996)
Handcrafted • ANDR
1495QXC4181 • **Value $53**

⑧ 1989 Happy Holidays® BARBIE® (2nd, club edition, 1997)
Handcrafted • ANDR
1595QXC5162 • **Value $15.95**

Hockey Greats

	Price Paid	Value of My Collection
1.		

Holiday BARBIE™

2.		
3.		
4.		
5.		
6.		

Holiday BARBIE™ – Collector's Club

7.		
8.		

Holiday Heirloom

9.		
10.		
11.		

Holiday Wildlife

12.		
13.		
14.		
15.		
16.		
17.		
18.		

⑨ Holiday Heirloom (1st, LE-34,600, 1987)
Crystal/Silver-Plated • UNRU
2500QX4857 • **Value $30**

⑩ Holiday Heirloom (2nd, club edition, LE-34,600, 1988)
Crystal/Silver-Plated • N/A
2500QX4064 • **Value $31**

⑪ Holiday Heirloom (3rd & final, club edition, LE-34,600, 1989)
Crystal/Silver-Plated • N/A
2500QXC4605 • **Value $33**

⑫ Cardinalis (1st, 1982)
Wood • N/A
700QX3133 • **Value $400**

⑬ Black-Capped Chickadees (2nd, 1983)
Wood • N/A
700QX3099 • **Value $75**

⑭ Ring-Necked Pheasant (3rd, 1984)
Wood • N/A
725QX3474 • **Value $26**

⑮ California Partridge (4th, 1985)
Wood • N/A
750QX3765 • **Value $24**

⑯ Cedar Waxwing (5th, 1986)
Wood • N/A
750QX3216 • **Value $24**

⑰ Snow Goose (6th, 1987)
Wood • VOTR
750QX3717 • **Value $18**

⑱ Purple Finch (7th & final, 1988)
Wood • N/A
775QX3711 • **Value $19**

\ PENCIL TOTALS

VALUE GUIDE — HALLMARK KEEPSAKE ORNAMENTS

(1) Shaquille O'Neal
(1st, 1995)
Handcrafted • N/A
1495QXI5517 • **Value $30**

(2) Larry Bird (2nd, 1996)
Handcrafted • N/A
1495QXI5014 • **Value $25**

(3) NEW!
Magic Johnson
(3rd, 1997)
Handcrafted • N/A
1495QXI6832 • **Value $14.95**

(4) Murray® "Champion"
(1st, 1994)
Die-Cast Metal • PALM
1395QX5426 • **Value $60**

(5) Murray® Fire Truck
(2nd, 1995)
Die-Cast Metal • PALM
1395QX5027 • **Value $30**

(6) Murray® Airplane
(3rd, 1996)
Die-Cast Metal • PALM
1395QX5364 • **Value $24**

(7) 1937 Steelcraft Auburn
by Murray®
(club edition, 1996)
Die-Cast Metal • PALM
1595QXC4174 • **Value $55**

(8) NEW!
Murray® Dump Truck
(4th, 1997)
Die-Cast Metal • PALM
1395QX6195 • **Value $13.95**

(9) NEW!
1937 Steelcraft Airflow
by Murray®
(club edition, 1997)
Die-Cast Metal • PALM
1595QXC5185 • **Value $15.95**

(10) Pansy (1st, 1996)
Handcrafted • TAGU
1595QK1171 • **Value $75**

(11) NEW!
Snowdrop Angel
(2nd, 1997)
Handcrafted • TAGU
1595QX1095 • **Value $15.95**

(12) 700E Hudson Steam
Locomotive (1st, 1996)
Die-Cast Metal • N/A
1895QX5531 • **Value $45**

(13) NEW!
1950 Santa Fe F3 Diesel
Locomotive (2nd, 1997)
Die-Cast Metal • N/A
1895QX6145 • **Value $18.95**

(14) Cinderella – 1995
(1st, 1996)
Handcrafted • FRAN
1495QX6311 • **Value $29**

(15) NEW!
Little Red Riding Hood
– 1991 (2nd, 1997)
Handcrafted • FRAN
1495QX6155 • **Value $14.95**

(16) NEW!
Snowshoe Rabbits in
Winter, Mark Newman
(1st, 1997)
Handcrafted • N/A
1295QX5694 • **Value $12.95**

HOOP STARS		
	Price Paid	Value of My Collection
1.		
2.		
3.		
KIDDIE CAR CLASSICS		
4.		
5.		
6.		
7.		
8.		
9.		
THE LANGUAGE OF FLOWERS		
10.		
11.		
LIONEL® TRAIN		
12.		
13.		
MADAME ALEXANDER™		
14.		
15.		
MAJESTIC WILDERNESS		
16.		
PENCIL TOTALS		

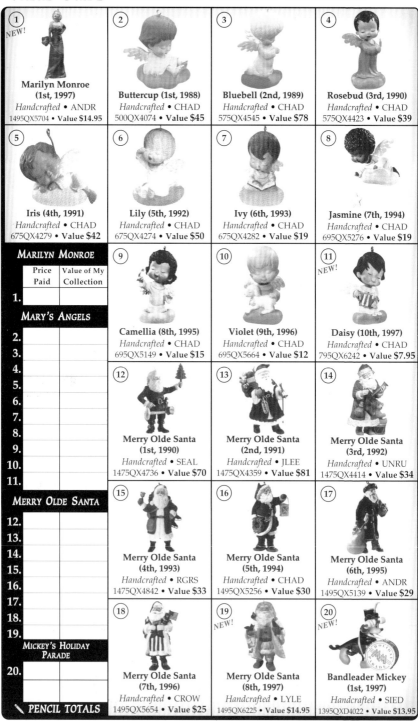

(1) NEW!
Marilyn Monroe (1st, 1997)
Handcrafted • ANDR
1495QX5704 • **Value $14.95**

(2)
Buttercup (1st, 1988)
Handcrafted • CHAD
500QX4074 • **Value $45**

(3)
Bluebell (2nd, 1989)
Handcrafted • CHAD
575QX4545 • **Value $78**

(4)
Rosebud (3rd, 1990)
Handcrafted • CHAD
575QX4423 • **Value $39**

(5)
Iris (4th, 1991)
Handcrafted • CHAD
675QX4279 • **Value $42**

(6)
Lily (5th, 1992)
Handcrafted • CHAD
675QX4274 • **Value $50**

(7)
Ivy (6th, 1993)
Handcrafted • CHAD
675QX4282 • **Value $19**

(8)
Jasmine (7th, 1994)
Handcrafted • CHAD
695QX5276 • **Value $19**

(9)
Camellia (8th, 1995)
Handcrafted • CHAD
695QX5149 • **Value $15**

(10)
Violet (9th, 1996)
Handcrafted • CHAD
695QX5664 • **Value $12**

(11) NEW!
Daisy (10th, 1997)
Handcrafted • CHAD
795QX6242 • **Value $7.95**

(12)
Merry Olde Santa (1st, 1990)
Handcrafted • SEAL
1475QX4736 • **Value $70**

(13)
Merry Olde Santa (2nd, 1991)
Handcrafted • JLEE
1475QX4359 • **Value $81**

(14)
Merry Olde Santa (3rd, 1992)
Handcrafted • UNRU
1475QX4414 • **Value $34**

(15)
Merry Olde Santa (4th, 1993)
Handcrafted • RGRS
1475QX4842 • **Value $33**

(16)
Merry Olde Santa (5th, 1994)
Handcrafted • CHAD
1495QX5256 • **Value $30**

(17)
Merry Olde Santa (6th, 1995)
Handcrafted • ANDR
1495QX5139 • **Value $29**

(18)
Merry Olde Santa (7th, 1996)
Handcrafted • CROW
1495QX5654 • **Value $25**

(19) NEW!
Merry Olde Santa (8th, 1997)
Handcrafted • LYLE
1495QX6225 • **Value $14.95**

(20) NEW!
Bandleader Mickey (1st, 1997)
Handcrafted • SIED
1395QXD4022 • **Value $13.95**

MARILYN MONROE

	Price Paid	Value of My Collection
1.		

MARY'S ANGELS

2.		
3.		
4.		
5.		
6.		
7.		
8.		
9.		
10.		
11.		

MERRY OLDE SANTA

12.		
13.		
14.		
15.		
16.		
17.		
18.		
19.		

MICKEY'S HOLIDAY PARADE

20.		

PENCIL TOTALS

VALUE GUIDE – HALLMARK KEEPSAKE ORNAMENTS

1 Miniature Crèche (1st, 1985) — *Wood/Straw* • SEAL — 875QX4825 • **Value $30**

2 Miniature Crèche (2nd, 1986) — *Porcelain* • SEAL — 900QX4076 • **Value $55**

3 Miniature Crèche (3rd, 1987) — *Brass* • SEAL — 900QX4819 • **Value $30**

4 Miniature Crèche (4th, 1988) — *Acrylic* • UNRU — 850QX4034 • **Value $23**

5 Miniature Crèche (5th & final, 1989) — *Handcrafted* • RGRS — 925QX4592 • **Value $21**

6 Humpty Dumpty (1st, 1993) — *Handcrafted* • SEAL/VOTR — 1375QX5282 • **Value $38**

7 Hey Diddle, Diddle (2nd, 1994) — *Handcrafted* • SEAL — 1395QX5213 • **Value $38**

8 Jack and Jill (3rd, 1995) — *Handcrafted* • SEAL/VOTR — 1395QX5099 • **Value $28**

9 Mary Had a Little Lamb (4th, 1996) — *Handcrafted* • SEAL/VOTR — 1395QX5644 • **Value $26**

10 Little Boy Blue (5th & final, 1997) NEW! — *Handcrafted* • SEAL/VOTR — 1395QX6215 • **Value $13.95**

11 Merry Mistletoe Time (1st, 1986) — *Handcrafted* • UNRU — 1300QX4026 • **Value $105**

12 Home Cooking (2nd, 1987) — *Handcrafted* • UNRU — 1325QX4837 • **Value $59**

13 Shall We Dance (3rd, 1988) — *Handcrafted* • UNRU — 1300QX4011 • **Value $50**

14 Holiday Duet (4th, 1989) — *Handcrafted* • UNRU — 1325QX4575 • **Value $48**

15 Popcorn Party (5th, 1990) — *Handcrafted* • UNRU — 1375QX4393 • **Value $70**

16 Checking His List (6th, 1991) — *Handcrafted* • UNRU — 1375QX4339 • **Value $34**

17 Gift Exchange (7th, 1992) — *Handcrafted* • UNRU — 1475QX4294 • **Value $30**

18 A Fitting Moment (8th, 1993) — *Handcrafted* • FRAN — 1475QX4202 • **Value $34**

19 A Handwarming Present (9th, 1994) — *Handcrafted* • UNRU — 1495QX5283 • **Value $33**

20 Christmas Eve Kiss (10th & final, 1995) — *Handcrafted* • UNRU — 1495QX5157 • **Value $26**

MINIATURE CRECHE

	Price Paid	Value of My Collection
1.		
2.		
3.		
4.		
5.		

MOTHER GOOSE

6.		
7.		
8.		
9.		
10.		

MR. AND MRS. CLAUS

11.		
12.		
13.		
14.		
15.		
16.		
17.		
18.		
19.		
20.		

PENCIL TOTALS

1
Santa's Visitors
(1st, 1980)
Cameo • N/A
650QX3061 • **Value** $225

2
The Carolers (2nd, 1981)
Cameo • N/A
850QX5115 • **Value** $43

3
Filling the Stockings
(3rd, 1982)
Cameo • N/A
850QX3053 • **Value** $27

4
Dress Rehearsal
(4th, 1983)
Cameo • N/A
750QX3007 • **Value** $37

5
Caught Napping
(5th, 1984)
Cameo • MCGE
750QX3411 • **Value** $33

6
Jolly Postman (6th, 1985)
Cameo • MCGE
750QX3745 • **Value** $27

7
Checking Up (7th, 1986)
Cameo • PIKE
775QX3213 • **Value** $23

8
The Christmas Dance
(8th, 1987)
Cameo • PALM
775QX3707 • **Value** $22

NORMAN ROCKWELL

	Price Paid	Value of My Collection
1.		
2.		
3.		
4.		
5.		
6.		
7.		
8.		
9.		

NOSTALGIC HOUSES AND SHOPS

10.		
11.		
12.		
13.		
14.		
15.		
16.		
17.		
18.		
19.		
20.		

\ PENCIL TOTALS

9
And to All a Good
Night (9th & final, 1988)
Cameo • N/A
775QX3704 • **Value** $19

10
Victorian Dollhouse
(1st, 1984)
Handcrafted • DLEE
1300QX4481 • **Value** $195

11
Old-Fashioned Toy
Shop (2nd, 1985)
Handcrafted • DLEE
1375QX4975 • **Value** $110

12
Christmas Candy
Shoppe (3rd, 1986)
Handcrafted • DLEE
1375QX4033 • **Value** $280

13
House on Main St.
(4th, 1987)
Handcrafted • DLEE
1400QX4839 • **Value** $75

14
Hall Bro's Card Shop
(5th, 1988)
Handcrafted • DLEE
1450QX4014 • **Value** $55

15
U.S. Post Office
(6th, 1989)
Handcrafted • DLEE
1425QX4582 • **Value** $64

16
Holiday Home
(7th, 1990)
Handcrafted • DLEE
1475QX4696 • **Value** $73

17
Fire Station (8th, 1991)
Handcrafted • DLEE
1475QX4139 • **Value** $63

18
Five and Ten Cent
Store (9th, 1992)
Handcrafted • DLEE
1475QX4254 • **Value** $38

19
Cozy Home (10th, 1993)
Handcrafted • DLEE
1475QX4175 • **Value** $42

20
Tannenbaum's Dept.
Store (complements
the series, 1993)
Handcrafted • DLEE
2600QX5612 • **Value** $55

(1) **Neighborhood Drugstore (11th, 1994)**
Handcrafted • DLEE
1495QX5286 • **Value $35**

(2) **Town Church (12th, 1995)**
Handcrafted • PALM
1495QX5159 • **Value $25**

(3) **Accessories for Nostalgic Houses and Shops (set/3, 1995)**
Handcrafted • JLEE
895QX5089 • **Value $10**

(4) **Victorian Painted Lady (13th, 1996)**
Handcrafted • PALM
1495QX5671 • **Value $28**

(5) NEW! **Cafe (14th, 1997)**
Handcrafted • PALM
1695QX6245 • **Value $16.95**

(6) **Owliver (1st, 1992)**
Handcrafted • SIED
775QX4544 • **Value $17**

(7) **Owliver (2nd, 1993)**
Handcrafted • SIED
775QX5425 • **Value $15**

(8) **Owliver (3rd & final, 1994)**
Handcrafted • SIED
795QX5226 • **Value $16**

(9) **Italy (1st, 1991)**
Handcrafted • SICK
1175QX5129 • **Value $25**

(10) **Spain (2nd, 1992)**
Handcrafted • SICK
1175QX5174 • **Value $22**

(11) **Poland (3rd & final, 1993)**
Handcrafted • SICK
1175QX5242 • **Value $22**

(12) **PEANUTS® (1st, 1993)**
Handcrafted • RHOD
975QX5315 • **Value $50**

(13) **The PEANUTS® Gang (2nd, 1994)**
Handcrafted • BISH
995QX5203 • **Value $24**

(14) **The PEANUTS® Gang (3rd, 1995)**
Handcrafted • SIED
995QX5059 • **Value $25**

(15) **The PEANUTS® Gang (4th & final, 1996)**
Handcrafted • FRAN
995QX5381 • **Value $19**

(16) **Cinnamon Teddy (1st, 1983)**
Porcelain • DUTK
700QX4289 • **Value $75**

(17) **Cinnamon Bear (2nd, 1984)**
Porcelain • N/A
700QX4541 • **Value $43**

(18) **Porcelain Bear (3rd, 1985)**
Porcelain • DUTK
750QX4792 • **Value $55**

(19) **Porcelain Bear (4th, 1986)**
Porcelain • N/A
775QX4056 • **Value $37**

(20) **Porcelain Bear (5th, 1987)**
Porcelain • N/A
775QX4427 • **Value $29**

NOSTALGIC HOUSES AND SHOPS		
	Price Paid	Value of My Collection
1.		
2.		
3.		
4.		
5.		

OWLIVER		
6.		
7.		
8.		

PEACE ON EARTH		
9.		
10.		
11.		

THE PEANUTS® GANG		
12.		
13.		
14.		
15.		

PORCELAIN BEAR		
16.		
17.		
18.		
19.		
20.		

PENCIL TOTALS

Value Guide — Hallmark Keepsake Ornaments

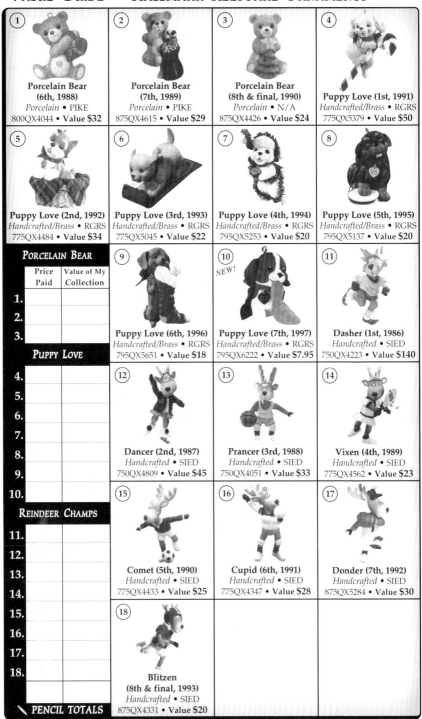

(1) Porcelain Bear (6th, 1988)
Porcelain • PIKE
800QX4044 • **Value $32**

(2) Porcelain Bear (7th, 1989)
Porcelain • PIKE
875QX4615 • **Value $29**

(3) Porcelain Bear (8th & final, 1990)
Porcelain • N/A
875QX4426 • **Value $24**

(4) Puppy Love (1st, 1991)
Handcrafted/Brass • RGRS
775QX5379 • **Value $50**

(5) Puppy Love (2nd, 1992)
Handcrafted/Brass • RGRS
775QX4484 • **Value $34**

(6) Puppy Love (3rd, 1993)
Handcrafted/Brass • RGRS
775QX5045 • **Value $22**

(7) Puppy Love (4th, 1994)
Handcrafted/Brass • RGRS
795QX5253 • **Value $20**

(8) Puppy Love (5th, 1995)
Handcrafted/Brass • RGRS
795QX5137 • **Value $20**

(9) Puppy Love (6th, 1996)
Handcrafted/Brass • RGRS
795QX5651 • **Value $18**

(10) NEW! Puppy Love (7th, 1997)
Handcrafted/Brass • RGRS
795QX6222 • **Value $7.95**

(11) Dasher (1st, 1986)
Handcrafted • SIED
750QX4223 • **Value $140**

(12) Dancer (2nd, 1987)
Handcrafted • SIED
750QX4809 • **Value $45**

(13) Prancer (3rd, 1988)
Handcrafted • SIED
750QX4051 • **Value $33**

(14) Vixen (4th, 1989)
Handcrafted • SIED
775QX4562 • **Value $23**

(15) Comet (5th, 1990)
Handcrafted • SIED
775QX4433 • **Value $25**

(16) Cupid (6th, 1991)
Handcrafted • SIED
775QX4347 • **Value $28**

(17) Donder (7th, 1992)
Handcrafted • SIED
875QX5284 • **Value $30**

(18) Blitzen (8th & final, 1993)
Handcrafted • SIED
875QX4331 • **Value $20**

Porcelain Bear

	Price Paid	Value of My Collection
1.		
2.		
3.		

Puppy Love

4.		
5.		
6.		
7.		
8.		
9.		
10.		

Reindeer Champs

11.		
12.		
13.		
14.		
15.		
16.		
17.		
18.		

Pencil Totals

VALUE GUIDE – HALLMARK KEEPSAKE ORNAMENTS

(1) Rocking Horse (1st, 1981)
Handcrafted • SICK
900QX4222 • **Value $580**

(2) Rocking Horse (2nd, 1982)
Handcrafted • SICK
1000QX5023 • **Value $350**

(3) Rocking Horse (3rd, 1983)
Handcrafted • SICK
1000QX4177 • **Value $295**

(4) Rocking Horse (4th, 1984)
Handcrafted • SICK
1000QX4354 • **Value $73**

(5) Rocking Horse (5th, 1985)
Handcrafted • SICK
1075QX4932 • **Value $70**

(6) Rocking Horse (6th, 1986)
Handcrafted • SICK
1075QX4016 • **Value $64**

(7) Rocking Horse (7th, 1987)
Handcrafted • SICK
1075QX4829 • **Value $62**

(8) Rocking Horse (8th, 1988)
Handcrafted • SICK
1075QX4024 • **Value $57**

(9) Rocking Horse (9th, 1989)
Handcrafted • SICK
1075QX4622 • **Value $45**

(10) Rocking Horse (10th, 1990)
Handcrafted • SICK
1075QX4646 • **Value $85**

(11) Rocking Horse (11th, 1991)
Handcrafted • SICK
1075QX4147 • **Value $38**

(12) Rocking Horse (12th, 1992)
Handcrafted • SICK
1075QX4261 • **Value $30**

(13) Rocking Horse (13th, 1993)
Handcrafted • SICK
1075QX4162 • **Value $32**

(14) Rocking Horse (14th, 1994)
Handcrafted • SICK
1095QX5016 • **Value $26**

(15) Rocking Horse (15th, 1995)
Handcrafted • SICK
1095QX5167 • **Value $27**

(16) Pewter Rocking Horse (15th Anniversary Edition, 1995)
Pewter • SICK
2000QX6167 • **Value $45**

(17) Rocking Horse (16th & final, 1996)
Handcrafted • SICK
1095QX5674 • **Value $28**

(18) Scarlett O'Hara™ (1st, 1997) NEW!
Handcrafted • ANDR
1495QX6125 • **Value $14.95**

(19) The Flight at Kitty Hawk (1st, 1997) NEW!
Handcrafted • NORT
1495QX5574 • **Value $14.95**

ROCKING HORSE

	Price Paid	Value of My Collection
1.		
2.		
3.		
4.		
5.		
6.		
7.		
8.		
9.		
10.		
11.		
12.		
13.		
14.		
15.		
16.		
17.		

SCARLETT O'HARA™

18.		

SKY'S THE LIMIT

19.		

PENCIL TOTALS

Value Guide — Hallmark Keepsake Ornaments

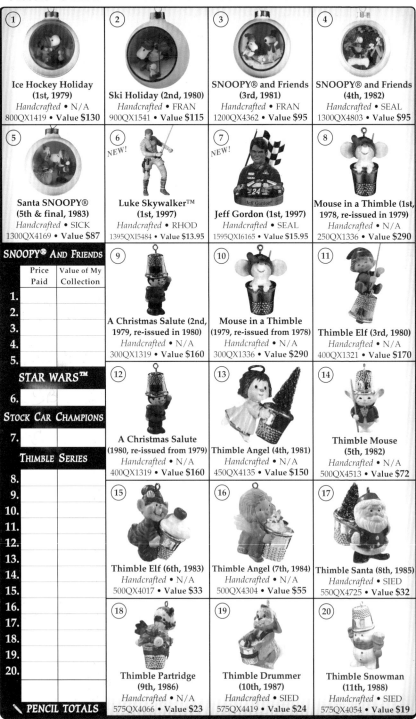

1 Ice Hockey Holiday (1st, 1979) · Handcrafted • N/A · 800QX1419 • Value **$130**

2 Ski Holiday (2nd, 1980) · Handcrafted • FRAN · 900QX1541 • Value **$115**

3 SNOOPY® and Friends (3rd, 1981) · Handcrafted • FRAN · 1200QX4362 • Value **$95**

4 SNOOPY® and Friends (4th, 1982) · Handcrafted • SEAL · 1300QX4803 • Value **$95**

5 Santa SNOOPY® (5th & final, 1983) · Handcrafted • SICK · 1300QX4169 • Value **$87**

6 NEW! Luke Skywalker™ (1st, 1997) · Handcrafted • RHOD · 1395QXI5484 • Value **$13.95**

7 NEW! Jeff Gordon (1st, 1997) · Handcrafted • SEAL · 1595QXI6165 • Value **$15.95**

8 Mouse in a Thimble (1st, 1978, re-issued in 1979) · Handcrafted • N/A · 250QX1336 • Value **$290**

9 A Christmas Salute (2nd, 1979, re-issued in 1980) · Handcrafted • N/A · 300QX1319 • Value **$160**

10 Mouse in a Thimble (1979, re-issued from 1978) · Handcrafted • N/A · 300QX1336 • Value **$290**

11 Thimble Elf (3rd, 1980) · Handcrafted • N/A · 400QX1321 • Value **$170**

12 A Christmas Salute (1980, re-issued from 1979) · Handcrafted • N/A · 400QX1319 • Value **$160**

13 Thimble Angel (4th, 1981) · Handcrafted • N/A · 450QX4135 • Value **$150**

14 Thimble Mouse (5th, 1982) · Handcrafted • N/A · 500QX4513 • Value **$72**

15 Thimble Elf (6th, 1983) · Handcrafted • N/A · 500QX4017 • Value **$33**

16 Thimble Angel (7th, 1984) · Handcrafted • N/A · 500QX4304 • Value **$55**

17 Thimble Santa (8th, 1985) · Handcrafted • SIED · 550QX4725 • Value **$32**

18 Thimble Partridge (9th, 1986) · Handcrafted • N/A · 575QX4066 • Value **$23**

19 Thimble Drummer (10th, 1987) · Handcrafted • SIED · 575QX4419 • Value **$24**

20 Thimble Snowman (11th, 1988) · Handcrafted • SIED · 575QX4054 • Value **$19**

SNOOPY® AND FRIENDS / **STAR WARS™** / **STOCK CAR CHAMPIONS** / **THIMBLE SERIES**

	Price Paid	Value of My Collection
1.		
2.		
3.		
4.		
5.		
6.		
7.		
8.		
9.		
10.		
11.		
12.		
13.		
14.		
15.		
16.		
17.		
18.		
19.		
20.		
PENCIL TOTALS		

48 · *Collectible Series – Keepsake*

1
**Thimble Puppy
(12th & final, 1989)**
Handcrafted • RGRS
575QX4552 • Value **$25**

2 NEW!
**Victorian Christmas
Thomas Kinkade, Painter
of Light™ (1st, 1997)**
Porcelain • SEAL
1095QXI6135 • Value **$10.95**

3
Tin Locomotive (1st, 1982)
Pressed Tin • SICK
1300QX4603 • Value **$560**

4
Tin Locomotive (2nd, 1983)
Pressed Tin • SICK
1300QX4049 • Value **$275**

5
Tin Locomotive (3rd, 1984)
Pressed Tin • SICK
1400QX4404 • Value **$85**

6
Tin Locomotive (4th, 1985)
Pressed Tin • SICK
1475QX4972 • Value **$74**

7
Tin Locomotive (5th, 1986)
Pressed Tin • SICK
1475QX4036 • Value **$71**

8
Tin Locomotive (6th, 1987)
Pressed Tin • SICK
1475QX4849 • Value **$59**

9
Tin Locomotive (7th, 1988)
Pressed Tin • SICK
1475QX4004 • Value **$50**

10
**Tin Locomotive
(8th & final, 1989)**
Pressed Tin • SICK
1475QX4602 • Value **$50**

11
**Tobin Fraley Carousel
(1st, 1992)**
Porcelain/Brass • FRAL
2800QX4891 • Value **$49**

12
**Tobin Fraley Carousel
(2nd, 1993)**
Porcelain/Brass • FRAL
2800QX5502 • Value **$47**

13
**Tobin Fraley Carousel
(3rd, 1994)**
Porcelain/Brass • FRAL
2800QX5223 • Value **$53**

14
**Tobin Fraley Carousel
(4th & final, 1995)**
Porcelain • FRAL
2800QX5069 • Value **$47**

15
The Fireman (1st, 1995)
Die-Cast Metal • CROW
1695QK1027 • Value **$38**

16
Uncle Sam (2nd, 1996)
Die-Cast Metal • CROW
1695QK1084 • Value **$30**

17 NEW!
**Santa Claus
(3rd & final, 1997)**
Die-Cast Metal • CROW
1695QX1215 • Value **$16.95**

	Price Paid	Value of My Collection
THIMBLE SERIES		
1.		
THOMAS KINKADE		
2.		
TIN LOCOMOTIVE		
3.		
4.		
5.		
6.		
7.		
8.		
9.		
10.		
TOBIN FRALEY CAROUSEL		
11.		
12.		
13.		
14.		
TURN-OF-THE-CENTURY PARADE		
15.		
16.		
17.		
PENCIL TOTALS		

VALUE GUIDE — HALLMARK KEEPSAKE ORNAMENTS

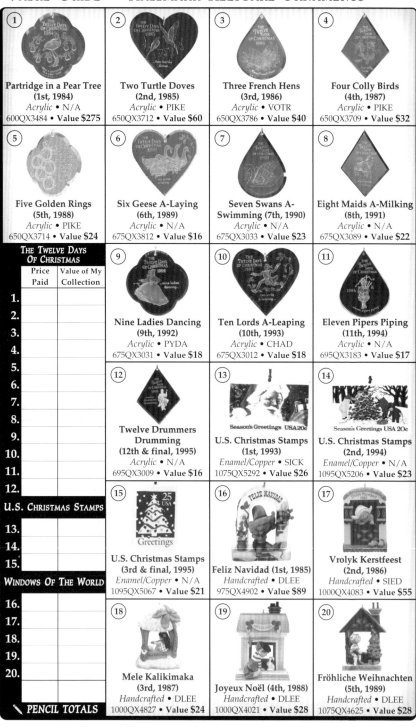

(1) Partridge in a Pear Tree
(1st, 1984)
Acrylic • N/A
600QX3484 • **Value $275**

(2) Two Turtle Doves
(2nd, 1985)
Acrylic • PIKE
650QX3712 • **Value $60**

(3) Three French Hens
(3rd, 1986)
Acrylic • VOTR
650QX3786 • **Value $40**

(4) Four Colly Birds
(4th, 1987)
Acrylic • PIKE
650QX3709 • **Value $32**

(5) Five Golden Rings
(5th, 1988)
Acrylic • PIKE
650QX3714 • **Value $24**

(6) Six Geese A-Laying
(6th, 1989)
Acrylic • N/A
675QX3812 • **Value $16**

(7) Seven Swans A-Swimming (7th, 1990)
Acrylic • N/A
675QX3033 • **Value $23**

(8) Eight Maids A-Milking
(8th, 1991)
Acrylic • N/A
675QX3089 • **Value $22**

(9) Nine Ladies Dancing
(9th, 1992)
Acrylic • PYDA
675QX3031 • **Value $18**

(10) Ten Lords A-Leaping
(10th, 1993)
Acrylic • CHAD
675QX3012 • **Value $18**

(11) Eleven Pipers Piping
(11th, 1994)
Acrylic • N/A
695QX3183 • **Value $17**

(12) Twelve Drummers Drumming
(12th & final, 1995)
Acrylic • N/A
695QX3009 • **Value $16**

(13) U.S. Christmas Stamps
(1st, 1993)
Enamel/Copper • SICK
1075QX5292 • **Value $26**

(14) U.S. Christmas Stamps
(2nd, 1994)
Enamel/Copper • N/A
1095QX5206 • **Value $23**

(15) U.S. Christmas Stamps
(3rd & final, 1995)
Enamel/Copper • N/A
1095QX5067 • **Value $21**

(16) Feliz Navidad (1st, 1985)
Handcrafted • DLEE
975QX4902 • **Value $89**

(17) Vrolyk Kerstfeest
(2nd, 1986)
Handcrafted • SIED
1000QX4083 • **Value $55**

(18) Mele Kalikimaka
(3rd, 1987)
Handcrafted • DLEE
1000QX4827 • **Value $24**

(19) Joyeux Noël (4th, 1988)
Handcrafted • DLEE
1000QX4021 • **Value $28**

(20) Fröhliche Weihnachten
(5th, 1989)
Handcrafted • DLEE
1075QX4625 • **Value $28**

THE TWELVE DAYS OF CHRISTMAS

	Price Paid	Value of My Collection
1.		
2.		
3.		
4.		
5.		
6.		
7.		
8.		
9.		
10.		
11.		
12.		

U.S. CHRISTMAS STAMPS

13.		
14.		
15.		

WINDOWS OF THE WORLD

16.		
17.		
18.		
19.		
20.		

PENCIL TOTALS

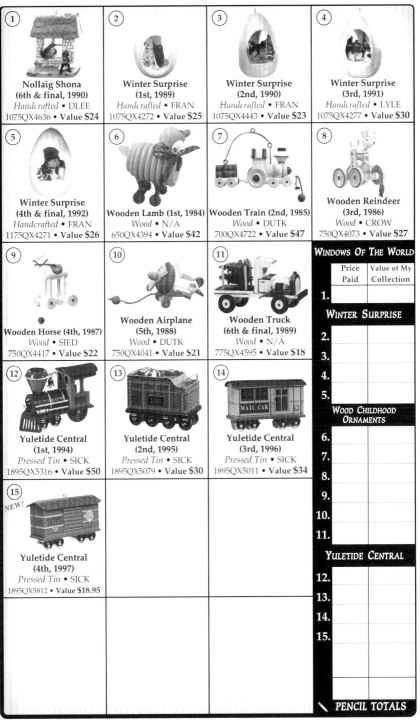

(1)

Nollaig Shona
(6th & final, 1990)
Handcrafted • DLEE
1075QX4636 • **Value $24**

(2)
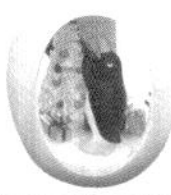
Winter Surprise
(1st, 1989)
Handcrafted • FRAN
1075QX4272 • **Value $25**

(3)
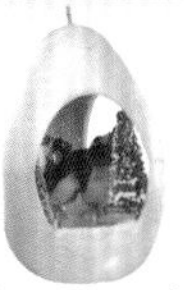
Winter Surprise
(2nd, 1990)
Handcrafted • FRAN
1075QX4443 • **Value $23**

(4)

Winter Surprise
(3rd, 1991)
Handcrafted • LYLE
1075QX4277 • **Value $30**

(5)

Winter Surprise
(4th & final, 1992)
Handcrafted • FRAN
1175QX4271 • **Value $26**

(6)

Wooden Lamb (1st, 1984)
Wood • N/A
650QX4394 • **Value $42**

(7)
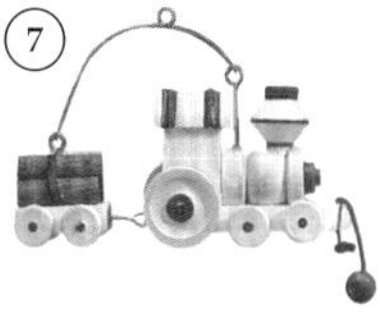
Wooden Train (2nd, 1985)
Wood • DUTK
700QX4722 • **Value $47**

(8)

Wooden Reindeer
(3rd, 1986)
Wood • CROW
750QX4073 • **Value $27**

(9)

Wooden Horse (4th, 1987)
Wood • SIED
750QX4417 • **Value $22**

(10)

Wooden Airplane
(5th, 1988)
Wood • DUTK
750QX4041 • **Value $21**

(11)

Wooden Truck
(6th & final, 1989)
Wood • N/A
775QX4595 • **Value $18**

(12)

Yuletide Central
(1st, 1994)
Pressed Tin • SICK
1895QX5316 • **Value $50**

(13)

Yuletide Central
(2nd, 1995)
Pressed Tin • SICK
1895QX5079 • **Value $30**

(14)

Yuletide Central
(3rd, 1996)
Pressed Tin • SICK
1895QX5011 • **Value $34**

(15)
NEW!

Yuletide Central
(4th, 1997)
Pressed Tin • SICK
1895QX5812 • **Value $18.95**

	Price Paid	Value of My Collection
WINDOWS OF THE WORLD		
1.		
WINTER SURPRISE		
2.		
3.		
4.		
5.		
WOOD CHILDHOOD ORNAMENTS		
6.		
7.		
8.		
9.		
10.		
11.		
YULETIDE CENTRAL		
12.		
13.		
14.		
15.		
PENCIL TOTALS		

Magic Series

There have been 8 Magic collectible series since the ornaments featuring light and motion debuted in 1984. Three series are ongoing. "Lighthouse Greetings" is a brand new series for 1997 and the long-running "Chris Mouse" series features its 13th and final edition in 1997.

Chris Mouse (1st, 1985)
Handcrafted • SIED
1250QLX7032 • **Value $75**

Chris Mouse Dreams (2nd, 1986)
Handcrafted • DUTK
1300QLX7056 • **Value $69**

Chris Mouse Glow (3rd, 1987)
Handcrafted • SIED
1100QLX7057 • **Value $58**

Chris Mouse Star (4th, 1988)
Handcrafted • SIED
875QLX7154 • **Value $58**

Chris Mouse Cookout (5th, 1989)
Handcrafted • RGRS
950QLX7225 • **Value $59**

Chris Mouse Wreath (6th, 1990)
Handcrafted • RGRS
1000QLX7296 • **Value $40**

Chris Mouse Mail (7th, 1991)
Handcrafted • SIED
1000QLX7207 • **Value $37**

Chris Mouse Tales (8th, 1992)
Handcrafted • RGRS
1200QLX7074 • **Value $25**

Chris Mouse Flight (9th, 1993)
Handcrafted • RGRS
1200QLX7152 • **Value $28**

Chris Mouse Jelly (10th, 1994)
Handcrafted • RGRS
1200QLX7393 • **Value $26**

Chris Mouse Tree (11th, 1995)
Handcrafted • RGRS
1250QLX7307 • **Value $25**

Chris Mouse Inn (12th, 1996)
Handcrafted • SIED
1450QLX7371 • **Value $28**

NEW!
Chris Mouse Luminaria (13th & final, 1997)
Handcrafted • SIED
1495QLX7525 • **Value $14.95**

The Nutcracker Ballet – Sugarplum Fairy (1st, 1986)
Handcrafted • N/A
1750QLX7043 • **Value $85**

A Christmas Carol (2nd, 1987)
Handcrafted • N/A
1600QLX7029 • **Value $63**

Night Before Christmas (3rd, 1988)
Handcrafted • DLEE
1500QLX7161 • **Value $40**

Little Drummer Boy (4th, 1989)
Handcrafted • DLEE
1350QLX7242 • **Value $35**

CHRIS MOUSE	Price Paid	Value of My Collection
1.		
2.		
3.		
4.		
5.		
6.		
7.		
8.		
9.		
10.		
11.		
12.		
13.		
CHRISTMAS CLASSICS		
14.		
15.		
16.		
17.		
PENCIL TOTALS		

VALUE GUIDE — HALLMARK KEEPSAKE ORNAMENTS

(1) The Littlest Angel
(5th & final, 1990)
Handcrafted • FRAN
1400QLX7303 • **Value $44**

(2) Forest Frolics (1st, 1989)
Handcrafted • PIKE
2450QLX7282 • **Value $88**

(3) Forest Frolics (2nd, 1990)
Handcrafted • PIKE
2500QLX7236 • **Value $70**

(4) Forest Frolics (3rd, 1991)
Handcrafted • PIKE
2500QLX7219 • **Value $61**

(5) Forest Frolics (4th, 1992)
Handcrafted • PIKE
2800QLX7254 • **Value $56**

(6) Forest Frolics (5th, 1993)
Handcrafted • PIKE
2500QLX7165 • **Value $45**

(7) Forest Frolics (6th, 1994)
Handcrafted • PIKE
2800QLX7436 • **Value $54**

(8) Forest Frolics
(7th & final, 1995)
Handcrafted • PIKE
2800QLX7299 • **Value $50**

(9) Freedom 7 (1st, 1996)
Handcrafted • SEAL
2400QLX7524 • **Value $41**

(10) NEW!
Friendship 7 (2nd, 1997)
Handcrafted • SEAL
2400QLX7532 • **Value $24**

(11) NEW!
Lighthouse Greetings
(1st, 1997)
Handcrafted • FRAN
2400QLX7442 • **Value $24**

(12) PEANUTS® (1st, 1991)
Handcrafted • RHOD
1800QLX7229 • **Value $65**

(13) PEANUTS® (2nd, 1992)
Handcrafted • RHOD
1800QLX7214 • **Value $50**

(14) PEANUTS® (3rd, 1993)
Handcrafted • RHOD
1800QLX7155 • **Value $38**

(15) PEANUTS® (4th, 1994)
Handcrafted • RHOD
2000QLX7406 • **Value $41**

(16) PEANUTS®
(5th & final, 1995)
Handcrafted • RHOD
2450QLX7277 • **Value $44**

(17) Lighting the Tree
(1st, 1986)
Handcrafted • N/A
2200QLX7033 • **Value $100**

(18) Perfect Portrait
(2nd, 1987)
Handcrafted • N/A
1950QLX7019 • **Value $64**

(19) On With the Show
(3rd & final, 1988)
Handcrafted • DLEE
1950QLX7191 • **Value $40**

CHRISTMAS CLASSICS	Price Paid	Value of My Collection
1.		
FOREST FROLICS		
2.		
3.		
4.		
5.		
6.		
7.		
8.		
JOURNEYS INTO SPACE		
9.		
10.		
LIGHTHOUSE GREETINGS		
11.		
PEANUTS®		
12.		
13.		
14.		
15.		
16.		
SANTA AND SPARKY		
17.		
18.		
19.		
PENCIL TOTALS		

①	②	③
Tobin Fraley Holiday Carousel (1st, 1994) *Handcrafted* • UNRU 3200QLX7496 • **Value $57**	**Tobin Fraley Holiday Carousel (2nd, 1995)** *Handcrafted* • FRAL 3200QLX7269 • **Value $53**	**Tobin Fraley Holiday Carousel (3rd & final, 1996)** *Handcrafted* • FRAN 3200QLX7461 • **Value $47**

Miniature Series

Of the 25 Miniature collectible series introduced since 1988, 16 are ongoing. There are 4 new series being introduced in 1997 and the two longest-running series, "Old English Village" and "Rocking Horse," are among the 3 series concluding in 1997.

④ **Alice in Wonderland (1st, 1995)** *Handcrafted* • ANDR 675QXM4777 • **Value $16**

TOBIN FRALEY HOLIDAY CAROUSEL

	Price Paid	Value of My Collection
1.		
2.		
3.		

ALICE IN WONDERLAND

4.		
5.		
6.		

ANTIQUE TRACTORS

7.		

THE BEARYMORES

8.		
9.		
10.		

CENTURIES OF SANTA

11.		
12.		
13.		
14.		

⑤ **Mad Hatter (2nd, 1996)** *Handcrafted* • ANDR 675QXM4074 • **Value $14**

⑥ NEW! **White Rabbit (3rd, 1997)** *Handcrafted* • ANDR 695QXM4142 • **Value $6.95**

⑦ NEW! **Antique Tractors (1st, 1997)** *Die-Cast Metal* • SICK 695QXM4185 • **Value $6.95**

⑧ **The Bearymores (1st, 1992)** *Handcrafted* • RGRS 575QXM5544 • **Value $17**

⑨ **The Bearymores (2nd, 1993)** *Handcrafted* • RGRS 575QXM5125 • **Value $15**

⑩ **The Bearymores (3rd & final, 1994)** *Handcrafted* • RGRS 575QXM5133 • **Value $13**

⑪ **Centuries of Santa (1st, 1994)** *Handcrafted* • SICK 600QXM5153 • **Value $20**

⑫ **Centuries of Santa (2nd, 1995)** *Handcrafted* • SICK 575QXM4789 • **Value $14**

⑬ **Centuries of Santa (3rd, 1996)** *Handcrafted* • SICK 575QXM4091 • **Value $13**

⑭ NEW! **Centuries of Santa (4th, 1997)** *Handcrafted* • SICK 595QXM4295 • **Value $5.95**

PENCIL TOTALS

VALUE GUIDE — HALLMARK KEEPSAKE ORNAMENTS

	1	**2**	**3**	**4**

1 Christmas Bells (1st, 1995)
Handcrafted/Metal • SEAL
475QXM4007 • **Value $16**

2 Christmas Bells (2nd, 1996)
Handcrafted/Metal • SEAL
475QXM4071 • **Value $12**

3 NEW! Christmas Bells (3rd, 1997)
Handcrafted/Metal • SEAL
495QXM4162 • **Value $4.95**

4 Kittens in Toyland (1st, 1988)
Handcrafted • CROW
500QXM5621 • **Value $25**

5 Kittens in Toyland (2nd, 1989)
Handcrafted • CROW
450QXM5612 • **Value $18**

6 Kittens in Toyland (3rd, 1990)
Handcrafted • CROW
450QXM5736 • **Value $18**

7 Kittens in Toyland (4th, 1991)
Handcrafted • CROW
450QXM5639 • **Value $16**

8 Kittens in Toyland (5th & final, 1992)
Handcrafted • CROW
450QXM5391 • **Value $15**

9 The Kringles (1st, 1989)
Handcrafted • RGRS
600QXM5625 • **Value $28**

10 The Kringles (2nd, 1990)
Handcrafted • RGRS
600QXM5753 • **Value $24**

11 The Kringles (3rd, 1991)
Handcrafted • RGRS
600QXM5647 • **Value $24**

12 The Kringles (4th, 1992)
Handcrafted • RGRS
600QXM5381 • **Value $17**

13 The Kringles (5th & final, 1993)
Handcrafted • RGRS
575QXM5135 • **Value $15**

14 March of the Teddy Bears (1st, 1993)
Handcrafted • UNRU
450QXM4005 • **Value $18**

15 March of the Teddy Bears (2nd, 1994)
Handcrafted • UNRU
450QXM5106 • **Value $13**

16 March of the Teddy Bears (3rd, 1995)
Handcrafted • UNRU
475QXM4799 • **Value $12**

17 March of the Teddy Bears (4th & final, 1996)
Handcrafted • UNRU
475QXM4094 • **Value $11**

18 Miniature Clothespin Soldier (1st, 1995)
Handcrafted • SICK
375QXM4097 • **Value $15**

19 Miniature Clothespin Soldier (2nd, 1996)
Handcrafted • SICK
475QXM4144 • **Value $11**

20 NEW! Miniature Clothespin Soldier (3rd, 1997)
Handcrafted • SICK
495QXM4155 • **Value $4.95**

MINIATURE SERIES

	Price Paid	Value of My Collection
CHRISTMAS BELLS		
1.		
2.		
3.		
KITTENS IN TOYLAND		
4.		
5.		
6.		
7.		
8.		
THE KRINGLES		
9.		
10.		
11.		
12.		
13.		
MARCH OF THE TEDDY BEARS		
14.		
15.		
16.		
17.		
MINIATURE CLOTHESPIN SOLDIER		
18.		
19.		
20.		
PENCIL TOTALS		

Value Guide — Hallmark Keepsake Ornaments

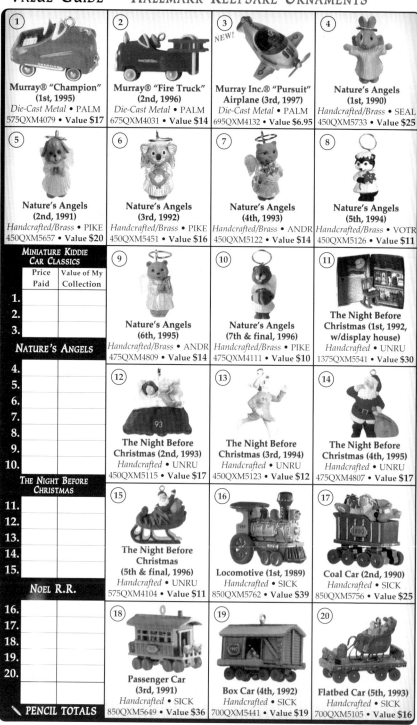

1. Murray® "Champion" (1st, 1995)
Die-Cast Metal • PALM
575QXM4079 • **Value $17**

2. Murray® "Fire Truck" (2nd, 1996)
Die-Cast Metal • PALM
675QXM4031 • **Value $14**

3. Murray Inc.® "Pursuit" Airplane (3rd, 1997)
NEW!
Die-Cast Metal • PALM
695QXM4132 • **Value $6.95**

4. Nature's Angels (1st, 1990)
Handcrafted/Brass • SEAL
450QXM5733 • **Value $25**

5. Nature's Angels (2nd, 1991)
Handcrafted/Brass • PIKE
450QXM5657 • **Value $20**

6. Nature's Angels (3rd, 1992)
Handcrafted/Brass • PIKE
450QXM5451 • **Value $16**

7. Nature's Angels (4th, 1993)
Handcrafted/Brass • ANDR
450QXM5122 • **Value $14**

8. Nature's Angels (5th, 1994)
Handcrafted/Brass • VOTR
450QXM5126 • **Value $11**

9. Nature's Angels (6th, 1995)
Handcrafted/Brass • ANDR
475QXM4809 • **Value $14**

10. Nature's Angels (7th & final, 1996)
Handcrafted/Brass • PIKE
475QXM4111 • **Value $10**

11. The Night Before Christmas (1st, 1992, w/display house)
Handcrafted • UNRU
1375QXM5541 • **Value $30**

12. The Night Before Christmas (2nd, 1993)
Handcrafted • UNRU
450QXM5115 • **Value $17**

13. The Night Before Christmas (3rd, 1994)
Handcrafted • UNRU
450QXM5123 • **Value $12**

14. The Night Before Christmas (4th, 1995)
Handcrafted • UNRU
475QXM4807 • **Value $17**

15. The Night Before Christmas (5th & final, 1996)
Handcrafted • UNRU
575QXM4104 • **Value $11**

16. Locomotive (1st, 1989)
Handcrafted • SICK
850QXM5762 • **Value $39**

17. Coal Car (2nd, 1990)
Handcrafted • SICK
850QXM5756 • **Value $25**

18. Passenger Car (3rd, 1991)
Handcrafted • SICK
850QXM5649 • **Value $36**

19. Box Car (4th, 1992)
Handcrafted • SICK
700QXM5441 • **Value $19**

20. Flatbed Car (5th, 1993)
Handcrafted • SICK
700QXM5105 • **Value $16**

Miniature Kiddie Car Classics

	Price Paid	Value of My Collection
1.		
2.		
3.		

Nature's Angels

4.		
5.		
6.		
7.		
8.		
9.		
10.		

The Night Before Christmas

11.		
12.		
13.		
14.		
15.		

Noel R.R.

16.		
17.		
18.		
19.		
20.		

PENCIL TOTALS

56

VALUE GUIDE – HALLMARK KEEPSAKE ORNAMENTS

(1) Stock Car (6th, 1994)
Handcrafted • SICK
700QXM5113 • **Value $17**

(2) Milk Tank Car (7th, 1995)
Handcrafted • SICK
675QXM4817 • **Value $14**

(3) Cookie Car (8th, 1996)
Handcrafted • SICK
675QXM4114 • **Value $14**

(4) NEW! Candy Car (9th, 1997)
Handcrafted • SICK
695QXM4175 • **Value $6.95**

(5) The Nutcracker Ballet (1st, 1996, w/display stage)
Handcrafted • VOTR
1475QXM4064 • **Value $26**

(6) NEW! Herr Drosselmeyer (2nd, 1997)
Handcrafted • VOTR
595QXM4135 • **Value $5.95**

(7) Nutcracker Guild (1st, 1994)
Handcrafted • SICK
575QXM5146 • **Value $15**

(8) Nutcracker Guild (2nd, 1995)
Handcrafted • SICK
575QXM4787 • **Value $14**

(9) Nutcracker Guild (3rd, 1996)
Handcrafted • SICK
575QXM4084 • **Value $13**

(10) NEW! Nutcracker Guild (4th, 1997)
Handcrafted • SICK
695QXM4165 • **Value $6.95**

(11) Family Home (1st, 1988)
Handcrafted • DLEE
850QXM5634 • **Value $38**

(12) Sweet Shop (2nd, 1989)
Handcrafted • JLEE
850QXM5615 • **Value $29**

(13) School (3rd, 1990)
Handcrafted • JLEE
850QXM5763 • **Value $20**

(14) Inn (4th, 1991)
Handcrafted • JLEE
850QXM5627 • **Value $24**

(15) Church (5th, 1992)
Handcrafted • JLEE
700QXM5384 • **Value $24**

(16) Toy Shop (6th, 1993)
Handcrafted • JLEE
700QXM5132 • **Value $16**

(17) Hat Shop (7th, 1994)
Handcrafted • ANDR
700QXM5143 • **Value $15**

(18) Tudor House (8th, 1995)
Handcrafted • JLEE
675QXM4819 • **Value $15**

(19) Village Mill (9th, 1996)
Handcrafted • RHOD
675QXM4124 • **Value $14**

(20) NEW! Village Depot (10th & final, 1997)
Handcrafted • LARS
695QXM4182 • **Value $6.95**

NOEL R.R.	Price Paid	Value of My Collection
1.		
2.		
3.		
4.		
THE NUTCRACKER BALLET		
5.		
6.		
NUTCRACKER GUILD		
7.		
8.		
9.		
10.		
OLD ENGLISH VILLAGE		
11.		
12.		
13.		
14.		
15.		
16.		
17.		
18.		
19.		
20.		
PENCIL TOTALS		

①

On The Road (1st, 1993)
Pressed Tin • SICK
575QXM4002 • **Value** $16

②

On The Road (2nd, 1994)
Pressed Tin • SICK
575QXM5103 • **Value** $13

③

On the Road (3rd, 1995)
Pressed Tin • SICK
575QXM4797 • **Value** $13

④

On the Road (4th, 1996)
Pressed Tin • SICK
575QXM4101 • **Value** $12

⑤
NEW!

On The Road (5th, 1997)
Pressed Tin • SICK
595QXM4172 • **Value** $5.95

⑥

Penguin Pal (1st, 1988)
Handcrafted • SIED
375QXM5631 • **Value** $24

⑦

Penguin Pal (2nd, 1989)
Handcrafted • N/A
450QXM5602 • **Value** $18

⑧

Penguin Pal (3rd, 1990)
Handcrafted • N/A
450QXM5746 • **Value** $16

On The Road

	Price Paid	Value of My Collection
1.		
2.		
3.		
4.		
5.		

Penguin Pal

6.		
7.		
8.		
9.		

Rocking Horse

10.		
11.		
12.		
13.		
14.		
15.		
16.		
17.		
18.		
19.		

⑨

**Penguin Pal
(4th & final, 1991)**
Handcrafted • SIED
450QXM5629 • **Value** $15

⑩

**Rocking Horse
(1st, 1988)**
Handcrafted • SICK
450QXM5624 • **Value** $40

⑪

**Rocking Horse
(2nd, 1989)**
Handcrafted • SICK
450QXM5605 • **Value** $28

⑫

**Rocking Horse
(3rd, 1990)**
Handcrafted • SICK
450QXM5743 • **Value** $22

⑬

**Rocking Horse
(4th, 1991)**
Handcrafted • SICK
450QXM5637 • **Value** $25

⑭

**Rocking Horse
(5th, 1992)**
Handcrafted • SICK
450QXM5454 • **Value** $17

⑮

**Rocking Horse
(6th, 1993)**
Handcrafted • SICK
450QXM5112 • **Value** $13

⑯

**Rocking Horse
(7th, 1994)**
Handcrafted • SICK
450QXM5116 • **Value** $14

⑰

**Rocking Horse
(8th, 1995)**
Handcrafted • SICK
450QXM4827 • **Value** $13

⑱

**Rocking Horse
(9th, 1996)**
Handcrafted • SICK
475QXM4121 • **Value** $14

⑲
NEW!

**Rocking Horse
(10th & final, 1997)**
Handcrafted • SICK
495QXM4302 • **Value** $4.95

PENCIL TOTALS

Value Guide — Hallmark Keepsake Ornaments

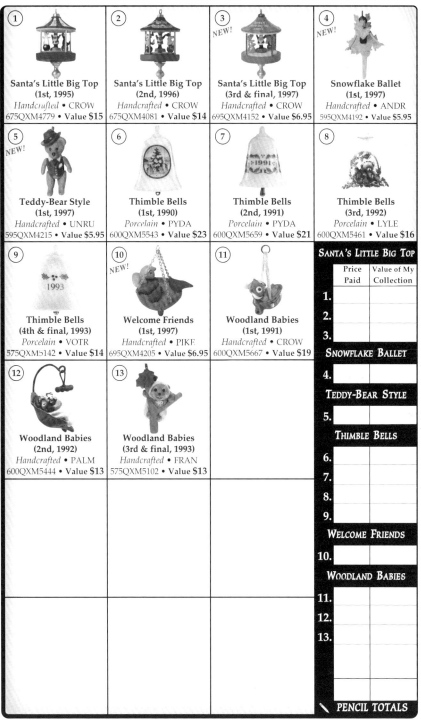

(1) Santa's Little Big Top
(1st, 1995)
Handcrafted • CROW
675QXM4779 • **Value $15**

(2) Santa's Little Big Top
(2nd, 1996)
Handcrafted • CROW
675QXM4081 • **Value $14**

(3) Santa's Little Big Top
(3rd & final, 1997) NEW!
Handcrafted • CROW
695QXM4152 • **Value $6.95**

(4) Snowflake Ballet
(1st, 1997) NEW!
Handcrafted • ANDR
595QXM4192 • **Value $5.95**

(5) Teddy-Bear Style
(1st, 1997) NEW!
Handcrafted • UNRU
595QXM4215 • **Value $5.95**

(6) Thimble Bells
(1st, 1990)
Porcelain • PYDA
600QXM5543 • **Value $23**

(7) Thimble Bells
(2nd, 1991)
Porcelain • PYDA
600QXM5659 • **Value $21**

(8) Thimble Bells
(3rd, 1992)
Porcelain • LYLE
600QXM5461 • **Value $16**

(9) Thimble Bells
(4th & final, 1993)
Porcelain • VOTR
575QXM5142 • **Value $14**

(10) Welcome Friends
(1st, 1997) NEW!
Handcrafted • PIKE
695QXM4205 • **Value $6.95**

(11) Woodland Babies
(1st, 1991)
Handcrafted • CROW
600QXM5667 • **Value $19**

(12) Woodland Babies
(2nd, 1992)
Handcrafted • PALM
600QXM5444 • **Value $13**

(13) Woodland Babies
(3rd & final, 1993)
Handcrafted • FRAN
575QXM5102 • **Value $13**

	Price Paid	Value of My Collection
SANTA'S LITTLE BIG TOP		
1.		
2.		
3.		
SNOWFLAKE BALLET		
4.		
TEDDY-BEAR STYLE		
5.		
THIMBLE BELLS		
6.		
7.		
8.		
9.		
WELCOME FRIENDS		
10.		
WOODLAND BABIES		
11.		
12.		
13.		
PENCIL TOTALS		

1997

Among 1997's highlights are a new collection of Disney ornaments and several ornaments based on the STAR WARS movies. The 1997 collection features 143 Keepsake ornaments, 17 Magic ornaments and 36 Miniature ornaments. See collectible series section for more 1997 ornaments.

1 1997 Corvette
Handcrafted • PALM
1395QXI6455 • **Value $13.95**

2 All-Round Sports Fan
Handcrafted • WILL
895QX6392 • **Value $8.95**

3 All-Weather Walker
Handcrafted • WILL
895QX6415 • **Value $8.95**

4 Angel Friend
Handcrafted • FRAN
1495QX6762 • **Value $14.95**

5 Ariel, The Little Mermaid
Handcrafted • BRIC
1295QXI4072 • **Value $12.95**

6 Baby's First Christmas
Handcrafted • N/A
795QX6482 • **Value $7.95**

7 Baby's First Christmas
Handcrafted • CROW
795QX6495 • **Value $7.95**

8 Baby's First Christmas
Handcrafted • VOTR
995QX6485 • **Value $9.95**

9 Baby's First Christmas
Handcrafted • ANDR
995QX6492 • **Value $9.95**

10 Baby's First Christmas
Porcelain • VOTR
1495QX6535 • **Value $14.95**

11 Baby's Second Christmas
Handcrafted • CROW
795QX6502 • **Value $7.95**

12 Biking Buddies
Handcrafted • PALM
1295QX6682 • **Value $12.95**

13 Book of the Year
Handcrafted • BRIC
795QX6645 • **Value $7.95**

14 Breezin' Along
Handcrafted • SEAL
895QX6722 • **Value $8.95**

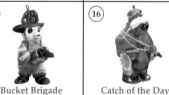
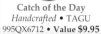

15 Bucket Brigade
Handcrafted • FRAN
895QX6382 • **Value $8.95**

16 Catch of the Day
Handcrafted • TAGU
995QX6712 • **Value $9.95**

17 Child's Fifth Christmas
Handcrafted • CROW
795QX6515 • **Value $7.95**

GENERAL KEEPSAKE		
	Price Paid	Value of My Collection
1.		
2.		
3.		
4.		
5.		
6.		
7.		
8.		
9.		
10.		
11.		
12.		
13.		
14.		
15.		
16.		
17.		
PENCIL TOTALS		

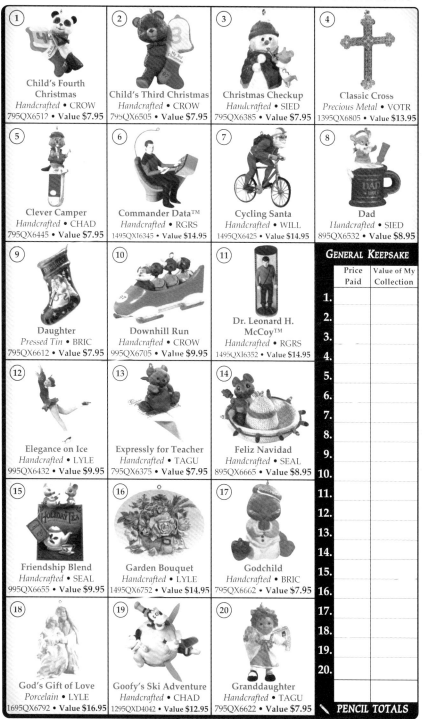

1997

1. Child's Fourth Christmas
Handcrafted • CROW
795QX6512 • **Value $7.95**

2. Child's Third Christmas
Handcrafted • CROW
795QX6505 • **Value $7.95**

3. Christmas Checkup
Handcrafted • SIED
795QX6385 • **Value $7.95**

4. Classic Cross
Precious Metal • VOTR
1395QX6805 • **Value $13.95**

5. Clever Camper
Handcrafted • CHAD
795QX6445 • **Value $7.95**

6. Commander Data™
Handcrafted • RGRS
1495QXI6345 • **Value $14.95**

7. Cycling Santa
Handcrafted • WILL
1495QX6425 • **Value $14.95**

8. Dad
Handcrafted • SIED
895QX6532 • **Value $8.95**

9. Daughter
Pressed Tin • BRIC
795QX6612 • **Value $7.95**

10. Downhill Run
Handcrafted • CROW
995QX6705 • **Value $9.95**

11. Dr. Leonard H. McCoy™
Handcrafted • RGRS
1495QXI6352 • **Value $14.95**

12. Elegance on Ice
Handcrafted • LYLE
995QX6432 • **Value $9.95**

13. Expressly for Teacher
Handcrafted • TAGU
795QX6375 • **Value $7.95**

14. Feliz Navidad
Handcrafted • SEAL
895QX6665 • **Value $8.95**

15. Friendship Blend
Handcrafted • SEAL
995QX6655 • **Value $9.95**

16. Garden Bouquet
Handcrafted • LYLE
1495QX6752 • **Value $14.95**

17. Godchild
Handcrafted • BRIC
795QX6662 • **Value $7.95**

18. God's Gift of Love
Porcelain • LYLE
1695QX6792 • **Value $16.95**

19. Goofy's Ski Adventure
Handcrafted • CHAD
1295QXD4042 • **Value $12.95**

20. Granddaughter
Handcrafted • TAGU
795QX6622 • **Value $7.95**

GENERAL KEEPSAKE		
	Price Paid	Value of My Collection
1.		
2.		
3.		
4.		
5.		
6.		
7.		
8.		
9.		
10.		
11.		
12.		
13.		
14.		
15.		
16.		
17.		
18.		
19.		
20.		
PENCIL TOTALS		

(1) Grandma
Handcrafted • PIKE
895QX6625 • **Value $8.95**

(2) Grandson
Handcrafted • TAGU
795QX6615 • **Value $7.95**

(3) Gus & Jaq, Cinderella
Handcrafted • CROW
1295QXD4052 • **Value $12.95**

(4) Heavenly Song
Acrylic • VOTR
1295QX6795 • **Value $12.95**

(5) Hercules
Handcrafted • WILL
1295QXI4005 • **Value $12.95**

(6) Honored Guests
Handcrafted • FRAN
1495QX6745 • **Value $14.95**

(7) Howdy Doody™
Handcrafted • LARS
1295QX6272 • **Value $12.95**

(8) The Incredible Hulk®
Handcrafted • N/A
1295QX5471 • **Value $12.95**

(9) Jasmine & Aladdin, Aladdin & the King of Thieves
Handcrafted • RGRS
1495QXD4062 • **Value $14.95**

(10) Jingle Bell Jester
Handcrafted • PIKE
995QX6695 • **Value $9.95**

(11) Juggling Stars
Handcrafted • TAGU
995QX6595 • **Value $9.95**

(12) King Noor – First King
Handcrafted • ANDR
1295QX6552 • **Value $12.95**

(13) Leading The Way
Handcrafted • SICK
1695QX6782 • **Value $16.95**

(14) Lion and Lamb
Handcrafted • WILL
795QX6602 • **Value $7.95**

(15) The Lone Ranger™
Pressed Tin • N/A
1295QX6265 • **Value $12.95**

(16) Love to Sew
Handcrafted • TAGU
795QX6435 • **Value $7.95**

(17) Madonna del Rosario
Handcrafted • SICK
1295QX6545 • **Value $12.95**

(18) Marbles Champion
Handcrafted • UNRU
1095QX6342 • **Value $10.95**

(19) Meadow Snowman
Pressed Tin • SICK
1295QX6715 • **Value $12.95**

(20) Megara and Pegasus
Handcrafted • CROW
1695QXI4012 • **Value $16.95**

General Keepsake

	Price Paid	Value of My Collection
1.		
2.		
3.		
4.		
5.		
6.		
7.		
8.		
9.		
10.		
11.		
12.		
13.		
14.		
15.		
16.		
17.		
18.		
19.		
20.		
PENCIL TOTALS		

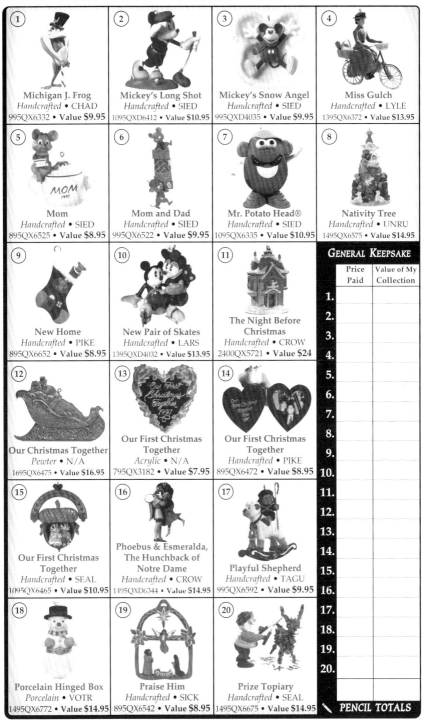

1 Michigan J. Frog
Handcrafted • CHAD
995QX6332 • **Value $9.95**

2 Mickey's Long Shot
Handcrafted • SIED
1095QXD6412 • **Value $10.95**

3 Mickey's Snow Angel
Handcrafted • SIED
995QXD4035 • **Value $9.95**

4 Miss Gulch
Handcrafted • LYLE
1395QX6372 • **Value $13.95**

5 Mom
Handcrafted • SIED
895QX6525 • **Value $8.95**

6 Mom and Dad
Handcrafted • SIED
995QX6522 • **Value $9.95**

7 Mr. Potato Head®
Handcrafted • SIED
1095QX6335 • **Value $10.95**

8 Nativity Tree
Handcrafted • UNRU
1495QX6575 • **Value $14.95**

9 New Home
Handcrafted • PIKE
895QX6652 • **Value $8.95**

10 New Pair of Skates
Handcrafted • LARS
1395QXD4032 • **Value $13.95**

11 The Night Before Christmas
Handcrafted • CROW
2400QX5721 • **Value $24**

12 Our Christmas Together
Pewter • N/A
1695QX6475 • **Value $16.95**

13 Our First Christmas Together
Acrylic • N/A
795QX3182 • **Value $7.95**

14 Our First Christmas Together
Handcrafted • PIKE
895QX6472 • **Value $8.95**

15 Our First Christmas Together
Handcrafted • SEAL
1095QX6465 • **Value $10.95**

16 Phoebus & Esmeralda, The Hunchback of Notre Dame
Handcrafted • CROW
1495QXD6344 • **Value $14.95**

17 Playful Shepherd
Handcrafted • TAGU
995QX6592 • **Value $9.95**

18 Porcelain Hinged Box
Porcelain • VOTR
1495QX6772 • **Value $14.95**

19 Praise Him
Handcrafted • SICK
895QX6542 • **Value $8.95**

20 Prize Topiary
Handcrafted • SEAL
1495QX6675 • **Value $14.95**

1997

General Keepsake

	Price Paid	Value of My Collection
1.		
2.		
3.		
4.		
5.		
6.		
7.		
8.		
9.		
10.		
11.		
12.		
13.		
14.		
15.		
16.		
17.		
18.		
19.		
20.		
PENCIL TOTALS		

(1) Sailor Bear
Handcrafted • UNRU
1495QX6765 • **Value $14.95**

(2) Santa Mail
Handcrafted • WILL
1095QX6702 • **Value $10.95**

(3) Santa's Friend
Handcrafted • UNRU
1295QX6685 • **Value $12.95**

(4) Santa's Magical Sleigh
Handcrafted • UNRU
2400QX6672 • **Value $24**

(5) Santa's Merry Path
Handcrafted • SICK
1695QX6785 • **Value $16.95**

(6) Santa's Polar Friend
Handcrafted • CHAD
1695QX6755 • **Value $16.95**

(7) Santa's Ski Adventure
Handcrafted • CHAD
1295QX6422 • **Value $12.95**

(8) Sister to Sister
Handcrafted • PIKE
995QX6635 • **Value $9.95**

(9) Snow Bowling
Handcrafted • WILL
695QX6395 • **Value $6.95**

(10) Snow White, Anniversary Edition (set/2)
Handcrafted • ESCH
1695QXD4055 • **Value $16.95**

(11) Snowgirl
Handcrafted • TAGU
795QX6562 • **Value $7.95**

(12) Son
Pressed Tin • BRIC
795QX6605 • **Value $7.95**

(13) Special Dog
Handcrafted • BRIC
795QX6632 • **Value $7.95**

(14) The Spirit of Christmas
Handcrafted • LARS
995QX6585 • **Value $9.95**

(15) Stealing a Kiss
Handcrafted • TAGU
1495QX6555 • **Value $14.95**

(16) Sweet Discovery
Handcrafted • SICK
1195QX6325 • **Value $11.95**

(17) Sweet Dreamer
Handcrafted • BRIC
695QX6732 • **Value $6.95**

(18) Swinging in the Snow
Handcrafted/Glass • TAGU
1295QX6775 • **Value $12.95**

(19) Taking A Break
Handcrafted • UNRU
1495QX6305 • **Value $14.95**

(20) Timon & Pumbaa, The Lion King
Handcrafted • WILL
1295QXD4065 • **Value $12.95**

GENERAL KEEPSAKE

	Price Paid	Value of My Collection
1.		
2.		
3.		
4.		
5.		
6.		
7.		
8.		
9.		
10.		
11.		
12.		
13.		
14.		
15.		
16.		
17.		
18.		
19.		
20.		
PENCIL TOTALS		

(1) Tomorrow's Leader
Ceramic • N/A
995QX6452 • **Value $9.95**

(2) Tonka® Mighty Front Loader
Die-cast Metal • N/A
1395QX6362 • **Value $13.95**

(3) Two-Tone, 101 Dalmatians
Handcrafted • CHAD
995QXD4015 • **Value $9.95**

(4) Waitin' on Santa – Winnie the Pooh
Handcrafted • SIED
1295QXD6365 • **Value $12.95**

(5) What a Deal!
Handcrafted • PIKE
895QX6442 • **Value $8.95**

(6) Yoda™
Handcrafted • BRIC
995QXI6355 • **Value $9.95**

(7) Darth Vader™
Handcrafted • RHOD
2400QXI7531 • **Value $24**

(8) Decorator Taz
Handcrafted • CHAD
3000QLX7502 • **Value $30**

(9) Glowing Angel
Handcrafted • VOTR
1895QLX7435 • **Value $18.95**

(10) Holiday Serenade
Handcrafted • FRAN
2400QLX7485 • **Value $24**

(11) Joy to the World
Handcrafted • TAGU
1495QLX7512 • **Value $14.95**

(12) The Lincoln Memorial
Handcrafted • SEAL
2400QLX7522 • **Value $24**

(13) Madonna and Child
Handcrafted • LYLE
1995QLX7425 • **Value $19.95**

(14) Motorcycle Chums
Handcrafted • SEAL
2400QLX7495 • **Value $24**

(15) Santa's Secret Gift
Handcrafted • CHAD
2400QLX7455 • **Value $24**

(16) Santa's Showboat
Handcrafted • CROW
4200QLX7465 • **Value $42**

(17) SNOOPY Plays Santa
Handcrafted • RGRS
2200QLX7475 • **Value $22**

(18) Teapot Party
Handcrafted • TAGU
1895QLX7482 • **Value $18.95**

(19) U.S.S. Defiant™
Handcrafted • NORT
2400QXI7481 • **Value $24**

(20) The Warmth of Home
Handcrafted • LARS
1895QXI7545 • **Value $18.95**

1997

GENERAL KEEPSAKE		
	Price Paid	Value of My Collection
1.		
2.		
3.		
4.		
5.		
6.		
GENERAL MAGIC		
7.		
8.		
9.		
10.		
11.		
12.		
13.		
14.		
15.		
16.		
17.		
18.		
19.		
20.		
PENCIL TOTALS		

(1) C-3PO™ and R2-D2™ (set/2)
Handcrafted • RHOD
1295QXI4265 • **Value $12.95**

(2) Casablanca™ (set/3)
Handcrafted • ANDR
1995QXM4272 • **Value $19.95**

(3) Future Star
Handcrafted • PIKE
595QXM4232 • **Value $5.95**

(4) Gentle Giraffes
Handcrafted • SICK
595QXM4221 • **Value $5.95**

(5) He Is Born
Handcrafted • VOTR
795QXM4235 • **Value $7.95**

(6) Heavenly Music
Handcrafted • TAGU
595QXM4292 • **Value $5.95**

(7) Home Sweet Home
Handcrafted • SEAL
595QXM4222 • **Value $5.95**

(8) Honey of a Gift – Winnie the Pooh
Handcrafted • LARS
695QXD4255 • **Value $6.95**

(9) Ice Cold Coca-Cola®
Handcrafted • CHAD
695QXM4252 • **Value $6.95**

(10) King of the Forest (set/4)
Handcrafted • RGRS
2400QXM4262 • **Value $24**

(11) Miniature 1997 Corvette
Handcrafted • PALM
695QXI4322 • **Value $6.95**

(12) Our Lady of Guadalupe
Pewter • CHAD
895QXM4275 • **Value $8.95**

(13) Peppermint Painter
Handcrafted • TAGU
495QXM4312 • **Value $4.95**

(14) Polar Buddies
Handcrafted • FRAN
495QXM4332 • **Value $4.95**

(15) Seeds of Joy
Handcrafted • TAGU
695QXM4242 • **Value $6.95**

(16) Sew Talented
Handcrafted • SEAL
595QXM4195 • **Value $5.95**

(17) Shutterbug
Handcrafted • TAGU
595QXM4212 • **Value $5.95**

(18) Snowboard Bunny
Handcrafted • TAGU
495QXM4315 • **Value $4.95**

(19) Tiny Home Improvers (set/6)
Handcrafted • SEAL
2900QXM4282 • **Value $29**

(20) Victorian Skater
Handcrafted • UNRU
595QXM4305 • **Value $5.95**

GENERAL MINIATURE

	Price Paid	Value of My Collection
1.		
2.		
3.		
4.		
5.		
6.		
7.		
8.		
9.		
10.		
11.		
12.		
13.		
14.		
15.		
16.		
17.		
18.		
19.		
20.		

PENCIL TOTALS

1 Away to the Window
(keepsake of membership)
Handcrafted • WILL
QXC5135 • **Value N/E**

2 Farmer's Market,
Tender Touches
(club edition)
Handcrafted • SEAL
1500QXC5182 • **Value $15**

3 Happy Christmas to All!
(keepsake of membership)
Handcrafted • WILL
QXC5132 • **Value N/E**

4 Jolly Old Santa
(keepsake of membership,
miniature)
Handcrafted • WILL
QXC5145 • **Value N/E**

5 Ready for Santa
(keepsake of membership,
miniature)
Handcrafted • WILL
QXC5142 • **Value N/E**

6 The Perfect Tree,
Tender Touches
Handcrafted • SEAL
1500QX6572 • **Value $15**

7 Mrs. Claus's Story
Handcrafted • ESCH/KLIN
($14.95) N/A • **Value $14.95**

8 Trimming Santa's Tree
(set/2, Studio Edition)
Handcrafted • VARI
($55.00) N/A • **Value $55**

9 BARBIE™ Lapel Pin
(re-issued from 1996)
Handcrafted • N/A
495XLP3544 • **Value $4.95**

10 Holiday BARBIE™
Stocking Hanger
(re-issued from 1996)
Handcrafted • N/A
1995XSH3101 • **Value $19.95**

11 Holiday Traditions™
BARBIE® Doll (1st in
*Holiday Homecoming
Collector Series™*)
Vinyl • N/A
5000QHB3402 • **Value $50**

12 Holiday Traditions™
BARBIE™ Ornament
Handcrafted • N/A
1495QHB6002 • **Value $14.95**

13 Holiday Traditions™
BARBIE™ Porcelain
Figurine
Porcelain • N/A
4500QHB6001 • **Value $45**

14 Holiday Traditions™
BARBIE™ Porcelain Plate
Porcelain • N/A
3000QHB6003 • **Value $30**

15 Victorian Elegance™
BARBIE™ Ornament
Handcrafted • N/A
1495QHB6004 • **Value $14.95**

16 Victorian Elegance™
BARBIE™ Porcelain Plate
Porcelain • N/A
3000QHB6005 • **Value $30**

17 CHICAGO BULLS
NBA COLLECTION
(10 assorted)
Ceramic • N/A

	Price Paid	Value of My Collection
COLLECTOR'S CLUB		
1.		
2.		
3.		
4.		
5.		
PREMIERE ORNAMENTS		
6.		
ARTISTS ON TOUR PIECES		
7.		
8.		
BARBIE™ COLLECTIBLES		
9.		
10.		
11.		
12.		
13.		
14.		
15.		
16.		
NBA COLLECTION		
17.		
PENCIL TOTALS		

1. Charlotte Hornets™
995QSR1222 • **Value $9.95**

2. Chicago Bulls™
995QSR1232 • **Value $9.95**

3. Detroit Pistons™
995QSR1242 • **Value $9.95**

4. Houston Rockets™
995QSR1245 • **Value $9.95**

5. Indiana Pacers™
995QSR1252 • **Value $9.95**

6. Los Angeles Lakers™
995QSR1262 • **Value $9.95**

7. New York
Knickerbockers™
995QSR1272 • **Value $9.95**

8. Orlando Magic™
995QSR1282 • **Value $9.95**

9. Phoenix Suns™
995QSR1292 • **Value $9.95**

10. Seattle Supersonics™
995QSR1295 • **Value $9.95**

1997

NFL COLLECTION
(30 assorted)
Handcrafted • SIED

1. **Arizona Cardinals™**
995QSR5505 • **Value $9.95**
2. **Atlanta Falcons™**
995QSR5305 • **Value $9.95**
3. **Baltimore Ravens™**
995QSR5352 • **Value $9.95**
4. **Buffalo Bills™**
995QSR5312 • **Value $9.95**
5. **Carolina Panthers™**
995QSR5315 • **Value $9.95**
6. **Chicago Bears™**
995QSR5322 • **Value $9.95**
7. **Cincinnati Bengals™**
995QSR5325 • **Value $9.95**
8. **Dallas Cowboys™**
995QSR5355 • **Value $9.95**
9. **Denver Broncos™**
995QSR5362 • **Value $9.95**
10. **Detroit Lions™**
995QSR5365 • **Value $9.95**

11. **Green Bay Packers™**
995QSR5372 • **Value $9.95**
12. **Houston Oilers™**
995QSR5375 • **Value $9.95**
13. **Indianapolis Colts™**
995QSR5411 • **Value $9.95**
14. **Jacksonville Jaguars™**
995QSR5415 • **Value $9.95**
15. **Kansas City Chiefs™**
995QSR5302 • **Value $9.95**
16. **Miami Dolphins™**
995QSR5472 • **Value $9.95**
17. **Minnesota Vikings™**
995QSR5475 • **Value $9.95**
18. **New England Patriots™**
995QSR5482 • **Value $9.95**
19. **New Orleans Saints™**
995QSR5485 • **Value $9.95**
20. **New York Giants™**
995QSR5492 • **Value $9.95**

21. **New York Jets™**
995QSR5495 • **Value $9.95**
22. **Oakland Raiders™**
995QSR5422 • **Value $9.95**
23. **Philadelphia Eagles™**
995QSR5502 • **Value $9.95**
24. **Pittsburgh Steelers™**
995QSR5512 • **Value $9.95**
25. **St. Louis Rams™**
995QSR5425 • **Value $9.95**
26. **San Diego Chargers™**
995QSR5515 • **Value $9.95**
27. **San Francisco 49ers™**
995QSR5522 • **Value $9.95**
28. **Seattle Seahawks™**
995QSR5525 • **Value $9.95**
29. **Tampa Bay Buccaneers™**
995QSR5532 • **Value $9.95**
30. **Washington Redskins™**
995QSR5535 • **Value $9.95**

NFL COLLECTION

	Price Paid	Value of My Collection
1.		

GENERAL KEEPSAKE

2.		
3.		
4.		
5.		
6.		
7.		
8.		
9.		
10.		

\ PENCIL TOTALS

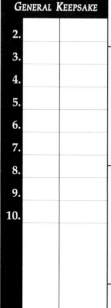

1996

Hallmark introduced several ornaments and collectibles commemorating the Centennial Olympic Games in Atlanta, Georgia in 1996. Overall, there were 135 Keepsake ornaments in the collection, as well as 23 Magic, 13 Showcase and 34 Miniature ornaments. See collectible series section for more 1996 ornaments.

101 Dalmatians
Handcrafted • N/A
1295QX16544 • **Value $20**

Antlers Aweigh!
Handcrafted • CHAD
995QX5901 • **Value $17**

Apple for Teacher
Handcrafted • AUBE
795QX6121 • **Value $15**

Baby's First Christmas
Handcrafted • SEAL
795QX5761 • **Value $12**

Baby's First Christmas
Handcrafted • CROW
795QX5764 • **Value $17**

Baby's First Christmas
Handcrafted • ANDR
995QX5754 • **Value $18**

Baby's First Christmas
Porcelain • N/A
1095QX5751 • **Value $22**

Baby's First Christmas
Porcelain • VOTR
1895QX5744 • **Value $26**

Baby's Second Christmas
Handcrafted • CROW
795QX5771 • **Value $15**

Value Guide — Hallmark Keepsake Ornaments

1 Bounce Pass
Handcrafted • SIED
795QX6031 • **Value $13**

2 Bowl 'em Over
Handcrafted • SIED
795QX6014 • **Value $13**

3 Child Care Giver
Handcrafted • SIED
895QX6071 • **Value $12**

4 Child's Fifth Christmas
Handcrafted • RHOD
695QX5784 • **Value $13**

5 Child's Fourth Christmas
Handcrafted • CROW
795QX5781 • **Value $13**

6 Child's Third Christmas
Handcrafted • CROW
795QX5774 • **Value $13**

7 Christmas Joy
Handcrafted • UNRU
1495QX6241 • **Value $24**

8 Christmas Snowman
Handcrafted • UNRU
995QX6214 • **Value $18**

9 Close-Knit Friends
Handcrafted • BRIC
995QX5874 • **Value $14**

10 Come All Ye Faithful
Handcrafted • CROW
1295QX6244 • **Value $20**

11 Commander William T. Riker™
Handcrafted • RGRS
1495QXI5551 • **Value $22**

12 Dad
Handcrafted • SIED
795QX5831 • **Value $14**

13 Daughter
Handcrafted • PALM
895QX6077 • **Value $14**

14 Esmeralda and Djali
Handcrafted • CROW
1495QXI6351 • **Value $20**

15 Evergreen Santa
Handcrafted • LYLE
2200QX5714 • **Value $30**

16 Fan-tastic Season
Handcrafted • CHAD
995QX5924 • **Value $18**

17 Feliz Navidad
Handcrafted • SICK
995QX6304 • **Value $19**

18 Foghorn Leghorn and Henery Hawk (set/2)
Handcrafted • CHAD
1395QX5444 • **Value $20**

19 Glad Tidings
Handcrafted • LYLE
1495QX6231 • **Value $25**

20 Goal Line Glory (set/2)
Handcrafted • SEAL
1295QX6001 • **Value $20**

General Keepsake

	Price Paid	Value of My Collection
1.		
2.		
3.		
4.		
5.		
6.		
7.		
8.		
9.		
10.		
11.		
12.		
13.		
14.		
15.		
16.		
17.		
18.		
19.		
20.		
PENCIL TOTALS		

1996

1
Godchild
Handcrafted • RGRS
895QX5841 • **Value $12**

2
Granddaughter
Handcrafted • RGRS
795QX5697 • **Value $12**

3
Grandma
Handcrafted • VOTR
895QX5844 • **Value $15**

4
Grandpa
Handcrafted • VOTR
895QX5851 • **Value $15**

5
Grandson
Handcrafted • RGRS
795QX5699 • **Value $12**

6
Growth of a Leader
Ceramic • N/A
995QX5541 • **Value $16**

7
Happy Holi-doze
Handcrafted • RHOD
995QX5904 • **Value $18**

8
Hearts Full of Love
Handcrafted • RHOD
995QX5814 • **Value $16**

9
High Style
Handcrafted • CHAD
895QX6064 • **Value $17**

10
Hillside Express
Handcrafted • AUBE
1295QX6134 • **Value $19**

11
Holiday Haul
Handcrafted • SICK
1495QX6201 • **Value $25**

12
Hurrying Downstairs
Handcrafted • FRAN
895QX6074 • **Value $16**

13
I Dig Golf
Handcrafted • RHOD
1095QX5891 • **Value $17**

14
Invitation to the Games (set/2)
Ceramic • MCGE
1495QXE5511 • **Value $24**

15
It's A Wonderful Life™
Handcrafted • CROW
1495QXI6531 • **Value $27**

16
IZZY™ – The Mascot
Handcrafted • PALM
995QXE5724 • **Value $18**

17
Jackpot Jingle
Handcrafted • SIED
995QX5911 • **Value $18**

18
Jolly Wolly Ark
Handcrafted • CROW
1295QX6221 • **Value $23**

19
Kindly Shepherd
Handcrafted • ANDR
1295QX6274 • **Value $21**

20
Laverne, Victor and Hugo
Handcrafted • CROW
1295QXI6354 • **Value $17**

General Keepsake

	Price Paid	Value of My Collection
1.		
2.		
3.		
4.		
5.		
6.		
7.		
8.		
9.		
10.		
11.		
12.		
13.		
14.		
15.		
16.		
17.		
18.		
19.		
20.		
PENCIL TOTALS		

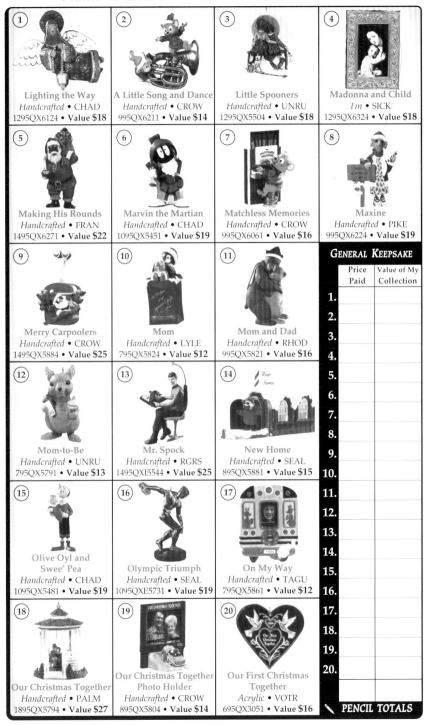

1. Lighting the Way
Handcrafted • CHAD
1295QX6124 • **Value $18**

2. A Little Song and Dance
Handcrafted • CROW
995QX6211 • **Value $14**

3. Little Spooners
Handcrafted • UNRU
1295QX5504 • **Value $18**

4. Madonna and Child
Tin • SICK
1295QX6324 • **Value $18**

5. Making His Rounds
Handcrafted • FRAN
1495QX6271 • **Value $22**

6. Marvin the Martian
Handcrafted • CHAD
1095QX5451 • **Value $19**

7. Matchless Memories
Handcrafted • CROW
995QX6061 • **Value $16**

8. Maxine
Handcrafted • PIKE
995QX6224 • **Value $19**

9. Merry Carpoolers
Handcrafted • CROW
1495QX5884 • **Value $25**

10. Mom
Handcrafted • LYLE
795QX5824 • **Value $12**

11. Mom and Dad
Handcrafted • RHOD
995QX5821 • **Value $16**

12. Mom-to-Be
Handcrafted • UNRU
795QX5791 • **Value $13**

13. Mr. Spock
Handcrafted • RGRS
1495QXI5544 • **Value $25**

14. New Home
Handcrafted • SEAL
895QX5881 • **Value $15**

15. Olive Oyl and Swee' Pea
Handcrafted • CHAD
1095QX5481 • **Value $19**

16. Olympic Triumph
Handcrafted • SEAL
1095QXE5731 • **Value $19**

17. On My Way
Handcrafted • TAGU
795QX5861 • **Value $12**

18. Our Christmas Together
Handcrafted • PALM
1895QX5794 • **Value $27**

19. Our Christmas Together Photo Holder
Handcrafted • CROW
895QX5804 • **Value $14**

20. Our First Christmas Together
Acrylic • VOTR
695QX3051 • **Value $16**

1996

GENERAL KEEPSAKE		
	Price Paid	Value of My Collection
1.		
2.		
3.		
4.		
5.		
6.		
7.		
8.		
9.		
10.		
11.		
12.		
13.		
14.		
15.		
16.		
17.		
18.		
19.		
20.		
PENCIL TOTALS		

VALUE GUIDE – HALLMARK KEEPSAKE ORNAMENTS

(1) Our First Christmas Together
Handcrafted • PALM
995QX5811 • **Value $16**

(2) Our First Christmas Together Collector's Plate
Porcelain • N/A
1095QX5801 • **Value $19**

(3) Parade of Nations
Porcelain • N/A
1095QXE5741 • **Value $22**

(4) Peppermint Surprise
Handcrafted • PIKE
795QX6234 • **Value $14**

(5) Percy the Small Engine – No. 6
Handcrafted • RHOD
995QX6314 • **Value $18**

(6) PEZ® Snowman
Handcrafted • N/A
795QX6534 • **Value $13**

(7) Polar Cycle
Handcrafted • UNRU
1295QX6034 • **Value $20**

(8) Prayer for Peace
Handcrafted • LYLE
795QX6261 • **Value $12**

(9) Precious Child
Handcrafted • VOTR
895QX6251 • **Value $13**

(10) Pup-Tenting
Handcrafted • PALM
795QX6011 • **Value $14**

(11) Quasimodo
Handcrafted • CROW
995QXI6341 • **Value $14**

(12) Regal Cardinal
Handcrafted • FRAN
995QX6204 • **Value $16**

(13) Sew Sweet
Handcrafted • AUBE
895QX5921 • **Value $14**

(14) Sister to Sister
Handcrafted • LYLE
995QX5834 • **Value $14**

(15) Son
Handcrafted • PALM
895QX6079 • **Value $13**

(16) Special Dog
Handcrafted • TAGU
795QX5864 • **Value $23**

(17) SPIDER-MAN™
Handcrafted • CHAD
1295QX5757 • **Value $24**

(18) Star of the Show
Handcrafted • AUBE
895QX6004 • **Value $16**

(19) Tamika
Handcrafted • BRIC
795QX6301 • **Value $12**

GENERAL KEEPSAKE

	Price Paid	Value of My Collection
1.		
2.		
3.		
4.		
5.		
6.		
7.		
8.		
9.		
10.		
11.		
12.		
13.		
14.		
15.		
16.		
17.		
18.		
19.		
PENCIL TOTALS		

1996 Collection

VALUE GUIDE – HALLMARK KEEPSAKE ORNAMENTS

1. Tender Lovin' Care
Handcrafted • SEAL
795QX6114 • **Value $13**

2. Thank You, Santa
Handcrafted • BRIC
795QX5854 • **Value $12**

3. This Big!
Handcrafted • SEAL
995QX5914 • **Value $16**

4. Time for a Treat
Handcrafted • SICK
1195QX5464 • **Value $19**

5. Tonka® Mighty Dump Truck
Die-Cast Metal • N/A
1395QX6321 • **Value $24**

6. A Tree for SNOOPY
Handcrafted • SIED
895QX5507 • **Value $14**

7. Welcome Guest
Handcrafted • UNRU
1495QX5394 • **Value $25**

8. Welcome Him
Handcrafted • TAGU
895QX6264 • **Value $14**

9. Winnie the Pooh and Piglet
Handcrafted • SIED
1295QX5454 • **Value $28**

10. Witch of the West
Handcrafted • LYLE
1395QX5554 • **Value $28**

11. WONDER WOMAN™
Handcrafted • RGRS
1295QX5941 • **Value $22**

12. Woodland Santa
Pressed Tin • SICK
1295QX6131 • **Value $20**

13. Yogi Bear™ and Boo Boo™
Handcrafted • RGRS
1295QX5521 • **Value $19**

14. Yuletide Cheer
Handcrafted • VOTR
795QX6054 • **Value $14**

15. Ziggy®
Handcrafted • CHAD
995QX6524 • **Value $17**

16. Baby's First Christmas
Handcrafted • FRAN
2200QLX7404 • **Value $43**

17. Chicken Coop Chorus
Handcrafted • CROW
2450QLX7491 • **Value $40**

18. Emerald City
Handcrafted • CROW
3200QLX7454 • **Value $55**

19. Father Time
Handcrafted • CHAD
2450QLX7391 • **Value $43**

20. THE JETSONS™
Handcrafted • CROW
2800QLX7411 • **Value $45**

1996

GENERAL KEEPSAKE		
	Price Paid	Value of My Collection
1.		
2.		
3.		
4.		
5.		
6.		
7.		
8.		
9.		
10.		
11.		
12.		
13.		
14.		
15.		
GENERAL MAGIC		
16.		
17.		
18.		
19.		
20.		
PENCIL TOTALS		

(1) Jukebox Party
Handcrafted • PALM
2450QLX7339 • **Value $48**

(2) Let Us Adore Him
Handcrafted • LYLE
1650QLX7381 • **Value $26**

(3) Lighting the Flame
Handcrafted • UNRU
2800QXE7444 • **Value $43**

(4) Millennium Falcon™
Handcrafted • N/A
2400QLX7474 • **Value $42**

(5) North Pole Volunteers
Handcrafted • SEAL
4200QLX7471 • **Value $79**

(6) Over the Rooftops
Handcrafted • SEAL
1450QLX7374 • **Value $23**

(7) PEANUTS®
Handcrafted • CHAD
1850QLX7394 • **Value $34**

(8) Pinball Wonder
Handcrafted • CROW
2800QLX7451 • **Value $45**

(9) Sharing a Soda
Handcrafted • CROW
2450QLX7424 • **Value $41**

(10) Slippery Day
Handcrafted • SIED
2450QLX7414 • **Value $43**

(11) STAR TREK®, 30 Years
(set/2, w/display base)
Handcrafted • NORT/RHOD
4500QXI7534 • **Value $63**

(12) The Statue of Liberty
Handcrafted • SEAL
2450QLX7421 • **Value $42**

(13) Treasured Memories
Handcrafted • SICK
1850QLX7384 • **Value $30**

(14) U.S.S. Voyager™
Handcrafted • NORT
2400QXI7544 • **Value $34**

(15) Video Party
Handcrafted • SIED
2800QLX7431 • **Value $48**

(16) Carmen
Cookie Jar Friends
Porcelain • RGRS
1595QK1164 • **Value $23**

(17) Clyde
Cookie Jar Friends
Porcelain • AUBE
1595QK1161 • **Value $18**

(18) Caroling Angel
Folk Art Americana
Handcrafted/Copper • SICK
1695QK1134 • **Value $27**

(19) Mrs. Claus
Folk Art Americana
Handcrafted/Copper • SICK
1895QK1204 • **Value $27**

(20) Santa's Gifts
Folk Art Americana
Handcrafted/Copper • SICK
1895QK1124 • **Value $34**

GENERAL MAGIC

	Price Paid	Value of My Collection
1.		
2.		
3.		
4.		
5.		
6.		
7.		
8.		
9.		
10.		
11.		
12.		
13.		
14.		
15.		

GENERAL SHOWCASE

16.		
17.		
18.		
19.		
20.		

PENCIL TOTALS

74

Value Guide – Hallmark Keepsake Ornaments

1. Balthasar (Frankincense)
Magi Bells
Porcelain • VOTR
1395QK1174 • **Value $18**

2. Caspar (Myrrh)
Magi Bells
Porcelain • VOTR
1395QK1184 • **Value $18**

3. Melchoir (Gold)
Magi Bells
Porcelain • VOTR
1395QK1181 • **Value $18**

4. The Birds' Christmas Tree
Nature's Sketchbook
Handcrafted • UNRU
1895QK1114 • **Value $24**

5. Christmas Bunny
Nature's Sketchbook
Handcrafted • FRAN
1895QK1104 • **Value $29**

6. The Holly Basket
Nature's Sketchbook
Handcrafted • LYLE
1895QK1094 • **Value $24**

7. Madonna and Child
Sacred Masterworks
Handcrafted • SICK
1595QK1144 • **Value $23**

8. Praying Madonna
Sacred Masterworks
Handcrafted • SICK
1595QK1154 • **Value $23**

9. African Elephants
Handcrafted • SICK
575QXM4224 • **Value $15**

10. Baby Sylvester
Handcrafted • PALM
575QXM4154 • **Value $15**

11. Baby Tweety
Handcrafted • PALM
575QXM4014 • **Value $26**

12. A Child's Gifts
Handcrafted • ANDR
675QXM4234 • **Value $11**

13. Christmas Bear
Handcrafted • SEAL
475QXM4241 • **Value $10**

14. Cloisonné Medallion
Cloisonné • MCGE
975QXE4041 • **Value $17**

15. Cool Delivery
Coca-Cola®
Handcrafted • PIKE
575QXM4021 • **Value $11**

16. GONE WITH THE
WIND™ (set/3)
Handcrafted • ANDR
1995QXM4211 • **Value $29**

17. Hattie Chapeau
Handcrafted • RHOD
475QXM4251 • **Value $10**

18. Joyous Angel
Handcrafted • ANDR
475QXM4231 • **Value $9**

19. Long Winter's Nap
Handcrafted • ANDR
575QXM4244 • **Value $11**

20. Message for Santa
Handcrafted • SEAL
675QXM4254 • **Value $12**

1996

General Showcase

	Price Paid	Value of My Collection
1.		
2.		
3.		
4.		
5.		
6.		
7.		
8.		

General Miniature

9.		
10.		
11.		
12.		
13.		
14.		
15.		
16.		
17.		
18.		
19.		
20.		
PENCIL TOTALS		

Value Guide – Hallmark Keepsake Ornaments

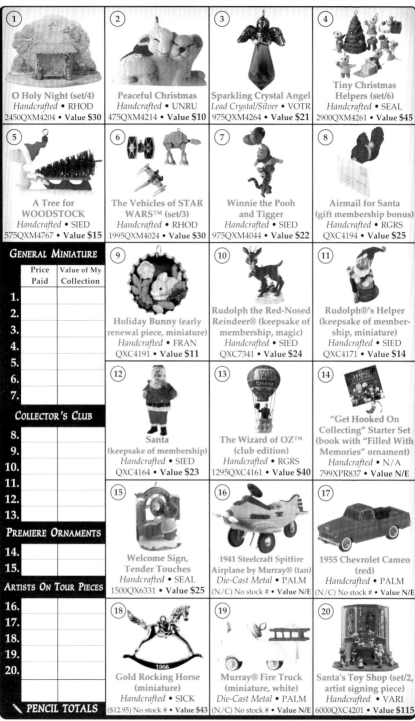

1. O Holy Night (set/4) — Handcrafted • RHOD — 2450QXM4204 • Value $30

2. Peaceful Christmas — Handcrafted • UNRU — 475QXM4214 • Value $10

3. Sparkling Crystal Angel — Lead Crystal/Silver • VOTR — 975QXM4264 • Value $21

4. Tiny Christmas Helpers (set/6) — Handcrafted • SEAL — 2900QXM4261 • Value $45

5. A Tree for WOODSTOCK — Handcrafted • SIED — 575QXM4767 • Value $15

6. The Vehicles of STAR WARS™ (set/3) — Handcrafted • RHOD — 1995QXM4024 • Value $30

7. Winnie the Pooh and Tigger — Handcrafted • SIED — 975QXM4044 • Value $22

8. Airmail for Santa (gift membership bonus) — Handcrafted • RGRS — QXC4194 • Value $25

9. Holiday Bunny (early renewal piece, miniature) — Handcrafted • FRAN — QXC4191 • Value $11

10. Rudolph the Red-Nosed Reindeer® (keepsake of membership, magic) — Handcrafted • SIED — QXC7341 • Value $24

11. Rudolph®'s Helper (keepsake of membership, miniature) — Handcrafted • SIED — QXC4171 • Value $14

12. Santa (keepsake of membership) — Handcrafted • SIED — QXC4164 • Value $23

13. The Wizard of OZ™ (club edition) — Handcrafted • RGRS — 1295QXC4161 • Value $40

14. "Get Hooked On Collecting" Starter Set (book with "Filled With Memories" ornament) — Handcrafted • N/A — 799XPR837 • Value N/E

15. Welcome Sign, Tender Touches — Handcrafted • SEAL — 1500QX6331 • Value $25

16. 1941 Steelcraft Spitfire Airplane by Murray® (tan) — Die-Cast Metal • PALM — (N/C) No stock # • Value N/E

17. 1955 Chevrolet Cameo (red) — Handcrafted • PALM — (N/C) No stock # • Value N/E

18. Gold Rocking Horse (miniature) — Handcrafted • SICK — ($12.95) No stock # • Value $43

19. Murray® Fire Truck (miniature, white) — Die-Cast Metal • PALM — (N/C) No stock # • Value N/E

20. Santa's Toy Shop (set/2, artist signing piece) — Handcrafted • VARI — 6000QXC4201 • Value $115

General Miniature / Collector's Club / Premiere Ornaments / Artists On Tour Pieces — Price Paid / Value of My Collection — 1–20 — Pencil Totals

76 — *1996 Collection*

Value Guide – Hallmark Keepsake Ornaments

(1) Toy Shop Santa
Handcrafted • UNRU
($14.95) No stock # • **Value $32**

(2) BARBIE™ Lapel Pin (re-issued in 1997)
Handcrafted • N/A
495XLP3544 • **Value $4.95**

(3) Holiday BARBIE™ Stocking Hanger (re-issued in 1997)
Handcrafted • N/A
1995XSH3101 • **Value $19.95**

(4) Yuletide Romance ™ BARBIE® Doll (3rd & final in series)
Vinyl • N/A
5000QHX3401 • **Value N/E**

(5) Reindeer Rooters
Handcrafted • CROW
(N/C) No stock # • **Value N/E**

(6) Golden Age Batman and Robin™ "The Dynamic Duo™"
Handcrafted • UNRU
7000QHF3103 • **Value N/E**

(7) Golden Age Superman™ "Man of Steel™" (LE-14,500)
Handcrafted • N/A
8000QHF3101 • **Value N/E**

(8) Golden Age Wonder Woman™ "Champion of Freedom"
Handcrafted • RGRS
3500QHF3107 • **Value N/E**

(9) Modern Era Batman™ "Guardian of Gotham City™"
Handcrafted • CHAD
5500QHF3104 • **Value N/E**

(10) Modern Era Robin™ "World's Bravest Teenager"
Handcrafted • CHAD
4000QHF3105 • **Value N/E**

(11) Modern Era Superman™ "In A Single Bound"
Handcrafted • N/A
6000QHF3102 • **Value N/E**

(12) Modern Era Wonder Woman™ "Warrior of Strength and Wisdom"
Handcrafted • RGRS
3500QHF3106 • **Value N/E**

(13) NFL COLLECTION (14 assorted)
Glass • N/A

1. Buffalo Bills™
595BIL2035 • **Value N/E**
2. Carolina Panthers™ (re-issued from 1995)
595PNA2035 • **Value N/E**
3. Chicago Bears™ (re-issued from 1995)
595BRS2035 • **Value N/E**
4. Dallas Cowboys™ (re-issued from 1995)
595COW2035 • **Value N/E**
5. Green Bay Packers™
595PKR2035 • **Value N/E**
6. Kansas City Chiefs™ (re-issued from 1995)
595CHF2035 • **Value N/E**
7. Los Angeles Raiders™ (re-issued from 1995)
595RDR2035 • **Value N/E**

8. Minnesota Vikings™ (re-issued from 1995)
595VIK2035 • **Value N/E**
9. New England Patriots™ (re-issued from 1995)
595NEP2035 • **Value N/E**
10. Philadelphia Eagles™ (re-issued from 1995)
595EAG2035 • **Value N/E**
11. Pittsburgh Steelers™
595PIT2035 • **Value N/E**
12. St. Louis Rams™
595RAM2035 • **Value N/E**
13. San Francisco 49ers™ (re-issued from 1995)
595FOR2035 • **Value N/E**
14. Washington Redskins™ (re-issued from 1995)
595RSK2035 • **Value N/E**

(14) NFL COLLECTION (30 assorted)
Handcrafted • UNRU

1. Arizona Cardinals™
995QSR6484 • **Value N/E**
2. Atlanta Falcons™
995QSR6364 • **Value N/E**
3. Browns™
995QSR6391 • **Value N/E**
4. Buffalo Bills™
995QSR6371 • **Value N/E**
5. Carolina Panthers™
995QSR6374 • **Value N/E**
6. Chicago Bears™
995QSR6381 • **Value N/E**

7. Cincinnati Bengals™
995QSR6384 • **Value N/E**
8. Dallas Cowboys™
995QSR6394 • **Value N/E**
9. Denver Broncos™
995QSR6411 • **Value N/E**
10. Detroit Lions™
995QSR6414 • **Value N/E**
11. Green Bay Packers™
995QSR6421 • **Value N/E**
12. Indianapolis Colts™
995QSR6431 • **Value N/E**

1996

Artists On Tour Pieces

	Price Paid	Value of My Collection
1.		

BARBIE™ Collectibles

2.		
3.		
4.		

Club Tour Ornament

5.		

D.C. Super Heroes Figurines

6.		
7.		
8.		
9.		
10.		
11.		
12.		

NFL Collection

13.		
14.		

PENCIL TOTALS

Value Guide — Hallmark Keepsake Ornaments

13. Jacksonville Jaguars™ 995QSR6434 • **Value N/E** 14. Kansas City Chiefs™ 995QSR6361 • **Value N/E** 15. Miami Dolphins™ 995QSR6451 • **Value N/E** 16. Minnesota Vikings™ 995QSR6454 • **Value N/E** 17. New England Patriots™ 995QSR6461 • **Value N/E** 18. New Orleans Saints™ 995QSR6464 • **Value N/E**	19. New York Giants™ 995QSR6471 • **Value N/E** 20. New York Jets™ 995QSR6474 • **Value N/E** 21. Oakland Raiders™ 995QSR6441 • **Value N/E** 22. Oilers™ 995QSR6424 • **Value N/E** 23. Philadelphia Eagles™ 995QSR6481 • **Value N/E** 24. Pittsburgh Steelers™ 995QSR6491 • **Value N/E**	25. St. Louis Rams™ 995QSR6444 • **Value N/E** 26. San Diego Chargers™ 995QSR6494 • **Value N/E** 27. San Francisco 49ers™ 995QSR6501 • **Value N/E** 28. Seattle Seahawks™ 995QSR6504 • **Value N/E** 29. Tampa Bay Buccaneers™ 995QSR6511 • **Value N/E** 30. Washington Redskins™ 995QSR6514 • **Value N/E**

Gymnastics Figurine
Handcrafted • LYLE
1750QHC8204 • **Value N/E**

**Olympic Triumph
Figurine (LE-24,500)**
Handcrafted • UNRU
5000QHC8191 • **Value N/E**

Parade of Nations Plate
Porcelain • N/A
3000QHC8194 • **Value N/E**

Swimming Figurine
Handcrafted • CHAD
1750QHC8211 • **Value N/E**

**Track and Field
Figurine**
Handcrafted • N/A
1750QHC8201 • **Value N/E**

Olympic Collectibles

	Price Paid	Value of My Collection
1.		
2.		
3.		
4.		
5.		

General Keepsake

6.		
7.		
8.		
9.		
10.		
11.		
12.		
13.		
14.		

\ PENCIL TOTALS

1995

More great BARBIE™, STAR TREK™ and sports figure ornaments were released in 1995 as well as a record number of Showcase ornaments. In the 1995 line, there were 146 Keepsake, 20 Magic, 20 Showcase and 36 Miniature ornaments. See collectible series section for more 1995 ornaments.

Acorn 500
Handcrafted • SIED
1095QX5929 • **Value $21**

Across the Miles
Handcrafted • FRAN
895QX5847 • **Value $17**

Air Express
Handcrafted • SEAL
795QX5977 • **Value $17**

Anniversary Year
Handcrafted • UNRU
895QX5819 • **Value $15**

Baby's First Christmas
Handcrafted • VOTR
795QX5549 • **Value $16**

Baby's First Christmas
Handcrafted • CROW
795QX5559 • **Value $18**

Baby's First Christmas
Handcrafted • ANDR
995QX5557 • **Value $18**

Baby's First Christmas
Handcrafted • ANDR
1895QX5547 • **Value $44**

**Baby's First Christmas
– Baby Boy**
Glass • N/A
500QX2319 • **Value $13**

1
Baby's First Christmas
– Baby Girl
Glass • N/A
500QX2317 • **Value $13**

2
Baby's Second
Christmas
Handcrafted • CROW
795QX5567 • **Value $18**

3
Barrel-Back Rider
Handcrafted • FRAN
995QX5189 • **Value $24**

4
Batmobile
Handcrafted • PALM
1495QX5739 • **Value $27**

5
Betty and Wilma
Handcrafted • RHOD
1495QX5417 • **Value $25**

6
Beverly and Teddy
Handcrafted • UNRU
2175QX5259 • **Value $38**

7
Bingo Bear
Handcrafted • VOTR
795QX5919 • **Value $15**

8
Bobbin' Along
Handcrafted • CROW
895QX5879 • **Value $33**

9
Brother
Handcrafted • LYLE
695QX5679 • **Value $12**

10
Bugs Bunny
Handcrafted • CHAD
895QX5019 • **Value $22**

11
Captain James T. Kirk
Handcrafted • RGRS
1395QXI5539 • **Value $23**

12
Captain Jean-Luc Picard
Handcrafted • RGRS
1395QXI5737 • **Value $23**

13
Captain John Smith
and Meeko
Handcrafted • CROW
1295QXI6169 • **Value $20**

14
Catch the Spirit
Handcrafted • SIED
795QX5899 • **Value $18**

15
Child's Fifth Christmas
Handcrafted • RHOD
695QX5637 • **Value $16**

16
Child's Fourth
Christmas
Handcrafted • FRAN
695QX5629 • **Value $17**

17
Child's Third Christmas
Handcrafted • CROW
795QX5627 • **Value $17**

18
Christmas Fever
Handcrafted • AUBE
795QX5967 • **Value $16**

19
Christmas Morning
Handcrafted • FRAN
1095QX5997 • **Value $17**

20
Christmas Patrol
Handcrafted • ANDR
795QX5959 • **Value $16**

1995

General Keepsake

	Price Paid	Value of My Collection
1.		
2.		
3.		
4.		
5.		
6.		
7.		
8.		
9.		
10.		
11.		
12.		
13.		
14.		
15.		
16.		
17.		
18.		
19.		
20.		

PENCIL TOTALS

Value Guide — Hallmark Keepsake Ornaments

(1) Colorful World
Handcrafted • CROW
1095QX5519 • **Value $25**

(2) Cows of Bali
Handcrafted • ANDR
895QX5999 • **Value $16**

(3) Dad
Handcrafted • SIED
795QX5649 • **Value $14**

(4) Dad-to-Be
Handcrafted • RHOD
795QX5667 • **Value $12**

(5) Daughter
Handcrafted • PALM
695QX5677 • **Value $14**

(6) Delivering Kisses
Handcrafted • SICK
1095QX4107 • **Value $23**

(7) Dream On
Handcrafted • FRAN
1095QX6007 • **Value $18**

(8) Dudley the Dragon
Handcrafted • PIKE
1095QX6209 • **Value $20**

(9) Faithful Fan
Handcrafted • SIED
895QX5897 • **Value $18**

(10) Feliz Navidad
Handcrafted • RHOD
795QX5869 • **Value $18**

(11) For My Grandma
Handcrafted • PALM
695QX5729 • **Value $12**

(12) Forever Friends Bear
Handcrafted • BRWN
895QX5258 • **Value $20**

(13) Friendly Boost
Handcrafted • PALM
895QX5827 • **Value $20**

(14) GARFIELD®
Handcrafted • N/A
1095QX5007 • **Value $24**

(15) Glinda, Witch of the North
Handcrafted • LYLE
1395QX5749 • **Value $28**

(16) Godchild
Handcrafted/Brass • PALM
795QX5707 • **Value $19**

(17) Godparent
Glass • VOTR
500QX2417 • **Value $9**

(18) Gopher Fun
Handcrafted • SIED
995QX5887 • **Value $20**

(19) Grandchild's First Christmas
Handcrafted • FRAN
795QX5777 • **Value $15**

(20) Granddaughter
Handcrafted • RGRS
695QX5779 • **Value $14**

General Keepsake

	Price Paid	Value of My Collection
1.		
2.		
3.		
4.		
5.		
6.		
7.		
8.		
9.		
10.		
11.		
12.		
13.		
14.		
15.		
16.		
17.		
18.		
19.		
20.		

PENCIL TOTALS

80

1995 Collection

1 Grandmother
Handcrafted • ANDR
795QX5767 • **Value $18**

2 Grandpa
Handcrafted • CROW
895QX5769 • **Value $15**

3 Grandparents
Glass • LYLE
500QX2419 • **Value $10**

4 Grandson
Handcrafted • RGRS
695QX5787 • **Value $13**

5 Happy Wrappers (set/2)
Handcrafted • CROW
1095QX6037 • **Value $19**

6 Heaven's Gift (set/2)
Handcrafted • ANDR
2000QX6057 • **Value $35**

7 Hockey Pup
Handcrafted • CROW
995QX5917 • **Value $23**

8 Important Memo
Handcrafted • SICK
895QX5947 • **Value $15**

9 In a Heartbeat
Handcrafted • ANDR
895QX5817 • **Value $17**

10 In Time With Christmas
Handcrafted • CROW
1295QX6049 • **Value $24**

11 Joy to the World
Handcrafted • ANDR
895QX5867 • **Value $18**

12 LEGO® Fireplace
With Santa
Handcrafted • CROW
1095QX4769 • **Value $23**

13 Lou Rankin Bear
Handcrafted • SIED
995QX4069 • **Value $20**

14 The Magic School Bus™
Handcrafted • RHOD
1095QX5849 • **Value $18**

15 Mary Engelbreit
Glass • N/A
500QX2409 • **Value $14**

16 Merry RV
Handcrafted • PALM
1295QX6027 • **Value $23**

17 Mom
Handcrafted • SIED
795QX5647 • **Value $15**

18 Mom and Dad
Handcrafted • RGRS
995QX5657 • **Value $23**

19 Mom-to-Be
Handcrafted • RHOD
795QX5659 • **Value $13**

20 Muletide Greetings
Handcrafted • CHAD
795QX6009 • **Value $14**

1995

GENERAL KEEPSAKE

	Price Paid	Value of My Collection
1.		
2.		
3.		
4.		
5.		
6.		
7.		
8.		
9.		
10.		
11.		
12.		
13.		
14.		
15.		
16.		
17.		
18.		
19.		
20.		
PENCIL TOTALS		

1 New Home
Handcrafted • ANDR
895QX5839 • **Value $15**

2 North Pole 911
Handcrafted • SEAL
1095QX5957 • **Value $22**

3 Number One Teacher
Handcrafted • SEAL
795QX5949 • **Value $14**

4 The Olympic Spirit
Centennial Games
Atlanta 1996
Acrylic • N/A
795QX3169 • **Value $18**

5 On the Ice
Handcrafted • CROW
795QX6047 • **Value $21**

6 Our Christmas Together
Handcrafted • LYLE
995QX5809 • **Value $17**

7 Our Family
Handcrafted • CHAD
795QX5709 • **Value $15**

8 Our First Christmas
Together
Acrylic • LYLE
695QX3177 • **Value $19**

9 Our First Christmas
Together
Handcrafted • SIED
895QX5799 • **Value $19**

10 Our First Christmas
Together
Handcrafted • SEAL
895QX5807 • **Value $17**

11 Our First Christmas
Together
Handcrafted • LYLE
1695QX5797 • **Value $28**

12 Our Little Blessings
Handcrafted • CROW
1295QX5209 • **Value $23**

13 Packed With Memories
Handcrafted • SEAL
795QX5639 • **Value $13**

14 Percy, Flit and Meeko
Handcrafted • CROW
995QXI6179 • **Value $20**

15 Perfect Balance
Handcrafted • SIED
795QX5927 • **Value $14**

16 PEZ® Santa
Handcrafted • FRAN
795QX5267 • **Value $17**

17 Pocahontas
Handcrafted • CROW
1295QXI6177 • **Value $21**

18 Pocahontas and Captain
John Smith
Handcrafted • CROW
1495QXI6197 • **Value $23**

19 Polar Coaster
Handcrafted • CROW
895QX6117 • **Value $24**

20 Popeye®
Handcrafted • CHAD
1095QX5257 • **Value $27**

General Keepsake

	Price Paid	Value of My Collection
1.		
2.		
3.		
4.		
5.		
6.		
7.		
8.		
9.		
10.		
11.		
12.		
13.		
14.		
15.		
16.		
17.		
18.		
19.		
20.		

PENCIL TOTALS

1 Refreshing Gift
Handcrafted • UNRU
1495QX4067 • **Value $28**

2 Rejoice!
Handcrafted • LYLE
1095QX5987 • **Value $23**

3 Roller Whiz
Handcrafted • SEAL
795QX5937 • **Value $17**

4 Santa In Paris
Handcrafted • SICK
895QX5877 • **Value $25**

5 Santa's Serenade
Handcrafted • CROW
895QX6017 • **Value $18**

6 Santa's Visitors
Glass • N/A
500QX2407 • **Value $14**

7 Simba, Pumbaa and Timon
Handcrafted • CROW
1295QX6159 • **Value $14**

8 Sister
Handcrafted • LYLE
695QX5687 • **Value $13**

9 Sister to Sister
Handcrafted • VOTR
895QX5689 • **Value $15**

10 Ski Hound
Handcrafted • RHOD
895QX5909 • **Value $15**

11 Son
Handcrafted • PALM
695QX5669 • **Value $13**

12 Special Cat
Handcrafted • CHAD
795QX5717 • **Value $13**

13 Special Dog
Handcrafted • CHAD
795QX5719 • **Value $13**

14 Surfin' Santa
Handcrafted • CROW
995QX6019 • **Value $20**

15 Sylvester and Tweety (set/2)
Handcrafted • CHAD
1395QX5017 • **Value $26**

16 Takin' a Hike
Handcrafted • FRAN
795QX6029 • **Value $17**

17 Tennis, Anyone?
Handcrafted • AUBE
795QX5907 • **Value $17**

18 Thomas the Tank Engine – No. 1
Handcrafted • RHOD
995QX5857 • **Value $25**

19 Three Wishes
Handcrafted • ANDR
795QX5979 • **Value $18**

20 Two for Tea
Handcrafted • JLEE
995QX5829 • **Value $27**

1995

General Keepsake

	Price Paid	Value of My Collection
1.		
2.		
3.		
4.		
5.		
6.		
7.		
8.		
9.		
10.		
11.		
12.		
13.		
14.		
15.		
16.		
17.		
18.		
19.		
20.		
PENCIL TOTALS		

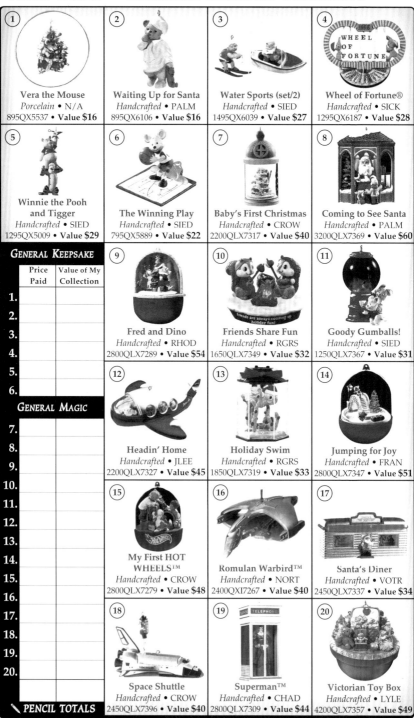

1

Vera the Mouse
Porcelain • N/A
895QX5537 • **Value $16**

2

Waiting Up for Santa
Handcrafted • PALM
895QX6106 • **Value $16**

3

Water Sports (set/2)
Handcrafted • SIED
1495QX6039 • **Value $27**

4

Wheel of Fortune®
Handcrafted • SICK
1295QX6187 • **Value $28**

5

**Winnie the Pooh
and Tigger**
Handcrafted • SIED
1295QX5009 • **Value $29**

6

The Winning Play
Handcrafted • SIED
795QX5889 • **Value $22**

7

Baby's First Christmas
Handcrafted • CROW
2200QLX7317 • **Value $40**

8

Coming to See Santa
Handcrafted • PALM
3200QLX7369 • **Value $60**

9

Fred and Dino
Handcrafted • RHOD
2800QLX7289 • **Value $54**

10

Friends Share Fun
Handcrafted • RGRS
1650QLX7349 • **Value $32**

11

Goody Gumballs!
Handcrafted • SIED
1250QLX7367 • **Value $31**

12

Headin' Home
Handcrafted • JLEE
2200QLX7327 • **Value $45**

13

Holiday Swim
Handcrafted • RGRS
1850QLX7319 • **Value $33**

14

Jumping for Joy
Handcrafted • FRAN
2800QLX7347 • **Value $51**

15

**My First HOT
WHEELS™**
Handcrafted • CROW
2800QLX7279 • **Value $48**

16

Romulan Warbird™
Handcrafted • NORT
2400QXI7267 • **Value $40**

17

Santa's Diner
Handcrafted • VOTR
2450QLX7337 • **Value $34**

18

Space Shuttle
Handcrafted • CROW
2450QLX7396 • **Value $40**

19

Superman™
Handcrafted • CHAD
2800QLX7309 • **Value $44**

20

Victorian Toy Box
Handcrafted • LYLE
4200QLX7357 • **Value $49**

General Keepsake

	Price Paid	Value of My Collection
1.		
2.		
3.		
4.		
5.		
6.		

General Magic

7.		
8.		
9.		
10.		
11.		
12.		
13.		
14.		
15.		
16.		
17.		
18.		
19.		
20.		

◥ PENCIL TOTALS

1. Wee Little Christmas
Handcrafted • CROW
2200QLX7329 • **Value $38**

2. Winnie the Pooh
Too Much Hunny
Handcrafted • SIED
2450QLX7297 • **Value $41**

3. Angel of Light
All Is Bright
Handcrafted • ANDR
1195QK1159 • **Value $21**

4. Gentle Lullaby
All Is Bright
Handcrafted • ANDR
1195QK1157 • **Value $21**

5. Carole
Angel Bells
Porcelain • VOTR
1295QK1147 • **Value $20**

6. Joy
Angel Bells
Porcelain • VOTR
1295QK1137 • **Value $26**

7. Noelle
Angel Bells
Porcelain • VOTR
1295QK1139 • **Value $20**

8. Fetching the Firewood
Folk Art Americana
Handcrafted • SICK
1595QK1057 • **Value $33**

9. Fishing Party
Folk Art Americana
Handcrafted • SICK
1595QK1039 • **Value $33**

10. Guiding Santa
Folk Art Americana
Handcrafted • SICK
1895QK1037 • **Value $50**

11. Learning to Skate
Folk Art Americana
Handcrafted • SICK
1495QK1047 • **Value $36**

12. Away in a Manger
Holiday Enchantment
Porcelain • N/A
1395QK1097 • **Value $24**

13. Following the Star
Holiday Enchantment
Porcelain • VOTR
1395QK1099 • **Value $24**

14. Cozy Cottage Teapot
Invitation To Tea
Handcrafted • ANDR
1595QK1127 • **Value $26**

15. European Castle Teapot
Invitation To Tea
Handcrafted • ANDR
1595QK1129 • **Value $26**

16. Victorian Home Teapot
Invitation To Tea
Handcrafted • ANDR
1595QK1119 • **Value $33**

17. Backyard Orchard
Nature's Sketchbook
Handcrafted • FRAN
1895QK1069 • **Value $29**

18. Christmas Cardinal
Nature's Sketchbook
Handcrafted • LYLE
1895QK1077 • **Value $39**

19. Raising a Family
Nature's Sketchbook
Handcrafted • LYLE
1895QK1067 • **Value $27**

20. Violets and Butterflies
Nature's Sketchbook
Handcrafted • LYLE
1695QK1079 • **Value $27**

1995

GENERAL MAGIC	Price Paid	Value of My Collection
1.		
2.		
GENERAL SHOWCASE		
3.		
4.		
5.		
6.		
7.		
8.		
9.		
10.		
11.		
12.		
13.		
14.		
15.		
16.		
17.		
18.		
19.		
20.		
PENCIL TOTALS		

Value Guide – Hallmark Keepsake Ornaments

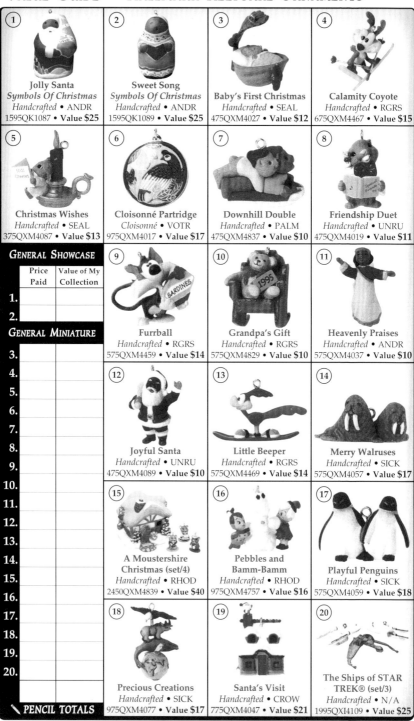

1. Jolly Santa
Symbols Of Christmas
Handcrafted • ANDR
1595QK1087 • **Value $25**

2. Sweet Song
Symbols Of Christmas
Handcrafted • ANDR
1595QK1089 • **Value $25**

3. Baby's First Christmas
Handcrafted • SEAL
475QXM4027 • **Value $12**

4. Calamity Coyote
Handcrafted • RGRS
675QXM4467 • **Value $15**

5. Christmas Wishes
Handcrafted • SEAL
375QXM4087 • **Value $13**

6. Cloisonné Partridge
Cloisonné • VOTR
975QXM4017 • **Value $17**

7. Downhill Double
Handcrafted • PALM
475QXM4837 • **Value $10**

8. Friendship Duet
Handcrafted • UNRU
475QXM4019 • **Value $11**

9. Furrball
Handcrafted • RGRS
575QXM4459 • **Value $14**

10. Grandpa's Gift
Handcrafted • RGRS
575QXM4829 • **Value $10**

11. Heavenly Praises
Handcrafted • ANDR
575QXM4037 • **Value $10**

12. Joyful Santa
Handcrafted • UNRU
475QXM4089 • **Value $10**

13. Little Beeper
Handcrafted • RGRS
575QXM4469 • **Value $14**

14. Merry Walruses
Handcrafted • SICK
575QXM4057 • **Value $17**

15. A Moustershire Christmas (set/4)
Handcrafted • RHOD
2450QXM4839 • **Value $40**

16. Pebbles and Bamm-Bamm
Handcrafted • RHOD
975QXM4757 • **Value $16**

17. Playful Penguins
Handcrafted • SICK
575QXM4059 • **Value $18**

18. Precious Creations
Handcrafted • SICK
975QXM4077 • **Value $17**

19. Santa's Visit
Handcrafted • CROW
775QXM4047 • **Value $21**

20. The Ships of STAR TREK® (set/3)
Handcrafted • N/A
1995QXI4109 • **Value $25**

GENERAL SHOWCASE

	Price Paid	Value of My Collection
1.		
2.		

GENERAL MINIATURE

3.		
4.		
5.		
6.		
7.		
8.		
9.		
10.		
11.		
12.		
13.		
14.		
15.		
16.		
17.		
18.		
19.		
20.		

PENCIL TOTALS

86

1995 Collection

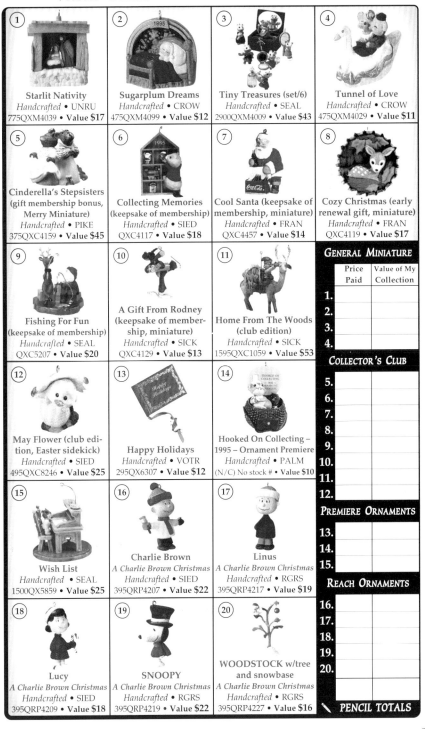

1995

1. Starlit Nativity
Handcrafted • UNRU
775QXM4039 • **Value $17**

2. Sugarplum Dreams
Handcrafted • CROW
475QXM4099 • **Value $12**

3. Tiny Treasures (set/6)
Handcrafted • SEAL
2900QXM4009 • **Value $43**

4. Tunnel of Love
Handcrafted • CROW
475QXM4029 • **Value $11**

5. Cinderella's Stepsisters
(gift membership bonus, Merry Miniature)
Handcrafted • PIKE
375QXC4159 • **Value $45**

6. Collecting Memories
(keepsake of membership)
Handcrafted • SIED
QXC4117 • **Value $18**

7. Cool Santa (keepsake of membership, miniature)
Handcrafted • FRAN
QXC4457 • **Value $14**

8. Cozy Christmas (early renewal gift, miniature)
Handcrafted • FRAN
QXC4119 • **Value $17**

9. Fishing For Fun
(keepsake of membership)
Handcrafted • SEAL
QXC5207 • **Value $20**

10. A Gift From Rodney
(keepsake of membership, miniature)
Handcrafted • SICK
QXC4129 • **Value $13**

11. Home From The Woods
(club edition)
Handcrafted • SICK
1595QXC1059 • **Value $53**

12. May Flower (club edition, Easter sidekick)
Handcrafted • SIED
495QXC8246 • **Value $25**

13. Happy Holidays
Handcrafted • VOTR
295QX6307 • **Value $12**

14. Hooked On Collecting – 1995 – Ornament Premiere
Handcrafted • PALM
(N/C) No stock # • **Value $10**

15. Wish List
Handcrafted • SEAL
1500QX5859 • **Value $25**

16. Charlie Brown
A Charlie Brown Christmas
Handcrafted • SIED
395QRP4207 • **Value $22**

17. Linus
A Charlie Brown Christmas
Handcrafted • RGRS
395QRP4217 • **Value $19**

18. Lucy
A Charlie Brown Christmas
Handcrafted • SIED
395QRP4209 • **Value $18**

19. SNOOPY
A Charlie Brown Christmas
Handcrafted • RGRS
395QRP4219 • **Value $22**

20. WOODSTOCK w/tree and snowbase
A Charlie Brown Christmas
Handcrafted • RGRS
395QRP4227 • **Value $16**

General Miniature

	Price Paid	Value of My Collection
1.		
2.		
3.		
4.		

Collector's Club

5.		
6.		
7.		
8.		
9.		
10.		
11.		
12.		

Premiere Ornaments

13.		
14.		
15.		

Reach Ornaments

16.		
17.		
18.		
19.		
20.		

Pencil Totals

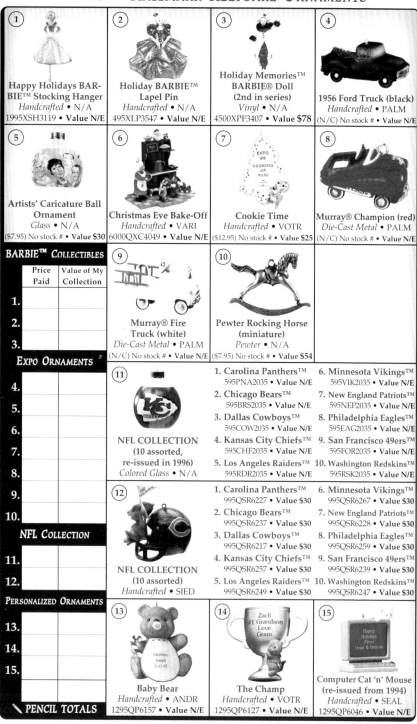

(1) Happy Holidays BAR-BIE™ Stocking Hanger
Handcrafted • N/A
1995XSH3119 • **Value N/E**

(2) Holiday BARBIE™ Lapel Pin
Handcrafted • N/A
495XLP3547 • **Value N/E**

(3) Holiday Memories™ BARBIE® Doll (2nd in series)
Vinyl • N/A
4500XPF3407 • **Value $78**

(4) 1956 Ford Truck (black)
Handcrafted • PALM
(N/C) No stock # • **Value N/E**

(5) Artists' Caricature Ball Ornament
Glass • N/A
($7.95) No stock # • **Value $30**

(6) Christmas Eve Bake-Off
Handcrafted • VARI
6000QXC4049 • **Value N/E**

(7) Cookie Time
Handcrafted • VOTR
($12.95) No stock # • **Value $25**

(8) Murray® Champion (red)
Die-Cast Metal • PALM
(N/C) No stock # • **Value N/E**

(9) Murray® Fire Truck (white)
Die-Cast Metal • PALM
(N/C) No stock # • **Value N/E**

(10) Pewter Rocking Horse (miniature)
Pewter • N/A
($7.95) No stock # • **Value $54**

BARBIE™ COLLECTIBLES

	Price Paid	Value of My Collection
1.		
2.		
3.		

EXPO ORNAMENTS

4.		
5.		
6.		
7.		
8.		
9.		
10.		

NFL COLLECTION

11.		
12.		

PERSONALIZED ORNAMENTS

13.		
14.		
15.		

PENCIL TOTALS

(11) NFL COLLECTION (10 assorted, re-issued in 1996)
Colored Glass • N/A

1. Carolina Panthers™ 595PNA2035 • **Value N/E**
2. Chicago Bears™ 595BRS2035 • **Value N/E**
3. Dallas Cowboys™ 595COW2035 • **Value N/E**
4. Kansas City Chiefs™ 595CHF2035 • **Value N/E**
5. Los Angeles Raiders™ 595RDR2035 • **Value N/E**
6. Minnesota Vikings™ 595VIK2035 • **Value N/E**
7. New England Patriots™ 595NEP2035 • **Value N/E**
8. Philadelphia Eagles™ 595EAG2035 • **Value N/E**
9. San Francisco 49ers™ 595FOR2035 • **Value N/E**
10. Washington Redskins™ 595RSK2035 • **Value N/E**

(12) NFL COLLECTION (10 assorted)
Handcrafted • SIED

1. Carolina Panthers™ 995QSR6227 • **Value $30**
2. Chicago Bears™ 995QSR6237 • **Value $30**
3. Dallas Cowboys™ 995QSR6217 • **Value $30**
4. Kansas City Chiefs™ 995QSR6257 • **Value $30**
5. Los Angeles Raiders™ 995QSR6249 • **Value $30**
6. Minnesota Vikings™ 995QSR6267 • **Value $30**
7. New England Patriots™ 995QSR6228 • **Value $30**
8. Philadelphia Eagles™ 995QSR6259 • **Value $30**
9. San Francisco 49ers™ 995QSR6239 • **Value $30**
10. Washington Redskins™ 995QSR6247 • **Value $30**

(13) Baby Bear
Handcrafted • ANDR
1295QP6157 • **Value N/E**

(14) The Champ
Handcrafted • VOTR
1295QP6127 • **Value N/E**

(15) Computer Cat 'n' Mouse (re-issued from 1994)
Handcrafted • SEAL
1295QP6046 • **Value N/E**

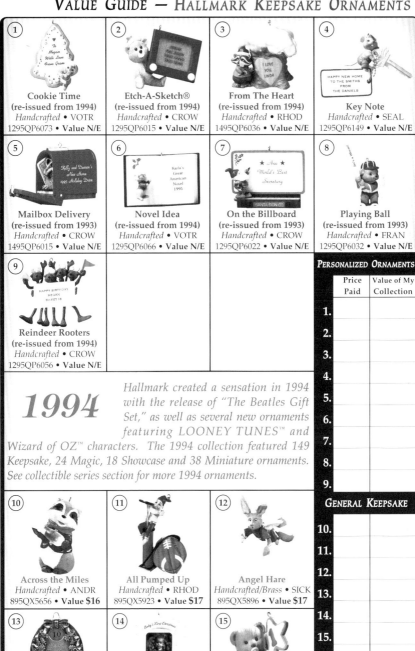

1
Cookie Time
(re-issued from 1994)
Handcrafted • VOTR
1295QP6073 • **Value N/E**

2
Etch-A-Sketch®
(re-issued from 1994)
Handcrafted • CROW
1295QP6015 • **Value N/E**

3
From The Heart
(re-issued from 1994)
Handcrafted • RHOD
1495QP6036 • **Value N/E**

4
Key Note
Handcrafted • SEAL
1295QP6149 • **Value N/E**

5
Mailbox Delivery
(re-issued from 1993)
Handcrafted • CROW
1495QP6015 • **Value N/E**

6
Novel Idea
(re-issued from 1994)
Handcrafted • VOTR
1295QP6066 • **Value N/E**

7
On the Billboard
(re-issued from 1993)
Handcrafted • CROW
1295QP6022 • **Value N/E**

8
Playing Ball
(re-issued from 1993)
Handcrafted • FRAN
1295QP6032 • **Value N/E**

9
Reindeer Rooters
(re-issued from 1994)
Handcrafted • CROW
1295QP6056 • **Value N/E**

1994

1994

Hallmark created a sensation in 1994 with the release of "The Beatles Gift Set," as well as several new ornaments featuring LOONEY TUNES™ and Wizard of OZ™ characters. The 1994 collection featured 149 Keepsake, 24 Magic, 18 Showcase and 38 Miniature ornaments. See collectible series section for more 1994 ornaments.

	Price Paid	Value of My Collection
PERSONALIZED ORNAMENTS		
1.		
2.		
3.		
4.		
5.		
6.		
7.		
8.		
9.		
GENERAL KEEPSAKE		
10.		
11.		
12.		
13.		
14.		
15.		
PENCIL TOTALS		

10
Across the Miles
Handcrafted • ANDR
895QX5656 • **Value $16**

11
All Pumped Up
Handcrafted • RHOD
895QX5923 • **Value $17**

12
Angel Hare
Handcrafted/Brass • SICK
895QX5896 • **Value $17**

13
Anniversary Year
Brass/Chrome • BISH
1095QX5683 • **Value $18**

14
Baby's First Christmas
Handcrafted • VOTR
795QX5636 • **Value $19**

15
Baby's First Christmas
Handcrafted • N/A
795QX5713 • **Value $27**

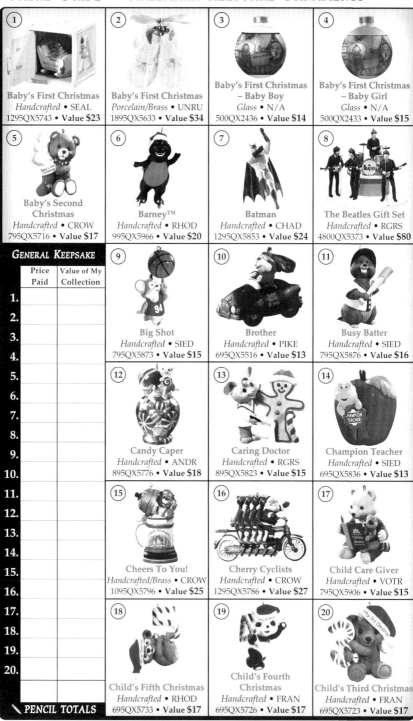

(1)
Baby's First Christmas
Handcrafted • SEAL
1295QX5743 • **Value $23**

(2)
Baby's First Christmas
Porcelain/Brass • UNRU
1895QX5633 • **Value $34**

(3)
Baby's First Christmas
– Baby Boy
Glass • N/A
500QX2436 • **Value $14**

(4)
Baby's First Christmas
– Baby Girl
Glass • N/A
500QX2433 • **Value $15**

(5)
Baby's Second
Christmas
Handcrafted • CROW
795QX5716 • **Value $17**

(6)
Barney™
Handcrafted • RHOD
995QX5966 • **Value $20**

(7)
Batman
Handcrafted • CHAD
1295QX5853 • **Value $24**

(8)
The Beatles Gift Set
Handcrafted • RGRS
4800QX5373 • **Value $80**

(9)
Big Shot
Handcrafted • SIED
795QX5873 • **Value $15**

(10)
Brother
Handcrafted • PIKE
695QX5516 • **Value $13**

(11)
Busy Batter
Handcrafted • SIED
795QX5876 • **Value $16**

(12)
Candy Caper
Handcrafted • ANDR
895QX5776 • **Value $18**

(13)
Caring Doctor
Handcrafted • RGRS
895QX5823 • **Value $15**

(14)
Champion Teacher
Handcrafted • SIED
695QX5836 • **Value $13**

(15)
Cheers To You!
Handcrafted/Brass • CROW
1095QX5796 • **Value $25**

(16)
Cherry Cyclists
Handcrafted • CROW
1295QX5786 • **Value $27**

(17)
Child Care Giver
Handcrafted • VOTR
795QX5906 • **Value $15**

(18)
Child's Fifth Christmas
Handcrafted • RHOD
695QX5733 • **Value $17**

(19)
Child's Fourth
Christmas
Handcrafted • FRAN
695QX5726 • **Value $17**

(20)
Child's Third Christmas
Handcrafted • FRAN
695QX5723 • **Value $17**

GENERAL KEEPSAKE

	Price Paid	Value of My Collection
1.		
2.		
3.		
4.		
5.		
6.		
7.		
8.		
9.		
10.		
11.		
12.		
13.		
14.		
15.		
16.		
17.		
18.		
19.		
20.		
PENCIL TOTALS		

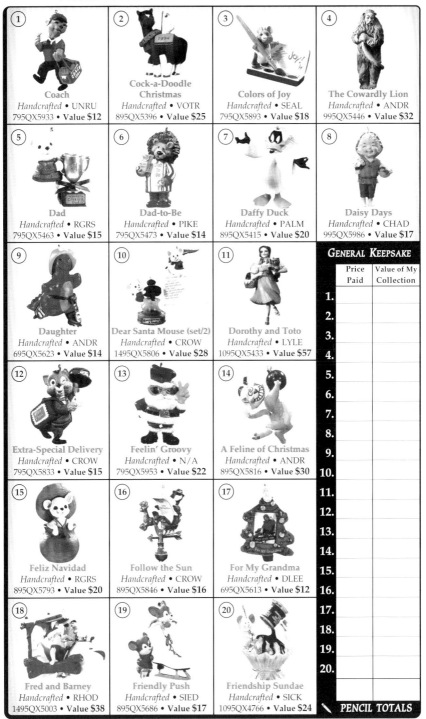

1. Coach
Handcrafted • UNRU
795QX5933 • Value **$12**

2. Cock-a-Doodle Christmas
Handcrafted • VOTR
895QX5396 • Value **$25**

3. Colors of Joy
Handcrafted • SEAL
795QX5893 • Value **$18**

4. The Cowardly Lion
Handcrafted • ANDR
995QX5446 • Value **$32**

5. Dad
Handcrafted • RGRS
795QX5463 • Value **$15**

6. Dad-to-Be
Handcrafted • PIKE
795QX5473 • Value **$14**

7. Daffy Duck
Handcrafted • PALM
895QX5415 • Value **$20**

8. Daisy Days
Handcrafted • CHAD
995QX5986 • Value **$17**

9. Daughter
Handcrafted • ANDR
695QX5623 • Value **$14**

10. Dear Santa Mouse (set/2)
Handcrafted • CROW
1495QX5806 • Value **$28**

11. Dorothy and Toto
Handcrafted • LYLE
1095QX5433 • Value **$57**

12. Extra-Special Delivery
Handcrafted • CROW
795QX5833 • Value **$15**

13. Feelin' Groovy
Handcrafted • N/A
795QX5953 • Value **$22**

14. A Feline of Christmas
Handcrafted • ANDR
895QX5816 • Value **$30**

15. Feliz Navidad
Handcrafted • RGRS
895QX5793 • Value **$20**

16. Follow the Sun
Handcrafted • CROW
895QX5846 • Value **$16**

17. For My Grandma
Handcrafted • DLEE
695QX5613 • Value **$12**

18. Fred and Barney
Handcrafted • RHOD
1495QX5003 • Value **$38**

19. Friendly Push
Handcrafted • SIED
895QX5686 • Value **$17**

20. Friendship Sundae
Handcrafted • SICK
1095QX4766 • Value **$24**

1994

GENERAL KEEPSAKE

	Price Paid	Value of My Collection
1.		
2.		
3.		
4.		
5.		
6.		
7.		
8.		
9.		
10.		
11.		
12.		
13.		
14.		
15.		
16.		
17.		
18.		
19.		
20.		
PENCIL TOTALS		

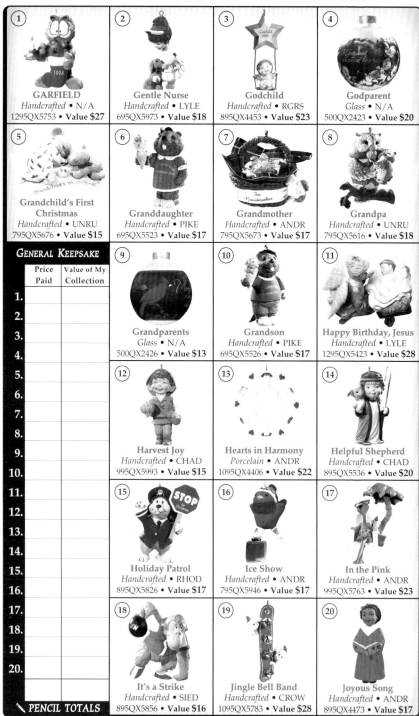

(1) GARFIELD
Handcrafted • N/A
1295QX5753 • **Value $27**

(2) Gentle Nurse
Handcrafted • LYLE
695QX5973 • **Value $18**

(3) Godchild
Handcrafted • RGRS
895QX4453 • **Value $23**

(4) Godparent
Glass • N/A
500QX2423 • **Value $20**

(5) Grandchild's First Christmas
Handcrafted • UNRU
795QX5676 • **Value $15**

(6) Granddaughter
Handcrafted • PIKE
695QX5523 • **Value $17**

(7) Grandmother
Handcrafted • ANDR
795QX5673 • **Value $17**

(8) Grandpa
Handcrafted • UNRU
795QX5616 • **Value $18**

(9) Grandparents
Glass • N/A
500QX2426 • **Value $13**

(10) Grandson
Handcrafted • PIKE
695QX5526 • **Value $17**

(11) Happy Birthday, Jesus
Handcrafted • LYLE
1295QX5423 • **Value $28**

(12) Harvest Joy
Handcrafted • CHAD
995QX5993 • **Value $15**

(13) Hearts in Harmony
Porcelain • ANDR
1095QX4406 • **Value $22**

(14) Helpful Shepherd
Handcrafted • CHAD
895QX5536 • **Value $20**

(15) Holiday Patrol
Handcrafted • RHOD
895QX5826 • **Value $17**

(16) Ice Show
Handcrafted • ANDR
795QX5946 • **Value $17**

(17) In the Pink
Handcrafted • ANDR
995QX5763 • **Value $23**

(18) It's a Strike
Handcrafted • SIED
895QX5856 • **Value $16**

(19) Jingle Bell Band
Handcrafted • CROW
1095QX5783 • **Value $28**

(20) Joyous Song
Handcrafted • ANDR
895QX4473 • **Value $17**

GENERAL KEEPSAKE

	Price Paid	Value of My Collection
1.		
2.		
3.		
4.		
5.		
6.		
7.		
8.		
9.		
10.		
11.		
12.		
13.		
14.		
15.		
16.		
17.		
18.		
19.		
20.		
PENCIL TOTALS		

1. Jump-along Jackalope
Handcrafted • FRAN
895QX5756 • **Value $17**

2. Keep on Mowin'
Handcrafted • SIED
895QX5413 • **Value $18**

3. Kickin' Roo
Handcrafted • SIED
795QX5916 • **Value $16**

4. Kitty's Catamaran
Handcrafted • SEAL
1095QX5416 • **Value $18**

5. Kringle's Kayak
Handcrafted • SEAL
795QX5886 • **Value $19**

6. Lou Rankin Seal
Handcrafted • BISH
995QX5456 • **Value $22**

7. Lucinda and Teddy
Handcrafted/Fabric • UNRU
2175QX4813 • **Value $45**

8. Magic Carpet Ride
Handcrafted • SEAL
795QX5883 • **Value $25**

9. Making It Bright
Handcrafted • RHOD
895QX5403 • **Value $18**

10. Mary Engelbreit
Glass • N/A
500QX2416 • **Value $17**

11. Merry Fishmas
Handcrafted • PALM
895QX5913 • **Value $19**

12. Mistletoe Surprise (set/2)
Handcrafted • SEAL
1295QX5996 • **Value $28**

13. Mom
Handcrafted • RGRS
795QX5466 • **Value $13**

14. Mom and Dad
Handcrafted • SIED
995QX5666 • **Value $18**

15. Mom-to-Be
Handcrafted • PIKE
795QX5506 • **Value $16**

16. Mufasa and Simba
Handcrafted • CROW
1495QX5406 • **Value $30**

17. Nephew
Handcrafted • FRAN
795QX5546 • **Value $12**

18. New Home
Handcrafted • ANDR
895QX5663 • **Value $20**

19. Niece
Handcrafted • FRAN
795QX5543 • **Value $12**

20. Norman Rockwell Art
Glass • LYLE
500QX2413 • **Value $18**

1994

GENERAL KEEPSAKE

	Price Paid	Value of My Collection
1.		
2.		
3.		
4.		
5.		
6.		
7.		
8.		
9.		
10.		
11.		
12.		
13.		
14.		
15.		
16.		
17.		
18.		
19.		
20.		
PENCIL TOTALS		

VALUE GUIDE — HALLMARK KEEPSAKE ORNAMENTS

(1) Open-and-Shut Holiday
Handcrafted • SIED
995QX5696 • **Value $22**

(2) Our Christmas Together
Handcrafted • RGRS
995QX4816 • **Value $21**

(3) Our Family
Handcrafted • ANDR
795QX5576 • **Value $13**

(4) Our First Christmas Together
Acrylic • VOTR
695QX3186 • **Value $16**

(5) Our First Christmas Together
Brass/Fabric • ANDR
1895QX5706 • **Value $38**

(6) Our First Christmas Together
Handcrafted • PALM
895QX5653 • **Value $19**

(7) Our First Christmas Together
Handcrafted • BISH
995QX5643 • **Value $23**

(8) Out of This World Teacher
Handcrafted • UNRU
795QX5766 • **Value $18**

(9) Practice Makes Perfect
Handcrafted • PALM
895QX5863 • **Value $15**

(10) Red Hot Holiday
Handcrafted • RGRS
795QX5843 • **Value $18**

(11) Reindeer Pro
Handcrafted • RHOD
795QX5926 • **Value $15**

(12) Relaxing Moment
Handcrafted • FRAN
1495QX5356 • **Value $30**

(13) Road Runner and Wile E. Coyote
Handcrafted • CHAD
1295QX5602 • **Value $27**

(14) Santa's LEGO® Sleigh
Handcrafted • CROW
1095QX5453 • **Value $29**

(15) The Scarecrow
Handcrafted • UNRU
995QX5436 • **Value $35**

(16) Secret Santa
Handcrafted • UNRU
795QX5736 • **Value $14**

(17) A Sharp Flat
Handcrafted • CROW
1095QX5773 • **Value $24**

(18) Simba and Nala (set/2)
Handcrafted • CROW
1295QX5303 • **Value $26**

(19) Sister
Handcrafted • PIKE
695QX5513 • **Value $16**

(20) Sister to Sister
Handcrafted • RHOD
995QX5533 • **Value $19**

GENERAL KEEPSAKE

	Price Paid	Value of My Collection
1.		
2.		
3.		
4.		
5.		
6.		
7.		
8.		
9.		
10.		
11.		
12.		
13.		
14.		
15.		
16.		
17.		
18.		
19.		
20.		
PENCIL TOTALS		

94

1994 Collection

1
Son
Handcrafted • ANDR
695QX5626 • **Value $12**

2
Special Cat
Acrylic • RHOD
795QX5606 • **Value $14**

3
CANINE EDITION
Dog of the Year in '94!
Special Dog
Handcrafted • RHOD
795QX5603 • **Value $14**

4
Speedy Gonzales
Handcrafted • PALM
895QX5343 • **Value $20**

5
ASAP
A Santa-Approved Person
Stamp of Approval
Handcrafted • SICK
795QX5703 • **Value $15**

6
Sweet Greeting (set/2)
Handcrafted • PALM
1095QX5803 • **Value $20**

7
The Tale of Peter Rabbit
BEATRIX POTTER
Glass • N/A
500QX2443 • **Value $16**

8
Tasmanian Devil
Handcrafted • PALM
895QX5605 • **Value $54**

1994

9
Thick 'n' Thin
Handcrafted • RGRS
1095QX5693 • **Value $20**

10
Thrill a Minute
Handcrafted • SIED
895QX5866 • **Value $17**

11
PEACE
Time of Peace
Handcrafted • ANDR
795QX5813 • **Value $15**

12
Timon and Pumbaa
Handcrafted • CROW
895QX5366 • **Value $21**

13
The Tin Man
Handcrafted • UNRU
995QX5443 • **Value $35**

14
Tou Can Love
Handcrafted • RGRS
895QX5646 • **Value $18**

15
Tulip Time
Handcrafted • CHAD
995QX5983 • **Value $15**

16
Winnie the Pooh
and Tigger
Handcrafted • SIED
1295QX5746 • **Value $32**

17
Yosemite Sam
Handcrafted • PALM
895QX5346 • **Value $18**

18
Yuletide Cheer
Handcrafted • CHAD
995QX5976 • **Value $17**

19
Away in a Manger
Handcrafted • LYLE
1600QLX7383 • **Value $42**

20
Baby's First Christmas
Handcrafted • FRAN
2000QLX7466 • **Value $43**

General Keepsake

	Price Paid	Value of My Collection
1.		
2.		
3.		
4.		
5.		
6.		
7.		
8.		
9.		
10.		
11.		
12.		
13.		
14.		
15.		
16.		
17.		
18.		

General Magic

19.		
20.		

PENCIL TOTALS

VALUE GUIDE — HALLMARK KEEPSAKE ORNAMENTS

1 Barney™
Handcrafted • N/A
2400QLX7506 • **Value $40**

2 Candy Cane Lookout
Handcrafted • FRAN
1800QLX7376 • **Value $68**

3 Conversations With Santa
Handcrafted • SEAL
2800QLX7426 • **Value $50**

4 Country Showtime
Handcrafted • SICK
2200QLX7416 • **Value $41**

5 The Eagle Has Landed
Handcrafted • SEAL
2400QLX7486 • **Value $46**

6 Feliz Navidad
Handcrafted • CROW
2800QLX7433 • **Value $63**

7 Gingerbread Fantasy
Handcrafted • PALM
4400QLX7382 • **Value $93**

8 Klingon Bird of Prey™
Handcrafted • NORT
2400QLX7386 • **Value $45**

9 Kringle Trolley
Handcrafted • CROW
2000QLX7413 • **Value $44**

10 Maxine
Handcrafted • SICK
2000QLX7503 • **Value $42**

11 Peekaboo Pup
Handcrafted • RGRS
2000QLX7423 • **Value $37**

12 Rock Candy Miner
Handcrafted • SIED
2000QLX7403 • **Value $38**

13 Santa's Sing-Along
Handcrafted • CROW
2400QLX7473 • **Value $50**

14 Simba, Sarabi and Mufasa
Handcrafted • CROW
2000QLX7516 • **Value $40**

15 Simba, Sarabi and Mufasa (recalled due to defective sound)
Handcrafted • CROW
3200QLX7513 • **Value $73**

16 Very Merry Minutes
Handcrafted • VOTR
2400QLX7443 • **Value $45**

17 White Christmas
Handcrafted • DLEE
2800QLX7463 • **Value $65**

18 Winnie the Pooh Parade
Handcrafted • CROW
3200QLX7493 • **Value $65**

19 Home for the Holidays
Christmas Lights
Porcelain • PALM
1575QK1123 • **Value $20**

20 Moonbeams
Christmas Lights
Porcelain • ANDR
1575QK1116 • **Value $20**

GENERAL MAGIC

	Price Paid	Value of My Collection
1.		
2.		
3.		
4.		
5.		
6.		
7.		
8.		
9.		
10.		
11.		
12.		
13.		
14.		
15.		
16.		
17.		
18.		

GENERAL SHOWCASE

19.		
20.		

PENCIL TOTALS

VALUE GUIDE — HALLMARK KEEPSAKE ORNAMENTS

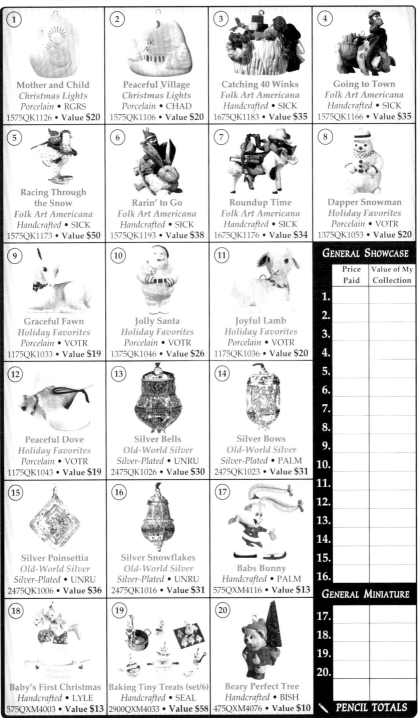

1. Mother and Child
Christmas Lights
Porcelain • RGRS
1575QK1126 • **Value $20**

2. Peaceful Village
Christmas Lights
Porcelain • CHAD
1575QK1106 • **Value $20**

3. Catching 40 Winks
Folk Art Americana
Handcrafted • SICK
1675QK1183 • **Value $35**

4. Going to Town
Folk Art Americana
Handcrafted • SICK
1575QK1166 • **Value $35**

5. Racing Through
the Snow
Folk Art Americana
Handcrafted • SICK
1575QK1173 • **Value $50**

6. Rarin' to Go
Folk Art Americana
Handcrafted • SICK
1575QK1193 • **Value $38**

7. Roundup Time
Folk Art Americana
Handcrafted • SICK
1675QK1176 • **Value $34**

8. Dapper Snowman
Holiday Favorites
Porcelain • VOTR
1375QK1053 • **Value $20**

9. Graceful Fawn
Holiday Favorites
Porcelain • VOTR
1175QK1033 • **Value $19**

10. Jolly Santa
Holiday Favorites
Porcelain • VOTR
1375QK1046 • **Value $26**

11. Joyful Lamb
Holiday Favorites
Porcelain • VOTR
1175QK1036 • **Value $20**

12. Peaceful Dove
Holiday Favorites
Porcelain • VOTR
1175QK1043 • **Value $19**

13. Silver Bells
Old-World Silver
Silver-Plated • UNRU
2475QK1026 • **Value $30**

14. Silver Bows
Old-World Silver
Silver-Plated • PALM
2475QK1023 • **Value $31**

15. Silver Poinsettia
Old-World Silver
Silver-Plated • UNRU
2475QK1006 • **Value $36**

16. Silver Snowflakes
Old-World Silver
Silver-Plated • UNRU
2475QK1016 • **Value $31**

17. Babs Bunny
Handcrafted • PALM
575QXM4116 • **Value $13**

18. Baby's First Christmas
Handcrafted • LYLE
575QXM4003 • **Value $13**

19. Baking Tiny Treats (set/6)
Handcrafted • SEAL
2900QXM4033 • **Value $58**

20. Beary Perfect Tree
Handcrafted • BISH
475QXM4076 • **Value $10**

1994

GENERAL SHOWCASE

	Price Paid	Value of My Collection
1.		
2.		
3.		
4.		
5.		
6.		
7.		
8.		
9.		
10.		
11.		
12.		
13.		
14.		
15.		
16.		

GENERAL MINIATURE

17.		
18.		
19.		
20.		
PENCIL TOTALS		

(1) Buster Bunny
Handcrafted • PALM
575QXM5163 • **Value $12**

(2) Corny Elf
Handcrafted • RHOD
450QXM4063 • **Value $9**

(3) Cute as a Button
Handcrafted • CROW
375QXM4103 • **Value $13**

(4) Dazzling Reindeer
Handcrafted • VOTR
975QXM4026 • **Value $20**

(5) Dizzy Devil
Handcrafted • PALM
575QXM4133 • **Value $12**

(6) Friends Need Hugs
Handcrafted • LYLE
450QXM4016 • **Value $13**

(7) Graceful Carousel Horse
Pewter • BISH
775QXM4056 • **Value $17**

(8) Hamton
Handcrafted • PALM
575QXM4126 • **Value $12**

(9) Have a Cookie
Handcrafted • DLEE
575QXM5166 • **Value $12**

(10) Hearts A-Sail
Handcrafted • BISH
575QXM4006 • **Value $11**

(11) Jolly Visitor
Handcrafted • SICK
575QXM4053 • **Value $13**

(12) Jolly Wolly Snowman
Handcrafted • VOTR
375QXM4093 • **Value $11**

(13) Journey to Bethlehem
Handcrafted • LYLE
575QXM4036 • **Value $16**

(14) Just My Size
Handcrafted • BISH
375QXM4086 • **Value $9**

(15) Love Was Born
Handcrafted • SICK
450QXM4043 • **Value $14**

(16) Melodic Cherub
Handcrafted • RGRS
375QXM4066 • **Value $9**

(17) A Merry Flight
Handcrafted • CROW
575QXM4073 • **Value $11**

(18) Mom
Handcrafted • RGRS
450QXM4013 • **Value $12**

(19) Noah's Ark (set/3)
Handcrafted • SICK
2450QXM4106 • **Value $55**

(20) Plucky Duck
Handcrafted • PALM
575QXM4123 • **Value $11**

General Miniature

	Price Paid	Value of My Collection
1.		
2.		
3.		
4.		
5.		
6.		
7.		
8.		
9.		
10.		
11.		
12.		
13.		
14.		
15.		
16.		
17.		
18.		
19.		
20.		

\ PENCIL TOTALS

Value Guide — Hallmark Keepsake Ornaments

1
Pour Some More
Handcrafted • CHAD
575QXM5156 • **Value $11**

2
Scooting Along
Handcrafted • FRAN
675QXM5173 • **Value $15**

3
Sweet Dreams
Handcrafted • CROW
300QXM4096 • **Value $11**

4
Tea With Teddy
Handcrafted • RGRS
725QXM4046 • **Value $16**

5
First Hello
(gift membership bonus)
Handcrafted • RGRS
QXC4846 • **Value N/E**

6
Happy Collecting
(early renewal piece,
Merry Miniature)
Handcrafted • N/A
QXC4803 • **Value $27**

7
Holiday Pursuit
(keepsake of membership)
Handcrafted • FRAN
QXC4823 • **Value $25**

8
Jolly Holly Santa
(club edition)
Handcrafted • LYLE
2200QXC4833 • **Value $50**

9
Majestic Deer
(club edition)
Porcelain/Pewter • UNRU
2500QXC4836 • **Value $50**

10
On Cloud Nine
(club edition)
Handcrafted • DLEE
1200QXC4853 • **Value $30**

11
Sweet Bouquet
(keepsake of member-
ship, miniature)
Handcrafted • N/A
QXC4806 • **Value $25**

12
Tilling Time
(Easter sidekick gift)
Handcrafted • SEAL
QXC8256 • **Value $28**

13
Collector's Survival Kit
Premiere '94
Handcrafted • RGRS
(N/C) No stock # • **Value $20**

14
Eager for Christmas
Handcrafted • SEAL
1500QX5336 • **Value $21**

15
The Country Church
Sarah, Plain and Tall
Handcrafted • BAUR
795XPR9450 • **Value $18**

16
The Hays Train Station
Sarah, Plain and Tall
Handcrafted • BAUR
795XPR9452 • **Value $18**

17
Mrs. Parkley's
General Store
Sarah, Plain and Tall
Handcrafted • BAUR
795XPR9451 • **Value $18**

18
Sarah's Maine Home
Sarah, Plain and Tall
Handcrafted • BAUR
795XPR9454 • **Value $21**

19
Sarah's Prairie Home
Sarah, Plain and Tall
Handcrafted • BAUR
795XPR9453 • **Value $19**

20
Victorian Elegance™
BARBIE® Doll
(1st in series)
Vinyl • N/A
4000XPF3546 • **Value $95**

1994

GENERAL MINIATURE	Price Paid	Value of My Collection
1.		
2.		
3.		
4.		

COLLECTOR'S CLUB		
5.		
6.		
7.		
8.		
9.		
10.		
11.		
12.		

PREMIERE ORNAMENTS		
13.		
14.		

REACH FIGURINES		
15.		
16.		
17.		
18.		
19.		

BARBIE™ COLLECTIBLES		
20.		

| PENCIL TOTALS | | |

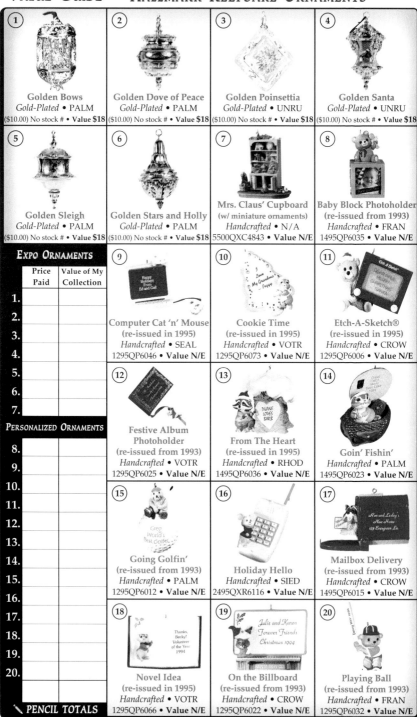

1. Golden Bows
Gold-Plated • PALM
($10.00) No stock # • **Value $18**

2. Golden Dove of Peace
Gold-Plated • PALM
($10.00) No stock # • **Value $18**

3. Golden Poinsettia
Gold-Plated • UNRU
($10.00) No stock # • **Value $18**

4. Golden Santa
Gold-Plated • UNRU
($10.00) No stock # • **Value $18**

5. Golden Sleigh
Gold-Plated • PALM
($10.00) No stock # • **Value $18**

6. Golden Stars and Holly
Gold-Plated • PALM
($10.00) No stock # • **Value $18**

7. Mrs. Claus' Cupboard
(w/ miniature ornaments)
Handcrafted • N/A
5500QXC4843 • **Value N/E**

8. Baby Block Photoholder
(re-issued from 1993)
Handcrafted • FRAN
1495QP6035 • **Value N/E**

Expo Ornaments

	Price Paid	Value of My Collection
1.		
2.		
3.		
4.		
5.		
6.		
7.		

Personalized Ornaments

8.		
9.		
10.		
11.		
12.		
13.		
14.		
15.		
16.		
17.		
18.		
19.		
20.		

PENCIL TOTALS

9. Computer Cat 'n' Mouse
(re-issued in 1995)
Handcrafted • SEAL
1295QP6046 • **Value N/E**

10. Cookie Time
(re-issued in 1995)
Handcrafted • VOTR
1295QP6073 • **Value N/E**

11. Etch-A-Sketch®
(re-issued in 1995)
Handcrafted • CROW
1295QP6006 • **Value N/E**

12. Festive Album Photoholder
(re-issued from 1993)
Handcrafted • VOTR
1295QP6025 • **Value N/E**

13. From The Heart
(re-issued in 1995)
Handcrafted • RHOD
1495QP6036 • **Value N/E**

14. Goin' Fishin'
Handcrafted • PALM
1495QP6023 • **Value N/E**

15. Going Golfin'
(re-issued from 1993)
Handcrafted • PALM
1295QP6012 • **Value N/E**

16. Holiday Hello
Handcrafted • SIED
2495QXR6116 • **Value N/E**

17. Mailbox Delivery
(re-issued from 1993)
Handcrafted • CROW
1495QP6015 • **Value N/E**

18. Novel Idea
(re-issued in 1995)
Handcrafted • VOTR
1295QP6066 • **Value N/E**

19. On the Billboard
(re-issued from 1993)
Handcrafted • CROW
1295QP6022 • **Value N/E**

20. Playing Ball
(re-issued from 1993)
Handcrafted • FRAN
1295QP6032 • **Value N/E**

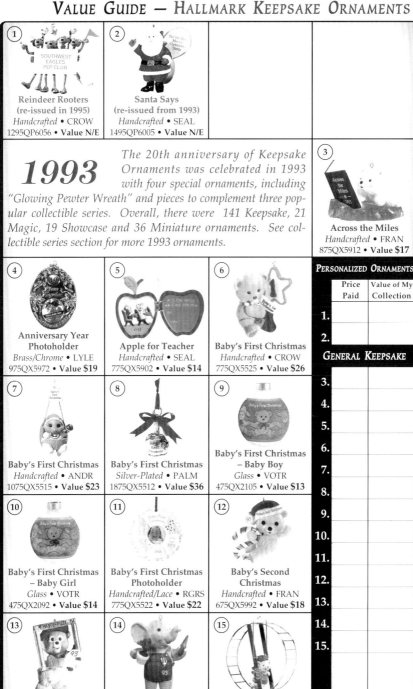

1
Reindeer Rooters
(re-issued in 1995)
Handcrafted • CROW
1295QP6056 • **Value N/E**

2
Santa Says
(re-issued from 1993)
Handcrafted • SEAL
1495QP6005 • **Value N/E**

1993

The 20th anniversary of Keepsake Ornaments was celebrated in 1993 with four special ornaments, including "Glowing Pewter Wreath" and pieces to complement three popular collectible series. Overall, there were 141 Keepsake, 21 Magic, 19 Showcase and 36 Miniature ornaments. See collectible series section for more 1993 ornaments.

3
Across the Miles
Handcrafted • FRAN
875QX5912 • **Value $17**

1993

4
Anniversary Year
Photoholder
Brass/Chrome • LYLE
975QX5972 • **Value $19**

5
Apple for Teacher
Handcrafted • SEAL
775QX5902 • **Value $14**

6
Baby's First Christmas
Handcrafted • CROW
775QX5525 • **Value $26**

7
Baby's First Christmas
Handcrafted • ANDR
1075QX5515 • **Value $23**

8
Baby's First Christmas
Silver-Plated • PALM
1875QX5512 • **Value $36**

9
Baby's First Christmas
– Baby Boy
Glass • VOTR
475QX2105 • **Value $13**

10
Baby's First Christmas
– Baby Girl
Glass • VOTR
475QX2092 • **Value $14**

11
Baby's First Christmas
Photoholder
Handcrafted/Lace • RGRS
775QX5522 • **Value $22**

12
Baby's Second
Christmas
Handcrafted • FRAN
675QX5992 • **Value $18**

13
Beary Gifted
Handcrafted • CROW
775QX5762 • **Value $15**

14
Big on Gardening
Handcrafted • VOTR
975QX5842 • **Value $15**

15
Big Roller
Handcrafted • SIED
875QX5352 • **Value $16**

Personalized Ornaments		
	Price Paid	Value of My Collection
1.		
2.		
General Keepsake		
3.		
4.		
5.		
6.		
7.		
8.		
9.		
10.		
11.		
12.		
13.		
14.		
15.		
Pencil Totals		

(1) Bird-Watcher
Handcrafted • JLEE
975QX5252 • **Value $16**

(2) Bowling for ZZZs
Handcrafted • FRAN
775QX5565 • **Value $16**

(3) Brother
Handcrafted • RGRS
675QX5542 • **Value $12**

(4) Bugs Bunny
Handcrafted • SICK
875QX5412 • **Value $23**

(5) Caring Nurse
Handcrafted • FRAN
675QX5785 • **Value $16**

(6) A Child's Christmas
Handcrafted • FRAN
975QX5882 • **Value $21**

(7) Child's Fifth Christmas
Handcrafted • RHOD
675QX5222 • **Value $15**

(8) Child's Fourth Christmas
Handcrafted • FRAN
675QX5215 • **Value $15**

(9) Child's Third Christmas
Handcrafted • FRAN
675QX5995 • **Value $16**

(10) Christmas Break
Handcrafted • SEAL
775QX5825 • **Value $23**

(11) Clever Cookie
Handcrafted/Tin • SICK
775QX5662 • **Value $23**

(12) Coach
Handcrafted • PALM
675QX5935 • **Value $13**

(13) Curly 'n' Kingly
Handcrafted/Brass • CROW
1075QX5285 • **Value $20**

(14) Dad
Handcrafted • JLEE
775QX5855 • **Value $16**

(15) Dad-to-Be
Handcrafted • JLEE
675QX5532 • **Value $14**

(16) Daughter
Handcrafted • VOTR
675QX5872 • **Value $19**

(17) Dickens Caroler Bell – Lady Daphne
Porcelain • CHAD
2175QX5505 • **Value $45**

(18) Dunkin' Roo
Handcrafted • SIED
775QX5575 • **Value $14**

(19) Eeyore
Handcrafted • SIED
975QX5712 • **Value $21**

(20) Elmer Fudd
Handcrafted • LYLE
875QX5495 • **Value $20**

	GENERAL KEEPSAKE	
	Price Paid	Value of My Collection
1.		
2.		
3.		
4.		
5.		
6.		
7.		
8.		
9.		
10.		
11.		
12.		
13.		
14.		
15.		
16.		
17.		
18.		
19.		
20.		
PENCIL TOTALS		

Value Guide — Hallmark Keepsake Ornaments

(1) **Faithful Fire Fighter** *Handcrafted* • VOTR 775QX5782 • **Value $16**	**(2)** **Feliz Navidad** *Handcrafted/Brass* • DLEE 875QX5365 • **Value $18**

(1) **Faithful Fire Fighter**
Handcrafted • VOTR
775QX5782 • **Value $16**

(2) **Feliz Navidad**
Handcrafted/Brass • DLEE
875QX5365 • **Value $18**

(3) **Fills the Bill**
Handcrafted • SIED
875QX5572 • **Value $16**

(4) **Glowing Pewter Wreath**
Pewter • UNRU
1875QX5302 • **Value $39**

(5) **Godchild**
Handcrafted • CHAD
875QX5875 • **Value $18**

(6) **Grandchild's First Christmas**
Handcrafted • FRAN
675QX5552 • **Value $13**

(7) **Granddaughter**
Handcrafted • CHAD
675QX5635 • **Value $13**

(8) **Grandmother**
Handcrafted • ANDR
675QX5665 • **Value $14**

(9) **Grandparents**
Glass • VOTR
475QX2085 • **Value $13**

(10) **Grandson**
Handcrafted • CHAD
675QX5632 • **Value $13**

(11) **Great Connections (set/2)**
Handcrafted • RGRS
1075QX5402 • **Value $25**

(12) **He Is Born**
Handcrafted • LYLE
975QX5362 • **Value $38**

(13) **High Top-Purr**
Handcrafted • SEAL
875QX5332 • **Value $23**

(14) **Home for Christmas**
Handcrafted • SIED
775QX5562 • **Value $16**

(15) **Howling Good Time**
Handcrafted • RGRS
975QX5255 • **Value $19**

(16) **Icicle Bicycle**
Handcrafted • JLEE
975QX5835 • **Value $19**

(17) **Julianne and Teddy**
Handcrafted • UNRU
2175QX5295 • **Value $40**

(18) **Kanga and Roo**
Handcrafted • SIED
975QX5672 • **Value $21**

(19) **Little Drummer Boy**
Handcrafted • PALM
875QX5372 • **Value $20**

(20) **Look for the Wonder**
Handcrafted • DLEE
1275QX5685 • **Value $27**

General Keepsake

	Price Paid	Value of My Collection
1.		
2.		
3.		
4.		
5.		
6.		
7.		
8.		
9.		
10.		
11.		
12.		
13.		
14.		
15.		
16.		
17.		
18.		
19.		
20.		
PENCIL TOTALS		

1993

Value Guide — Hallmark Keepsake Ornaments

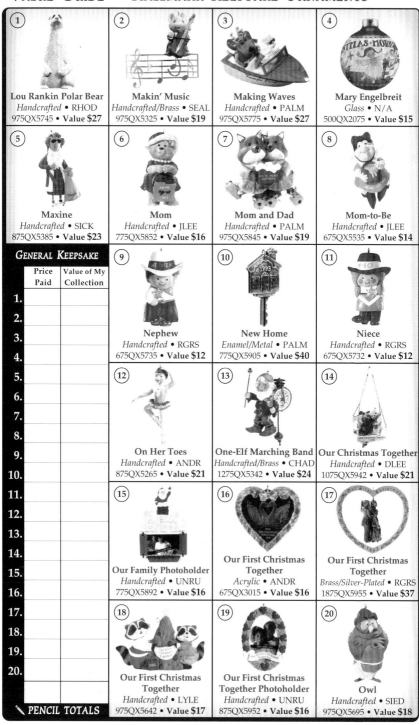

(1) Lou Rankin Polar Bear
Handcrafted • RHOD
975QX5745 • **Value $27**

(2) Makin' Music
Handcrafted/Brass • SEAL
975QX5325 • **Value $19**

(3) Making Waves
Handcrafted • PALM
975QX5775 • **Value $27**

(4) Mary Engelbreit
Glass • N/A
500QX2075 • **Value $15**

(5) Maxine
Handcrafted • SICK
875QX5385 • **Value $23**

(6) Mom
Handcrafted • JLEE
775QX5852 • **Value $16**

(7) Mom and Dad
Handcrafted • PALM
975QX5845 • **Value $19**

(8) Mom-to-Be
Handcrafted • JLEE
675QX5535 • **Value $14**

(9) Nephew
Handcrafted • RGRS
675QX5735 • **Value $12**

(10) New Home
Enamel/Metal • PALM
775QX5905 • **Value $40**

(11) Niece
Handcrafted • RGRS
675QX5732 • **Value $12**

(12) On Her Toes
Handcrafted • ANDR
875QX5265 • **Value $21**

(13) One-Elf Marching Band
Handcrafted/Brass • CHAD
1275QX5342 • **Value $24**

(14) Our Christmas Together
Handcrafted • DLEE
1075QX5942 • **Value $21**

(15) Our Family Photoholder
Handcrafted • UNRU
775QX5892 • **Value $16**

(16) Our First Christmas Together
Acrylic • ANDR
675QX3015 • **Value $16**

(17) Our First Christmas Together
Brass/Silver-Plated • RGRS
1875QX5955 • **Value $37**

(18) Our First Christmas Together
Handcrafted • LYLE
975QX5642 • **Value $17**

(19) Our First Christmas Together Photoholder
Handcrafted • UNRU
875QX5952 • **Value $16**

(20) Owl
Handcrafted • SIED
975QX5695 • **Value $18**

General Keepsake

	Price Paid	Value of My Collection
1.		
2.		
3.		
4.		
5.		
6.		
7.		
8.		
9.		
10.		
11.		
12.		
13.		
14.		
15.		
16.		
17.		
18.		
19.		
20.		
PENCIL TOTALS		

1993 Collection

VALUE GUIDE – HALLMARK KEEPSAKE ORNAMENTS

1
PEANUTS®
Glass • N/A
500QX2072 • **Value $25**

2
Peek-a-Boo Tree
Handcrafted • CROW
1075QX5245 • **Value $24**

3
Peep Inside
Handcrafted • DLEE
1375QX5322 • **Value $23**

4
People Friendly
Handcrafted • SEAL
875QX5932 • **Value $16**

5
Perfect Match
Handcrafted • SIED
875QX5772 • **Value $16**

6
The Pink Panther
Handcrafted • PALM
1275QX5755 • **Value $23**

7
Playful Pals
Handcrafted • RGRS
1475QX5742 • **Value $29**

8
**Popping Good Times
(set/2)**
Handcrafted • CHAD
1475QX5392 • **Value $27**

9
Porky Pig
Handcrafted • ANDR
875QX5652 • **Value $18**

10
Putt-Putt Penguin
Handcrafted • JLEE
975QX5795 • **Value $18**

11
Quick as a Fox
Handcrafted • CROW
875QX5792 • **Value $17**

12
Rabbit
Handcrafted • SIED
975QX5702 • **Value $19**

13
Ready for Fun
Handcrafted/Tin • LYLE
775QX5124 • **Value $15**

14
Room for One More
Handcrafted • CROW
875QX5382 • **Value $50**

15
Silvery Noel
Silver-Plated • LYLE
1275QX5305 • **Value $30**

16
Sister
Handcrafted • RGRS
675QX5545 • **Value $17**

17
Sister to Sister
Handcrafted • SEAL
975QX5885 • **Value $50**

18
**Smile! It's Christmas
Photoholder**
Handcrafted • SEAL
975QX5335 • **Value $19**

19
Snow Bear Angel
Handcrafted • JLEE
775QX5355 • **Value $18**

20
Snowbird
Handcrafted • JLEE
775QX5765 • **Value $16**

1993

GENERAL KEEPSAKE		
	Price Paid	Value of My Collection
1.		
2.		
3.		
4.		
5.		
6.		
7.		
8.		
9.		
10.		
11.		
12.		
13.		
14.		
15.		
16.		
17.		
18.		
19.		
20.		
PENCIL TOTALS		

VALUE GUIDE – HALLMARK KEEPSAKE ORNAMENTS

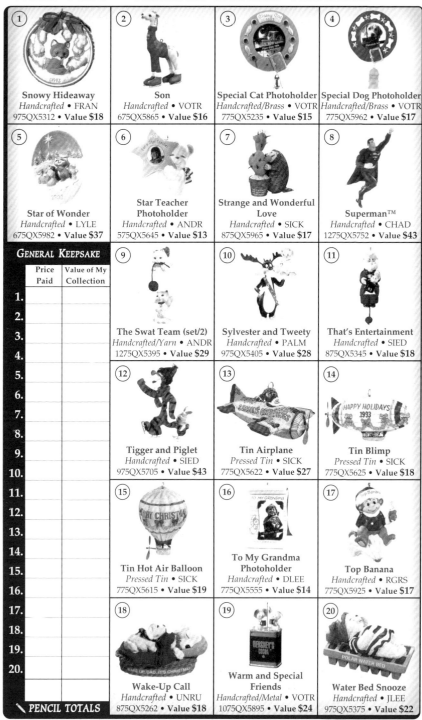

(1)
Snowy Hideaway
Handcrafted • FRAN
975QX5312 • **Value $18**

(2)
Son
Handcrafted • VOTR
675QX5865 • **Value $16**

(3)
Special Cat Photoholder
Handcrafted/Brass • VOTR
775QX5235 • **Value $15**

(4)
Special Dog Photoholder
Handcrafted/Brass • VOTR
775QX5962 • **Value $17**

(5)
Star of Wonder
Handcrafted • LYLE
675QX5982 • **Value $37**

(6)
Star Teacher Photoholder
Handcrafted • ANDR
575QX5645 • **Value $13**

(7)
Strange and Wonderful Love
Handcrafted • SICK
875QX5965 • **Value $17**

(8)
Superman™
Handcrafted • CHAD
1275QX5752 • **Value $43**

GENERAL KEEPSAKE

	Price Paid	Value of My Collection
1.		
2.		
3.		
4.		
5.		
6.		
7.		
8.		
9.		
10.		
11.		
12.		
13.		
14.		
15.		
16.		
17.		
18.		
19.		
20.		
PENCIL TOTALS		

(9)
The Swat Team (set/2)
Handcrafted/Yarn • ANDR
1275QX5395 • **Value $29**

(10)
Sylvester and Tweety
Handcrafted • PALM
975QX5405 • **Value $28**

(11)
That's Entertainment
Handcrafted • SIED
875QX5345 • **Value $18**

(12)
Tigger and Piglet
Handcrafted • SIED
975QX5705 • **Value $43**

(13)
Tin Airplane
Pressed Tin • SICK
775QX5622 • **Value $27**

(14)
Tin Blimp
Pressed Tin • SICK
775QX5625 • **Value $18**

(15)
Tin Hot Air Balloon
Pressed Tin • SICK
775QX5615 • **Value $19**

(16)
To My Grandma Photoholder
Handcrafted • DLEE
775QX5555 • **Value $14**

(17)
Top Banana
Handcrafted • RGRS
775QX5925 • **Value $17**

(18)
Wake-Up Call
Handcrafted • UNRU
875QX5262 • **Value $18**

(19)
Warm and Special Friends
Handcrafted/Metal • VOTR
1075QX5895 • **Value $24**

(20)
Water Bed Snooze
Handcrafted • JLEE
975QX5375 • **Value $22**

1 Winnie the Pooh
Handcrafted • SIED
975QX5715 • **Value $30**

2 Baby's First Christmas
Handcrafted • FRAN
2200QLX7365 • **Value $45**

3 Bells Are Ringing
Handcrafted • CROW
2800QLX7402 • **Value $62**

4 Dog's Best Friend
Handcrafted • JLEE
1200QLX7172 • **Value $24**

5 Dollhouse Dreams
Handcrafted • CROW
2200QLX7372 • **Value $50**

6 Home on the Range
Handcrafted • SICK
3200QLX7395 • **Value $63**

7 The Lamplighter
Handcrafted • PALM
1800QLX7192 • **Value $39**

8 Last Minute Shopping
Handcrafted • VOTR
2800QLX7385 • **Value $55**

1993

9 Messages of Christmas
Handcrafted • SIED
3500QLX7476 • **Value $49**

10 North Pole Merrython
Handcrafted • SEAL
2500QLX7392 • **Value $50**

11 Our First Christmas Together
Handcrafted • CHAD
2000QLX7355 • **Value $37**

12 Radio News Flash
Handcrafted • DLEE
2200QLX7362 • **Value $45**

13 Raiding the Fridge
Handcrafted • RGRS
1600QLX7185 • **Value $33**

14 Road Runner and Wile E. Coyote™
Handcrafted • CHAD
3000QLX7415 • **Value $65**

15 Santa's Snow-Getter
Handcrafted • CROW
1800QLX7352 • **Value $39**

16 Santa's Workshop
Handcrafted • SIED
2800QLX7375 • **Value $56**

17 Song of the Chimes
Handcrafted/Brass • ANDR
2500QLX7405 • **Value $50**

18 U.S.S. Enterprise™ THE NEXT GENERATION™
Handcrafted • NORT
2400QLX7412 • **Value $49**

19 Winnie the Pooh
Handcrafted • SIED
2400QLX7422 • **Value $44**

	Price Paid	Value of My Collection
General Keepsake		
1.		
General Magic		
2.		
3.		
4.		
5.		
6.		
7.		
8.		
9.		
10.		
11.		
12.		
13.		
14.		
15.		
16.		
17.		
18.		
19.		
PENCIL TOTALS		

1

Angel in Flight
Folk Art Americana
Handcrafted • SICK
1575QK1052 • **Value $50**

2

Polar Bear Adventure
Folk Art Americana
Handcrafted • SICK
1500QK1055 • **Value $68**

3

Riding in the Woods
Folk Art Americana
Handcrafted • SICK
1575QK1065 • **Value $69**

4

Riding the Wind
Folk Art Americana
Handcrafted • SICK
1575QK1045 • **Value $63**

5

Santa Claus
Folk Art Americana
Handcrafted • SICK
1675QK1072 • **Value $210**

6

Angelic Messengers
Holiday Enchantment
Porcelain • VOTR
1375QK1032 • **Value $40**

7

Bringing Home the Tree
Holiday Enchantment
Porcelain • CHAD
1375QK1042 • **Value $35**

8

Journey to the Forest
Holiday Enchantment
Porcelain • N/A
1375QK1012 • **Value $32**

General Showcase

	Price Paid	Value of My Collection
1.		
2.		
3.		
4.		
5.		
6.		
7.		
8.		
9.		
10.		
11.		
12.		
13.		
14.		
15.		
16.		
17.		
18.		
19.		

\ PENCIL TOTALS

9

The Magi
Holiday Enchantment
Porcelain • N/A
1375QK1025 • **Value $38**

10

Visions of Sugarplums
Holiday Enchantment
Porcelain • N/A
1375QK1005 • **Value $34**

11

Silver Dove of Peace
Old-World Silver
Silver-Plated • PALM
2475QK1075 • **Value $36**

12

Silver Santa
Old-World Silver
Silver-Plated • UNRU
2475QK1092 • **Value $60**

13

Silver Sleigh
Old-World Silver
Silver-Plated • PALM
2475QK1082 • **Value $37**

14

Silver Stars and Holly
Old-World Silver
Silver-Plated • PALM
2475QK1085 • **Value $36**

15

Christmas Feast
Portraits in Bisque
Porcelain • PIKE
1575QK1152 • **Value $33**

16

Joy of Sharing
Portraits in Bisque
Porcelain • LYLE
1575QK1142 • **Value $33**

17

Mistletoe Kiss
Portraits in Bisque
Porcelain • PIKE
1575QK1145 • **Value $32**

18

**Norman Rockwell
– Filling the Stockings**
Portraits in Bisque
Porcelain • DUTK
1575QK1155 • **Value $35**

19

**Norman Rockwell
– Jolly Postman**
Portraits in Bisque
Porcelain • DUTK
1575QK1162 • **Value $35**

1. Baby's First Christmas
Handcrafted • VOTR
575QXM5145 • **Value $12**

2. Cheese Please
Handcrafted • SIED
375QXM4072 • **Value $9**

3. Christmas Castle
Handcrafted • SEAL
575QXM4085 • **Value $12**

4. Cloisonné Snowflake
Cloisonné/Brass • VOTR
975QXM4012 • **Value $19**

5. Country Fiddling
Handcrafted • FRAN
375QXM4062 • **Value $9**

6. Crystal Angel
Crystal/Gold-Plated • PALM
975QXM4015 • **Value $54**

7. Ears to Pals
Handcrafted • ANDR
375QXM4075 • **Value $9**

8. Grandma
Handcrafted • SEAL
450QXM5162 • **Value $11**

9. I Dream of Santa
Handcrafted • SICK
375QXM4055 • **Value $13**

10. Into the Woods
Handcrafted • SEAL
375QXM4045 • **Value $9**

11. Learning to Skate
Handcrafted • CHAD
300QXM4122 • **Value $9**

12. Lighting a Path
Handcrafted • CHAD
300QXM4115 • **Value $9**

13. Merry Mascot
Handcrafted • SIED
375QXM4042 • **Value $10**

14. Mom
Handcrafted • ANDR
450QXM5155 • **Value $13**

15. Monkey Melody
Handcrafted • SICK
575QXM4092 • **Value $15**

16. North Pole Fire Truck
Handcrafted • PALM
475QXM4105 • **Value $13**

17. Pear-Shaped Tones
Handcrafted • LYLE
375QXM4052 • **Value $10**

18. Pull Out a Plum
Handcrafted • FRAN
575QXM4095 • **Value $14**

19. Refreshing Flight
Handcrafted • CHAD
575QXM4112 • **Value $15**

20. 'Round the Mountain
Handcrafted • CROW
725QXM4025 • **Value $19**

1993

General Miniature

	Price Paid	Value of My Collection
1.		
2.		
3.		
4.		
5.		
6.		
7.		
8.		
9.		
10.		
11.		
12.		
13.		
14.		
15.		
16.		
17.		
18.		
19.		
20.		
PENCIL TOTALS		

Value Guide — Hallmark Keepsake Ornaments

① **Secret Pal** *Handcrafted* • RGRS 375QXM5172 • **Value $9**	**②** **Snuggle Birds** *Handcrafted* • ANDR 575QXM5182 • **Value $14**	**③** **Special Friends** *Handcrafted* • FRAN 450QXM5165 • **Value $10**	**④** **Tiny Green Thumbs** **(set/6)** *Handcrafted* • SEAL 2900QXM4032 • **Value $49**
⑤ **Visions of Sugarplums** *Pewter* • PALM 725QXM4022 • **Value $16**	**⑥** **Circle of Friendship** **(gift membership bonus)** *Glass* • N/A QXC2112 • **Value N/E**	**⑦** **Forty Winks (keepsake of membership, miniature)** *Handcrafted* • FRAN QXC5294 • **Value $25**	**⑧** **Gentle Tidings** **(club edition, LE-17,500)** *Porcelain* • ANDR 2500QXC5442 • **Value $55**

General Miniature

	Price Paid	Value of My Collection
1.		
2.		
3.		
4.		
5.		

Collector's Club

6.		
7.		
8.		
9.		
10.		
11.		

Premiere Ornaments

12.		

Reach Ornaments

13.		
14.		
15.		
16.		
17.		

Anniversary Bells

18.		
19.		

⑨ **It's in the Mail** **(keepsake of membership)** *Handcrafted* • SEAL QXC5272 • **Value $27**	**⑩** **Sharing Christmas** **(club edition, LE-16,500)** *Handcrafted* • LYLE 2000QXC5435 • **Value $49**	**⑪** **Trimmed With Memories (club edition)** *Handcrafted* • SICK 1200QXC5432 • **Value $42**
⑫ **You're Always Welcome** *Handcrafted* • SEAL 975QX5692 • **Value $60**	**⑬** **Abearnathy** *The Bearingers of Victoria Circle* *Handcrafted* • N/A 495XPR9747 • **Value $10**	**⑭** **Bearnadette** *The Bearingers of Victoria Circle* *Handcrafted* • N/A 495XPR9748 • **Value $10**
⑮ **Fireplace Base** *The Bearingers of Victoria Circle* *Handcrafted* • N/A 495XPR9749 • **Value $13**	**⑯** **Mama Bearinger** *The Bearingers of Victoria Circle* *Handcrafted* • N/A 495XPR9745 • **Value $10**	**⑰** **Papa Bearinger** *The Bearingers of Victoria Circle* *Handcrafted* • N/A 495XPR9746 • **Value $10**
⑱ *25 Years Together 1992* **25 Years Together** *Porcelain* • N/A 800AGA7687 • **Value $20**	**⑲** *50 Years Together 1992* **50 Years Together** *Porcelain* • N/A 800AGA7788 • **Value $20**	

PENCIL TOTALS

1. Our First Anniversary
Porcelain • N/A
1000AGA7865 • **Value $20**

2. Our Fifth Anniversary
Porcelain • N/A
1000AGA7866 • **Value $20**

3. Our Tenth Anniversary
Porcelain • N/A
1000AGA7867 • **Value $20**

4. 25 Years Together
Porcelain • N/A
1000AGA7686 • **Value $20**

5. 40 Years Together
Porcelain • N/A
1000AGA7868 • **Value $20**

6. 50 Years Together
Porcelain • N/A
1000AGA7787 • **Value $20**

7. Santa's Favorite Stop
Handcrafted • VARI
5500QXC4125 • **Value N/E**

8. Baby's Christening
Handcrafted • N/A
1200BBY2917 • **Value $20**

9. Baby's Christening Photoholder
Silver-Plated • N/A
1000BBY1335 • **Value $15**

10. Baby's First Christmas
Handcrafted • N/A
1200BBY2918 • **Value $20**

11. Baby's First Christmas
Handcrafted • N/A
1400BBY2919 • **Value $20**

12. Baby's First Christmas Photoholder
Silver-Plated • N/A
1000BBY1470 • **Value $15**

13. Granddaughter's First Christmas
Handcrafted • N/A
1400BBY2802 • **Value $20**

14. Grandson's First Christmas
Handcrafted • N/A
1400BBY2801 • **Value $20**

15. K.C. Angel
Silver-Plated • N/A
(N/C) No Stock # • **Value N/E**

16. Baby Block Photoholder (re-issued in 1994)
Handcrafted • FRAN
1475QP6035 • **Value N/E**

17. Cool Snowman
Glass • N/A
875QP6052 • **Value N/E**

18. Festive Album Photoholder (re-issued in 1994)
Handcrafted • VOTR
1275QP6025 • **Value N/E**

19. Filled With Cookies
Handcrafted • RGRS
1275QP6042 • **Value N/E**

20. Going Golfin' (re-issued in 1994)
Handcrafted • PALM
1275QP6012 • **Value N/E**

1993

ANNIVERSARY ORNAMENTS		
	Price Paid	Value of My Collection
1.		
2.		
3.		
4.		
5.		
6.		
ARTISTS ON TOUR PIECES		
7.		
BABY ORNAMENTS		
8.		
9.		
10.		
11.		
12.		
13.		
14.		
CONVENTION ORNAMENTS		
15.		
PERSONALIZED ORNAMENTS		
16.		
17.		
18.		
19.		
20.		
PENCIL TOTALS		

Value Guide – Hallmark Keepsake Ornaments

(1) **Here's Your Fortune** *Handcrafted* • SEAL 1075QP6002 • **Value N/E**	**(2)** **Mailbox Delivery** (re-issued in 1994 and 1995) *Handcrafted* • CROW 1475QP6015 • **Value N/E**

(3) **On the Billboard** (re-issued in 1994 and 1995) *Handcrafted* • CROW 1275QP6022 • **Value N/E**

(4) **PEANUTS®** *Glass* • N/A 900QP6045 • **Value N/E**

(5) **Playing Ball** (re-issued in 1994 and 1995) *Handcrafted* • FRAN 1275QP6032 • **Value N/E**

(6) **Reindeer in the Sky** *Glass* • N/A 895QP6055 • **Value N/E**

(7) **Santa Says** (re-issued in 1994) *Handcrafted* • SEAL 1475QP6005 • **Value N/E**

PERSONALIZED ORNAMENTS

	Price Paid	Value of My Collection
1.		
2.		
3.		
4.		
5.		
6.		
7.		

GENERAL KEEPSAKE

8.		
9.		
10.		
11.		
12.		
13.		
14.		
15.		
16.		

PENCIL TOTALS

1992

Of note in the 1992 collection was the debut of the "unofficial series" of hand-crafted Coca-Cola® Santa ornaments in the Keepsake and Miniature lines. For 1992, there were 126 Keepsake ornaments, 21 Magic ornaments and 48 Miniature ornaments. See collectible series section for more 1992 ornaments.

(8) **Across The Miles** *Acrylic* • RHOD 675QX3044 • **Value $14**

(9) **Anniversary Year Photoholder** *Chrome/Brass* • UNRU 975QX4851 • **Value $23**

(10) **Baby's First Christmas** *Handcrafted* • FRAN 775QX4644 • **Value $27**

(11) **Baby's First Christmas** *Porcelain* • ANDR 1875QX4581 • **Value $36**

(12) **Baby's First Christmas – Baby Boy** *Satin* • VOTR 475QX2191 • **Value $15**

(13) **Baby's First Christmas – Baby Girl** *Satin* • VOTR 475QX2204 • **Value $15**

(14) **Baby's First Christmas Photoholder** *Fabric* • VOTR 775QX4641 • **Value $22**

(15) **Baby's Second Christmas** *Handcrafted* • FRAN 675QX4651 • **Value $20**

(16) **Bear Bell Champ** *Handcrafted/Brass* • SEAL 775QX5071 • **Value $26**

1. Brother
Handcrafted • CROW
675QX4684 • **Value $14**

2. Cheerful Santa
Handcrafted • UNRU
975QX5154 • **Value $33**

3. A Child's Christmas
Handcrafted • FRAN
975QX4574 • **Value $19**

4. Child's Fifth Christmas
Handcrafted • RHOD
675QX4664 • **Value $16**

5. Child's Fourth Christmas
Handcrafted • FRAN
675QX4661 • **Value $24**

6. Child's Third Christmas
Handcrafted • FRAN
675QX4654 • **Value $19**

7. Cool Fliers (set/2)
Handcrafted • JLEE
1075QX5474 • **Value $22**

8. Dad
Handcrafted • SIED
775QX4674 • **Value $21**

9. Dad-to-Be
Handcrafted • JLEE
675QX4611 • **Value $15**

10. Daughter
Handcrafted • FRAN
675QX5031 • **Value $24**

11. Deck the Hogs
Handcrafted • FRAN
875QX5204 • **Value $20**

12. Dickens Caroler Bell – Lord Chadwick
Porcelain • CHAD
2175QX4554 • **Value $40**

13. Down-Under Holiday
Handcrafted • CROW
775QX5144 • **Value $16**

14. Egg Nog Nest
Handcrafted • N/A
775QX5121 • **Value $17**

15. Elfin Marionette
Handcrafted • CHAD
1175QX5931 • **Value $21**

16. Elvis
Brass-Plated • RHOD/LYLE
1475QX5624 • **Value $22**

17. Eric the Baker
Handcrafted • SICK
875QX5244 • **Value $19**

18. Feliz Navidad
Handcrafted • ANDR
675QX5181 • **Value $19**

19. For My Grandma Photoholder
Fabric • N/A
775QX5184 • **Value $15**

20. For The One I Love
Porcelain • LYLE
975QX4844 • **Value $22**

1992

	Price Paid	Value of My Collection
GENERAL KEEPSAKE		
1.		
2.		
3.		
4.		
5.		
6.		
7.		
8.		
9.		
10.		
11.		
12.		
13.		
14.		
15.		
16.		
17.		
18.		
19.		
20.		
PENCIL TOTALS		

1. Franz the Artist
Handcrafted • SICK
875QX5261 • **Value $25**

2. Frieda the Animals' Friend
Handcrafted • SICK
875QX5264 • **Value $20**

3. Friendly Greetings
Handcrafted • CHAD
775QX5041 • **Value $14**

4. Friendship Line
Handcrafted • SEAL
975QX5034 • **Value $27**

5. From Our Home to Yours
Glass • VOTR
475QX2131 • **Value $11**

6. Fun on a Big Scale
Handcrafted • CROW
1075QX5134 • **Value $21**

7. GARFIELD
Handcrafted • PALM
775QX5374 • **Value $18**

8. Genius at Work
Handcrafted • CROW
1075QX5371 • **Value $20**

9. Godchild
Handcrafted • UNRU
675QX5941 • **Value $18**

10. Golf's a Ball
Handcrafted • SCHU
675QX5984 • **Value $25**

11. Gone Wishin'
Handcrafted • DLEE
875QX5171 • **Value $18**

12. Granddaughter
Handcrafted • SEAL
675QX5604 • **Value $18**

13. Granddaughter's First Christmas
Handcrafted • SIED
675QX4634 • **Value $15**

14. Grandmother
Glass • N/A
475QX2011 • **Value $15**

15. Grandparents
Glass • N/A
475QX2004 • **Value $15**

16. Grandson
Handcrafted • SEAL
675QX5611 • **Value $16**

17. Grandson's First Christmas
Handcrafted • SIED
675QX4621 • **Value $16**

18. Green Thumb Santa
Handcrafted • PALM
775QX5101 • **Value $16**

19. Hello-Ho-Ho
Handcrafted • CROW
975QX5141 • **Value $23**

20. Holiday Memo
Handcrafted • RGRS
775QX5044 • **Value $16**

General Keepsake

	Price Paid	Value of My Collection
1.		
2.		
3.		
4.		
5.		
6.		
7.		
8.		
9.		
10.		
11.		
12.		
13.		
14.		
15.		
16.		
17.		
18.		
19.		
20.		

PENCIL TOTALS

Value Guide — Hallmark Keepsake Ornaments

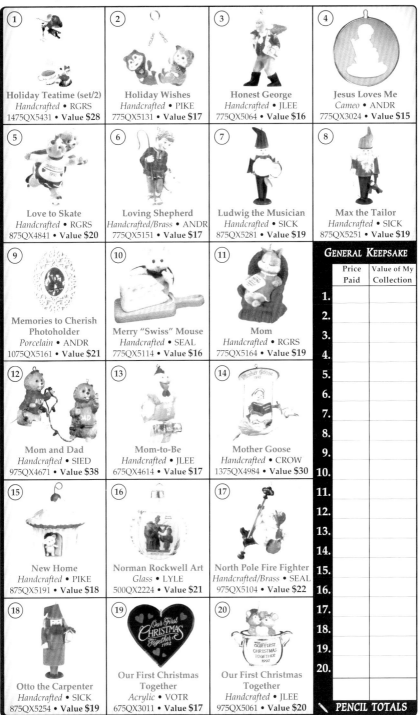

1. Holiday Teatime (set/2)
Handcrafted • RGRS
1475QX5431 • **Value $28**

2. Holiday Wishes
Handcrafted • PIKE
775QX5131 • **Value $17**

3. Honest George
Handcrafted • JLEE
775QX5064 • **Value $16**

4. Jesus Loves Me
Cameo • ANDR
775QX3024 • **Value $15**

5. Love to Skate
Handcrafted • RGRS
875QX4841 • **Value $20**

6. Loving Shepherd
Handcrafted/Brass • ANDR
775QX5151 • **Value $17**

7. Ludwig the Musician
Handcrafted • SICK
875QX5281 • **Value $19**

8. Max the Tailor
Handcrafted • SICK
875QX5251 • **Value $19**

9. Memories to Cherish
Photoholder
Porcelain • ANDR
1075QX5161 • **Value $21**

10. Merry "Swiss" Mouse
Handcrafted • SEAL
775QX5114 • **Value $16**

11. Mom
Handcrafted • RGRS
775QX5164 • **Value $19**

12. Mom and Dad
Handcrafted • SIED
975QX4671 • **Value $38**

13. Mom-to-Be
Handcrafted • JLEE
675QX4614 • **Value $17**

14. Mother Goose
Handcrafted • CROW
1375QX4984 • **Value $30**

15. New Home
Handcrafted • PIKE
875QX5191 • **Value $18**

16. Norman Rockwell Art
Glass • LYLE
500QX2224 • **Value $21**

17. North Pole Fire Fighter
Handcrafted/Brass • SEAL
975QX5104 • **Value $22**

18. Otto the Carpenter
Handcrafted • SICK
875QX5254 • **Value $19**

19. Our First Christmas
Together
Acrylic • VOTR
675QX3011 • **Value $17**

20. Our First Christmas
Together
Handcrafted • JLEE
975QX5061 • **Value $20**

1992

GENERAL KEEPSAKE		
	Price Paid	Value of My Collection
1.		
2.		
3.		
4.		
5.		
6.		
7.		
8.		
9.		
10.		
11.		
12.		
13.		
14.		
15.		
16.		
17.		
18.		
19.		
20.		
PENCIL TOTALS		

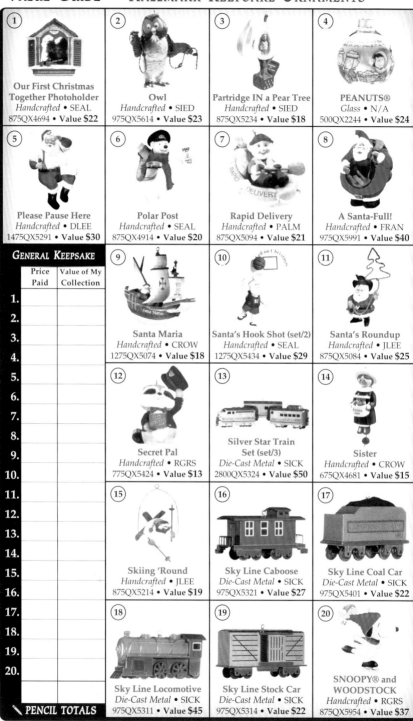

1
**Our First Christmas
Together Photoholder**
Handcrafted • SEAL
875QX4694 • **Value $22**

2
Owl
Handcrafted • SIED
975QX5614 • **Value $23**

3
Partridge IN a Pear Tree
Handcrafted • SIED
875QX5234 • **Value $18**

4
PEANUTS®
Glass • N/A
500QX2244 • **Value $24**

5
Please Pause Here
Handcrafted • DLEE
1475QX5291 • **Value $30**

6
Polar Post
Handcrafted • SEAL
875QX4914 • **Value $20**

7
Rapid Delivery
Handcrafted • PALM
875QX5094 • **Value $21**

8
A Santa-Full!
Handcrafted • FRAN
975QX5991 • **Value $40**

9
Santa Maria
Handcrafted • CROW
1275QX5074 • **Value $18**

10
Santa's Hook Shot (set/2)
Handcrafted • SEAL
1275QX5434 • **Value $29**

11
Santa's Roundup
Handcrafted • JLEE
875QX5084 • **Value $25**

12
Secret Pal
Handcrafted • RGRS
775QX5424 • **Value $13**

13
**Silver Star Train
Set (set/3)**
Die-Cast Metal • SICK
2800QX5324 • **Value $50**

14
Sister
Handcrafted • CROW
675QX4681 • **Value $15**

15
Skiing 'Round
Handcrafted • JLEE
875QX5214 • **Value $19**

16
Sky Line Caboose
Die-Cast Metal • SICK
975QX5321 • **Value $27**

17
Sky Line Coal Car
Die-Cast Metal • SICK
975QX5401 • **Value $22**

18
Sky Line Locomotive
Die-Cast Metal • SICK
975QX5311 • **Value $45**

19
Sky Line Stock Car
Die-Cast Metal • SICK
975QX5314 • **Value $22**

20
**SNOOPY® and
WOODSTOCK**
Handcrafted • RGRS
875QX5954 • **Value $37**

General Keepsake

	Price Paid	Value of My Collection
1.		
2.		
3.		
4.		
5.		
6.		
7.		
8.		
9.		
10.		
11.		
12.		
13.		
14.		
15.		
16.		
17.		
18.		
19.		
20.		

PENCIL TOTALS

Value Guide — Hallmark Keepsake Ornaments

1
Son
Handcrafted • FRAN
675QX5024 • **Value $21**

2
Special Cat Photoholder
Handcrafted • CHAD
775QX5414 • **Value $15**

3
Special Dog Photoholder
Handcrafted • CHAD
775QX5421 • **Value $27**

4
Spirit of Christmas Stress
Handcrafted • CHAD
875QX5231 • **Value $22**

5
Stocked With Joy
Pressed Tin • SICK
775QX5934 • **Value $23**

6
Tasty Christmas
Handcrafted • FRAN
975QX5994 • **Value $24**

7
Teacher
Glass • N/A
475QX2264 • **Value $15**

8
Toboggan Tail
Handcrafted • ANDR
775QX5459 • **Value $16**

9
Tread Bear
Handcrafted • SEAL
875QX5091 • **Value $24**

10
Turtle Dreams
Handcrafted • JLEE
875QX4991 • **Value $25**

11
Uncle Art's Ice Cream
Handcrafted • SIED
875QX5001 • **Value $24**

12
V.P. of Important Stuff
Handcrafted • SIED
675QX5051 • **Value $14**

13
World-Class Teacher
Handcrafted • SIED
775QX5054 • **Value $17**

14
Baby's First Christmas
Handcrafted • CROW
2200QLX7281 • **Value $90**

15
Christmas Parade
Handcrafted • SICK
3000QLX7271 • **Value $56**

16
Continental Express
Handcrafted • SICK
3200QLX7264 • **Value $65**

17
The Dancing Nutcracker
Handcrafted • VOTR
3000QLX7261 • **Value $53**

18
Enchanted Clock
Handcrafted • CROW
3000QLX7274 • **Value $60**

19
Feathered Friends
Handcrafted • SICK
1400QLX7091 • **Value $29**

20
Good Sledding Ahead
Handcrafted • PALM
2800QLX7244 • **Value $57**

General Keepsake

	Price Paid	Value of My Collection
1.		
2.		
3.		
4.		
5.		
6.		
7.		
8.		
9.		
10.		
11.		
12.		
13.		

General Magic

14.		
15.		
16.		
17.		
18.		
19.		
20.		

PENCIL TOTALS

1992

1 Lighting the Way
Handcrafted • ANDR
1800QLX7231 • **Value** $45

2 Look! It's Santa
Handcrafted • DLEE
1400QLX7094 • **Value** $40

3 Nut Sweet Nut
Handcrafted • CROW
1000QLX7081 • **Value** $23

4 Our First Christmas Together
Panorama Ball • CHAD
2000QLX7221 • **Value** $40

5 Santa Special
(re-issued from 1991)
Handcrafted • SEAL
4000QLX7167 • **Value** $75

6 Santa Sub
Handcrafted • CROW
1800QLX7321 • **Value** $40

7 Santa's Answering Machine
Handcrafted • JLEE
2200QLX7241 • **Value** $42

8 Shuttlecraft Galileo™ From the Starship Enterprise™
Handcrafted • RHOD
2400QLX7331 • **Value** $50

9 Under Construction
Handcrafted • PALM
1800QLX7324 • **Value** $39

10 Watch Owls
Porcelain • FRAN
1200QLX7084 • **Value** $24

11 Yuletide Rider
Handcrafted • SEAL
2800QLX7314 • **Value** $55

12 A+ Teacher
Handcrafted • UNRU
375QXM5511 • **Value** $8

13 Angelic Harpist
Handcrafted • LYLE
450QXM5524 • **Value** $14

14 Baby's First Christmas
Handcrafted/Brass • LYLE
450QXM5494 • **Value** $19

15 Black-Capped Chickadee
Handcrafted • FRAN
300QXM5484 • **Value** $14

16 Bright Stringers
Handcrafted • SEAL
375QXM5841 • **Value** $15

17 Buck-A-Roo
Handcrafted • CROW
450QXM5814 • **Value** $14

18 Christmas Bonus
Handcrafted • PALM
300QXM5811 • **Value** $9

19 Christmas Copter
Handcrafted • FRAN
575QXM5844 • **Value** $15

20 Coca-Cola® Santa
Handcrafted • UNRU
575QXM5884 • **Value** $17

General Magic

	Price Paid	Value of My Collection
1.		
2.		
3.		
4.		
5.		
6.		
7.		
8.		
9.		
10.		
11.		

General Miniature

12.		
13.		
14.		
15.		
16.		
17.		
18.		
19.		
20.		

PENCIL TOTALS

VALUE GUIDE – HALLMARK KEEPSAKE ORNAMENTS

1 Cool Uncle Sam
Handcrafted • JLEE
300QXM5561 • **Value $14**

2 Cozy Kayak
Handcrafted • JLEE
375QXM5551 • **Value $12**

3 Fast Finish
Handcrafted • RHOD
375QXM5301 • **Value $12**

4 Feeding Time
Handcrafted • CROW
575QXM5481 • **Value $15**

5 Friendly Tin Soldier
Pressed Tin • SICK
450QXM5874 • **Value $16**

6 Friends Are Tops
Handcrafted • CROW
450QXM5521 • **Value $10**

7 Gerbil Inc.
Handcrafted • SIED
375QXM5924 • **Value $10**

8 Going Places
Handcrafted • ANDR
375QXM5871 • **Value $10**

9 Grandchild's First
Christmas
Handcrafted • FRAN
575QXM5501 • **Value $13**

10 Grandma
Handcrafted • UNRU
450QXM5514 • **Value $15**

11 Harmony Trio (set/3)
Handcrafted • VOTR
1175QXM5471 • **Value $23**

12 Hickory, Dickory, Dock
Handcrafted • CHAD
375QXM5861 • **Value $12**

13 Holiday Holly
Gold-Plated • N/A
975QXM5364 • **Value $17**

14 Holiday Splash
Handcrafted • FRAN
575QXM5834 • **Value $14**

15 Hoop It Up
Handcrafted • CROW
450QXM5831 • **Value $13**

16 Inside Story
Handcrafted • SEAL
725QXM5881 • **Value $18**

17 Little Town of
Bethlehem
Handcrafted • SICK
300QXM5864 • **Value $19**

18 Minted for Santa
Copper • UNRU
375QXM5854 • **Value $14**

19 Mom
Handcrafted • ANDR
450QXM5504 • **Value $17**

20 Perfect Balance
Handcrafted • RGRS
300QXM5571 • **Value $11**

1992

GENERAL MINIATURE

	Price Paid	Value of My Collection
1.		
2.		
3.		
4.		
5.		
6.		
7.		
8.		
9.		
10.		
11.		
12.		
13.		
14.		
15.		
16.		
17.		
18.		
19.		
20.		
PENCIL TOTALS		

VALUE GUIDE — HALLMARK KEEPSAKE ORNAMENTS

(1) **Polar Polka** *Handcrafted* • SEAL 450QXM5534 • **Value $13**	**(2)** **Puppet Show** *Handcrafted* • SIED 300QXM5574 • **Value $12**	**(3)** **Sew, Sew Tiny (set/6)** *Handcrafted* • SEAL 2900QXM5794 • **Value $50**	**(4)** **Ski for Two** *Handcrafted* • ANDR 450QXM5821 • **Value $13**
(5) **Snowshoe Bunny** *Handcrafted* • VOTR 375QXM5564 • **Value $10**	**(6)** **Snug Kitty** *Handcrafted* • PIKE 375QXM5554 • **Value $12**	**(7)** **Spunky Monkey** *Handcrafted* • CHAD 300QXM5921 • **Value $14**	**(8)** **Visions of Acorns** *Handcrafted* • ANDR 450QXM5851 • **Value $14**

GENERAL MINIATURE

	Price Paid	Value of My Collection
1.		
2.		
3.		
4.		
5.		
6.		
7.		
8.		
9.		

COLLECTOR'S CLUB

10.		
11.		
12.		
13.		
14.		

PREMIERE ORNAMENTS

15.		

REACH ORNAMENTS

16.		
17.		
18.		
19.		
20.		

(9) **Wee Three Kings** *Handcrafted* • PALM 575QXM5531 • **Value $18**

(10) **Chipmunk Parcel Service (early renewal piece, miniature)** *Handcrafted* • SEAL QXC5194 • **Value $26**

(11) **Christmas Treasures (set/4, club edition, LE-15,500, miniature)** *Handcrafted* • CHAD 2200QXC5464 • **Value $160**

(12) **Rodney Takes Flight (keepsake of membership)** *Handcrafted* • DLEE QXC5081 • **Value $28**

(13) **Santa's Club List (club edition, magic)** *Handcrafted* • SEAL 1500QXC7291 • **Value $40**

(14) **Victorian Skater (club edition, LE-14,700)** *Porcelain* • UNRU 2500QXC4067 • **Value $68**

(15) **O Christmas Tree** *Porcelain* • VOTR 1075QX5411 • **Value $30**

(16) **Comet and Cupid** *Santa and His Reindeer* *Handcrafted/Brass* • CROW 495XPR9737 • **Value $18**

(17) **Dasher and Dancer** *Santa and His Reindeer* *Handcrafted/Brass* • CROW 495XPR9735 • **Value $29**

(18) **Donder and Blitzen** *Santa and His Reindeer* *Handcrafted/Brass* • CROW 495XPR9738 • **Value $29**

(19) **Prancer and Vixen** *Santa and His Reindeer* *Handcrafted/Brass* • CROW 495XPR9736 • **Value $18**

(20) **Santa Claus** *Santa and His Reindeer* *Handcrafted/Brass* • CROW 495XPR9739 • **Value $26**

\ PENCIL TOTALS

1992 Collection

Value Guide – Hallmark Keepsake Ornaments

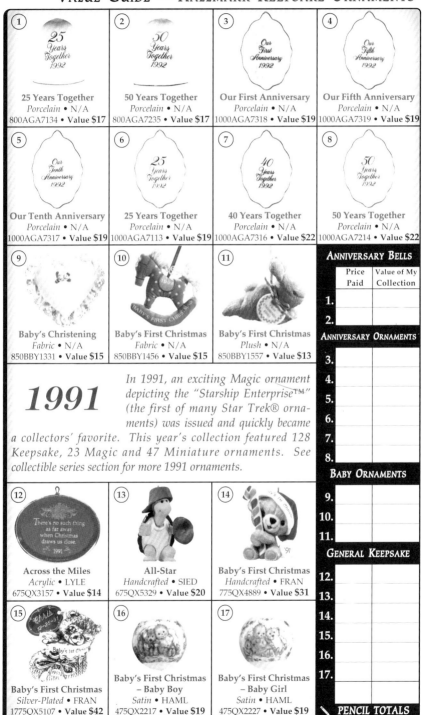

1

25 Years Together
Porcelain • N/A
800AGA7134 • **Value $17**

2

50 Years Together
Porcelain • N/A
800AGA7235 • **Value $17**

3

Our First Anniversary
Porcelain • N/A
1000AGA7318 • **Value $19**

4

Our Fifth Anniversary
Porcelain • N/A
1000AGA7319 • **Value $19**

5

Our Tenth Anniversary
Porcelain • N/A
1000AGA7317 • **Value $19**

6

25 Years Together
Porcelain • N/A
1000AGA7113 • **Value $19**

7

40 Years Together
Porcelain • N/A
1000AGA7316 • **Value $22**

8

50 Years Together
Porcelain • N/A
1000AGA7214 • **Value $22**

9

Baby's Christening
Fabric • N/A
850BBY1331 • **Value $15**

10

Baby's First Christmas
Fabric • N/A
850BBY1456 • **Value $15**

11

Baby's First Christmas
Plush • N/A
850BBY1557 • **Value $13**

1991

In 1991, an exciting Magic ornament depicting the "Starship Enterprise™" (the first of many Star Trek® ornaments) was issued and quickly became a collectors' favorite. This year's collection featured 128 Keepsake, 23 Magic and 47 Miniature ornaments. See collectible series section for more 1991 ornaments.

12

Across the Miles
Acrylic • LYLE
675QX3157 • **Value $14**

13

All-Star
Handcrafted • SIED
675QX5329 • **Value $20**

14

Baby's First Christmas
Handcrafted • FRAN
775QX4889 • **Value $31**

15

Baby's First Christmas
Silver-Plated • FRAN
1775QX5107 • **Value $42**

16

Baby's First Christmas – Baby Boy
Satin • HAML
475QX2217 • **Value $19**

17

Baby's First Christmas – Baby Girl
Satin • HAML
475QX2227 • **Value $19**

1991

Anniversary Bells

	Price Paid	Value of My Collection
1.		
2.		

Anniversary Ornaments

3.		
4.		
5.		
6.		
7.		
8.		

Baby Ornaments

9.		
10.		
11.		

General Keepsake

12.		
13.		
14.		
15.		
16.		
17.		

Pencil Totals

1
Baby's First Christmas
Photoholder
Fabric • VOTR
775QX4869 • **Value $28**

2
Baby's Second
Christmas
Handcrafted • FRAN
675QX4897 • **Value $34**

3
Basket Bell Players
Handcrafted/Wicker • SEAL
775QX5377 • **Value $23**

4
The Big Cheese
Handcrafted • SIED
675QX5327 • **Value $18**

5
Bob Cratchit
Porcelain • UNRU
1375QX4997 • **Value $34**

6
Brother
Handcrafted • SIED
675QX5479 • **Value $20**

7
A Child's Christmas
Handcrafted • FRAN
975QX4887 • **Value $15**

8
Child's Fifth Christmas
Handcrafted • RHOD
675QX4909 • **Value $17**

9
Child's Fourth
Christmas
Handcrafted • FRAN
675QX4907 • **Value $18**

10
Child's Third Christmas
Handcrafted • FRAN
675QX4899 • **Value $26**

11
Chilly Chap
Handcrafted • DLEE
675QX5339 • **Value $16**

12
Christmas Welcome
Handcrafted • SICK
975QX5299 • **Value $23**

13
Christopher Robin
Handcrafted • SIED
975QX5579 • **Value $36**

14
Cuddly Lamb
Handcrafted • RGRS
675QX5199 • **Value $18**

15
Dad
Handcrafted • JLEE
775QX5127 • **Value $18**

16
Dad-to-Be
Handcrafted • JLEE
575QX4879 • **Value $16**

17
Daughter
Handcrafted • SIED
575QX5477 • **Value $35**

18
Dickens Caroler Bell
– Mrs. Beaumont
Porcelain • CHAD
2175QX5039 • **Value $45**

19
Dinoclaus
Handcrafted • CHAD
775QX5277 • **Value $22**

20
Ebenezer Scrooge
Porcelain • UNRU
1375QX4989 • **Value $42**

General Keepsake

	Price Paid	Value of My Collection
1.		
2.		
3.		
4.		
5.		
6.		
7.		
8.		
9.		
10.		
11.		
12.		
13.		
14.		
15.		
16.		
17.		
18.		
19.		
20.		
PENCIL TOTALS		

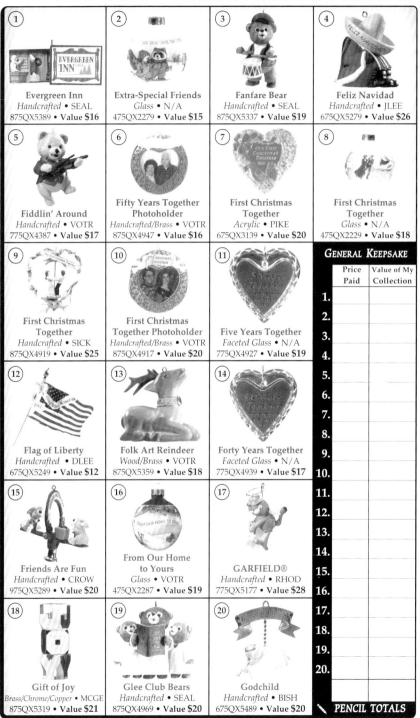

1 Evergreen Inn
Handcrafted • SEAL
875QX5389 • **Value $16**

2 Extra-Special Friends
Glass • N/A
475QX2279 • **Value $15**

3 Fanfare Bear
Handcrafted • SEAL
875QX5337 • **Value $19**

4 Feliz Navidad
Handcrafted • JLEE
675QX5279 • **Value $26**

5 Fiddlin' Around
Handcrafted • VOTR
775QX4387 • **Value $17**

6 Fifty Years Together Photoholder
Handcrafted/Brass • VOTR
875QX4947 • **Value $16**

7 First Christmas Together
Acrylic • PIKE
675QX3139 • **Value $20**

8 First Christmas Together
Glass • N/A
475QX2229 • **Value $18**

9 First Christmas Together
Handcrafted • SICK
875QX4919 • **Value $25**

10 First Christmas Together Photoholder
Handcrafted/Brass • VOTR
875QX4917 • **Value $20**

11 Five Years Together
Faceted Glass • N/A
775QX4927 • **Value $19**

12 Flag of Liberty
Handcrafted • DLEE
675QX5249 • **Value $12**

13 Folk Art Reindeer
Wood/Brass • VOTR
875QX5359 • **Value $18**

14 Forty Years Together
Faceted Glass • N/A
775QX4939 • **Value $17**

15 Friends Are Fun
Handcrafted • CROW
975QX5289 • **Value $20**

16 From Our Home to Yours
Glass • VOTR
475QX2287 • **Value $19**

17 GARFIELD®
Handcrafted • RHOD
775QX5177 • **Value $28**

18 Gift of Joy
Brass/Chrome/Copper • MCGE
875QX5319 • **Value $21**

19 Glee Club Bears
Handcrafted • SEAL
875QX4969 • **Value $20**

20 Godchild
Handcrafted • BISH
675QX5489 • **Value $20**

1991

General Keepsake

	Price Paid	Value of My Collection
1.		
2.		
3.		
4.		
5.		
6.		
7.		
8.		
9.		
10.		
11.		
12.		
13.		
14.		
15.		
16.		
17.		
18.		
19.		
20.		

PENCIL TOTALS

1. Granddaughter
Glass • PYDA
475QX2299 • **Value $25**

2. Granddaughter's First Christmas
Handcrafted • CHAD
675QX5119 • **Value $22**

3. Grandmother
Glass • N/A
475QX2307 • **Value $17**

4. Grandparents
Glass • PYDA
475QX2309 • **Value $13**

5. Grandson
Glass • PYDA
475QX2297 • **Value $22**

6. Grandson's First Christmas
Handcrafted • CHAD
675QX5117 • **Value $23**

7. Holiday Cafe
Handcrafted • SEAL
875QX5399 • **Value $13**

8. Hooked on Santa
Handcrafted • JLEE
775QX4109 • **Value $27**

9. Jesus Loves Me
Cameo • RHOD
775QX3147 • **Value $16**

10. Jolly Wolly Santa
Pressed Tin • SICK
775QX5419 • **Value $28**

11. Jolly Wolly Snowman
Pressed Tin • SICK
775QX5427 • **Value $23**

12. Jolly Wolly Soldier
Pressed Tin • SICK
775QX5429 • **Value $21**

13. Joyous Memories Photoholder
Handcrafted • VOTR
675QX5369 • **Value $25**

14. Kanga and Roo
Handcrafted • SIED
975QX5617 • **Value $45**

15. Look Out Below
Handcrafted • SEAL
875QX4959 • **Value $18**

16. Loving Stitches
Handcrafted • SEAL
875QX4987 • **Value $31**

17. Mary Engelbreit
Glass • N/A
475QX2237 • **Value $30**

18. Merry Carolers
Porcelain • UNRU
2975QX4799 • **Value $90**

19. Mom and Dad
Handcrafted • N/A
975QX5467 • **Value $23**

20. Mom-to-Be
Handcrafted • JLEE
575QX4877 • **Value $20**

General Keepsake

	Price Paid	Value of My Collection
1.		
2.		
3.		
4.		
5.		
6.		
7.		
8.		
9.		
10.		
11.		
12.		
13.		
14.		
15.		
16.		
17.		
18.		
19.		
20.		

PENCIL TOTALS

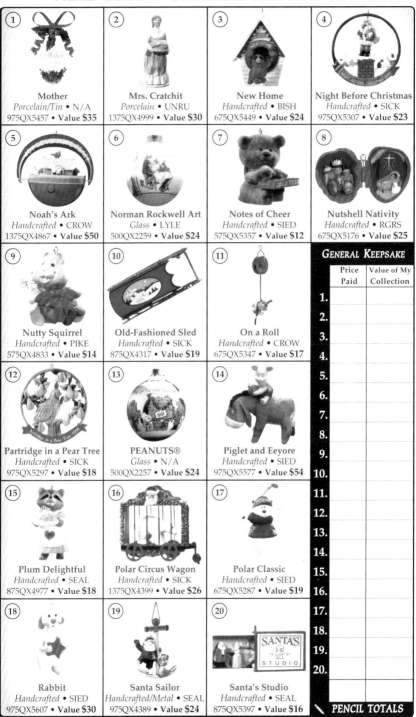

1. Mother
Porcelain/Tin • N/A
975QX5457 • **Value $35**

2. Mrs. Cratchit
Porcelain • UNRU
1375QX4999 • **Value $30**

3. New Home
Handcrafted • BISH
675QX5449 • **Value $24**

4. Night Before Christmas
Handcrafted • SICK
975QX5307 • **Value $23**

5. Noah's Ark
Handcrafted • CROW
1375QX4867 • **Value $50**

6. Norman Rockwell Art
Glass • LYLE
500QX2259 • **Value $24**

7. Notes of Cheer
Handcrafted • SIED
575QX5357 • **Value $12**

8. Nutshell Nativity
Handcrafted • RGRS
675QX5176 • **Value $25**

9. Nutty Squirrel
Handcrafted • PIKE
575QX4833 • **Value $14**

10. Old-Fashioned Sled
Handcrafted • SICK
875QX4317 • **Value $19**

11. On a Roll
Handcrafted • CROW
675QX5347 • **Value $17**

12. Partridge in a Pear Tree
Handcrafted • SICK
975QX5297 • **Value $18**

13. PEANUTS®
Glass • N/A
500QX2257 • **Value $24**

14. Piglet and Eeyore
Handcrafted • SIED
975QX5577 • **Value $54**

15. Plum Delightful
Handcrafted • SEAL
875QX4977 • **Value $18**

16. Polar Circus Wagon
Handcrafted • SICK
1375QX4399 • **Value $26**

17. Polar Classic
Handcrafted • SIED
675QX5287 • **Value $19**

18. Rabbit
Handcrafted • SIED
975QX5607 • **Value $30**

19. Santa Sailor
Handcrafted/Metal • SEAL
975QX4389 • **Value $24**

20. Santa's Studio
Handcrafted • SEAL
875QX5397 • **Value $16**

1991

General Keepsake

	Price Paid	Value of My Collection
1.		
2.		
3.		
4.		
5.		
6.		
7.		
8.		
9.		
10.		
11.		
12.		
13.		
14.		
15.		
16.		
17.		
18.		
19.		
20.		
PENCIL TOTALS		

(1) Sister *Handcrafted* • LYLE 675QX5487 • **Value $18**	**(2)** Ski Lift Bunny *Handcrafted* • JLEE 675QX5447 • **Value $19**	**(3)** SNOOPY® and WOODSTOCK *Handcrafted* • RHOD 675QX5197 • **Value $32**	**(4)** Snow Twins *Handcrafted* • SEAL 875QX4979 • **Value $20**
(5) Snowy Owl *Handcrafted* • SICK 775QX5269 • **Value $18**	**(6)** Son *Handcrafted* • SIED 575QX5469 • **Value $17**	**(7)** Sweet Talk *Handcrafted* • UNRU 875QX5367 • **Value $19**	**(8)** Sweetheart *Porcelain* • N/A 975QX4957 • **Value $24**

General Keepsake

	Price Paid	Value of My Collection
1.		
2.		
3.		
4.		
5.		
6.		
7.		
8.		
9.		
10.		
11.		
12.		
13.		
14.		
15.		
16.		
17.		
18.		
19.		

General Magic

20.		

\ **Pencil Totals**

(9) Teacher *Glass* • RGRS 475QX228-9 • **Value $12**	**(10)** Ten Years Together *Faceted Glass* • N/A 775QX4929 • **Value $18**	**(11)** Terrific Teacher *Handcrafted* • SICK 675QX5309 • **Value $15**
(12) Tigger *Handcrafted* • SIED 975QX5609 • **Value $125**	**(13)** Tiny Tim *Porcelain* • UNRU 1075QX5037 • **Value $35**	**(14)** Tramp and Laddie *Handcrafted* • FRAN 775QX4397 • **Value $40**
(15) Twenty-Five Years Together Photoholder *Handcrafted/Chrome* • VOTR 875QX4937 • **Value $18**	**(16)** Under the Mistletoe *Handcrafted* • PIKE 875QX4949 • **Value $19**	**(17)** Up 'N' Down Journey *Handcrafted* • CROW 975QX5047 • **Value $26**
(18) Winnie-the-Pooh *Handcrafted* • SIED 975QX5569 • **Value $55**	**(19)** Yule Logger *Handcrafted* • SEAL 875QX4967 • **Value $28**	**(20)** Arctic Dome *Handcrafted* • CROW 2500QLX7117 • **Value $50**

126

1
Baby's First Christmas
Handcrafted • SEAL
3000QLX7247 • **Value $90**

2
Bringing Home the Tree
Handcrafted • UNRU
2800QLX7249 • **Value $57**

3
Elfin Engineer
Handcrafted • CHAD
1000QLX7209 • **Value $24**

4
Father Christmas
Handcrafted • UNRU
1400QLX7147 • **Value $34**

5
Festive Brass Church
Brass • MCGE
1400QLX7179 • **Value $30**

6
First Christmas Together
Handcrafted • SICK
2500QLX7137 • **Value $55**

7
Friendship Tree
Handcrafted • DUTK
1000QLX7169 • **Value $23**

8
Holiday Glow
Panorama Ball • PIKE
1400QLX7177 • **Value $28**

9
It's a Wonderful Life
Handcrafted • DLEE
2000QLX7237 • **Value $70**

10
Jingle Bears
Handcrafted • JLEE
2500QLX7323 • **Value $50**

11
Kringle's Bumper Cars
Handcrafted • SICK
2500QLX7119 • **Value $54**

12
Mole Family Home
Handcrafted • JLEE
2000QLX7149 • **Value $40**

13
Salvation Army Band
Handcrafted • UNRU
3000QLX7273 • **Value $72**

14
Santa Special
(re-issued in 1992)
Handcrafted • SEAL
4000QLX7167 • **Value 63**

15
Santa's Hot Line
Handcrafted • CROW
1800QLX7159 • **Value $42**

16
Ski Trip
Handcrafted • SEAL
2800QLX7266 • **Value $55**

17
Sparkling Angel
Handcrafted • CHAD
1800QLX7157 • **Value $35**

18
Starship Enterprise™
Handcrafted • NORT
2000QLX7199 • **Value $350**

19
Toyland Tower
Handcrafted • CROW
2000QLX7129 • **Value $39**

20
All Aboard
Handcrafted • CHAD
450QXM5869 • **Value $15**

1991

GENERAL MAGIC

	Price Paid	Value of My Collection
1.		
2.		
3.		
4.		
5.		
6.		
7.		
8.		
9.		
10.		
11.		
12.		
13.		
14.		
15.		
16.		
17.		
18.		
19.		

GENERAL MINIATURE

20.		

PENCIL TOTALS

1 Baby's First Christmas
Handcrafted • FRAN
600QXM5799 • **Value $19**

2 Brass Bells
Brass • ANDR
300QXM5977 • **Value $9**

3 Brass Church
Brass • N/A
300QXM5979 • **Value $9**

4 Brass Soldier
Brass • N/A
300QXM5987 • **Value $9**

5 Bright Boxers
Handcrafted • RHOD
450QXM5877 • **Value $15**

6 Busy Bear
Wood • RHOD
450QXM5939 • **Value $12**

7 Cardinal Cameo
Handcrafted • LYLE
600QXM5957 • **Value $16**

8 Caring Shepherd
Porcelain • FRAN
600QXM5949 • **Value $17**

General Miniature

	Price Paid	Value of My Collection
1.		
2.		
3.		
4.		
5.		
6.		
7.		
8.		
9.		
10.		
11.		
12.		
13.		
14.		
15.		
16.		
17.		
18.		
19.		
20.		

PENCIL TOTALS

9 Cool 'n Sweet
Porcelain • PIKE
450QXM5867 • **Value $20**

10 Country Sleigh
Enamel • VOTR
450QXM5999 • **Value $13**

11 Courier Turtle
Handcrafted • PIKE
450QXM5857 • **Value $13**

12 Fancy Wreath
Handcrafted • LYLE
450QXM5917 • **Value $12**

13 Feliz Navidad
Handcrafted/Straw • RGRS
600QXM5887 • **Value $15**

14 First Christmas Together
Handcrafted/Brass • UNRU
600QXM5819 • **Value $15**

15 Fly By
Handcrafted • CROW
450QXM5859 • **Value $17**

16 Friendly Fawn
Handcrafted • JLEE
600QXM5947 • **Value $15**

17 Grandchild's First Christmas
Porcelain • RGRS
450QXM5697 • **Value $12**

18 Heavenly Minstrel
Handcrafted • DLEE
975QXM5687 • **Value $27**

19 Holiday Snowflake
Acrylic • RHOD
300QXM5997 • **Value $13**

20 Key to Love
Handcrafted • CROW
450QXM5689 • **Value $15**

1

Kitty in a Mitty
Handcrafted • ANDR
450QXM5879 • **Value $11**

2

Li'l Popper
Handcrafted • SICK
450QXM5897 • **Value $18**

3

1991

Love Is Born
Porcelain • VOTR
600QXM5959 • **Value $19**

4

Lulu & Family
Handcrafted • RGRS
600QXM5677 • **Value $20**

5

MOM
1991

Mom
Handcrafted • SIED
600QXM5699 • **Value $17**

6

1991

N. Pole Buddy
Handcrafted • PALM
450QXM5927 • **Value $16**

7
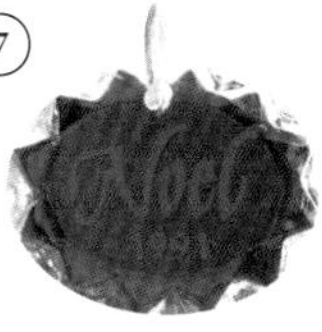
Noel
1991

Noel
Acrylic • N/A
300QXM5989 • **Value $11**

8

1991

Ring-A-Ding Elf
Handcrafted/Brass • CHAD
850QXM5669 • **Value $18**

9

Seaside Otter
Handcrafted • SIED
450QXM5909 • **Value $12**

10

Silvery Santa
Silver-Plated • JLEE
975QXM5679 • **Value $22**

11

SPECIAL FRIENDS

Special Friends
Handcrafted/Wicker • JLEE
850QXM5797 • **Value $19**

12

Tiny Tea Party Set (set/6)
Handcrafted/Porcelain • SEAL
2900QXM5827 • **Value $160**

13

1991

Top Hatter
Handcrafted • SEAL
600QXM5889 • **Value $17**

14

Treeland Trio
Handcrafted • CHAD
850QXM5899 • **Value $16**

15

Upbeat Bear
Handcrafted/Metal • FRAN
600QXM5907 • **Value $16**

16

Vision of Santa
Handcrafted • CHAD
450QXM5937 • **Value $13**

17

Wee Toymaker
Handcrafted • BISH
850QXM5967 • **Value $17**

18

Beary Artistic (club edition, magic)
Handcrafted/Acrylic • SIED
1000QXC7259 • **Value $36**

19

Hallmark
Keepsake
Ornament
COLLECTOR'S CLUB
Charter Member
FIVE YEARS TOGETHER
1991

Five Years Together (charter member gift)
Acrylic • N/A
QXC3159 • **Value $50**

20

Galloping Into Christmas (club edition, LE-28,400)
Pressed Tin • SICK
1975QXC4779 • **Value $110**

GENERAL MINIATURE

	Price Paid	Value of My Collection
1.		
2.		
3.		
4.		
5.		
6.		
7.		
8.		
9.		
10.		
11.		
12.		
13.		
14.		
15.		
16.		
17.		

COLLECTOR'S CLUB

18.		
19.		
20.		

PENCIL TOTALS

1991

VALUE GUIDE — HALLMARK KEEPSAKE ORNAMENTS

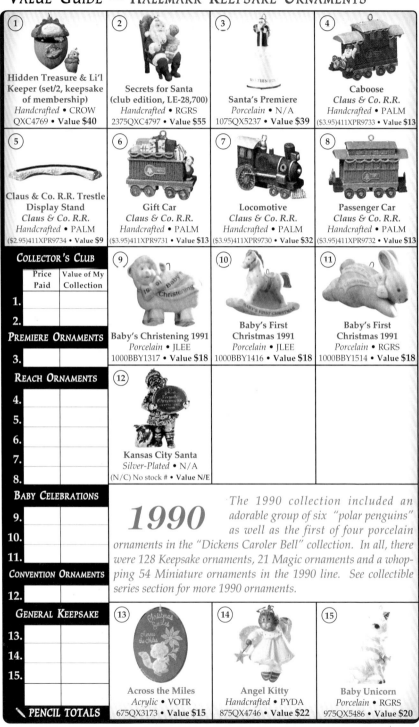

(1) Hidden Treasure & Li'l Keeper (set/2, keepsake of membership)
Handcrafted • CROW
QXC4769 • **Value $40**

(2) Secrets for Santa (club edition, LE-28,700)
Handcrafted • RGRS
2375QXC4797 • **Value $55**

(3) Santa's Premiere
Porcelain • N/A
1075QX5237 • **Value $39**

(4) Caboose
Claus & Co. R.R.
Handcrafted • PALM
($3.95)411XPR9733 • **Value $13**

(5) Claus & Co. R.R. Trestle Display Stand
Claus & Co. R.R.
Handcrafted • PALM
($2.95)411XPR9734 • **Value $9**

(6) Gift Car
Claus & Co. R.R.
Handcrafted • PALM
($3.95)411XPR9731 • **Value $13**

(7) Locomotive
Claus & Co. R.R.
Handcrafted • PALM
($3.95)411XPR9730 • **Value $32**

(8) Passenger Car
Claus & Co. R.R.
Handcrafted • PALM
($3.95)411XPR9732 • **Value $13**

(9) Baby's Christening 1991
Porcelain • JLEE
1000BBY1317 • **Value $18**

(10) Baby's First Christmas 1991
Porcelain • JLEE
1000BBY1416 • **Value $18**

(11) Baby's First Christmas 1991
Porcelain • RGRS
1000BBY1514 • **Value $18**

(12) Kansas City Santa
Silver-Plated • N/A
(N/C) No stock # • **Value N/E**

	Price Paid	Value of My Collection
COLLECTOR'S CLUB		
1.		
2.		
PREMIERE ORNAMENTS		
3.		
REACH ORNAMENTS		
4.		
5.		
6.		
7.		
8.		
BABY CELEBRATIONS		
9.		
10.		
11.		
CONVENTION ORNAMENTS		
12.		
GENERAL KEEPSAKE		
13.		
14.		
15.		
PENCIL TOTALS		

1990

The 1990 collection included an adorable group of six "polar penguins" as well as the first of four porcelain ornaments in the "Dickens Caroler Bell" collection. In all, there were 128 Keepsake ornaments, 21 Magic ornaments and a whopping 54 Miniature ornaments in the 1990 line. See collectible series section for more 1990 ornaments.

(13) Across the Miles
Acrylic • VOTR
675QX3173 • **Value $15**

(14) Angel Kitty
Handcrafted • PYDA
875QX4746 • **Value $22**

(15) Baby Unicorn
Porcelain • RGRS
975QX5486 • **Value $20**

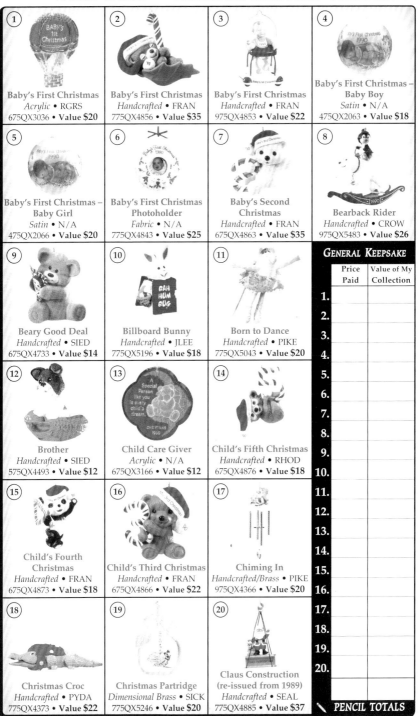

1
Baby's First Christmas
Acrylic • RGRS
675QX3036 • **Value $20**

2
Baby's First Christmas
Handcrafted • FRAN
775QX4856 • **Value $35**

3
Baby's First Christmas
Handcrafted • FRAN
975QX4853 • **Value $22**

4
Baby's First Christmas –
Baby Boy
Satin • N/A
475QX2063 • **Value $18**

5
Baby's First Christmas –
Baby Girl
Satin • N/A
475QX2066 • **Value $20**

6
Baby's First Christmas
Photoholder
Fabric • N/A
775QX4843 • **Value $25**

7
Baby's Second
Christmas
Handcrafted • FRAN
675QX4863 • **Value $35**

8
Bearback Rider
Handcrafted • CROW
975QX5483 • **Value $26**

1990

9
Beary Good Deal
Handcrafted • SIED
675QX4733 • **Value $14**

10
Billboard Bunny
Handcrafted • JLEE
775QX5196 • **Value $18**

11
Born to Dance
Handcrafted • PIKE
775QX5043 • **Value $20**

12
Brother
Handcrafted • SIED
575QX4493 • **Value $12**

13
Child Care Giver
Acrylic • N/A
675QX3166 • **Value $12**

14
Child's Fifth Christmas
Handcrafted • RHOD
675QX4876 • **Value $18**

15
Child's Fourth
Christmas
Handcrafted • FRAN
675QX4873 • **Value $18**

16
Child's Third Christmas
Handcrafted • FRAN
675QX4866 • **Value $22**

17
Chiming In
Handcrafted/Brass • PIKE
975QX4366 • **Value $20**

18
Christmas Croc
Handcrafted • PYDA
775QX4373 • **Value $22**

19
Christmas Partridge
Dimensional Brass • SICK
775QX5246 • **Value $20**

20
Claus Construction
(re-issued from 1989)
Handcrafted • SEAL
775QX4885 • **Value $37**

GENERAL KEEPSAKE

	Price Paid	Value of My Collection
1.		
2.		
3.		
4.		
5.		
6.		
7.		
8.		
9.		
10.		
11.		
12.		
13.		
14.		
15.		
16.		
17.		
18.		
19.		
20.		
PENCIL TOTALS		

Value Guide — Hallmark Keepsake Ornaments

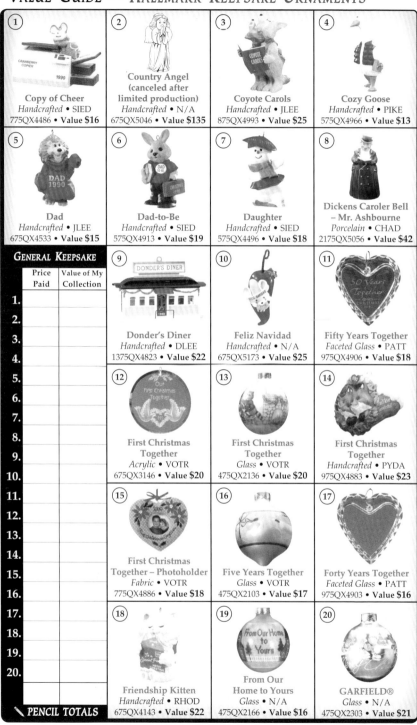

① Copy of Cheer
Handcrafted • SIED
775QX4486 • **Value $16**

② Country Angel
(canceled after
limited production)
Handcrafted • N/A
675QX5046 • **Value $135**

③ Coyote Carols
Handcrafted • JLEE
875QX4993 • **Value $25**

④ Cozy Goose
Handcrafted • PIKE
575QX4966 • **Value $13**

⑤ Dad
Handcrafted • JLEE
675QX4533 • **Value $15**

⑥ Dad-to-Be
Handcrafted • SIED
575QX4913 • **Value $19**

⑦ Daughter
Handcrafted • SIED
575QX4496 • **Value $18**

⑧ Dickens Caroler Bell
– Mr. Ashbourne
Porcelain • CHAD
2175QX5056 • **Value $42**

General Keepsake

	Price Paid	Value of My Collection
1.		
2.		
3.		
4.		
5.		
6.		
7.		
8.		
9.		
10.		
11.		
12.		
13.		
14.		
15.		
16.		
17.		
18.		
19.		
20.		

PENCIL TOTALS

⑨ Donder's Diner
Handcrafted • DLEE
1375QX4823 • **Value $22**

⑩ Feliz Navidad
Handcrafted • N/A
675QX5173 • **Value $25**

⑪ Fifty Years Together
Faceted Glass • PATT
975QX4906 • **Value $18**

⑫ First Christmas
Together
Acrylic • VOTR
675QX3146 • **Value $20**

⑬ First Christmas
Together
Glass • VOTR
475QX2136 • **Value $20**

⑭ First Christmas
Together
Handcrafted • PYDA
975QX4883 • **Value $23**

⑮ First Christmas
Together – Photoholder
Fabric • VOTR
775QX4886 • **Value $18**

⑯ Five Years Together
Glass • VOTR
475QX2103 • **Value $17**

⑰ Forty Years Together
Faceted Glass • PATT
975QX4903 • **Value $16**

⑱ Friendship Kitten
Handcrafted • RHOD
675QX4143 • **Value $22**

⑲ From Our
Home to Yours
Glass • N/A
475QX2166 • **Value $16**

⑳ GARFIELD®
Glass • N/A
475QX2303 • **Value $21**

1 Gentle Dreamers
Handcrafted • FRAN
875QX4756 • **Value $29**

2 Gingerbread Elf
Handcrafted • N/A
575QX5033 • **Value $19**

3 Godchild
Acrylic • FRAN
675QX3176 • **Value $14**

4 Golf's My Bag
Handcrafted • JLEE
775QX4963 • **Value $26**

5 Goose Cart
Handcrafted • N/A
775QX5236 • **Value $14**

6 Granddaughter
Glass • LYLE
475QX2286 • **Value $18**

7 Granddaughter's
First Christmas
Acrylic • FRAN
675QX3106 • **Value $16**

8 Grandmother
Glass • VOTR
475QX2236 • **Value $15**

9 Grandparents
Glass • N/A
475QX2253 • **Value $15**

10 Grandson
Glass • VOTR
475QX2293 • **Value $18**

11 Grandson's
First Christmas
Acrylic • FRAN
675QX3063 • **Value $16**

12 Hang in There
Handcrafted • SEAL
675QX4713 • **Value $20**

13 Happy Voices
Wood • VOTR
675QX4645 • **Value $14**

14 Happy Woodcutter
Handcrafted • JLEE
975QX4763 • **Value $20**

15 Holiday Cardinals
Dimensional Brass • LYLE
775QX5243 • **Value $22**

16 Home for the Owlidays
Handcrafted • N/A
675QX5183 • **Value $15**

17 Hot Dogger
Handcrafted • CROW
775QX4976 • **Value $18**

18 Jesus Loves Me
Acrylic • PATT
675QX3156 • **Value $13**

19 Jolly Dolphin
Handcrafted • RGRS
675QX4683 • **Value $29**

20 Joy is in the Air
Handcrafted • CROW
775QX5503 • **Value $25**

1990

General Keepsake

	Price Paid	Value of My Collection
1.		
2.		
3.		
4.		
5.		
6.		
7.		
8.		
9.		
10.		
11.		
12.		
13.		
14.		
15.		
16.		
17.		
18.		
19.		
20.		
PENCIL TOTALS		

(1) King Klaus
Handcrafted • SEAL
775QX4106 • **Value $20**

(2) Kitty's Best Pal
Handcrafted • FRAN
675QX4716 • **Value $21**

(3) Little Drummer Boy
Handcrafted • UNRU
775QX5233 • **Value $20**

(4) Long Winter's Nap
Handcrafted • RGRS
675QX4703 • **Value $22**

(5) Loveable Dears
Handcrafted • UNRU
875QX5476 • **Value $17**

(6) Meow Mart
Handcrafted • PIKE
775QX4446 • **Value $25**

(7) Mom and Dad
Handcrafted • CHAD
875QX4593 • **Value $22**

(8) Mom-to-Be
Handcrafted • SIED
575QX4916 • **Value $30**

General Keepsake

	Price Paid	Value of My Collection
1.		
2.		
3.		
4.		
5.		
6.		
7.		
8.		
9.		
10.		
11.		
12.		
13.		
14.		
15.		
16.		
17.		
18.		
19.		
20.		

PENCIL TOTALS

(9) Mooy Christmas
Handcrafted • N/A
675QX4933 • **Value $27**

(10) Mother
Ceramic/Bisque • VOTR
875QX4536 • **Value $20**

(11) Mouseboat
Handcrafted • SEAL
775QX4753 • **Value $14**

(12) New Home
Handcrafted • PYDA
675QX4343 • **Value $22**

(13) Norman Rockwell Art
Glass • LYLE
475QX2296 • **Value $23**

(14) Nutshell Chat
Handcrafted • N/A
675QX5193 • **Value $23**

(15) Nutshell Holiday
(re-issued from 1989)
Handcrafted • RGRS
575QX4652 • **Value $25**

(16) Peaceful Kingdom
Glass • N/A
475QX2106 • **Value $20**

(17) PEANUTS®
Glass • N/A
475QX2233 • **Value $28**

(18) Pepperoni Mouse
Handcrafted • SIED
675QX4973 • **Value $19**

(19) Perfect Catch
Handcrafted • SIED
775QX4693 • **Value $19**

(20) Polar Jogger
Handcrafted • SIED
575QX4666 • **Value $16**

134

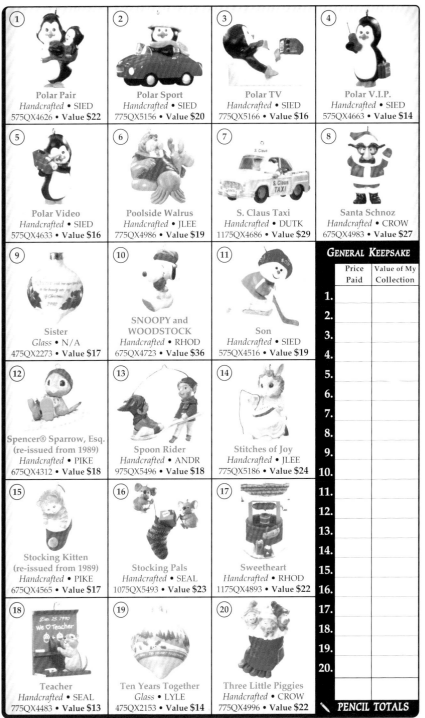

1 Polar Pair
Handcrafted • SIED
575QX4626 • **Value $22**

2 Polar Sport
Handcrafted • SIED
775QX5156 • **Value $20**

3 Polar TV
Handcrafted • SIED
775QX5166 • **Value $16**

4 Polar V.I.P.
Handcrafted • SIED
575QX4663 • **Value $14**

5 Polar Video
Handcrafted • SIED
575QX4633 • **Value $16**

6 Poolside Walrus
Handcrafted • JLEE
775QX4986 • **Value $19**

7 S. Claus Taxi
Handcrafted • DUTK
1175QX4686 • **Value $29**

8 Santa Schnoz
Handcrafted • CROW
675QX4983 • **Value $27**

9 Sister
Glass • N/A
475QX2273 • **Value $17**

10 SNOOPY and WOODSTOCK
Handcrafted • RHOD
675QX4723 • **Value $36**

11 Son
Handcrafted • SIED
575QX4516 • **Value $19**

12 Spencer® Sparrow, Esq.
(re-issued from 1989)
Handcrafted • PIKE
675QX4312 • **Value $18**

13 Spoon Rider
Handcrafted • ANDR
975QX5496 • **Value $18**

14 Stitches of Joy
Handcrafted • JLEE
775QX5186 • **Value $24**

15 Stocking Kitten
(re-issued from 1989)
Handcrafted • PIKE
675QX4565 • **Value $17**

16 Stocking Pals
Handcrafted • SEAL
1075QX5493 • **Value $23**

17 Sweetheart
Handcrafted • RHOD
1175QX4893 • **Value $22**

18 Teacher
Handcrafted • SEAL
775QX4483 • **Value $13**

19 Ten Years Together
Glass • LYLE
475QX2153 • **Value $14**

20 Three Little Piggies
Handcrafted • CROW
775QX4996 • **Value $22**

1990

GENERAL KEEPSAKE

	Price Paid	Value of My Collection
1.		
2.		
3.		
4.		
5.		
6.		
7.		
8.		
9.		
10.		
11.		
12.		
13.		
14.		
15.		
16.		
17.		
18.		
19.		
20.		
PENCIL TOTALS		

VALUE GUIDE – HALLMARK KEEPSAKE ORNAMENTS

(1) Time for Love
Glass • LYLE
475QX2133 • **Value $20**

(2) Twenty-Five Years Together
Faceted Glass • PATT
975QX4896 • **Value $17**

(3) Two Peas in a Pod
Handcrafted • ANDR
475QX4926 • **Value $35**

(4) Welcome, Santa
Handcrafted • CROW
1175QX4773 • **Value $24**

(5) Baby's First Christmas
Handcrafted • PALM
2800QLX7246 • **Value $65**

(6) Beary Short Nap
Handcrafted • SIED
1000QLX7326 • **Value $28**

(7) Blessings of Love
Panorama Ball • N/A
1400QLX7363 • **Value $50**

(8) Children's Express
Handcrafted • SICK
2800QLX7243 • **Value $68**

(9) Christmas Memories
Handcrafted • UNRU
2500QLX7276 • **Value $55**

(10) Deer Crossing
Handcrafted • SIED
1800QLX7213 • **Value $40**

(11) Elf of the Year
Handcrafted • ANDR
1000QLX7356 • **Value $20**

(12) Elfin Whittler
Handcrafted • CROW
2000QLX7265 • **Value $43**

(13) First Christmas Together
Handcrafted • DLEE
1800QLX7255 • **Value $42**

(14) Holiday Flash
Handcrafted • CHAD
1800QLX7333 • **Value $34**

(15) Hop 'N Pop Popper
Handcrafted • SIED
2000QLX7353 • **Value $95**

(16) Letter to Santa
Handcrafted • RGRS
1400QLX7226 • **Value $33**

(17) Mrs. Santa's Kitchen
Handcrafted • RHOD
2500QLX7263 • **Value $68**

(18) Partridges in a Pear
Dimensional Brass • LYLE
1400QLX7212 • **Value $30**

(19) Santa's Ho-Ho-Hoedown
Handcrafted • CROW
2500QLX7256 • **Value $84**

(20) Song and Dance
Handcrafted • RGRS
2000QLX7253 • **Value $88**

	Price Paid	Value of My Collection
GENERAL KEEPSAKE		
1.		
2.		
3.		
4.		
GENERAL MAGIC		
5.		
6.		
7.		
8.		
9.		
10. *B*		
11.		
12.		
13.		
14.		
15.		
16.		
17.		
18.		
19.		
20.		
＼ PENCIL TOTALS		

1990 Collection

1. Starlight Angel
Handcrafted • RGRS
1400QLX7306 • **Value $32**

2. Starship Christmas
Handcrafted • SIED
1800QLX7336 • **Value $45**

3. Acorn Squirrel
(re-issued from 1989)
Handcrafted • PIKE
450QXM5682 • **Value $10**

4. Acorn Wreath
Handcrafted • CROW
600QXM5686 • **Value $11**

5. Air Santa
Handcrafted • N/A
450QXM5656 • **Value $12**

6. Baby's First Christmas
Handcrafted • FRAN
850QXM5703 • **Value $16**

7. Basket Buddy
Handcrafted/Wicker • RGRS
600QXM5696 • **Value $11**

8. Bear Hug
Handcrafted • PALM
600QXM5633 • **Value $13**

9. Brass Bouquet
Brass • LYLE
600QXM5776 • **Value $7**

10. Brass Horn
Brass • N/A
300QXM5793 • **Value $7**

11. Brass Peace
Brass • N/A
300QXM5796 • **Value $7**

12. Brass Santa
Brass • PATT
300QXM5786 • **Value $8**

13. Brass Year
Brass • N/A
300QXM5833 • **Value $8**

14. Busy Carver
Handcrafted • CROW
450QXM5673 • **Value $8**

15. Christmas Dove
Handcrafted • SIED
450QXM5636 • **Value $16**

16. Cloisonné Poinsettia
Cloisonné • VOTR
1050QXM5533 • **Value $22**

17. Country Heart
Handcrafted • RGRS
450QXM5693 • **Value $8**

18. Cozy Skater
(re-issued from 1989)
Handcrafted • LYLE
450QXM5735 • **Value $11**

19. First Christmas Together
Porcelain • ANDR
600QXM5536 • **Value $13**

20. Going Sledding
Handcrafted • JLEE
450QXM5683 • **Value $14**

1990

GENERAL MAGIC	Price Paid	Value of My Collection
1.		
2.		
GENERAL MINIATURE		
3.		
4.		
5.		
6.		
7.		
8.		
9.		
10.		
11.		
12.		
13.		
14.		
15.		
16.		
17.		
18.		
19.		
20.		
PENCIL TOTALS		

Value Guide — Hallmark Keepsake Ornaments

1. Grandchild's First Christmas
Handcrafted • SIED
600QXM5723 • **Value $10**

2. Happy Bluebird
(re-issued from 1989)
Handcrafted • RGRS
450QXM5662 • **Value $13**

3. Holiday Cardinal
Acrylic • FRAN
300QXM5526 • **Value $11**

4. Lion and Lamb
Wood • SICK
450QXM5676 • **Value $10**

5. Little Soldier
(re-issued from 1989)
Handcrafted • SICK
450QXM5675 • **Value $10**

6. Loving Hearts
Acrylic • N/A
300QXM5523 • **Value $10**

7. Madonna and Child
Handcrafted • RGRS
600QXM5643 • **Value $12**

8. Mother
Cameo • LYLE
450QXM5716 • **Value $16**

9. Nativity
Handcrafted • UNRU
450QXM5706 • **Value $18**

10. Old-World Santa
(re-issued from 1989)
Handcrafted • SIED
300QXM5695 • **Value $9**

11. Panda's Surprise
Handcrafted • FRAN
450QXM5616 • **Value $12**

12. Perfect Fit
Handcrafted • CHAD
450QXM5516 • **Value $12**

13. Puppy Love
Handcrafted • PALM
600QXM5666 • **Value $14**

14. Roly-Poly Pig
(re-issued from 1989)
Handcrafted • PIKE
300QXM5712 • **Value $16**

15. Ruby Reindeer
Glass • PATT
600QXM5816 • **Value $12**

16. Santa's Journey
Handcrafted • SICK
850QXM5826 • **Value $18**

17. Santa's Streetcar
Handcrafted • DLEE
850QXM5766 • **Value $16**

18. Snow Angel
Handcrafted • JLEE
600QXM5773 • **Value $12**

19. Special Friends
Handcrafted • PIKE
600QXM5726 • **Value $13**

20. Stamp Collector
Handcrafted • CROW
450QXM5623 • **Value $9**

General Miniature

	Price Paid	Value of My Collection
1.		
2.		
3.		
4.		
5.		
6.		
7.		
8.		
9.		
10.		
11.		
12.		
13.		
14.		
15.		
16.		
17.		
18.		
19.		
20.		

PENCIL TOTALS

1990 Collection

VALUE GUIDE — HALLMARK KEEPSAKE ORNAMENTS

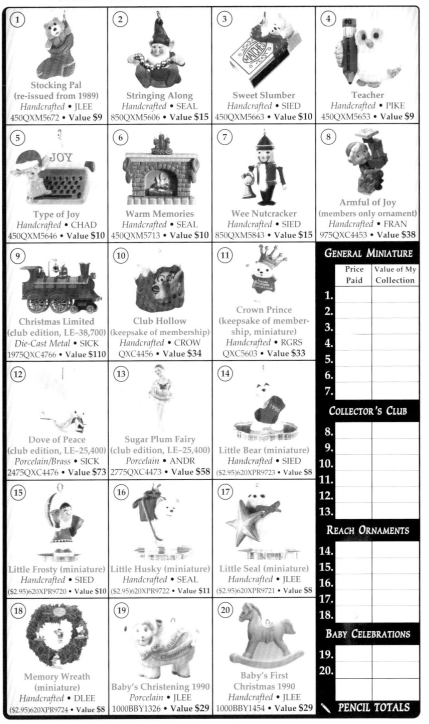

1. Stocking Pal
(re-issued from 1989)
Handcrafted • JLEE
450QXM5672 • **Value $9**

2. Stringing Along
Handcrafted • SEAL
850QXM5606 • **Value $15**

3. Sweet Slumber
Handcrafted • SIED
450QXM5663 • **Value $10**

4. Teacher
Handcrafted • PIKE
450QXM5653 • **Value $9**

5. Type of Joy
Handcrafted • CHAD
450QXM5646 • **Value $10**

6. Warm Memories
Handcrafted • SEAL
450QXM5713 • **Value $10**

7. Wee Nutcracker
Handcrafted • SIED
850QXM5843 • **Value $15**

8. Armful of Joy
(members only ornament)
Handcrafted • FRAN
975QXC4453 • **Value $38**

9. Christmas Limited
(club edition, LE–38,700)
Die-Cast Metal • SICK
1975QXC4766 • **Value $110**

10. Club Hollow
(keepsake of membership)
Handcrafted • CROW
QXC4456 • **Value $34**

11. Crown Prince
(keepsake of member-
ship, miniature)
Handcrafted • RGRS
QXC5603 • **Value $33**

12. Dove of Peace
(club edition, LE–25,400)
Porcelain/Brass • SICK
2475QXC4476 • **Value $73**

13. Sugar Plum Fairy
(club edition, LE–25,400)
Porcelain • ANDR
2775QXC4473 • **Value $58**

14. Little Bear (miniature)
Handcrafted • SIED
($2.95)620XPR9723 • **Value $8**

15. Little Frosty (miniature)
Handcrafted • SIED
($2.95)620XPR9720 • **Value $10**

16. Little Husky (miniature)
Handcrafted • SEAL
($2.95)620XPR9722 • **Value $11**

17. Little Seal (miniature)
Handcrafted • JLEE
($2.95)620XPR9721 • **Value $8**

18. Memory Wreath
(miniature)
Handcrafted • DLEE
($2.95)620XPR9724 • **Value $8**

19. Baby's Christening 1990
Porcelain • JLEE
1000BBY1326 • **Value $29**

20. Baby's First
Christmas 1990
Handcrafted • JLEE
1000BBY1454 • **Value $29**

1990

GENERAL MINIATURE		
	Price Paid	Value of My Collection
1.		
2.		
3.		
4.		
5.		
6.		
7.		
COLLECTOR'S CLUB		
8.		
9.		
10.		
11.		
12.		
13.		
REACH ORNAMENTS		
14.		
15.		
16.		
17.		
18.		
BABY CELEBRATIONS		
19.		
20.		
PENCIL TOTALS		

(1)
Baby's First
Christmas 1990
Porcelain • RGRS
1000BBY1554 • **Value $29**

1989

In 1989, Hallmark debuted a popular collection of dated teddy bear ornaments celebrating a child's first five Christmases. In the 1989 collection, there were 123 Keepsake ornaments, 19 Magic ornaments and 41 Miniature ornaments. See collectibles series section for more 1989 ornaments.

(2)
Baby Partridge
Handcrafted • FRAN
675QX4525 • **Value $14**

(3)
Baby's First Christmas
Acrylic • FRAN
675QX3815 • **Value $22**

(4)
Baby's First Christmas
Handcrafted • CHAD
725QX4492 • **Value $95**

(5)
Baby's First Christmas
– Baby Boy
Satin • VOTR
475QX2725 • **Value $22**

(6)
Baby's First Christmas
– Baby Girl
Satin • VOTR
475QX2722 • **Value $22**

(7)
Baby's First Christmas
Photoholder
Handcrafted • VOTR
625QX4682 • **Value $48**

(8)
Baby's Second
Christmas
Handcrafted • FRAN
675QX4495 • **Value $32**

(9)
Balancing Elf
Handcrafted • CHAD
675QX4895 • **Value $21**

(10)
Bear-i-Tone
Handcrafted • SIED
475QX4542 • **Value $18**

(11)
Brother
Handcrafted • LYLE
725QX4452 • **Value $18**

(12)
Cactus Cowboy
Handcrafted • DUTK
675QX4112 • **Value $39**

(13)
Camera Claus
Handcrafted • SIED
575QX5465 • **Value $18**

(14)
Carousel Zebra
Handcrafted • SICK
925QX4515 • **Value $19**

(15)
Cherry Jubilee
Handcrafted • SICK
500QX4532 • **Value $26**

(16)
Child's Fifth Christmas
Handcrafted • RHOD
675QX5435 • **Value $18**

(17)
Child's Fourth
Christmas
Handcrafted • FRAN
675QX5432 • **Value $18**

Baby Celebrations

	Price Paid	Value of My Collection
1.		

General Keepsake

2.		
3.		
4.		
5.		
6.		
7.		
8.		
9.		
10.		
11.		
12.		
13.		
14.		
15.		
16.		
17.		

PENCIL TOTALS

(1) Child's Third Christmas *Handcrafted* • FRAN 675QX4695 • **Value $19**	**(2)** Claus Construction (re-issued in 1990) *Handcrafted* • SEAL 775QX4885 • **Value $36**	**(3)** Cool Swing *Handcrafted* • CROW 625QX4875 • **Value $32**	**(4)** Country Cat *Handcrafted* • PYDA 625QX4672 • **Value $17**
(5) Cranberry Bunny *Handcrafted* • RGRS 575QX4262 • **Value $17**	**(6)** Dad *Handcrafted* • N/A 725QX4412 • **Value $15**	**(7)** Daughter *Handcrafted* • SICK 625QX4432 • **Value $18**	**(8)** Deer Disguise *Handcrafted* • SIED 575QX4265 • **Value $20**

1989

(9) Feliz Navidad *Handcrafted* • PYDA 675QX4392 • **Value $27**	**(10)** Festive Angel *Dimensional Brass* • N/A 675QX4635 • **Value $25**	**(11)** Festive Year *Acrylic* • VOTR 775QX3842 • **Value $22**	

GENERAL KEEPSAKE

	Price Paid	Value of My Collection
1.		
2.		
3.		
4.		
5.		
6.		
7.		
8.		
9.		
10.		
11.		
12.		
13.		
14.		
15.		
16.		
17.		
18.		
19.		
20.		

(12) Fifty Years Together Photoholder *Porcelain* • RGRS 875QX4862 • **Value $18**	**(13)** The First Christmas *Cameo* • N/A 775QX5475 • **Value $17**	**(14)** First Christmas Together *Acrylic* • RHOD 675QX3832 • **Value $23**
(15) First Christmas Together *Glass* • N/A 475QX2732 • **Value $24**	**(16)** First Christmas Together *Handcrafted* • RGRS 975QX4852 • **Value $24**	**(17)** Five Years Together *Glass* • N/A 475QX2735 • **Value $20**
(18) Forty Years Together Photoholder *Porcelain* • RGRS 875QX5452 • **Value $16**	**(19)** Friendship Time *Handcrafted* • N/A 975QX4132 • **Value $30**	**(20)** From Our Home to Yours *Acrylic* • N/A 625QX3845 • **Value $15**

PENCIL TOTALS

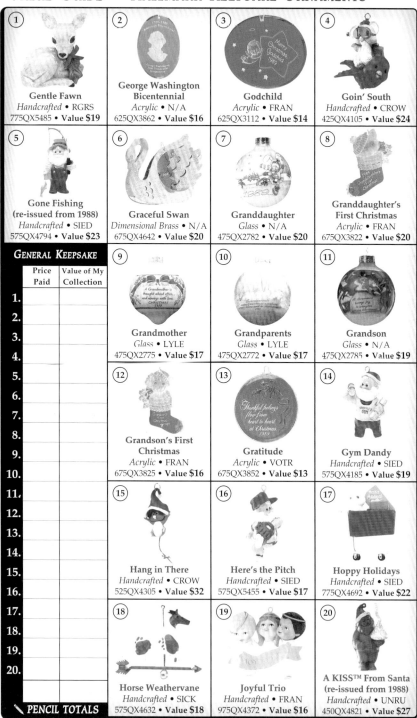

(1) **Gentle Fawn** *Handcrafted* • RGRS 775QX5485 • **Value $19**	**(2)** **George Washington Bicentennial** *Acrylic* • N/A 625QX3862 • **Value $16**	**(3)** **Godchild** *Acrylic* • FRAN 625QX3112 • **Value $14**	**(4)** **Goin' South** *Handcrafted* • CROW 425QX4105 • **Value $24**
(5) **Gone Fishing** **(re-issued from 1988)** *Handcrafted* • SIED 575QX4794 • **Value $23**	**(6)** **Graceful Swan** *Dimensional Brass* • N/A 675QX4642 • **Value $20**	**(7)** **Granddaughter** *Glass* • N/A 475QX2782 • **Value $20**	**(8)** **Granddaughter's First Christmas** *Acrylic* • FRAN 675QX3822 • **Value $20**

GENERAL KEEPSAKE

	Price Paid	Value of My Collection
1.		
2.		
3.		
4.		
5.		
6.		
7.		
8.		
9.		
10.		
11.		
12.		
13.		
14.		
15.		
16.		
17.		
18.		
19.		
20.		

PENCIL TOTALS

(9) **Grandmother** *Glass* • LYLE 475QX2775 • **Value $17**	**(10)** **Grandparents** *Glass* • LYLE 475QX2772 • **Value $17**	**(11)** **Grandson** *Glass* • N/A 475QX2785 • **Value $19**
(12) **Grandson's First Christmas** *Acrylic* • FRAN 675QX3825 • **Value $16**	**(13)** **Gratitude** *Acrylic* • VOTR 675QX3852 • **Value $13**	**(14)** **Gym Dandy** *Handcrafted* • SIED 575QX4185 • **Value $19**
(15) **Hang in There** *Handcrafted* • CROW 525QX4305 • **Value $32**	**(16)** **Here's the Pitch** *Handcrafted* • SIED 575QX5455 • **Value $17**	**(17)** **Hoppy Holidays** *Handcrafted* • SIED 775QX4692 • **Value $22**
(18) **Horse Weathervane** *Handcrafted* • SICK 575QX4632 • **Value $18**	**(19)** **Joyful Trio** *Handcrafted* • FRAN 975QX4372 • **Value $16**	**(20)** **A KISS™ From Santa** **(re-issued from 1988)** *Handcrafted* • UNRU 450QX4821 • **Value $27**

1989

1.
Kristy Claus
Handcrafted • SIED
575QX4245 • **Value $13**

2.
Language of Love
Acrylic • N/A
625QX3835 • **Value $24**

3.
Let's Play
Handcrafted • CROW
725QX4882 • **Value $27**

4.
Mail Call
Handcrafted • SEAL
875QX4522 • **Value $18**

5.
Merry-Go-Round Unicorn
Porcelain • RGRS
1075QX4472 • **Value $20**

6.
Mom and Dad
Handcrafted • PIKE
975QX4425 • **Value $22**

7.
Mother
Porcelain • N/A
975QX4405 • **Value $30**

8.
New Home
Glass • VOTR
475QX2755 • **Value $21**

9.
Norman Rockwell
Glass • LYLE
475QX2762 • **Value $20**

10.
North Pole Jogger
Handcrafted • SIED
575QX5462 • **Value $20**

11.
Nostalgic Lamb
Handcrafted • PYDA
675QX4665 • **Value $14**

12.
Nutshell Dreams
Handcrafted • CHAD
575QX4655 • **Value $21**

13.
Nutshell Holiday
(re-issued in 1990)
Handcrafted • RGRS
575QX4652 • **Value $24**

14.
Nutshell Workshop
Handcrafted • CHAD
575QX4872 • **Value $21**

15.
Old-World Gnome
Handcrafted • N/A
775QX4345 • **Value $23**

16.
On the Links
Handcrafted • SIED
575QX4192 • **Value $22**

17.
OREO® Chocolate Sandwich Cookies
(re-issued from 1988)
Handcrafted • UNRU
400QX4814 • **Value $20**

18.
The Ornament Express (set/3)
Handcrafted • SICK
2200QX5805 • **Value $43**

19.
Owliday Greetings
Handcrafted • PIKE
400QX4365 • **Value $17**

20.
Paddington™ Bear
Handcrafted • FRAN
575QX4292 • **Value $22**

General Keepsake

	Price Paid	Value of My Collection
1.		
2.		
3.		
4.		
5.		
6.		
7.		
8.		
9.		
10.		
11.		
12.		
13.		
14.		
15.		
16.		
17.		
18.		
19.		
20.		
PENCIL TOTALS		

1 Party Line
(re-issued from 1988)
Handcrafted • PIKE
875QX4761 • **Value $26**

2 PEANUTS® – A Charlie
Brown Christmas
Glass • N/A
475QX2765 • **Value $39**

3 Peek-a-Boo Kitties
(re-issued from 1988)
Handcrafted • CROW
750QX4871 • **Value $22**

4 Peppermint Clown
Porcelain • DUTK
2475QX4505 • **Value $40**

5 Playful Angel
Handcrafted • DLEE
675QX4535 • **Value $23**

6 Polar Bowler
(re-issued from 1988)
Handcrafted • SIED
575QX4784 • **Value $17**

7 Rodney Reindeer
Handcrafted • SIED
675QX4072 • **Value $16**

8 Rooster Weathervane
Handcrafted • SICK
575QX4675 • **Value $16**

9 Sea Santa
Handcrafted • SIED
575QX4152 • **Value $28**

10 Sister
Glass • N/A
475QX2792 • **Value $19**

11 SNOOPY and
WOODSTOCK
Handcrafted • RHOD
675QX4332 • **Value $36**

12 Snowplow Santa
Handcrafted • SIED
575QX4205 • **Value $20**

13 Son
Handcrafted • SICK
625QX4445 • **Value $19**

14 Sparkling Snowflake
Brass • LYLE
775QX5472 • **Value $21**

15 Special Delivery
Handcrafted • RGRS
525QX4325 • **Value $21**

16 Spencer® Sparrow, Esq.
(re-issued in 1990)
Handcrafted • PIKE
675QX4312 • **Value $19**

17 Stocking Kitten
(re-issued in 1990)
Handcrafted • PIKE
675QX4565 • **Value $18**

18 Sweet Memories
Photoholder
Handcrafted • N/A
675QX4385 • **Value $22**

19 Sweetheart
Handcrafted • SICK
975QX4865 • **Value $30**

20 Teacher
Handcrafted • SIED
575QX4125 • **Value $20**

General Keepsake

	Price Paid	Value of My Collection
1.		
2.		
3.		
4.		
5.		
6.		
7.		
8.		
9.		
10.		
11.		
12.		
13.		
14.		
15.		
16.		
17.		
18.		
19.		
20.		
PENCIL TOTALS		

144

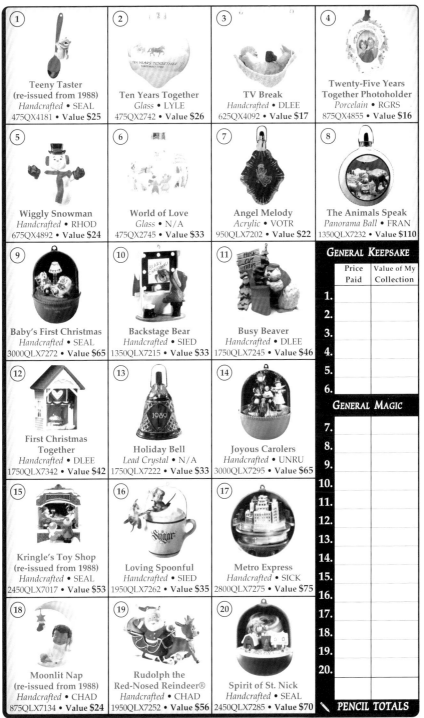

1
Teeny Taster
(re-issued from 1988)
Handcrafted • SEAL
475QX4181 • **Value $25**

2
Ten Years Together
Glass • LYLE
475QX2742 • **Value $26**

3
TV Break
Handcrafted • DLEE
625QX4092 • **Value $17**

4
Twenty-Five Years
Together Photoholder
Porcelain • RGRS
875QX4855 • **Value $16**

5
Wiggly Snowman
Handcrafted • RHOD
675QX4892 • **Value $24**

6
World of Love
Glass • N/A
475QX2745 • **Value $33**

7
Angel Melody
Acrylic • VOTR
950QLX7202 • **Value $22**

8
The Animals Speak
Panorama Ball • FRAN
1350QLX7232 • **Value $110**

1989

9
Baby's First Christmas
Handcrafted • SEAL
3000QLX7272 • **Value $65**

10
Backstage Bear
Handcrafted • SIED
1350QLX7215 • **Value $33**

11
Busy Beaver
Handcrafted • DLEE
1750QLX7245 • **Value $46**

12
First Christmas
Together
Handcrafted • DLEE
1750QLX7342 • **Value $42**

13
Holiday Bell
Lead Crystal • N/A
1750QLX7222 • **Value $33**

14
Joyous Carolers
Handcrafted • UNRU
3000QLX7295 • **Value $65**

15
Kringle's Toy Shop
(re-issued from 1988)
Handcrafted • SEAL
2450QLX7017 • **Value $53**

16
Loving Spoonful
Handcrafted • SIED
1950QLX7262 • **Value $35**

17
Metro Express
Handcrafted • SICK
2800QLX7275 • **Value $75**

18
Moonlit Nap
(re-issued from 1988)
Handcrafted • CHAD
875QLX7134 • **Value $24**

19
Rudolph the
Red-Nosed Reindeer®
Handcrafted • CHAD
1950QLX7252 • **Value $56**

20
Spirit of St. Nick
Handcrafted • SEAL
2450QLX7285 • **Value $70**

GENERAL KEEPSAKE	Price Paid	Value of My Collection
1.		
2.		
3.		
4.		
5.		
6.		
GENERAL MAGIC		
7.		
8.		
9.		
10.		
11.		
12.		
13.		
14.		
15.		
16.		
17.		
18.		
19.		
20.		
PENCIL TOTALS		

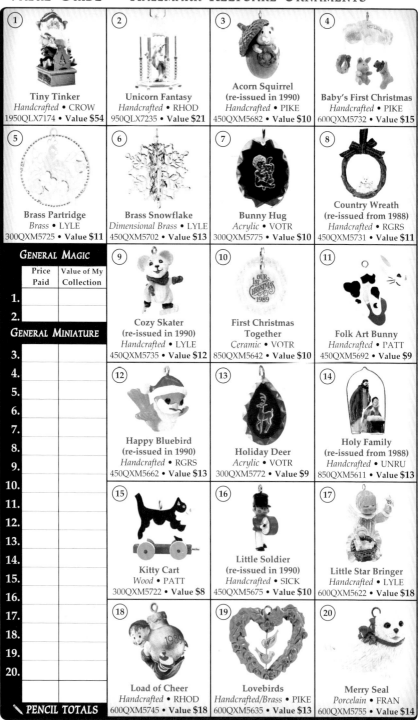

1
Tiny Tinker
Handcrafted • CROW
1950QLX7174 • **Value $54**

2
Unicorn Fantasy
Handcrafted • RHOD
950QLX7235 • **Value $21**

3
Acorn Squirrel
(re-issued in 1990)
Handcrafted • PIKE
450QXM5682 • **Value $10**

4
Baby's First Christmas
Handcrafted • PIKE
600QXM5732 • **Value $15**

5
Brass Partridge
Brass • LYLE
300QXM5725 • **Value $11**

6
Brass Snowflake
Dimensional Brass • LYLE
450QXM5702 • **Value $13**

7
Bunny Hug
Acrylic • VOTR
300QXM5775 • **Value $10**

8
Country Wreath
(re-issued from 1988)
Handcrafted • RGRS
450QXM5731 • **Value $11**

GENERAL MAGIC

	Price Paid	Value of My Collection
1.		
2.		

GENERAL MINIATURE

3.		
4.		
5.		
6.		
7.		
8.		
9.		
10.		
11.		
12.		
13.		
14.		
15.		
16.		
17.		
18.		
19.		
20.		

PENCIL TOTALS

9
Cozy Skater
(re-issued in 1990)
Handcrafted • LYLE
450QXM5735 • **Value $12**

10
First Christmas Together
Ceramic • VOTR
850QXM5642 • **Value $10**

11
Folk Art Bunny
Handcrafted • PATT
450QXM5692 • **Value $9**

12
Happy Bluebird
(re-issued in 1990)
Handcrafted • RGRS
450QXM5662 • **Value $13**

13
Holiday Deer
Acrylic • VOTR
300QXM5772 • **Value $9**

14
Holy Family
(re-issued from 1988)
Handcrafted • UNRU
850QXM5611 • **Value $13**

15
Kitty Cart
Wood • PATT
300QXM5722 • **Value $8**

16
Little Soldier
(re-issued in 1990)
Handcrafted • SICK
450QXM5675 • **Value $10**

17
Little Star Bringer
Handcrafted • LYLE
600QXM5622 • **Value $18**

18
Load of Cheer
Handcrafted • RHOD
600QXM5745 • **Value $18**

19
Lovebirds
Handcrafted/Brass • PIKE
600QXM5635 • **Value $13**

20
Merry Seal
Porcelain • FRAN
600QXM5755 • **Value $14**

VALUE GUIDE — HALLMARK KEEPSAKE ORNAMENTS

1. Mother
Cameo • N/A
600QXM5645 • **Value $13**

2. Old-World Santa
(re-issued in 1990)
Handcrafted • SIED
300QXM5695 • **Value $9**

3. Pinecone Basket
Handcrafted • RHOD
450QXM5734 • **Value $8**

4. Puppy Cart
Wood • SICK
300QXM5715 • **Value $8**

5. Rejoice
Acrylic • VOTR
300QXM5782 • **Value $9**

6. Roly-Poly Pig
(re-issued in 1990)
Handcrafted • PIKE
300QXM5712 • **Value $16**

7. Roly-Poly Ram
Handcrafted • N/A
300QXM5705 • **Value $13**

8. Santa's Magic Ride
Handcrafted • RGRS
850QXM5632 • **Value $18**

9. Santa's Roadster
Handcrafted • CROW
600QXM5665 • **Value $19**

10. Scrimshaw Reindeer
Handcrafted • VOTR
450QXM5685 • **Value $9**

11. Sharing a Ride
Handcrafted • DUTK
850QXM5765 • **Value $14**

12. Slow Motion
Handcrafted • SIED
600QXM5752 • **Value $15**

13. Special Friend
Handcrafted/Willow • N/A
450QXM5652 • **Value $12**

14. Starlit Mouse
Handcrafted • RHOD
450QXM5655 • **Value $15**

15. Stocking Pal
(re-issued in 1990)
Handcrafted • JLEE
450QXM5672 • **Value $9**

16. Strollin' Snowman
Porcelain • SIED
450QXM5742 • **Value $16**

17. Three Little Kitties
(re-issued from 1988)
Handcrafted/Willow • PIKE
600QXM5694 • **Value $17**

18. Christmas is Peaceful
(club edition, LE-49,900)
Bone China • SEAL
1850QXC4512 • **Value $42**

19. Collect a Dream
(club edition)
Handcrafted • PIKE
900QXC4285 • **Value $55**

20. Noelle
(club edition, LE-49,900)
Porcelain • UNRU
1975QXC4483 • **Value $55**

1989

GENERAL MINIATURE

	Price Paid	Value of My Collection
1.		
2.		
3.		
4.		
5.		
6.		
7.		
8.		
9.		
10.		
11.		
12.		
13.		
14.		
15.		
16.		
17.		

COLLECTOR'S CLUB

18.		
19.		
20.		

PENCIL TOTALS

Value Guide — Hallmark Keepsake Ornaments

1 Sitting Purrty (keepsake of membership, miniature)
Handcrafted • DUTK
QXC5812 • **Value $34**

2 Visit From Santa (keepsake of membership)
Handcrafted • CROW
QXC5802 • **Value $50**

3 Carousel Display Stand
Handcrafted/Brass • N/A
($1.00)629XPR9723 • **Value $9**

4 Ginger
Handcrafted/Brass • JLEE
($3.95)629XPR9721 • **Value $18**

5 Holly
Handcrafted/Brass • JLEE
($3.95)629XPR9722 • **Value $18**

6 Snow
Handcrafted/Brass • JLEE
($3.95)629XPR9719 • **Value $35**

7 Star
Handcrafted/Brass • JLEE
($3.95)629XPR9720 • **Value $18**

8 Baby's Christening Keepsake
Acrylic • N/A
700BBY1325 • **Value $33**

9 Baby's First Birthday
Acrylic • N/A
550BBY1729 • **Value $33**

10 Baby's First Christmas – Baby Boy (same as #475QX2725)
Satin • VOTR
475BBY1453 • **Value $15**

11 Baby's First Christmas – Baby Girl (same as #475QX2722)
Satin • VOTR
475BBY1553 • **Value $15**

1988

1988 was the year Hallmark introduced the Miniature ornaments to the collection. In its debut year, the Miniature line featured 27 ornaments, while the Keepsake line had 118 and Magic had 20. See collectible series section for more 1988 ornaments.

12 Americana Drum
Tin • SICK
775QX4881 • **Value $29**

13 Arctic Tenor
Handcrafted • SIED
400QX4721 • **Value $18**

14 Baby Redbird
Handcrafted • CHAD
500QX4101 • **Value $20**

15 Baby's First Christmas
Acrylic • PIKE
600QX3721 • **Value $20**

16 Baby's First Christmas
Handcrafted • CROW
975QX4701 • **Value $40**

17 Baby's First Christmas – Baby Boy
Satin • N/A
475QX2721 • **Value $24**

Collector's Club

	Price Paid	Value of My Collection
1.		
2.		

Reach Ornaments

3.		
4.		
5.		
6.		
7.		

Baby Celebrations

8.		
9.		
10.		
11.		

General Keepsake

12.		
13.		
14.		
15.		
16.		
17.		

Pencil Totals

148
1989 Collection / 1988 Collection

Value Guide – Hallmark Keepsake Ornaments

1
Baby's First Christmas
– Baby Girl
Satin • N/A
475QX2724 • **Value $24**

2
Baby's First Christmas
Photoholder
Fabric • N/A
750QX4704 • **Value $24**

3
Baby's Second
Christmas
Handcrafted • PIKE
600QX4711 • **Value $34**

4
Babysitter
Glass • SICK
475QX2791 • **Value $10**

5
Child's Third Christmas
Handcrafted • CHAD
600QX4714 • **Value $27**

6
Christmas Cardinal
Handcrafted • RGRS
475QX4941 • **Value $17**

7
Christmas Cuckoo
Handcrafted • CROW
800QX4801 • **Value $28**

8
Christmas Memories
Photoholder
Acrylic • PATT
650QX3724 • **Value $22**

9
Cool Juggler
Handcrafted • CROW
650QX4874 • **Value $21**

10
Cymbals of Christmas
Handcrafted/Acrylic • DLEE
550QX4111 • **Value $26**

11
Dad
Handcrafted • SIED
700QX4141 • **Value $23**

12
Daughter
Handcrafted • PATT
575QX4151 • **Value $53**

13
Feliz Navidad
Handcrafted • UNRU
675QX4161 • **Value $29**

14
Fifty Years Together
Acrylic • N/A
675QX3741 • **Value $17**

15
Filled With Fudge
Handcrafted • SEAL
475QX4191 • **Value $30**

16
First Christmas
Together
Acrylic • VOTR
675QX3731 • **Value $22**

17
First Christmas
Together
Glass • N/A
475QX2741 • **Value $24**

18
First Christmas
Together
Handcrafted • PIKE
900QX4894 • **Value $25**

19
Five Years Together
Glass • MCGE
475QX2744 • **Value $17**

20
From Our
Home to Yours
Glass • PATT
475QX2794 • **Value $17**

1988

General Keepsake

	Price Paid	Value of My Collection
1.		
2.		
3.		
4.		
5.		
6.		
7.		
8.		
9.		
10.		
11.		
12.		
13.		
14.		
15.		
16.		
17.		
18.		
19.		
20.		
PENCIL TOTALS		

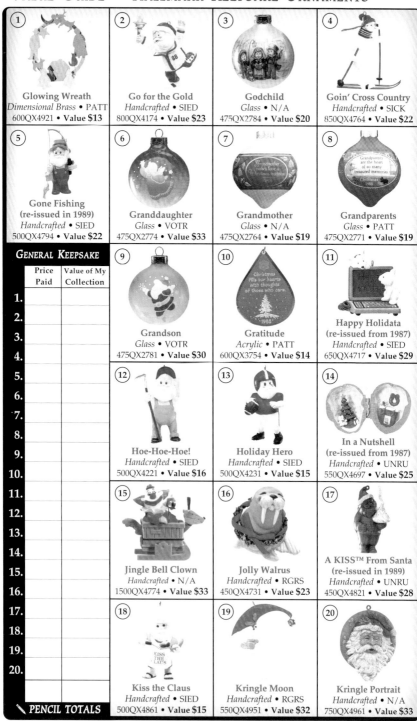

(1) Glowing Wreath
Dimensional Brass • PATT
600QX4921 • **Value $13**

(2) Go for the Gold
Handcrafted • SIED
800QX4174 • **Value $23**

(3) Godchild
Glass • N/A
475QX2784 • **Value $20**

(4) Goin' Cross Country
Handcrafted • SICK
850QX4764 • **Value $22**

(5) Gone Fishing
(re-issued in 1989)
Handcrafted • SIED
500QX4794 • **Value $22**

(6) Granddaughter
Glass • VOTR
475QX2774 • **Value $33**

(7) Grandmother
Glass • N/A
475QX2764 • **Value $19**

(8) Grandparents
Glass • PATT
475QX2771 • **Value $19**

(9) Grandson
Glass • VOTR
475QX2781 • **Value $30**

(10) Gratitude
Acrylic • PATT
600QX3754 • **Value $14**

(11) Happy Holidata
(re-issued from 1987)
Handcrafted • SIED
650QX4717 • **Value $29**

(12) Hoe-Hoe-Hoe!
Handcrafted • SIED
500QX4221 • **Value $16**

(13) Holiday Hero
Handcrafted • SIED
500QX4231 • **Value $15**

(14) In a Nutshell
(re-issued from 1987)
Handcrafted • UNRU
550QX4697 • **Value $25**

(15) Jingle Bell Clown
Handcrafted • N/A
1500QX4774 • **Value $33**

(16) Jolly Walrus
Handcrafted • RGRS
450QX4731 • **Value $23**

(17) A KISS™ From Santa
(re-issued in 1989)
Handcrafted • UNRU
450QX4821 • **Value $28**

(18) Kiss the Claus
Handcrafted • SIED
500QX4861 • **Value $15**

(19) Kringle Moon
Handcrafted • RGRS
550QX4951 • **Value $32**

(20) Kringle Portrait
Handcrafted • N/A
750QX4961 • **Value $33**

GENERAL KEEPSAKE

	Price Paid	Value of My Collection
1.		
2.		
3.		
4.		
5.		
6.		
7.		
8.		
9.		
10.		
11.		
12.		
13.		
14.		
15.		
16.		
17.		
18.		
19.		
20.		

PENCIL TOTALS

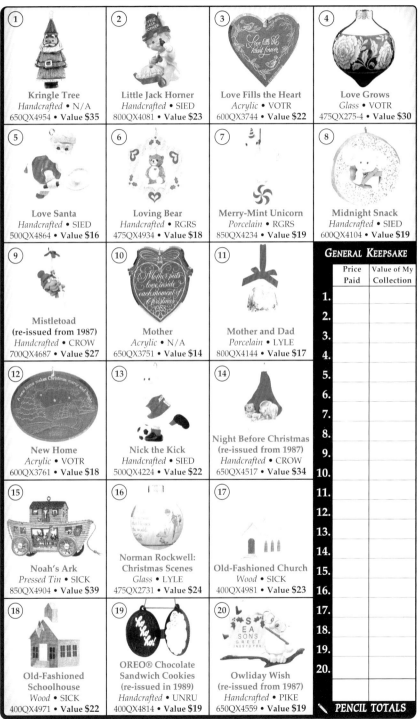

1988

(1) **Kringle Tree** *Handcrafted* • N/A 650QX4954 • **Value $35**	**(2)** **Little Jack Horner** *Handcrafted* • SIED 800QX4081 • **Value $23**	**(3)** **Love Fills the Heart** *Acrylic* • VOTR 600QX3744 • **Value $22**	**(4)** **Love Grows** *Glass* • VOTR 475QX275-4 • **Value $30**
(5) **Love Santa** *Handcrafted* • SIED 500QX4864 • **Value $16**	**(6)** **Loving Bear** *Handcrafted* • RGRS 475QX4934 • **Value $18**	**(7)** **Merry-Mint Unicorn** *Porcelain* • RGRS 850QX4234 • **Value $19**	**(8)** **Midnight Snack** *Handcrafted* • SIED 600QX4104 • **Value $19**
(9) **Mistletoad** **(re-issued from 1987)** *Handcrafted* • CROW 700QX4687 • **Value $27**	**(10)** **Mother** *Acrylic* • N/A 650QX3751 • **Value $14**	**(11)** **Mother and Dad** *Porcelain* • LYLE 800QX4144 • **Value $17**	

General Keepsake

	Price Paid	Value of My Collection
1.		
2.		
3.		
4.		
5.		
6.		
7.		
8.		
9.		
10.		
11.		
12.		
13.		
14.		
15.		
16.		
17.		
18.		
19.		
20.		

(12) **New Home** *Acrylic* • VOTR 600QX3761 • **Value $18**	**(13)** **Nick the Kick** *Handcrafted* • SIED 500QX4224 • **Value $22**	**(14)** **Night Before Christmas** **(re-issued from 1987)** *Handcrafted* • CROW 650QX4517 • **Value $34**
(15) **Noah's Ark** *Pressed Tin* • SICK 850QX4904 • **Value $39**	**(16)** **Norman Rockwell: Christmas Scenes** *Glass* • LYLE 475QX2731 • **Value $24**	**(17)** **Old-Fashioned Church** *Wood* • SICK 400QX4981 • **Value $23**
(18) **Old-Fashioned Schoolhouse** *Wood* • SICK 400QX4971 • **Value $22**	**(19)** **OREO® Chocolate Sandwich Cookies** **(re-issued in 1989)** *Handcrafted* • UNRU 400QX4814 • **Value $19**	**(20)** **Owliday Wish** **(re-issued from 1987)** *Handcrafted* • PIKE 650QX4559 • **Value $19**

PENCIL TOTALS

1. Par for Santa
Handcrafted • SIED
500QX4791 • **Value $18**

2. Party Line
(re-issued in 1989)
Handcrafted • PIKE
875QX4761 • **Value $26**

3. PEANUTS®
Glass • N/A
475QX2801 • **Value $43**

4. Peek-a-Boo Kitties
(re-issued in 1989)
Handcrafted • CROW
750QX4871 • **Value $22**

5. Polar Bowler
(re-issued in 1989)
Handcrafted • SIED
500QX4784 • **Value $17**

6. Purrfect Snuggle
Handcrafted • RGRS
625QX4744 • **Value $27**

7. Reindoggy
(re-issued from 1987)
Handcrafted • SIED
575QX4527 • **Value $33**

8. Sailing! Sailing!
Pressed Tin • SICK
850QX4911 • **Value $24**

9. St. Louie Nick
(re-issued from 1987)
Handcrafted • DUTK
775QX4539 • **Value $30**

10. Santa Flamingo
Handcrafted • PYDA
475QX4834 • **Value $34**

11. Shiny Sleigh
Dimensional Brass • PATT
575QX4924 • **Value $18**

12. Sister
Porcelain • VOTR
800QX4994 • **Value $30**

13. Slipper Spaniel
Handcrafted • CROW
425QX4724 • **Value $17**

14. SNOOPY® and WOODSTOCK
Handcrafted • UNRU
600QX4741 • **Value $43**

15. Soft Landing
Handcrafted • CHAD
700QX4751 • **Value $23**

16. Son
Handcrafted • PATT
575QX4154 • **Value $35**

17. Sparkling Tree
Dimensional Brass • PATT
600QX4931 • **Value $18**

18. Spirit of Christmas
Glass • LYLE
475QX2761 • **Value $23**

19. Squeaky Clean
Handcrafted • PIKE
675QX4754 • **Value $20**

20. Starry Angel
Handcrafted • RGRS
475QX4944 • **Value $19**

GENERAL KEEPSAKE

	Price Paid	Value of My Collection
1.		
2.		
3.		
4.		
5.		
6.		
7.		
8.		
9.		
10.		
11.		
12.		
13.		
14.		
15.		
16.		
17.		
18.		
19.		
20.		
PENCIL TOTALS		

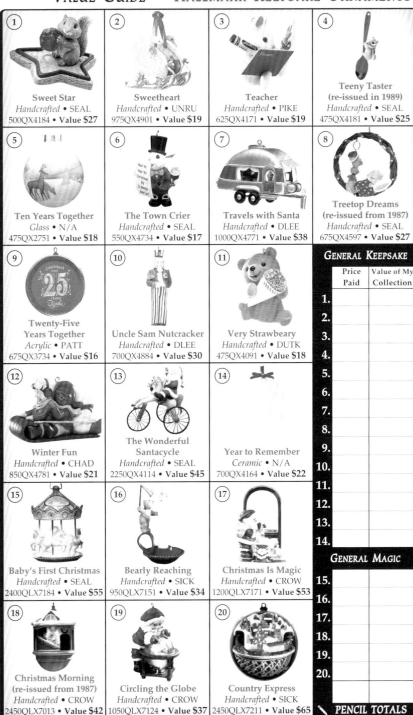

1. Sweet Star
Handcrafted • SEAL
500QX4184 • **Value $27**

2. Sweetheart
Handcrafted • UNRU
975QX4901 • **Value $19**

3. Teacher
Handcrafted • PIKE
625QX4171 • **Value $19**

4. Teeny Taster
(re-issued in 1989)
Handcrafted • SEAL
475QX4181 • **Value $25**

5. Ten Years Together
Glass • N/A
475QX2751 • **Value $18**

6. The Town Crier
Handcrafted • SEAL
550QX4734 • **Value $17**

7. Travels with Santa
Handcrafted • DLEE
1000QX4771 • **Value $38**

8. Treetop Dreams
(re-issued from 1987)
Handcrafted • SEAL
675QX4597 • **Value $27**

9. Twenty-Five
Years Together
Acrylic • PATT
675QX3734 • **Value $16**

10. Uncle Sam Nutcracker
Handcrafted • DLEE
700QX4884 • **Value $30**

11. Very Strawbeary
Handcrafted • DUTK
475QX4091 • **Value $18**

12. Winter Fun
Handcrafted • CHAD
850QX4781 • **Value $21**

13. The Wonderful
Santacycle
Handcrafted • SEAL
2250QX4114 • **Value $45**

14. Year to Remember
Ceramic • N/A
700QX4164 • **Value $22**

15. Baby's First Christmas
Handcrafted • SEAL
2400QLX7184 • **Value $55**

16. Bearly Reaching
Handcrafted • SICK
950QLX7151 • **Value $34**

17. Christmas Is Magic
Handcrafted • CROW
1200QLX7171 • **Value $53**

18. Christmas Morning
(re-issued from 1987)
Handcrafted • CROW
2450QLX7013 • **Value $42**

19. Circling the Globe
Handcrafted • CROW
1050QLX7124 • **Value $37**

20. Country Express
Handcrafted • SICK
2450QLX7211 • **Value $65**

1988

General Keepsake

	Price Paid	Value of My Collection
1.		
2.		
3.		
4.		
5.		
6.		
7.		
8.		
9.		
10.		
11.		
12.		
13.		
14.		

General Magic

15.		
16.		
17.		
18.		
19.		
20.		

PENCIL TOTALS

VALUE GUIDE — HALLMARK KEEPSAKE ORNAMENTS

(1) Festive Feeder
Handcrafted • SICK
1150QLX7204 • **Value $52**

(2) First Christmas Together
Handcrafted • SICK
1200QLX7027 • **Value $35**

(3) Heavenly Glow
Brass • PYDA
1175QLX7114 • **Value $27**

(4) Kitty Capers
Handcrafted • PIKE
1300QLX7164 • **Value $44**

(5) Last-Minute Hug
Handcrafted • UNRU
2200QLX7181 • **Value $45**

(6) Moonlit Nap (re-issued in 1989)
Handcrafted • CHAD
875QLX7134 • **Value $24**

(7) Parade of the Toys
Handcrafted • SICK
2450QLX7194 • **Value $43**

(8) Radiant Tree
Brass • LYLE
1175QLX7121 • **Value $22**

GENERAL MAGIC

	Price Paid	Value of My Collection
1.		
2.		
3.		
4.		
5.		
6.		
7.		
8.		
9.		
10.		
11.		

GENERAL MINIATURE

12.		
13.		
14.		
15.		
16.		
17.		
18.		
19.		
20.		

PENCIL TOTALS

(9) Skater's Waltz
Handcrafted • UNRU
2450QLX7201 • **Value $53**

(10) Song of Christmas
Acrylic • N/A
850QLX7111 • **Value $27**

(11) Tree of Friendship
Acrylic • N/A
850QLX7104 • **Value $24**

(12) Baby's First Christmas
Handcrafted • DLEE
600QXM5744 • **Value $12**

(13) Brass Angel
Brass • LYLE
150QXM5671 • **Value $17**

(14) Brass Star
Brass • LYLE
150QXM5664 • **Value $17**

(15) Brass Tree
Brass • LYLE
150QXM5674 • **Value $17**

(16) Candy Cane Elf
Handcrafted • SIED
300QXM5701 • **Value $19**

(17) Country Wreath (re-issued in 1989)
Handcrafted • RGRS
400QXM5731 • **Value $10**

(18) First Christmas Together
Wood/Straw • MCGE
400QXM5741 • **Value $11**

(19) Folk Art Lamb
Wood • PATT
275QXM5681 • **Value $21**

(20) Folk Art Reindeer
Wood • PATT
300QXM5684 • **Value $15**

Value Guide — Hallmark Keepsake Ornaments

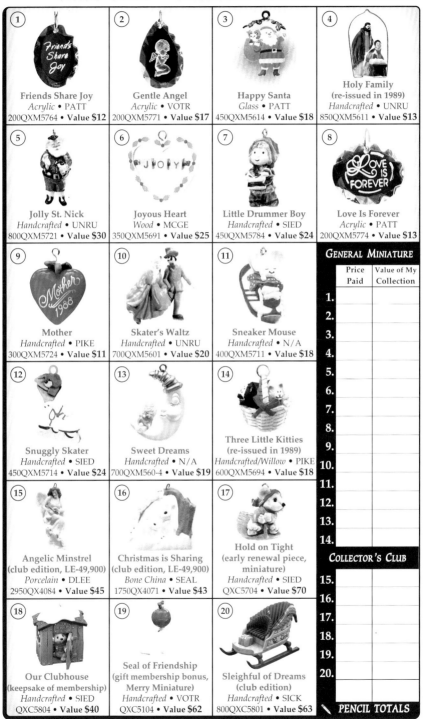

1. Friends Share Joy
Acrylic • PATT
200QXM5764 • **Value $12**

2. Gentle Angel
Acrylic • VOTR
200QXM5771 • **Value $17**

3. Happy Santa
Glass • PATT
450QXM5614 • **Value $18**

4. Holy Family (re-issued in 1989)
Handcrafted • UNRU
850QXM5611 • **Value $13**

5. Jolly St. Nick
Handcrafted • UNRU
800QXM5721 • **Value $30**

6. Joyous Heart
Wood • MCGE
350QXM5691 • **Value $25**

7. Little Drummer Boy
Handcrafted • SIED
450QXM5784 • **Value $24**

8. Love Is Forever
Acrylic • PATT
200QXM5774 • **Value $13**

9. Mother
Handcrafted • PIKE
300QXM5724 • **Value $11**

10. Skater's Waltz
Handcrafted • UNRU
700QXM5601 • **Value $20**

11. Sneaker Mouse
Handcrafted • N/A
400QXM5711 • **Value $18**

12. Snuggly Skater
Handcrafted • SIED
450QXM5714 • **Value $24**

13. Sweet Dreams
Handcrafted • N/A
700QXM560-4 • **Value $19**

14. Three Little Kitties (re-issued in 1989)
Handcrafted/Willow • PIKE
600QXM5694 • **Value $18**

15. Angelic Minstrel (club edition, LE-49,900)
Porcelain • DLEE
2950QX4084 • **Value $45**

16. Christmas is Sharing (club edition, LE-49,900)
Bone China • SEAL
1750QX4071 • **Value $43**

17. Hold on Tight (early renewal piece, miniature)
Handcrafted • SIED
QXC5704 • **Value $70**

18. Our Clubhouse (keepsake of membership)
Handcrafted • SIED
QXC5804 • **Value $40**

19. Seal of Friendship (gift membership bonus, Merry Miniature)
Handcrafted • VOTR
QXC5104 • **Value $62**

20. Sleighful of Dreams (club edition)
Handcrafted • SICK
800QXC5801 • **Value $63**

General Miniature

	Price Paid	Value of My Collection
1.		
2.		
3.		
4.		
5.		
6.		
7.		
8.		
9.		
10.		
11.		
12.		
13.		
14.		

Collector's Club

15.		
16.		
17.		
18.		
19.		
20.		
Pencil Totals		

1988

①

Kringle's Toy Shop
(re-issued in 1989, magic)
Handcrafted • SEAL
2450QLX7017 • **Value $50**

1987

Among the most sought-after ornaments from 1987 is "Bright Christmas Dreams," which is coveted by collectors of the "CRAYOLA® Crayon" collectible series, although it is not officially a part of that series. Overall, there were 122 Keepsake ornaments and 18 Magic ornaments. See collectible series section for more 1987 ornaments.

②

Baby Locket
Textured Metal • N/A
1500QX4617 • **Value $28**

③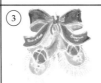

Baby's First Christmas
Acrylic • N/A
600QX3729 • **Value $18**

④

Baby's First Christmas
Handcrafted • DLEE
975QX4113 • **Value $27**

⑤

Baby's First Christmas
– Baby Boy
Satin • PATT
475QX2749 • **Value $29**

⑥

Baby's First Christmas
– Baby Girl
Satin • PATT
475QX2747 • **Value $26**

⑦

Baby's First Christmas
Photoholder
Fabric • N/A
750QX4619 • **Value $27**

⑧

Baby's Second
Christmas
Handcrafted • DLEE
575QX4607 • **Value $29**

⑨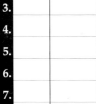

Babysitter
Glass • PIKE
475QX2797 • **Value $16**

⑩

Beary Special
Handcrafted • SIED
475QX4557 • **Value $23**

⑪

Bright
Christmas Dreams
Handcrafted • SIED
725QX4737 • **Value $95**

⑫

Child's Third Christmas
Handcrafted • CROW
575QX4599 • **Value $24**

⑬

Chocolate Chipmunk
Handcrafted • SEAL
600QX4567 • **Value $50**

⑭

Christmas Cuddle
Handcrafted • N/A
575QX4537 • **Value $33**

⑮

Christmas Fun Puzzle
Handcrafted • DLEE
800QX4679 • **Value $26**

⑯

Christmas is Gentle
(LE-24,700)
Bone China • SEAL
1750QX4449 • **Value $60**

⑰

Christmas Keys
Handcrafted • UNRU
575QX4739 • **Value $31**

Open House Ornaments

	Price Paid	Value of My Collection
1.		
General Keepsake		
2.		
3.		
4.		
5.		
6.		
7.		
8.		
9.		
10.		
11.		
12.		
13.		
14.		
15.		
16.		
17.		
PENCIL TOTALS		

1 Christmas Time Mime
(LE-24,700)
Porcelain • UNRU
2750QX4429 • **Value $53**

2 The Constitution
Acrylic • PATT
650QX3777 • **Value $25**

3 Country Wreath
Wood/Straw • PYDA
575QX4709 • **Value $23**

4 Currier & Ives:
American Farm Scene
Glass • LYLE
475QX2829 • **Value $28**

5 Dad
Handcrafted • SIED
600QX4629 • **Value $38**

6 Daughter
Handcrafted • SICK
575QX4637 • **Value $29**

7 December Showers
Handcrafted • DLEE
550QX4487 • **Value $29**

8 Doc Holiday
Handcrafted • SEAL
800QX4677 • **Value $45**

9 Dr. Seuss: The
Grinch's Christmas
Glass • N/A
475QX2783 • **Value $85**

10 Favorite Santa
Porcelain • DUTK
2250QX4457 • **Value $39**

11 Fifty Years Together
Porcelain • SEAL
800QX4437 • **Value $23**

12 First Christmas
Together
Acrylic • N/A
650QX3719 • **Value $17**

13 First Christmas
Together
Glass • LYLE
475QX2729 • **Value $28**

14 First Christmas
Together
Handcrafted • N/A
800QX4459 • **Value $37**

15 First Christmas
Together
Handcrafted • DLEE
950QX4467 • **Value $26**

16 First Christmas
Together
Textured Brass • N/A
1500QX4469 • **Value $27**

17 Folk Art Santa
Handcrafted • SICK
525QX4749 • **Value $30**

18 From Our
Home to Yours
Glass • PYDA
475QX2799 • **Value $32**

19 Fudge Forever
Handcrafted • DUTK
500QX4497 • **Value $33**

20 Godchild
Glass • PYDA
475QX2767 • **Value $19**

1987

GENERAL KEEPSAKE

	Price Paid	Value of My Collection
1.		
2.		
3.		
4.		
5.		
6.		
7.		
8.		
9.		
10.		
11.		
12.		
13.		
14.		
15.		
16.		
17.		
18.		
19.		
20.		
PENCIL TOTALS		

Value Guide — Hallmark Keepsake Ornaments

1. Goldfinch
Porcelain • SICK
700QX4649 • **Value $73**

2. Grandchild's First Christmas
Handcrafted • SEAL
900QX4609 • **Value $22**

3. Granddaughter
Bezeled Satin • VOTR
600QX3747 • **Value $17**

4. Grandmother
Glass • N/A
475QX2779 • **Value $14**

5. Grandparents
Glass • PIKE
475QX2777 • **Value $17**

6. Grandson
Glass • VOTR
475QX2769 • **Value $26**

7. Happy Holidata (re-issued in 1988)
Handcrafted • SIED
650QX4717 • **Value $29**

8. Happy Santa
Handcrafted • CROW
475QX4569 • **Value $28**

9. Heart in Blossom
Acrylic • VOTR
600QX3727 • **Value $21**

10. Heavenly Harmony
Handcrafted • CROW
1500QX4659 • **Value $32**

11. Holiday Greetings
Bezeled Foil • N/A
600QX3757 • **Value $11**

12. Holiday Hourglass
Handcrafted • UNRU
800QX4707 • **Value $25**

13. Hot Dogger
Handcrafted • UNRU
650QX4719 • **Value $23**

14. Husband
Cameo • VOTR
700QX3739 • **Value $10**

15. I Remember Santa
Glass • LYLE
475QX278-9 • **Value $33**

16. Icy Treat
Handcrafted • SIED
450QX4509 • **Value $24**

17. In a Nutshell (re-issued in 1988)
Handcrafted • UNRU
550QX4697 • **Value $25**

18. Jack Frosting
Handcrafted • SEAL
700QX4499 • **Value $53**

19. Jammie Pies™
Glass • N/A
475QX2839 • **Value $17**

20. Jogging Through the Snow
Handcrafted • DUTK
725QX4577 • **Value $35**

General Keepsake

	Price Paid	Value of My Collection
1.		
2.		
3.		
4.		
5.		
6.		
7.		
8.		
9.		
10.		
11.		
12.		
13.		
14.		
15.		
16.		
17.		
18.		
19.		
20.		

PENCIL TOTALS

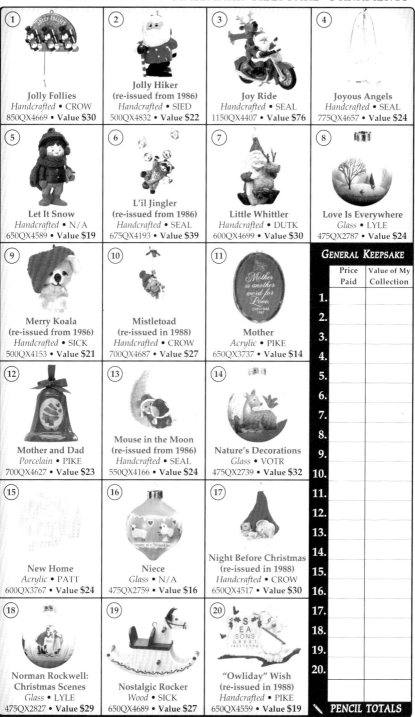

1

Jolly Follies
Handcrafted • CROW
850QX4669 • **Value $30**

2

Jolly Hiker
(re-issued from 1986)
Handcrafted • SIED
500QX4832 • **Value $22**

3

Joy Ride
Handcrafted • SEAL
1150QX4407 • **Value $76**

4

Joyous Angels
Handcrafted • SEAL
775QX4657 • **Value $24**

5

Let It Snow
Handcrafted • N/A
650QX4589 • **Value $19**

6

L'il Jingler
(re-issued from 1986)
Handcrafted • SEAL
675QX4193 • **Value $39**

7

Little Whittler
Handcrafted • DUTK
600QX4699 • **Value $30**

8

Love Is Everywhere
Glass • LYLE
475QX2787 • **Value $24**

9

Merry Koala
(re-issued from 1986)
Handcrafted • SICK
500QX4153 • **Value $21**

10

Mistletoad
(re-issued in 1988)
Handcrafted • CROW
700QX4687 • **Value $27**

11

Mother
Acrylic • PIKE
650QX3737 • **Value $14**

12

Mother and Dad
Porcelain • PIKE
700QX4627 • **Value $23**

13

Mouse in the Moon
(re-issued from 1986)
Handcrafted • SEAL
550QX4166 • **Value $24**

14

Nature's Decorations
Glass • VOTR
475QX2739 • **Value $32**

15

New Home
Acrylic • PATT
600QX3767 • **Value $24**

16

Niece
Glass • N/A
475QX2759 • **Value $16**

17

Night Before Christmas
(re-issued in 1988)
Handcrafted • CROW
650QX4517 • **Value $30**

18

Norman Rockwell:
Christmas Scenes
Glass • LYLE
475QX2827 • **Value $29**

19

Nostalgic Rocker
Wood • SICK
650QX4689 • **Value $27**

20

"Owliday" Wish
(re-issued in 1988)
Handcrafted • PIKE
650QX4559 • **Value $19**

General Keepsake

	Price Paid	Value of My Collection
1.		
2.		
3.		
4.		
5.		
6.		
7.		
8.		
9.		
10.		
11.		
12.		
13.		
14.		
15.		
16.		
17.		
18.		
19.		
20.		
PENCIL TOTALS		

1987

1. Paddington™ Bear
Handcrafted • PIKE
550QX4727 • **Value $34**

2. PEANUTS®
Glass • N/A
475QX2819 • **Value $35**

3. Pretty Kitty
Handcrafted/Glass • CROW
1100QX4489 • **Value $27**

4. Promise of Peace
Acrylic • PIKE
650QX3749 • **Value $20**

5. Raccoon Biker
Handcrafted • SIED
700QX4587 • **Value $26**

6. Reindoggy
(re-issued in 1988)
Handcrafted • SIED
575QX4527 • **Value $33**

7. St. Louie Nick
(re-issued in 1988)
Handcrafted • DUTK
775QX4539 • **Value $30**

8. Santa at the Bat
Handcrafted • SIED
775QX4579 • **Value $23**

9. Seasoned Greetings
Handcrafted • SEAL
625QX4549 • **Value $24**

10. Sister
Wood • SICK
600QX4747 • **Value $14**

11. Sleepy Santa
Handcrafted • CROW
625QX4507 • **Value $37**

12. SNOOPY and WOODSTOCK
Handcrafted • SIED
725QX4729 • **Value $49**

13. Son
Handcrafted • SICK
575QX4639 • **Value $45**

14. Special Memories Photoholder
Fabric • N/A
675QX4647 • **Value $22**

15. Spots 'n Stripes
Handcrafted • N/A
550QX4529 • **Value $23**

16. Sweetheart
Handcrafted • SICK
1100QX4479 • **Value $26**

17. Teacher
Handcrafted • SIED
575QX4667 • **Value $20**

18. Ten Years Together
Porcelain • VOTR
700QX4447 • **Value $18**

19. Three Men in a Tub
Handcrafted • DLEE
800QX4547 • **Value $26**

20. Time for Friends
Glass • VOTR
475QX2807 • **Value $22**

GENERAL KEEPSAKE

	Price Paid	Value of My Collection
1.		
2.		
3.		
4.		
5.		
6.		
7.		
8.		
9.		
10.		
11.		
12.		
13.		
14.		
15.		
16.		
17.		
18.		
19.		
20.		
PENCIL TOTALS		

VALUE GUIDE – HALLMARK KEEPSAKE ORNAMENTS

① Treetop Dreams (re-issued in 1988) *Handcrafted* • SEAL 675QX4597 • **Value $27**	**②** Treetop Trio (re-issued from 1986) *Handcrafted* • DLEE 1100QX4256 • **Value $30**	**③** Twenty-Five Years Together *Porcelain* • N/A 750QX4439 • **Value $22**	**④** Walnut Shell Rider (re-issued from 1986) *Handcrafted* • SEAL 600QX4196 • **Value $23**
⑤ Warmth of Friendship *Acrylic* • N/A 600QX3759 • **Value $11**	**⑥** Wee Chimney Sweep *Handcrafted* • SEAL 625QX4519 • **Value $23**	**⑦** Word of Love *Porcelain* • N/A 800QX4477 • **Value $22**	**⑧** Angelic Messengers *Panorama Ball* • UNRU 1875QLX7113 • **Value $55**

			GENERAL KEEPSAKE		
⑨ Baby's First Christmas *Handcrafted* • N/A 1350QLX7049 • **Value $34**	**⑩** Bright Noel *Acrylic* • VOTR 700QLX7059 • **Value $28**	**⑪** Christmas Morning *Handcrafted* • CROW 2450QLX7013 • **Value $42**		Price Paid	Value of My Collection
			1.		
			2.		
			3.		
			4.		

⑫ First Christmas Together *Handcrafted* • N/A 1150QLX7087 • **Value $43**	**⑬** Good Cheer Blimp *Handcrafted* • SICK 1600QLX7046 • **Value $56**	**⑭** Keep on Glowin'! (re-issued from 1986) *Handcrafted* • CROW 1000QLX7076 • **Value $43**	5.		
			6.		
			7.		

GENERAL MAGIC

⑮ Keeping Cozy *Handcrafted* • CROW 1175QLX7047 • **Value $31**	**⑯** Lacy Brass Snowflake *Brass* • N/A 1150QLX7097 • **Value $23**	**⑰** Loving Holiday *Handcrafted* • SEAL 2200QLX7016 • **Value $50**	8.		
			9.		
			10.		
			11.		
			12.		
			13.		
			14.		
⑱ Memories Are Forever Photoholder *Handcrafted* • SEAL 850QLX7067 • **Value $33**	**⑲** Meowy Christmas! *Handcrafted* • PIKE 1000QLX7089 • **Value $57**	**⑳** Season for Friendship *Acrylic* • N/A 850QLX7069 • **Value $18**	15.		
			16.		
			17.		
			18.		
			19.		
			20.		
			PENCIL TOTALS		

1987

① Train Station
Handcrafted • DLEE
1275QLX703-9 • **Value $46**

② Village Express
(re-issued from 1986)
Handcrafted • SICK
2450QLX7072 • **Value $100**

③ Carousel Reindeer
(club edition)
Handcrafted • SICK
800QXC5817 • **Value $59**

④ Wreath of Memories
(keepsake of membership)
Handcrafted • UNRU
QXC5809 • **Value $50**

⑤ North Pole Power
& Light
Handcrafted • CROW
($2.95)627XPR9333 • **Value $25**

1986

One of the biggest stories among Hallmark collectors in 1986 was the hard-to-find porcelain "Magical Unicorn" ornament which was limited to 24,700 pieces. The 1986 collection featured 120 Keepsake ornaments and 16 Magic ornaments. See collectible series section for more 1986 ornaments.

	Price Paid	Value of My Collection
GENERAL MAGIC		
1.		
2.		
COLLECTOR'S CLUB		
3.		
4.		
OPEN HOUSE ORNAMENTS		
5.		
GENERAL KEEPSAKE		
6.		
7.		
8.		
9.		
10.		
11.		
12.		
13.		
14.		
15.		
16.		
17.		
PENCIL TOTALS		

⑥ Acorn Inn
Handcrafted • UNRU
850QX4243 • **Value $28**

⑦ Baby Locket
Textured Brass • MCGE
1600QX1123 • **Value $26**

⑧ Baby's First Christmas
Acrylic • PALM
600QX3803 • **Value $25**

⑨ Baby's First Christmas
Handcrafted • SICK
900QX4126 • **Value $39**

⑩ Baby's First Christmas
Satin • PATT
550QX2713 • **Value $23**

⑪ Baby's First Christmas
Photoholder
Fabric • PATT
800QX3792 • **Value $24**

⑫ Baby's Second
Christmas
Handcrafted • SIED
650QX4133 • **Value $27**

⑬ Baby-Sitter
Glass • N/A
475QX2756 • **Value $8**

⑭ Beary Smooth Ride
(re-issued from 1985)
Handcrafted • SICK
650QX4805 • **Value $23**

⑮ Bluebird
Porcelain • SICK
725QX4283 • **Value $55**

⑯ Chatty Penguin
Plush • CROW
575QX4176 • **Value $24**

⑰ Child's Third Christmas
Fabric • VOTR
650QX4136 • **Value $24**

VALUE GUIDE – HALLMARK KEEPSAKE ORNAMENTS

1
Christmas Beauty
Lacquer • PATT
600QX3223 • **Value $8**

2
Christmas Guitar
Handcrafted • UNRU
700QX5126 • **Value $23**

3
Cookies for Santa
Handcrafted • MCGE
450QX4146 • **Value $27**

4
Country Sleigh
Handcrafted • SICK
1000QX5113 • **Value $24**

5
Daughter
Handcrafted • SEAL
575QX4306 • **Value $47**

6
Do Not Disturb Bear
(re-issued from 1985)
Handcrafted • SEAL
775QX4812 • **Value $28**

7
Father
Wood • VOTR
650QX4313 • **Value $12**

8
Favorite Tin Drum
Tin • SICK
850QX5143 • **Value $30**

9
Festive Treble Clef
Handcrafted • SIED
875QX5133 • **Value $22**

10
Fifty Years Together
Porcelain • PIKE
1000QX4006 • **Value $17**

11
First Christmas
Together
Acrylic • MCGE
700QX3793 • **Value $18**

12
First Christmas
Together
Glass • N/A
475QX2703 • **Value $19**

13
First Christmas
Together
Handcrafted • SICK
1200QX4096 • **Value $26**

14
First Christmas
Together
Textured Brass • N/A
1600QX4003 • **Value $22**

15
Friends Are Fun
Glass • CROW
475QX2723 • **Value $40**

16
Friendship Greeting
Fabric • N/A
800QX4273 • **Value $13**

17
Friendship's Gift
Acrylic • N/A
600QX3816 • **Value $15**

18
From Our
Home to Yours
Acrylic • N/A
600QX3833 • **Value $15**

19
Glowing
Christmas Tree
Acrylic • PATT
700QX4286 • **Value $15**

20
Godchild
Satin • N/A
475QX2716 • **Value $16**

1986

GENERAL KEEPSAKE

	Price Paid	Value of My Collection
1.		
2.		
3.		
4.		
5.		
6.		
7.		
8.		
9.		
10.		
11.		
12.		
13.		
14.		
15.		
16.		
17.		
18.		
19.		
20.		

PENCIL TOTALS

VALUE GUIDE – HALLMARK KEEPSAKE ORNAMENTS

(1) Grandchild's First Christmas
Handcrafted • N/A
1000QX4116 • **Value $13**

(2) Granddaughter
Glass • LYLE
475QX2736 • **Value $21**

(3) Grandmother
Satin • PATT
475QX2743 • **Value $14**

(4) Grandparents
Porcelain • PATT
750QX4323 • **Value $19**

(5) Grandson
Glass • VOTR
475QX2733 • **Value $23**

(6) Gratitude
Satin/Wood • PIKE
600QX4326 • **Value $10**

(7) Happy Christmas to Owl
Handcrafted • UNRU
600QX4183 • **Value $22**

(8) Heathcliff
Handcrafted • SEAL
750QX4363 • **Value $27**

(9) Heavenly Dreamer
Handcrafted • DLEE
575QX4173 • **Value $32**

(10) Heirloom Snowflake
Fabric • PATT
675QX5153 • **Value $18**

(11) Holiday Horn
Porcelain • UNRU
800QX5146 • **Value $32**

(12) Holiday Jingle Bell
Handcrafted • N/A
1600QX4046 • **Value $55**

(13) Husband
Cameo • PIKE
800QX3836 • **Value $12**

(14) Jolly Hiker
(re-issued in 1987)
Handcrafted • SIED
500QX4832 • **Value $22**

(15) Jolly St. Nick
Porcelain • UNRU
2250QX4296 • **Value $65**

(16) Joy of Friends
Bezeled Satin • PATT
675QX3823 • **Value $15**

(17) Joyful Carolers
Handcrafted • SICK
975QX5136 • **Value $35**

(18) Katybeth
Porcelain • N/A
700QX4353 • **Value $23**

(19) Kitty Mischief
(re-issued from 1985)
Handcrafted • DUTK
500QX4745 • **Value $30**

(20) Li'l Jingler
(re-issued in 1987)
Handcrafted • SEAL
675QX4193 • **Value $39**

GENERAL KEEPSAKE

	Price Paid	Value of My Collection
1.		
2.		
3.		
4.		
5.		
6.		
7.		
8.		
9.		
10.		
11.		
12.		
13.		
14.		
15.		
16.		
17.		
18.		
19.		
20.		
PENCIL TOTALS		

1986 Collection

VALUE GUIDE — HALLMARK KEEPSAKE ORNAMENTS

1 Little Drummers
Handcrafted • CROW
1250QX5116 • **Value $32**

2 Loving Memories
Handcrafted • SEAL
900QX4093 • **Value $32**

3 The Magi
Glass • PIKE
475QX2726 • **Value $19**

4 Magical Unicorn
(LE-24,700)
Porcelain • UNRU
2750QX4293 • **Value $100**

5 Marionette Angel
(canceled after
limited production)
Handcrafted • N/A
850QX4023 • **Value N/E**

6 Mary Emmerling:
American Country
Collection
Glass • N/A
795QX2752 • **Value $26**

7 Memories to Cherish
Ceramic • VOTR
750QX4276 • **Value $28**

8 Merry Koala
(re-issued in 1987)
Handcrafted • SICK
500QX4153 • **Value $21**

9 Merry Mouse
(re-issued from 1985)
Handcrafted • DUTK
450QX4032 • **Value $29**

10 Mother
Acrylic • N/A
700QX3826 • **Value $15**

11 Mother and Dad
Porcelain • PYDA
750QX4316 • **Value $17**

12 Mouse in the Moon
(re-issued in 1987)
Handcrafted • SEAL
550QX4166 • **Value $24**

13 Nephew
Bezeled Lacquer • N/A
625QX3813 • **Value $12**

14 New Home
Glass • CROW
475QX2746 • **Value $40**

15 Niece
Fabric/Wood • N/A
600QX4266 • **Value $10**

16 Norman Rockwell
Glass • PIKE
475QX2763 • **Value $25**

17 Nutcracker Santa
Handcrafted • UNRU
1000QX5123 • **Value $50**

18 Open Me First
Handcrafted • N/A
725QX4226 • **Value $29**

19 Paddington™ Bear
Handcrafted • SIED
600QX4356 • **Value $36**

20 PEANUTS®
Glass • N/A
475QX2766 • **Value $40**

GENERAL KEEPSAKE

	Price Paid	Value of My Collection
1.		
2.		
3.		
4.		
5.		
6.		
7.		
8.		
9.		
10.		
11.		
12.	B	
13.		
14.		
15.		
16.		
17.		
18.		
19.		
20.		
PENCIL TOTALS		

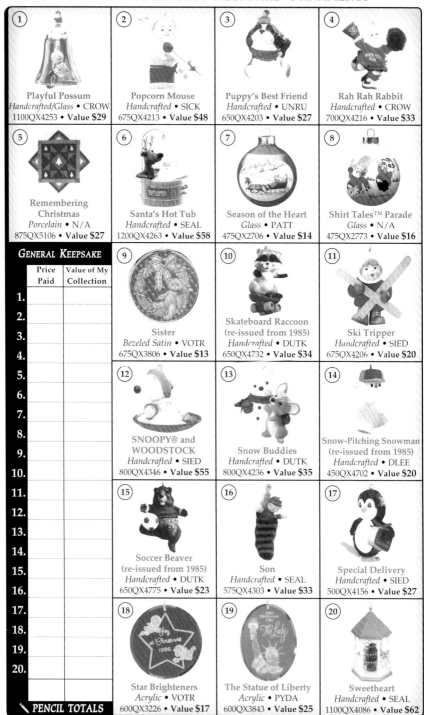

(1) Playful Possum
Handcrafted/Glass • CROW
1100QX4253 • **Value $29**

(2) Popcorn Mouse
Handcrafted • SICK
675QX4213 • **Value $48**

(3) Puppy's Best Friend
Handcrafted • UNRU
650QX4203 • **Value $27**

(4) Rah Rah Rabbit
Handcrafted • CROW
700QX4216 • **Value $33**

(5) Remembering Christmas
Porcelain • N/A
875QX5106 • **Value $27**

(6) Santa's Hot Tub
Handcrafted • SEAL
1200QX4263 • **Value $58**

(7) Season of the Heart
Glass • PATT
475QX2706 • **Value $14**

(8) Shirt Tales™ Parade
Glass • N/A
475QX2773 • **Value $16**

(9) Sister
Bezeled Satin • VOTR
675QX3806 • **Value $13**

(10) Skateboard Raccoon
(re-issued from 1985)
Handcrafted • DUTK
650QX4732 • **Value $34**

(11) Ski Tripper
Handcrafted • SIED
675QX4206 • **Value $20**

(12) SNOOPY® and WOODSTOCK
Handcrafted • SIED
800QX4346 • **Value $55**

(13) Snow Buddies
Handcrafted • DUTK
800QX4236 • **Value $35**

(14) Snow-Pitching Snowman
(re-issued from 1985)
Handcrafted • DLEE
450QX4702 • **Value $20**

(15) Soccer Beaver
(re-issued from 1985)
Handcrafted • DUTK
650QX4775 • **Value $23**

(16) Son
Handcrafted • SEAL
575QX4303 • **Value $33**

(17) Special Delivery
Handcrafted • SIED
500QX4156 • **Value $27**

(18) Star Brighteners
Acrylic • VOTR
600QX3226 • **Value $17**

(19) The Statue of Liberty
Acrylic • PYDA
600QX3843 • **Value $25**

(20) Sweetheart
Handcrafted • SEAL
1100QX4086 • **Value $62**

General Keepsake

	Price Paid	Value of My Collection
1.		
2.		
3.		
4.		
5.		
6.		
7.		
8.		
9.		
10.		
11.		
12.		
13.		
14.		
15.		
16.		
17.		
18.		
19.		
20.		
PENCIL TOTALS		

VALUE GUIDE — HALLMARK KEEPSAKE ORNAMENTS

1. Teacher
Glass • N/A
475QX2753 • **Value $12**

2. Ten Years Together
Porcelain • N/A
750QX4013 • **Value $14**

3. Timeless Love
Acrylic • VOTR
600QX3796 • **Value $25**

4. Tipping the Scales
Handcrafted • DUTK
675QX4186 • **Value $26**

5. Touchdown Santa
Handcrafted • DUTK
800QX4233 • **Value $40**

6. Treetop Trio
(re-issued in 1987)
Handcrafted • DLEE
1100QX4256 • **Value $30**

7. Twenty-Five Years Together
Porcelain • VOTR
800QX4103 • **Value $19**

8. Walnut Shell Rider
(re-issued in 1987)
Handcrafted • SEAL
600QX4196 • **Value $23**

9. Welcome, Christmas
Handcrafted • CROW
825QX5103 • **Value $30**

10. Wynken, Blynken and Nod
Handcrafted • DLEE
975QX4246 • **Value $43**

11. Baby's First Christmas
Panorama Ball • CROW
1950QLX7103 • **Value $45**

12. Christmas Sleigh Ride
Handcrafted • SEAL
2450QLX7012 • **Value $120**

13. First Christmas Together
Handcrafted • SEAL
1400QLX7073 • **Value $40**

14. General Store
Handcrafted • DLEE
1575QLX7053 • **Value $53**

15. Gentle Blessings
Panorama Ball • SICK
1500QLX7083 • **Value $165**

16. Keep on Glowin'!
(re-issued in 1987)
Handcrafted • CROW
1000QLX7076 • **Value $43**

17. Merry Christmas Bell
Acrylic • VOTR
850QLX7093 • **Value $22**

18. Mr. and Mrs. Santa
(re-issued from 1985)
Handcrafted • N/A
1450QLX7052 • **Value $78**

19. Santa's On His Way
Panorama Ball • UNRU
1500QLX7115 • **Value $67**

20. Santa's Snack
Handcrafted • CROW
1000QLX7066 • **Value $57**

1986

GENERAL KEEPSAKE	Price Paid	Value of My Collection
1.		
2.		
3.		
4.		
5.		
6.		
7.		
8.		
9.		
10.		

GENERAL MAGIC		
11.		
12.		
13.		
14.		
15.		
16.		
17.		
18.		
19.		
20.		
PENCIL TOTALS		

(1) **Sharing Friendship**
Acrylic • VOTR
850QLX7063 • **Value** $20

(2) **Sugarplum Cottage**
(re-issued from 1984)
Handcrafted • N/A
1100QLX7011 • **Value** $43

(3) **Village Express**
(re-issued in 1987)
Handcrafted • SICK
2450QLX7072 • **Value** $105

(4) **On the Right Track**
Porcelain • DUTK
1500QSP4201 • **Value** $40

(5) **Coca-Cola® Santa**
Glass • N/A
475QXO2796 • **Value** $21

(6) **Old-Fashioned Santa**
Handcrafted • SICK
1275QXO4403 • **Value** $55

(7) **Santa and His Reindeer**
Handcrafted • N/A
975QXO4406 • **Value** $37

(8) **Santa's Panda Pal**
Handcrafted • N/A
500QXO4413 • **Value** $25

1985

Among the most popular pieces in 1985 were based on favorite themes such as Santa Claus, SNOOPY® and Norman Rockwell's art. For 1985, there were 114 Keepsake ornament designs and 14 Magic ornaments. See collectible series section for more 1985 ornaments.

	Price Paid	Value of My Collection
GENERAL MAGIC		
1.		
2.		
3.		
GOLD CROWN ORNAMENTS		
4.		
OPEN HOUSE ORNAMENTS		
5.		
6.		
7.		
8.		
GENERAL KEEPSAKE		
9.		
10.		
11.		
12.		
13.		
14.		
15.		
16.		
17.		
PENCIL TOTALS		

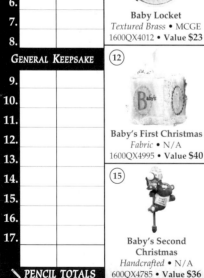

(9) **Baby Locket**
Textured Brass • MCGE
1600QX4012 • **Value** $23

(10) **Baby's First Christmas**
Acrylic • N/A
575QX3702 • **Value** $17

(11) **Baby's First Christmas**
Embroidered Fabric • N/A
700QX4782 • **Value** $14

(12) **Baby's First Christmas**
Fabric • N/A
1600QX4995 • **Value** $40

(13) **Baby's First Christmas**
Handcrafted • DLEE
1500QX4992 • **Value** $55

(14) **Baby's First Christmas**
Satin • VOTR
500QX2602 • **Value** $24

(15) **Baby's Second Christmas**
Handcrafted • N/A
600QX4785 • **Value** $36

(16) **Babysitter**
Glass • PYDA
475QX2642 • **Value** $11

(17) **Baker Elf**
Handcrafted • SEAL
575QX4912 • **Value** $30

VALUE GUIDE – HALLMARK KEEPSAKE ORNAMENTS

1. Beary Smooth Ride
(re-issued in 1986)
Handcrafted • SICK
650QX4805 • **Value $23**

2. Betsey Clark
Porcelain • N/A
850QX5085 • **Value $32**

3. Bottlecap Fun Bunnies
Handcrafted • SIED
775QX4815 • **Value $32**

4. Candle Cameo
Bezeled Cameo • PIKE
675QX3742 • **Value $14**

5. Candy Apple Mouse
Handcrafted • SICK
650QX4705 • **Value $60**

6. Charming Angel
Fabric • PYDA
975QX5125 • **Value $23**

7. Children in the Shoe
Handcrafted • SEAL
950QX4905 • **Value $48**

8. Child's Third Christmas
Handcrafted • SEAL
600QX4755 • **Value $29**

9. Christmas Treats
Bezeled Glass • N/A
550QX5075 • **Value $16**

10. Country Goose
Wood • PYDA
775QX5185 • **Value $14**

11. Dapper Penguin
Handcrafted • SEAL
500QX4772 • **Value $29**

12. Daughter
Wood • N/A
550QX5032 • **Value $15**

13. A DISNEY Christmas
Glass • N/A
475QX2712 • **Value $32**

14. Do Not Disturb Bear
(re-issued in 1986)
Handcrafted • SEAL
775QX4812 • **Value $28**

15. Doggy in a Stocking
Handcrafted • N/A
550QX4742 • **Value $38**

16. Engineering Mouse
Handcrafted • SIED
550QX4735 • **Value $26**

17. Father
Wood • VOTR
650QX3762 • **Value $9**

18. First Christmas
Together
Acrylic • N/A
675QX3705 • **Value $18**

19. First Christmas
Together
Brass • SEAL
1675QX4005 • **Value $27**

20. First Christmas
Together
Fabric/Wood • N/A
800QX5072 • **Value $12**

1985

GENERAL KEEPSAKE		
	Price Paid	Value of My Collection
1.		
2.		
3.		
4.		
5.		
6.		
7.		
8.		
9.		
10.		
11.		
12.		
13.		
14.		
15.		
16.		
17.		
18.		
19.		
20.		
PENCIL TOTALS		

VALUE GUIDE – HALLMARK KEEPSAKE ORNAMENTS

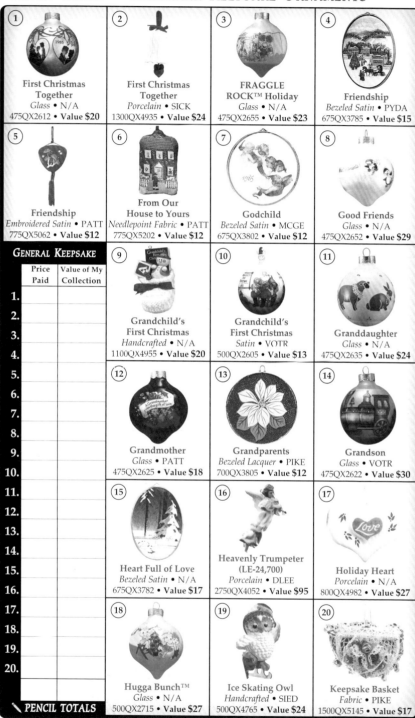

(1) First Christmas Together
Glass • N/A
475QX2612 • **Value $20**

(2) First Christmas Together
Porcelain • SICK
1300QX4935 • **Value $24**

(3) FRAGGLE ROCK™ Holiday
Glass • N/A
475QX2655 • **Value $23**

(4) Friendship
Bezeled Satin • PYDA
675QX3785 • **Value $15**

(5) Friendship
Embroidered Satin • PATT
775QX5062 • **Value $12**

(6) From Our House to Yours
Needlepoint Fabric • PATT
775QX5202 • **Value $12**

(7) Godchild
Bezeled Satin • MCGE
675QX3802 • **Value $12**

(8) Good Friends
Glass • N/A
475QX2652 • **Value $29**

(9) Grandchild's First Christmas
Handcrafted • N/A
1100QX4955 • **Value $20**

(10) Grandchild's First Christmas
Satin • VOTR
500QX2605 • **Value $13**

(11) Granddaughter
Glass • N/A
475QX2635 • **Value $24**

(12) Grandmother
Glass • PATT
475QX2625 • **Value $18**

(13) Grandparents
Bezeled Lacquer • PIKE
700QX3805 • **Value $12**

(14) Grandson
Glass • VOTR
475QX2622 • **Value $30**

(15) Heart Full of Love
Bezeled Satin • N/A
675QX3782 • **Value $17**

(16) Heavenly Trumpeter (LE-24,700)
Porcelain • DLEE
2750QX4052 • **Value $95**

(17) Holiday Heart
Porcelain • N/A
800QX4982 • **Value $27**

(18) Hugga Bunch™
Glass • N/A
500QX2715 • **Value $27**

(19) Ice Skating Owl
Handcrafted • SIED
500QX4765 • **Value $24**

(20) Keepsake Basket
Fabric • PIKE
1500QX5145 • **Value $17**

GENERAL KEEPSAKE

	Price Paid	Value of My Collection
1.		
2.		
3.		
4.		
5.		
6.		
7.		
8.		
9.		
10.		
11.		
12.		
13.		
14.		
15.		
16.		
17.		
18.		
19.		
20.		
PENCIL TOTALS		

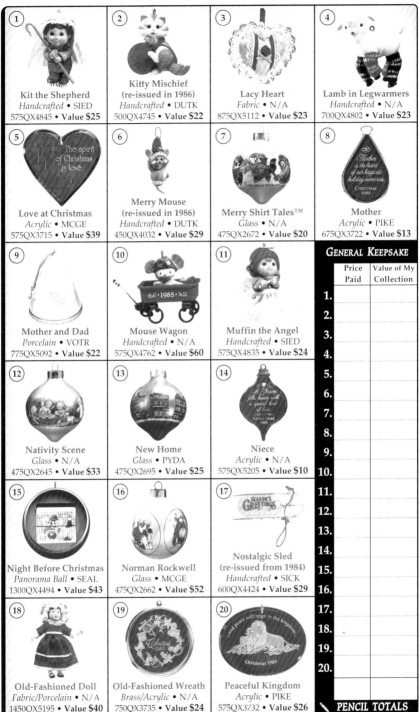

1. Kit the Shepherd
Handcrafted • SIED
575QX4845 • **Value $25**

2. Kitty Mischief
(re-issued in 1986)
Handcrafted • DUTK
500QX4745 • **Value $22**

3. Lacy Heart
Fabric • N/A
875QX5112 • **Value $23**

4. Lamb in Legwarmers
Handcrafted • N/A
700QX4802 • **Value $23**

5. Love at Christmas
Acrylic • MCGE
575QX3715 • **Value $39**

6. Merry Mouse
(re-issued in 1986)
Handcrafted • DUTK
450QX4032 • **Value $29**

7. Merry Shirt Tales™
Glass • N/A
475QX2672 • **Value $20**

8. Mother
Acrylic • PIKE
675QX3722 • **Value $13**

9. Mother and Dad
Porcelain • VOTR
775QX5092 • **Value $22**

10. Mouse Wagon
Handcrafted • N/A
575QX4762 • **Value $60**

11. Muffin the Angel
Handcrafted • SIED
575QX4835 • **Value $24**

12. Nativity Scene
Glass • N/A
475QX2645 • **Value $33**

13. New Home
Glass • PYDA
475QX2695 • **Value $25**

14. Niece
Acrylic • N/A
575QX5205 • **Value $10**

15. Night Before Christmas
Panorama Ball • SEAL
1300QX4494 • **Value $43**

16. Norman Rockwell
Glass • MCGE
475QX2662 • **Value $52**

17. Nostalgic Sled
(re-issued from 1984)
Handcrafted • SICK
600QX4424 • **Value $29**

18. Old-Fashioned Doll
Fabric/Porcelain • N/A
1450QX5195 • **Value $40**

19. Old-Fashioned Wreath
Brass/Acrylic • N/A
750QX3735 • **Value $24**

20. Peaceful Kingdom
Acrylic • PIKE
575QX3732 • **Value $26**

1985

GENERAL KEEPSAKE		
	Price Paid	Value of My Collection
1.		
2.		
3.		
4.		
5.		
6.		
7.		
8.		
9.		
10.		
11.		
12.		
13.		
14.		
15.		
16.		
17.		
18.		
19.		
20.		
PENCIL TOTALS		

1
PEANUTS®
Glass • N/A
475QX2665 • **Value $35**

2
Porcelain Bird
Porcelain • SICK
650QX4795 • **Value $30**

3
Rainbow Brite™
and Friends
Glass • N/A
475QX2682 • **Value $25**

4
Rocking Horse
Memories
Fabric/Wood • VOTR
1000QX5182 • **Value $13**

5
Roller Skating Rabbit
(re-issued from 1984)
Handcrafted • SEAL
500QX4571 • **Value $32**

6
Santa Pipe
Handcrafted • DUTK
950QX4942 • **Value $23**

7
Santa's Ski Trip
Handcrafted • SEAL
1200QX4962 • **Value $60**

8
Sewn Photoholder
Embroidered Fabric • PIKE
700QX3795 • **Value $32**

General Keepsake

	Price Paid	Value of My Collection
1.		
2.		
3.		
4.		
5.		
6.		
7.		
8.		
9.		
10.		
11.		
12.		
13.		
14.		
15.		
16.		
17.		
18.		
19.		
20.		

PENCIL TOTALS

9
Sheep at Christmas
Handcrafted • SICK
825QX5175 • **Value $25**

10
Sister
Porcelain • PATT
725QX5065 • **Value $22**

11
Skateboard Raccoon
(re-issued in 1986)
Handcrafted • DUTK
650QX4732 • **Value $34**

12
SNOOPY® and
WOODSTOCK
Handcrafted • SIED
750QX4915 • **Value $65**

13
Snowflake
Fabric • PATT
650QX5105 • **Value $20**

14
Snow-Pitching Snowman
(re-issued in 1986)
Handcrafted • DLEE
450QX4702 • **Value $20**

15
Snowy Seal
(re-issued from 1984)
Handcrafted • SEAL
400QX4501 • **Value $23**

16
Soccer Beaver
(re-issued in 1986)
Handcrafted • DUTK
650QX4775 • **Value $23**

17
Son
Handcrafted • SIED
550QX5025 • **Value $44**

18
Special Friends
Arylic • PALM
575QX3725 • **Value $10**

19
The Spirit of
Santa Claus
Handcrafted • DLEE
2250QX4985 • **Value $90**

20
Stardust Angel
Handcrafted • DLEE
575QX4752 • **Value $34**

VALUE GUIDE – HALLMARK KEEPSAKE ORNAMENTS

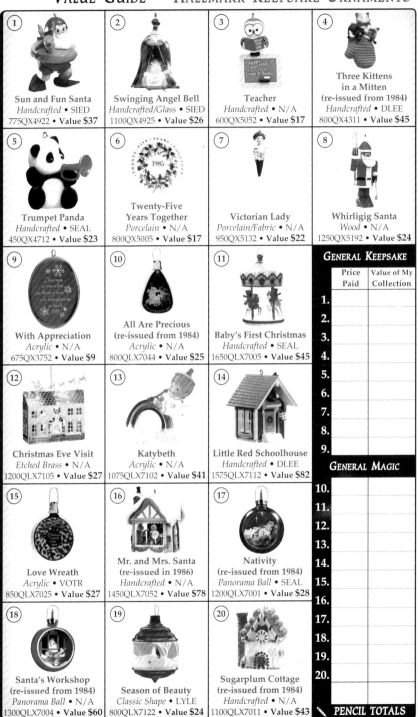

1985

#	Name	Details	Item/Value
1	**Sun and Fun Santa**	*Handcrafted* • SIED	775QX4922 • **Value $37**
2	**Swinging Angel Bell**	*Handcrafted/Glass* • SIED	1100QX4925 • **Value $26**
3	**Teacher**	*Handcrafted* • N/A	600QX5052 • **Value $17**
4	**Three Kittens in a Mitten** (re-issued from 1984)	*Handcrafted* • DLEE	800QX4311 • **Value $45**
5	**Trumpet Panda**	*Handcrafted* • SEAL	450QX4712 • **Value $23**
6	**Twenty-Five Years Together**	*Porcelain* • N/A	800QX5005 • **Value $17**
7	**Victorian Lady**	*Porcelain/Fabric* • N/A	950QX5132 • **Value $22**
8	**Whirligig Santa**	*Wood* • N/A	1250QX5192 • **Value $24**
9	**With Appreciation**	*Acrylic* • N/A	675QX3752 • **Value $9**
10	**All Are Precious** (re-issued from 1984)	*Acrylic* • N/A	800QLX7044 • **Value $25**
11	**Baby's First Christmas**	*Handcrafted* • SEAL	1650QLX7005 • **Value $45**
12	**Christmas Eve Visit**	*Etched Brass* • N/A	1200QLX7105 • **Value $27**
13	**Katybeth**	*Acrylic* • N/A	1075QLX7102 • **Value $41**
14	**Little Red Schoolhouse**	*Handcrafted* • DLEE	1575QLX7112 • **Value $82**
15	**Love Wreath**	*Acrylic* • VOTR	850QLX7025 • **Value $27**
16	**Mr. and Mrs. Santa** (re-issued in 1986)	*Handcrafted* • N/A	1450QLX7052 • **Value $78**
17	**Nativity** (re-issued from 1984)	*Panorama Ball* • SEAL	1200QLX7001 • **Value $28**
18	**Santa's Workshop** (re-issued from 1984)	*Panorama Ball* • N/A	1300QLX7004 • **Value $60**
19	**Season of Beauty**	*Classic Shape* • LYLE	800QLX7122 • **Value $24**
20	**Sugarplum Cottage** (re-issued from 1984)	*Handcrafted* • N/A	1100QLX7011 • **Value $43**

GENERAL KEEPSAKE

	Price Paid	Value of My Collection
1.		
2.		
3.		
4.		
5.		
6.		
7.		
8.		
9.		

GENERAL MAGIC

	Price Paid	Value of My Collection
10.		
11.		
12.		
13.		
14.		
15.		
16.		
17.		
18.		
19.		
20.		

PENCIL TOTALS

① 
Swiss Cheese Lane
Handcrafted • N/A
1300QLX7065 • **Value $40**

**② **
Village Church
(re-issued from 1984)
Handcrafted • DLEE
1500QLX7021 • **Value $48**

**③ **
Santa Claus
Lacquer • N/A
675QX3005 • **Value $10**

④ 
Santa's Village
Lacquer • N/A
675QX3002• **Value $10**

1984

1984 was a landmark year for Hallmark ornaments with the debut of lighted Magic ornaments (then called "Lighted Ornaments"). In later years, these ornaments would also incorporate motion and sound. There were 10 Magic ornaments issued in 1984 as well as 110 Keepsake designs. See collectible series section for more 1984 ornaments.

⑤ 
Alpine Elf
Handcrafted • SEAL
600QX4521 • **Value $35**

GENERAL MAGIC

	Price Paid	Value of My Collection
1.		
2.		

SANTA CLAUS – THE MOVIE

3.		
4.		

GENERAL KEEPSAKE

5.		
6.		
7.		
8.		
9.		
10.		
11.		
12.		
13.		
14.		
15.		
16.		
17.		

PENCIL TOTALS

⑥
Amanda
Fabric/Porcelain • N/A
900QX4321 • **Value $28**

⑦
Baby's First Christmas
Acrylic • N/A
600QX3401 • **Value $39**

⑧
Baby's First Christmas
Classic Shape • DLEE
1600QX9041 • **Value $47**

⑨
Baby's First Christmas
Handcrafted • N/A
1400QX4381 • **Value $48**

⑩
Baby's First Christmas – Boy
Satin • N/A
450QX2404 • **Value $27**

⑪
Baby's First Christmas – Girl
Satin • N/A
450QX2401 • **Value $28**

⑫
Baby's First Christmas – Photoholder
Fabric • N/A
700QX3001 • **Value $18**

⑬
Baby's Second Christmas
Satin • N/A
450QX2411 • **Value $37**

⑭
Baby-sitter
Glass • N/A
450QX2531 • **Value $12**

⑮
Bell Ringer Squirrel
Handcrafted/Glass • SEAL
1000QX4431 • **Value $33**

⑯
Betsey Clark Angel
Porcelain • N/A
900QX4624 • **Value $32**

⑰
Chickadee
Porcelain • SICK
600QX4514 • **Value $38**

Value Guide – Hallmark Keepsake Ornaments

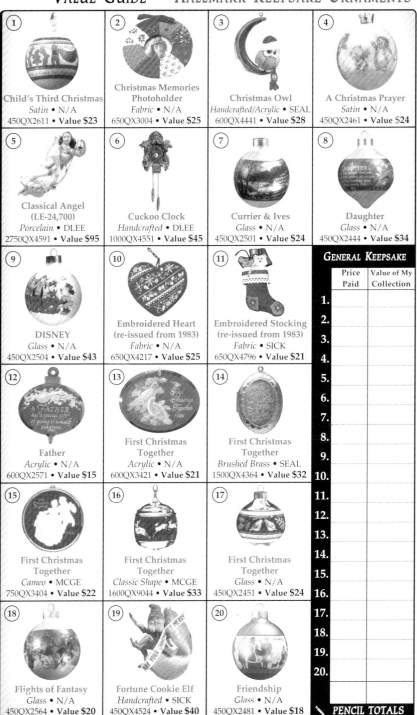

(1) Child's Third Christmas
Satin • N/A
450QX2611 • **Value $23**

(2) Christmas Memories
Photoholder
Fabric • N/A
650QX3004 • **Value $25**

(3) Christmas Owl
Handcrafted/Acrylic • SEAL
600QX4441 • **Value $28**

(4) A Christmas Prayer
Satin • N/A
450QX2461 • **Value $24**

(5) Classical Angel
(LE-24,700)
Porcelain • DLEE
2750QX4591 • **Value $95**

(6) Cuckoo Clock
Handcrafted • DLEE
1000QX4551 • **Value $45**

(7) Currier & Ives
Glass • N/A
450QX2501 • **Value $24**

(8) Daughter
Glass • N/A
450QX2444 • **Value $34**

(9) DISNEY
Glass • N/A
450QX2504 • **Value $43**

(10) Embroidered Heart
(re-issued from 1983)
Fabric • N/A
650QX4217 • **Value $25**

(11) Embroidered Stocking
(re-issued from 1983)
Fabric • SICK
650QX4796 • **Value $21**

(12) Father
Acrylic • N/A
600QX2571 • **Value $15**

(13) First Christmas
Together
Acrylic • N/A
600QX3421 • **Value $21**

(14) First Christmas
Together
Brushed Brass • SEAL
1500QX4364 • **Value $32**

(15) First Christmas
Together
Cameo • MCGE
750QX3404 • **Value $22**

(16) First Christmas
Together
Classic Shape • MCGE
1600QX9044 • **Value $33**

(17) First Christmas
Together
Glass • N/A
450QX2451 • **Value $24**

(18) Flights of Fantasy
Glass • N/A
450QX2564 • **Value $20**

(19) Fortune Cookie Elf
Handcrafted • SICK
450QX4524 • **Value $40**

(20) Friendship
Glass • N/A
450QX2481 • **Value $18**

General Keepsake

	Price Paid	Value of My Collection
1.		
2.		
3.		
4.		
5.		
6.		
7.		
8.		
9.		
10.		
11.		
12.		
13.		
14.		
15.		
16.		
17.		
18.		
19.		
20.		

PENCIL TOTALS

1984

VALUE GUIDE – HALLMARK KEEPSAKE ORNAMENTS

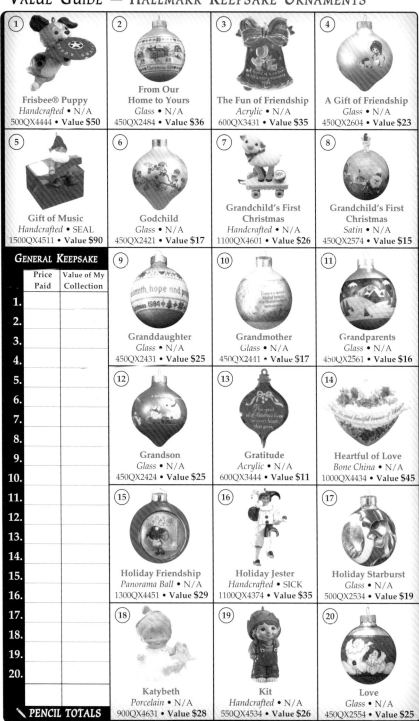

1 Frisbee® Puppy
Handcrafted • N/A
500QX4444 • **Value $50**

2 From Our
Home to Yours
Glass • N/A
450QX2484 • **Value $36**

3 The Fun of Friendship
Acrylic • N/A
600QX3431 • **Value $35**

4 A Gift of Friendship
Glass • N/A
450QX2604 • **Value $23**

5 Gift of Music
Handcrafted • SEAL
1500QX4511 • **Value $90**

6 Godchild
Glass • N/A
450QX2421 • **Value $17**

7 Grandchild's First
Christmas
Handcrafted • N/A
1100QX4601 • **Value $26**

8 Grandchild's First
Christmas
Satin • N/A
450QX2574 • **Value $15**

9 Granddaughter
Glass • N/A
450QX2431 • **Value $25**

10 Grandmother
Glass • N/A
450QX2441 • **Value $17**

11 Grandparents
Glass • N/A
450QX2561 • **Value $16**

12 Grandson
Glass • N/A
450QX2424 • **Value $25**

13 Gratitude
Acrylic • N/A
600QX3444 • **Value $11**

14 Heartful of Love
Bone China • N/A
1000QX4434 • **Value $45**

15 Holiday Friendship
Panorama Ball • N/A
1300QX4451 • **Value $29**

16 Holiday Jester
Handcrafted • SICK
1100QX4374 • **Value $35**

17 Holiday Starburst
Glass • N/A
500QX2534 • **Value $19**

18 Katybeth
Porcelain • N/A
900QX4631 • **Value $28**

19 Kit
Handcrafted • N/A
550QX4534 • **Value $26**

20 Love
Glass • N/A
450QX2554 • **Value $25**

GENERAL KEEPSAKE

	Price Paid	Value of My Collection
1.		
2.		
3.		
4.		
5.		
6.		
7.		
8.		
9.		
10.		
11.		
12.		
13.		
14.		
15.		
16.		
17.		
18.		
19.		
20.		
PENCIL TOTALS		

1. Love ... the Spirit
of Christmas
Glass • N/A
450QX2474 • **Value $37**

2. Madonna and Child
Acrylic • PALM
600QX3441 • **Value $48**

3. Marathon Santa
Handcrafted • SEAL
800QX4564 • **Value $40**

4. The Miracle of Love
Acrylic • N/A
600QX3424 • **Value $32**

5. Mother
Acrylic • N/A
600QX3434 • **Value $16**

6. Mother and Dad
Bone China • N/A
650QX2581 • **Value $23**

7. Mountain
Climbing Santa
(re-issued from 1983)
Handcrafted • SEAL
650QX4077 • **Value $36**

8. Muffin
Handcrafted • DLEE
550QX4421 • **Value $27**

1984

9. The MUPPETS™
Glass • N/A
450QX2514 • **Value $35**

10. Musical Angel
Handcrafted • DLEE
550QX1344 • **Value $70**

11. Napping Mouse
Handcrafted • N/A
550QX4351 • **Value $50**

12. Needlepoint Wreath
Fabric • PIKE
650QX4594 • **Value $13**

13. New Home
Glass • N/A
450QX2454 • **Value $50**

14. Norman Rockwell
Glass • MCGE
450QX2511 • **Value $32**

15. Nostalgic Sled
(re-issued in 1985)
Handcrafted • SICK
600QX4424 • **Value $29**

16. Old Fashioned
Rocking Horse
Acrylic/Brass • N/A
750QX3464 • **Value $19**

17. Peace on Earth
Cameo • N/A
750QX3414 • **Value $30**

18. PEANUTS®
Satin • N/A
450QX2521 • **Value $34**

19. Peppermint 1984
Handcrafted • DLEE
450QX4561 • **Value $53**

20. Polar Bear Drummer
Handcrafted • SEAL
450QX4301 • **Value $27**

GENERAL KEEPSAKE

	Price Paid	Value of My Collection
1.		
2.		
3.		
4.		
5.		
6.		
7.		
8.		
9.		
10.		
11.		
12.		
13.		
14.		
15.		
16.		
17.		
18.		
19.		
20.		
PENCIL TOTALS		

(1) Raccoon's Christmas
Handcrafted • SEAL
900QX4474 • **Value $53**

(2) Reindeer Racetrack
Glass • N/A
450QX2544 • **Value $24**

(3) Roller Skating Rabbit
(re-issued in 1985)
Handcrafted • SEAL
500QX4571 • **Value $32**

(4) Santa
Fabric • N/A
750QX4584 • **Value $18**

(5) Santa Mouse
Handcrafted • SIED
450QX4334 • **Value $52**

(6) Santa Star
Handcrafted • N/A
550QX4504 • **Value $36**

(7) Santa Sulky Driver
Etched Brass • N/A
900QX4361 • **Value $33**

(8) A Savior is Born
Glass • N/A
450QX2541 • **Value $32**

(9) Shirt Tales™
Satin • N/A
450QX2524 • **Value $18**

(10) Sister
Bone China • N/A
650QX2594 • **Value $30**

(11) SNOOPY® and WOODSTOCK
Handcrafted • SEAL
750QX4391 • **Value $95**

(12) Snowmobile Santa
Handcrafted • N/A
650QX4314 • **Value $36**

(13) Snowshoe Penguin
Handcrafted • SICK
650QX4531 • **Value $49**

(14) Snowy Seal
(re-issued in 1985)
Handcrafted • SEAL
400QX4501 • **Value $23**

(15) Son
Glass • N/A
450QX2434 • **Value $30**

(16) Teacher
Glass • N/A
450QX2491 • **Value $13**

(17) Ten Years Together
Bone China • N/A
650QX2584 • **Value $19**

(18) Three Kittens in a Mitten (re-issued in 1985)
Handcrafted • DLEE
800QX4311 • **Value $47**

(19) Twelve Days of Christmas
Handcrafted • SEAL
1500QX4159 • **Value $100**

(20) Twenty-Five Years Together
Bone China • N/A
650QX2591 • **Value $22**

General Keepsake

	Price Paid	Value of My Collection
1.		
2.		
3.		
4.		
5.		
6.		
7.		
8.		
9.		
10.		
11.		
12.		
13.		
14.		
15.		
16.		
17.		
18.		
19.		
20.		
PENCIL TOTALS		

VALUE GUIDE – HALLMARK KEEPSAKE ORNAMENTS

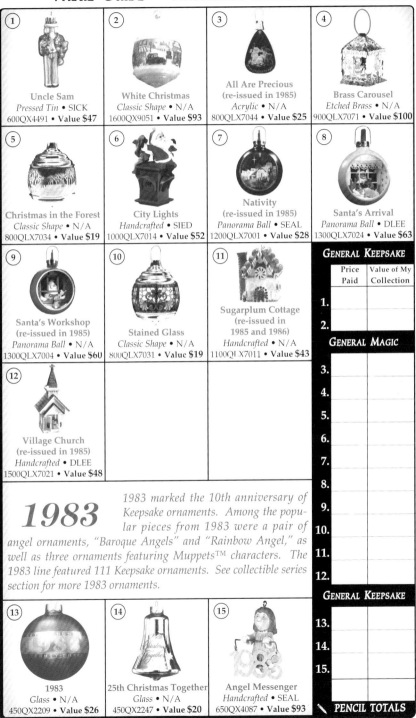

1
Uncle Sam
Pressed Tin • SICK
600QX4491 • **Value $47**

2
White Christmas
Classic Shape • N/A
1600QX9051 • **Value $93**

3
All Are Precious
(re-issued in 1985)
Acrylic • N/A
800QLX7044 • **Value $25**

4
Brass Carousel
Etched Brass • N/A
900QLX7071 • **Value $100**

5
Christmas in the Forest
Classic Shape • N/A
800QLX7034 • **Value $19**

6
City Lights
Handcrafted • SIED
1000QLX7014 • **Value $52**

7
Nativity
(re-issued in 1985)
Panorama Ball • SEAL
1200QLX7001 • **Value $28**

8
Santa's Arrival
Panorama Ball • DLEE
1300QLX7024 • **Value $63**

9
Santa's Workshop
(re-issued in 1985)
Panorama Ball • N/A
1300QLX7004 • **Value $60**

10
Stained Glass
Classic Shape • N/A
800QLX7031 • **Value $19**

11
Sugarplum Cottage
(re-issued in
1985 and 1986)
Handcrafted • N/A
1100QLX7011 • **Value $43**

12
Village Church
(re-issued in 1985)
Handcrafted • DLEE
1500QLX7021 • **Value $48**

1983

1983 marked the 10th anniversary of Keepsake ornaments. Among the popular pieces from 1983 were a pair of angel ornaments, "Baroque Angels" and "Rainbow Angel," as well as three ornaments featuring Muppets™ characters. The 1983 line featured 111 Keepsake ornaments. See collectible series section for more 1983 ornaments.

13
1983
Glass • N/A
450QX2209 • **Value $26**

14
25th Christmas Together
Glass • N/A
450QX2247 • **Value $20**

15
Angel Messenger
Handcrafted • SEAL
650QX4087 • **Value $93**

1983

	Price Paid	Value of My Collection
GENERAL KEEPSAKE		
1.		
2.		
GENERAL MAGIC		
3.		
4.		
5.		
6.		
7.		
8.		
9.		
10.		
11.		
12.		
GENERAL KEEPSAKE		
13.		
14.		
15.		
PENCIL TOTALS		

1. Angels
Glass • N/A
500QX2197 • **Value $24**

2. The Annunciation
Glass • N/A
450QX2167 • **Value $29**

3. Baby's First Christmas
Acrylic • N/A
700QX3029 • **Value $22**

4. Baby's First Christmas
Cameo • SICK
750QX3019 • **Value $16**

5. Baby's First Christmas
Handcrafted • DLEE
1400QX4027 • **Value $37**

6. Baby's First Christmas – Boy
Satin • N/A
450QX2009 • **Value $25**

7. Baby's First Christmas – Girl
Satin • N/A
450QX2007 • **Value $25**

8. Baby's Second Christmas
Satin • N/A
450QX2267 • **Value $35**

9. Baroque Angels
Handcrafted • DLEE
1300QX4229 • **Value $125**

10. Bell Wreath
Brass • SICK
650QX4209 • **Value $33**

11. Betsey Clark
Handcrafted • SEAL
650QX4047 • **Value $31**

12. Betsey Clark
Porcelain • N/A
900QX4401 • **Value $33**

13. Brass Santa
Brass • SEAL
900QX4239 • **Value $20**

14. Caroling Owl
Handcrafted • SEAL
450QX4117 • **Value $38**

15. Child's Third Christmas
Satin Piqué • N/A
450QX2269 • **Value $23**

16. Christmas Joy
Satin • N/A
450QX2169 • **Value $27**

17. Christmas Kitten
(re-issued from 1982)
Handcrafted • N/A
400QX4543 • **Value $35**

18. Christmas Koala
Handcrafted • SEAL
400QX4199 • **Value $30**

19. Christmas Stocking
Acrylic • N/A
600QX3039 • **Value $37**

20. Christmas Wonderland
Glass • N/A
450QX2219 • **Value $115**

GENERAL KEEPSAKE

	Price Paid	Value of My Collection
1.		
2.		
3.		
4.		
5.		
6.		
7.		
8.		
9.		
10.		
11.		
12.		
13.		
14.		
15.		
16.		
17.		
18.		
19.		
20.		

PENCIL TOTALS

1983

1. Currier & Ives
Glass • N/A
450QX2159 • **Value $22**

2. Cycling Santa
(re-issued from 1982)
Handcrafted • N/A
2000QX4355 • **Value $145**

3. Daughter
Glass • N/A
450QX2037 • **Value $38**

4. DISNEY
Glass • N/A
450QX2129 • **Value $50**

5. Embroidered Heart
(re-issued in 1984)
Fabric • N/A
650QX4217 • **Value $25**

6. Embroidered Stocking
(re-issued in 1984)
Fabric • SICK
650QX4796 • **Value $21**

7. Enameled Christmas
Wreath
Enameled • N/A
900QX3119 • **Value $14**

8. First Christmas
Together
Acrylic • N/A
600QX3069 • **Value $22**

9. First Christmas
Together
Cameo • N/A
750QX3017 • **Value $21**

10. First Christmas
Together
Classic Shape • N/A
600QX3107 • **Value $36**

11. First Christmas
Together
Glass • SICK
450QX2089 • **Value $28**

12. First Christmas
Together – Brass Locket
Brass • SEAL
1500QX4329 • **Value $37**

13. Friendship
Acrylic • N/A
600QX3059 • **Value $19**

14. Friendship
Glass • N/A
450QX2077 • **Value $18**

15. Godchild
Glass • N/A
450QX2017 • **Value $15**

16. Grandchild's First
Christmas
Classic Shape • N/A
600QX3129 • **Value $21**

17. Grandchild's First
Christmas
Handcrafted • N/A
1400QX4309 • **Value $37**

18. Granddaughter
Glass • N/A
450QX2027 • **Value $29**

19. Grandmother
Glass • N/A
450QX2057 • **Value $15**

20. Grandparents
Ceramic • N/A
650QX4299 • **Value $16**

General Keepsake	Price Paid	Value of My Collection
1.		
2.		
3.		
4.		
5.		
6.		
7.		
8.		
9.		
10.		
11.		
12.		
13.		
14.		
15.		
16.		
17.		
18.		
19.		
20.		
PENCIL TOTALS		

Value Guide — Hallmark Keepsake Ornaments

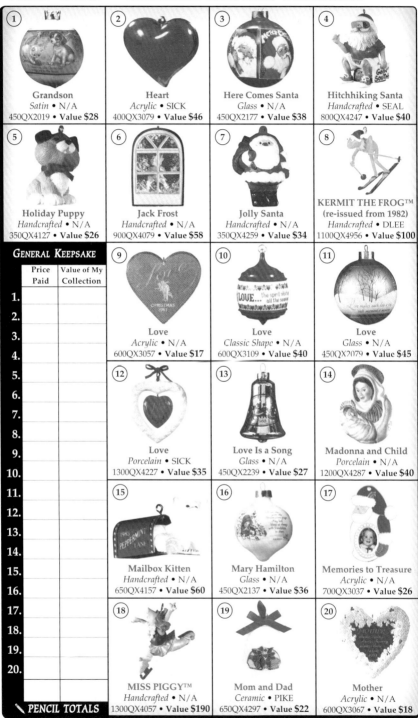

1	2	3	4
Grandson *Satin • N/A* 450QX2019 • **Value $28**	**Heart** *Acrylic • SICK* 400QX3079 • **Value $46**	**Here Comes Santa** *Glass • N/A* 450QX2177 • **Value $38**	**Hitchhiking Santa** *Handcrafted • SEAL* 800QX4247 • **Value $40**

5	6	7	8
Holiday Puppy *Handcrafted • N/A* 350QX4127 • **Value $26**	**Jack Frost** *Handcrafted • N/A* 900QX4079 • **Value $58**	**Jolly Santa** *Handcrafted • N/A* 350QX4259 • **Value $34**	**KERMIT THE FROG™** (re-issued from 1982) *Handcrafted • DLEE* 1100QX4956 • **Value $100**

GENERAL KEEPSAKE

	Price Paid	Value of My Collection
1.		
2.		
3.		
4.		
5.		
6.		
7.		
8.		
9.		
10.		
11.		
12.		
13.		
14.		
15.		
16.		
17.		
18.		
19.		
20.		

PENCIL TOTALS

9	10	11
Love *Acrylic • N/A* 600QX3057 • **Value $17**	**Love** *Classic Shape • N/A* 600QX3109 • **Value $40**	**Love** *Glass • N/A* 450QX2079 • **Value $45**

12	13	14
Love *Porcelain • SICK* 1300QX4227 • **Value $35**	**Love Is a Song** *Glass • N/A* 450QX2239 • **Value $27**	**Madonna and Child** *Porcelain • N/A* 1200QX4287 • **Value $40**

15	16	17
Mailbox Kitten *Handcrafted • N/A* 650QX4157 • **Value $60**	**Mary Hamilton** *Glass • N/A* 450QX2137 • **Value $36**	**Memories to Treasure** *Acrylic • N/A* 700QX3037 • **Value $26**

18	19	20
MISS PIGGY™ *Handcrafted • N/A* 1300QX4057 • **Value $190**	**Mom and Dad** *Ceramic • PIKE* 650QX4297 • **Value $22**	**Mother** *Acrylic • N/A* 600QX3067 • **Value $18**

182

1983 Collection

1983

#	Ornament	Details	
1	**Mother and Child**	Cameo • N/A	750QX3027 • **Value $38**
2	**Mountain Climbing Santa** (re-issued in 1984)	Handcrafted • SEAL	650QX4077 • **Value $36**
3	**Mouse in Bell**	Handcrafted/Glass • N/A	1000QX4197 • **Value $65**
4	**Mouse on Cheese**	Handcrafted • SICK	650QX4137 • **Value $47**
5	**The MUPPETS™**	Satin • N/A	450QX2147 • **Value $50**
6	**New Home**	Satin • N/A	450QX2107 • **Value $33**
7	**Norman Rockwell**	Glass • N/A	450QX2157 • **Value $53**
8	**An Old Fashioned Christmas**	Glass • N/A	450QX2179 • **Value $30**
9	**Old-Fashioned Santa**	Handcrafted • SICK	1100QX4099 • **Value $65**
10	**Oriental Butterflies**	Glass • N/A	450QX2187 • **Value $29**
11	**PEANUTS®**	Satin • N/A	450QX2127 • **Value $36**
12	**Peppermint Penguin**	Handcrafted • N/A	650QX4089 • **Value $42**
13	**Porcelain Doll, Diana**	Porcelain/Fabric • DLEE	900QX4237 • **Value $26**
14	**Rainbow Angel**	Handcrafted • DLEE	550QX4167 • **Value $105**
15	**Santa**	Acrylic • N/A	400QX3087 • **Value $32**
16	**Santa's Many Faces**	Classic Shape • N/A	600QX3117 • **Value $30**
17	**Santa's on His Way**	Handcrafted • N/A	1000QX4269 • **Value $34**
18	**Santa's Workshop** (re-issued from 1982)	Handcrafted • DLEE	1000QX4503 • **Value $78**
19	**Scrimshaw Reindeer**	Handcrafted • SEAL	800QX4249 • **Value $33**
20	**Season's Greetings**	Glass • N/A	450QX2199 • **Value $22**

GENERAL KEEPSAKE

	Price Paid	Value of My Collection
1.		
2.		
3.		
4.		
5.		
6.		
7.		
8.		
9.		
10.		
11.		
12.		
13.		
14.		
15.		
16.		
17.		
18.		
19.		
20.		

PENCIL TOTALS

VALUE GUIDE — HALLMARK KEEPSAKE ORNAMENTS

(1) SHIRT TALES™
Glass • N/A
450QX2149 • **Value $24**

(2) Sister
Glass • N/A
450QX2069 • **Value $22**

(3) Skating Rabbit
Handcrafted • N/A
800QX4097 • **Value $50**

(4) Ski Lift Santa
Handcrafted/Brass • N/A
800QX4187 • **Value $70**

(5) Skiing Fox
Handcrafted • DLEE
800QX4207 • **Value $38**

(6) Sneaker Mouse
Handcrafted • SEAL
450QX4009 • **Value $40**

(7) Son
Satin • N/A
450QX2029 • **Value $36**

(8) Star of Peace
Acrylic • SEAL
600QX3047 • **Value $18**

(9) Teacher
Acrylic • N/A
600QX3049 • **Value $12**

(10) Teacher
Glass • N/A
450QX2249 • **Value $16**

(11) Tenth Christmas Together
Ceramic • N/A
650QX4307 • **Value $23**

(12) Time for Sharing
Acrylic • N/A
600QX3077 • **Value $37**

(13) Tin Rocking Horse
Pressed Tin • SICK
650QX4149 • **Value $50**

(14) Unicorn
Porcelain • N/A
1000QX4267 • **Value $63**

(15) The Wise Men
Glass • N/A
450QX2207 • **Value $55**

(16) Baby's First Christmas
Classic Shape • N/A
1600QMB9039 • **Value $95**

(17) Friendship
Classic Shape • N/A
1600QMB9047 • **Value $115**

(18) Nativity
Classic Shape • N/A
1600QMB9049 • **Value $125**

(19) Twelve Days of Christmas
Handcrafted • SEAL
1500QMB4159 • **Value $90**

GENERAL KEEPSAKE

	Price Paid	Value of My Collection
1.		
2.		
3.		
4.		
5.		
6.		
7.		
8.		
9.		
10.		
11.		
12.		
13.		
14.		
15.		

MUSICAL ORNAMENTS

16.		
17.		
18.		
19.		

PENCIL TOTALS

1983 Collection

1982

The 1982 collection was highlighted by the always-popular creations of Hallmark artist, Donna Lee. Among her sought-after 1982 designs were "Baroque Angel," "Pinecone Home" and "Raccoon Surprises." Overall, there were 104 Keepsake ornaments issued in 1982. See collectible series section for more 1982 ornaments.

(1)
25th Christmas Together
Glass • N/A
450QX2116 • **Value $17**

1982

(2)
50th Christmas Together
Glass • N/A
450QX2123 • **Value $18**

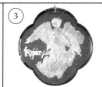

(3)
Angel
Acrylic • N/A
550QX3096 • **Value $36**

(4)
Angel Chimes
Chrome-Plated Brass • N/A
550QX5026 • **Value $30**

(5)
Arctic Penquin
Acrylic • N/A
400QX3003 • **Value $18**

(6)
Baby's First Christmas
Acrylic • SEAL
550QX3023 • **Value $39**

(7)
Baby's First Christmas
Handcrafted • SEAL
1300QX4553 • **Value $47**

(8)
Baby's First Christmas – Boy
Satin • N/A
450QX2163 • **Value $24**

(9)
Baby's First Christmas – Girl
Satin • N/A
450QX2073 • **Value $27**

(10)
Baby's First Christmas – Photoholder
Acrylic • N/A
650QX3126 • **Value $26**

(11)
Baroque Angel
Handcrafted/Brass • DLEE
1500QX4566 • **Value $170**

(12)
Bell Chimes
Chrome-Plated Brass • SICK
550QX4943 • **Value $28**

(13)
Betsey Clark
Cameo • N/A
850QX3056 • **Value $25**

(14)
Brass Bell
Brass • DLEE
1200QX4606 • **Value $25**

(15)
Christmas Angel
Glass • N/A
450QX2206 • **Value $25**

(16)
Christmas Fantasy
(re-issued from 1981)
Handcrafted/Brass • N/A
1300QX1554 • **Value $89**

(17)
Christmas Kitten
(re-issued in 1983)
Handcrafted • N/A
400QX4543 • **Value $35**

GENERAL KEEPSAKE

	Price Paid	Value of My Collection
1.		
2.		
3.		
4.		
5.		
6.		
7.		
8.		
9.		
10.		
11.		
12.		
13.		
14.		
15.		
16.		
17.		
PENCIL TOTALS		

VALUE GUIDE — HALLMARK KEEPSAKE ORNAMENTS

① Christmas Magic
Acrylic • N/A
550QX3113 • **Value $28**

② Christmas Memories – Photoholder
Acrylic • SICK
650QX3116 • **Value $23**

③ Christmas Owl (re-issued from 1980)
Handcrafted • N/A
400QX1314 • **Value $28**

④ Christmas Sleigh
Acrylic • N/A
550QX3093 • **Value $75**

⑤ Cloisonné Angel
Cloisonné • N/A
1200QX1454 • **Value $95**

⑥ Cookie Mouse
Handcrafted • SICK
450QX4546 • **Value $55**

⑦ Cowboy Snowman
Handcrafted • N/A
800QX4806 • **Value $52**

⑧ Currier & Ives
Glass • N/A
450QX2013 • **Value $24**

⑨ Cycling Santa (re-issued in 1983)
Handcrafted • N/A
2000QX4355 • **Value $145**

⑩ Daughter
Satin • N/A
450QX2046 • **Value $35**

⑪ DISNEY
Satin • N/A
450QX2173 • **Value $37**

⑫ THE DIVINE MISS PIGGY™ (re-issued from 1981)
Handcrafted • FRAN
1200QX4255 • **Value $90**

⑬ Dove Love
Acrylic • SICK
450QX4623 • **Value $53**

⑭ Elfin Artist
Handcrafted • SICK
900QX4573 • **Value $49**

⑮ Embroidered Tree
Fabric • N/A
650QX4946 • **Value $38**

⑯ Father
Satin • SICK
450QX2056 • **Value $18**

⑰ First Christmas Together
Acrylic • SEAL
550QX3026 • **Value $18**

⑱ First Christmas Together
Cameo • N/A
850QX3066 • **Value $45**

⑲ First Christmas Together
Glass • N/A
450QX2113 • **Value $38**

⑳ First Christmas Together – Locket
Brass • SEAL
1500QX4563 • **Value $29**

GENERAL KEEPSAKE	Price Paid	Value of My Collection
1.		
2.		
3.		
4.		
5.		
6.		
7.		
8.		
9.		
10.		
11.		
12.		
13.		
14.		
15.		
16.		
17.		
18.		
19.		
20.		
PENCIL TOTALS		

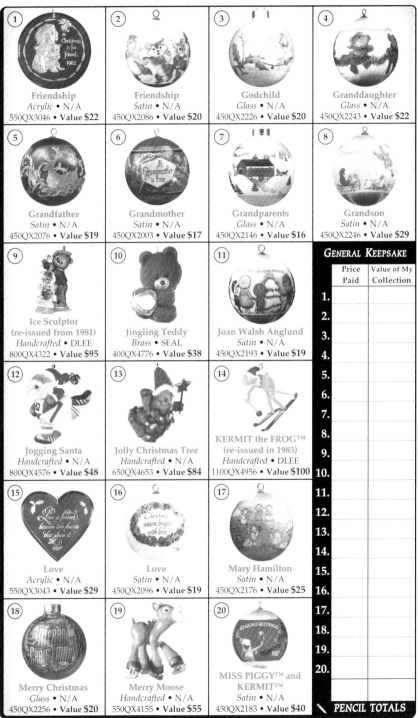

1
Friendship
Acrylic • N/A
550QX3046 • **Value $22**

2
Friendship
Satin • N/A
450QX2086 • **Value $20**

3
Godchild
Glass • N/A
450QX2226 • **Value $20**

4
Granddaughter
Glass • N/A
450QX2243 • **Value $22**

5
Grandfather
Satin • N/A
450QX2076 • **Value $19**

6
Grandmother
Satin • N/A
450QX2003 • **Value $17**

7
Grandparents
Glass • N/A
450QX2146 • **Value $16**

8
Grandson
Satin • N/A
450QX2246 • **Value $29**

9
Ice Sculptor
(re-issued from 1981)
Handcrafted • DLEE
800QX4322 • **Value $95**

10
Jingling Teddy
Brass • SEAL
400QX4776 • **Value $38**

11
Joan Walsh Anglund
Satin • N/A
450QX2193 • **Value $19**

12
Jogging Santa
Handcrafted • N/A
800QX4576 • **Value $48**

13
Jolly Christmas Tree
Handcrafted • N/A
650QX4653 • **Value $84**

14
KERMIT the FROG™
(re-issued in 1983)
Handcrafted • DLEE
1100QX4956 • **Value $100**

15
Love
Acrylic • N/A
550QX3043 • **Value $29**

16
Love
Satin • N/A
450QX2096 • **Value $19**

17
Mary Hamilton
Satin • N/A
450QX2176 • **Value $25**

18
Merry Christmas
Glass • N/A
450QX2256 • **Value $20**

19
Merry Moose
Handcrafted • N/A
550QX4155 • **Value $55**

20
MISS PIGGY™ and
KERMIT™
Satin • N/A
450QX2183 • **Value $40**

GENERAL KEEPSAKE

	Price Paid	Value of My Collection
1.		
2.		
3.		
4.		
5.		
6.		
7.		
8.		
9.		
10.		
11.		
12.		
13.		
14.		
15.		
16.		
17.		
18.		
19.		
20.		
PENCIL TOTALS		

1982

1 Moments of Love
Satin • N/A
450QX2093 • **Value $17**

2 Mother
Glass • N/A
450QX2053 • **Value $18**

3 Mother and Dad
Glass • N/A
450QX2223 • **Value $16**

4 MUPPETS™ Party
Satin • N/A
450QX2186 • **Value $40**

5 Musical Angel
Handcrafted • DLEE
550QX4596 • **Value $70**

6 Nativity
Acrylic • N/A
450QX3083 • **Value $48**

7 New Home
Satin • N/A
450QX2126 • **Value $19**

8 Norman Rockwell
Satin • N/A
450QX2023 • **Value $28**

9 Old Fashioned Christmas
Glass • N/A
450QX2276 • **Value $60**

10 Old World Angels
Glass • N/A
450QX2263 • **Value $23**

11 Patterns of Christmas
Glass • N/A
450QX2266 • **Value $19**

12 PEANUTS®
Satin • N/A
450QX2006 • **Value $37**

13 Peeking Elf
Handcrafted • N/A
650QX4195 • **Value $34**

14 Perky Penguin
(re-issued from 1981)
Handcrafted • N/A
400QX4095 • **Value $58**

15 Pinecone Home
Handcrafted • DLEE
800QX4613 • **Value $170**

16 Raccoon Surprises
Handcrafted • DLEE
900QX4793 • **Value $150**

17 Santa
Glass • BLAC
450QX2216 • **Value $19**

18 Santa and Reindeer
Handcrafted/Brass • SICK
900QX4676 • **Value $47**

19 Santa Bell
Porcelain • N/A
1500QX1487 • **Value $60**

20 Santa's Flight
Acrylic • N/A
450QX3086 • **Value $46**

General Keepsake

	Price Paid	Value of My Collection
1.		
2.		
3.		
4.		
5.		
6.		
7.		
8.		
9.		
10.		
11.		
12.		
13.		
14.		
15.		
16.		
17.		
18.		
19.		
20.		
PENCIL TOTALS		

VALUE GUIDE — HALLMARK KEEPSAKE ORNAMENTS

(1) **Santa's Sleigh** *Brass* • SEAL 900QX4786 • **Value $31**	**(2)** **Santa's Workshop (re-issued in 1983)** *Handcrafted* • DLEE 1000QX4503 • **Value $78**
(3) **Season for Caring** *Satin* • N/A 450QX2213 • **Value $22**	**(4)** **Sister** *Glass* • N/A 450QX2083 • **Value $26**

(5) **Snowy Seal** *Acrylic* • N/A 400QX3006 • **Value $19**

(6) **Son** *Satin* • N/A 450QX2043 • **Value $26**

(7) **The Spirit of Christmas** *Handcrafted* • SICK 1000QX4526 • **Value $135**

(8) **Stained Glass** *Glass* • N/A 450QX2283 • **Value $22**

(9) **Teacher** *Acrylic* • SICK 650QX3123 • **Value $17**

(10) **Teacher** *Glass* • N/A 450QX2143 • **Value $13**

(11) **Teacher – Apple** *Acrylic* • SEAL 550QX3016 • **Value $13**

(12) **Three Kings** *Cameo* • BLAC 850QX3073 • **Value $25**

(13) **Tin Soldier** *Pressed Tin* • SICK 650QX4836 • **Value $49**

(14) **Tree Chimes** *Stamped Brass* • SEAL 550QX4846 • **Value $50**

(15) **Twelve Days of Christmas** *Glass* • N/A 450QX2036 • **Value $24**

(16) **Dimensional Ornament** *Dimensional Brass* • N/A ($3.50) No stock # • **Value $37**

(17) **Baby's First Christmas** *Classic Shape* • N/A 1600QMB9007 • **Value $85**

(18) **First Christmas Together** *Classic Shape* • N/A 1600QMB9019 • **Value $80**

(19) **Love** *Classic Shape* • N/A 1600QMB9009 • **Value $85**

GENERAL KEEPSAKE

	Price Paid	Value of My Collection
1.		
2.		
3.		
4.		
5.		
6.		
7.		
8.		
9.		
10.		
11.		
12.		
13.		
14.		
15.		

EARLY PROMOTIONAL ORNAMENTS

16.		

MUSICAL ORNAMENTS

17.		
18.		
19.		

PENCIL TOTALS

1982

1982 Collection   189

1981

Santa Claus was well-represented in Hallmark's collection for 1981 with several coveted designs, including the handcrafted ornaments "Sailing Santa" and "Space Santa" as well as the ball ornament "Traditional (Black Santa)." The 1981 line featured 99 Keepsake ornaments. See collectible series section for more 1981 ornaments.

1
25th Christmas Together
Acrylic • N/A
550QX5042 • **Value $23**

2
25th Christmas Together
Glass • N/A
450QX7075 • **Value $21**

3
50th Christmas
Glass • N/A
450QX7082 • **Value $16**

4
Angel
Acrylic • N/A
400QX5095 • **Value $60**

5
Angel
Acrylic • N/A
450QX5075 • **Value $26**

6
Angel
(re-issued from 1980)
Yarn • N/A
300QX1621 • **Value $9**

7
Baby's First Christmas
Acrylic • N/A
550QX5162 • **Value $30**

8
Baby's First Christmas
Cameo • N/A
850QX5135 • **Value $19**

9
Baby's First Christmas
Handcrafted • N/A
1300QX4402 • **Value $50**

10
Baby's First Christmas – Black
Satin • N/A
450QX6022 • **Value $25**

11
Baby's First Christmas – Boy
Satin • N/A
450QX6015 • **Value $22**

12
Baby's First Christmas – Girl
Satin • N/A
450QX6002 • **Value $21**

13
Betsey Clark
Cameo • N/A
850QX5122 • **Value $27**

14
Betsey Clark
Handcrafted • FRAN
900QX4235 • **Value $75**

15
Calico Kitty
Fabric • N/A
300QX4035 • **Value $20**

16
Candyville Express
Handcrafted • N/A
750QX4182 • **Value $95**

17
Cardinal Cutie
Fabric • N/A
300QX4002 • **Value $21**

GENERAL KEEPSAKE

	Price Paid	Value of My Collection
1.		
2.		
3.		
4.		
5.		
6.		
7.		
8.		
9.		
10.		
11.		
12.		
13.		
14.		
15.		
16.		
17.		
PENCIL TOTALS		

Value Guide — Hallmark Keepsake Ornaments

1 Checking It Twice
(re-issued from 1980)
Handcrafted • BLAC
2250QX1584 • **Value $195**

2 Christmas 1981 –
Schneeberg
Satin • N/A
450QX8095 • **Value $24**

3 Christmas Dreams
Handcrafted • DLEE
1200QX4375 • **Value $215**

4 Christmas Fantasy
(re-issued in 1982)
Handcrafted • N/A
1300QX1554 • **Value $89**

5 Christmas in the Forest
Glass • N/A
450QX8135 • **Value $150**

6 Christmas Magic
Satin • N/A
450QX8102 • **Value $24**

7 Christmas Star
Acrylic • N/A
550QX5015 • **Value $26**

8 Christmas Teddy
Plush • N/A
550QX4042 • **Value $23**

9 Clothespin
Drummer Boy
Handcrafted • N/A
450QX4082 • **Value $42**

10 Daughter
Satin • N/A
450QX6075 • **Value $39**

11 DISNEY
Satin • N/A
450QX8055 • **Value $29**

12 THE DIVINE MISS
PIGGY™
(re-issued in 1982)
Handcrafted • FRAN
1200QX4255 • **Value $90**

13 Dough Angel
(re-issued from 1978)
Handcrafted • DLEE
550QX1396 • **Value $85**

14 Drummer Boy
Wood • N/A
250QX1481 • **Value $45**

15 Father
Satin • N/A
450QX6095 • **Value $17**

16 First Christmas Together
Acrylic • N/A
550QX5055 • **Value $23**

17 First Christmas Together
Glass • N/A
450QX7062 • **Value $26**

18 The Friendly Fiddler
Handcrafted • DLEE
800QX4342 • **Value $75**

19 Friendship
Acrylic • N/A
550QX5035 • **Value $30**

20 Friendship
Satin • N/A
450QX7042 • **Value $27**

1981

General Keepsake

	Price Paid	Value of My Collection
1.		
2.		
3.		
4.		
5.		
6.		
7.		
8.		
9.		
10.		
11.		
12.		
13.		
14.		
15.		
16.		
17.		
18.		
19.		
20.		
PENCIL TOTALS		

	1	2	3	4
	The Gift of Love *Glass* • N/A 450QX7055 • **Value $25**	**Gingham Dog** *Fabric* • N/A 300QX4022 • **Value $20**	**Godchild** *Satin* • N/A 450QX6035 • **Value $18**	**Granddaughter** *Satin* • N/A 450QX6055 • **Value $25**

	5	6	7	8
	Grandfather *Glass* • N/A 450QX7015 • **Value $19**	**Grandmother** *Satin* • N/A 450QX7022 • **Value $18**	**Grandparents** *Glass* • N/A 450QX7035 • **Value $18**	**Grandson** *Satin* • N/A 450QX6042 • **Value $24**

GENERAL KEEPSAKE

	Price Paid	Value of My Collection
1.		
2.		
3.		
4.		
5.		
6.		
7.		
8.		
9.		
10.		
11.		
12.		
13.		
14.		
15.		
16.		
17.		
18.		
19.		
20.		

PENCIL TOTALS

9	10	11
A Heavenly Nap **(re-issued from 1980)** *Handcrafted* • DLEE 650QX1394 • **Value $55**	**Home** *Satin* • N/A 450QX7095 • **Value $19**	**Ice Fairy** *Handcrafted* • DLEE 650QX4315 • **Value $98**

12	13	14
The Ice Sculptor **(re-issued in 1982)** *Handcrafted* • DLEE 800QX4322 • **Value $95**	**Joan Walsh Anglund** *Satin* • N/A 450QX8042 • **Value $28**	**Jolly Snowman** *Handcrafted* • N/A 350QX4075 • **Value $57**

15	16	17
KERMIT the FROG™ *Handcrafted* • FRAN 900QX4242 • **Value $95**	**Let Us Adore Him** *Glass* • N/A 450QX8115 • **Value $60**	**Love** *Acrylic* • N/A 550QX5022 • **Value $48**

18	19	20
Love and Joy **(Porcelain Chimes)** *Porcelain* • N/A 900QX4252 • **Value $92**	**Marty Links™** *Satin* • N/A 450QX8082 • **Value $19**	**Mary Hamilton** *Glass* • N/A 450QX8062 • **Value $18**

1981

1	**Merry Christmas** *Glass* • N/A 450QX8142 • **Value $24**
2	**Mother** *Satin* • N/A 450QX6082 • **Value $16**
3	**Mother and Dad** *Satin* • N/A 450QX7002 • **Value $14**
4	**Mouse** *Acrylic* • N/A 400QX5082 • **Value $24**
5	**Mr. & Mrs. Claus (set/2, re-issued from 1975)** *Handcrafted* • N/A 1200QX4485 • **Value $125**
6	**MUPPETS™** *Satin* • N/A 450QX8075 • **Value $32**
7	**PEANUTS®** *Satin* • N/A 450QX8035 • **Value $37**
8	**Peppermint Mouse** *Fabric* • N/A 300QX4015 • **Value $35**
9	**Perky Penquin (re-issued in 1982)** *Handcrafted* • N/A 350QX4095 • **Value $58**
10	**Puppy Love** *Handcrafted* • N/A 350QX4062 • **Value $37**
11	**Raccoon Tunes** *Plush* • N/A 550QX4055 • **Value $22**
12	**Sailing Santa** *Handcrafted* • N/A 1300QX4395 • **Value $275**
13	**St. Nicholas** *Pressed Tin* • SICK 550QX4462 • **Value $50**
14	**Santa (re-issued from 1980)** *Yarn* • N/A 300QX1614 • **Value $23**
15	**Santa Mobile (re-issued from 1980)** *Chrome Plate* • N/A 550QX1361 • **Value $47**
16	**Santa's Coming** *Satin* • N/A 450QX8122 • **Value $26**
17	**Santa's Surprise** *Satin* • N/A 450QX8155 • **Value $24**
18	**Shepherd Scene** *Acrylic* • N/A 550QX5002 • **Value $27**
19	**Snowflake Chimes (re-issued from 1980)** *Chrome Plate* • SICK 550QX1654 • **Value $33**
20	**Snowman** *Acrylic* • N/A 400QX5102 • **Value $24**

GENERAL KEEPSAKE

	Price Paid	Value of My Collection
1.		
2.		
3.		
4.		
5.		
6.		
7.		
8.		
9.		
10.		
11.		
12.		
13.		
14.		
15.		
16.		
17.		
18.		
19.		
20.		

PENCIL TOTALS

Value Guide – Hallmark Keepsake Ornaments

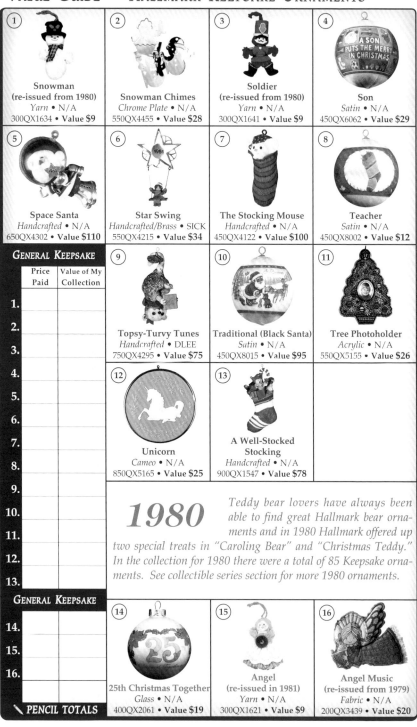

1 Snowman
(re-issued from 1980)
Yarn • N/A
300QX1634 • **Value $9**

2 Snowman Chimes
Chrome Plate • N/A
550QX4455 • **Value $28**

3 Soldier
(re-issued from 1980)
Yarn • N/A
300QX1641 • **Value $9**

4 Son
Satin • N/A
450QX6062 • **Value $29**

5 Space Santa
Handcrafted • N/A
650QX4302 • **Value $110**

6 Star Swing
Handcrafted/Brass • SICK
550QX4215 • **Value $34**

7 The Stocking Mouse
Handcrafted • N/A
450QX4122 • **Value $100**

8 Teacher
Satin • N/A
450QX8002 • **Value $12**

9 Topsy-Turvy Tunes
Handcrafted • DLEE
750QX4295 • **Value $75**

10 Traditional (Black Santa)
Satin • N/A
450QX8015 • **Value $95**

11 Tree Photoholder
Acrylic • N/A
550QX5155 • **Value $26**

12 Unicorn
Cameo • N/A
850QX5165 • **Value $25**

13 A Well-Stocked
Stocking
Handcrafted • N/A
900QX1547 • **Value $78**

14 25th Christmas Together
Glass • N/A
400QX2061 • **Value $19**

15 Angel
(re-issued in 1981)
Yarn • N/A
300QX1621 • **Value $9**

16 Angel Music
(re-issued from 1979)
Fabric • N/A
200QX3439 • **Value $20**

General Keepsake

	Price Paid	Value of My Collection
1.		
2.		
3.		
4.		
5.		
6.		
7.		
8.		
9.		
10.		
11.		
12.		
13.		

General Keepsake

14.		
15.		
16.		
PENCIL TOTALS		

1980

Teddy bear lovers have always been able to find great Hallmark bear ornaments and in 1980 Hallmark offered up two special treats in "Caroling Bear" and "Christmas Teddy." In the collection for 1980 there were a total of 85 Keepsake ornaments. See collectible series section for more 1980 ornaments.

VALUE GUIDE — HALLMARK KEEPSAKE ORNAMENTS

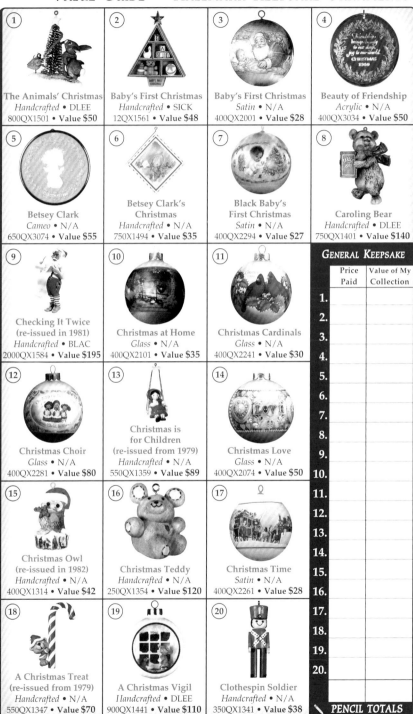

1 The Animals' Christmas
Handcrafted • DLEE
800QX1501 • **Value $50**

2 Baby's First Christmas
Handcrafted • SICK
12QX1561 • **Value $48**

3 Baby's First Christmas
Satin • N/A
400QX2001 • **Value $28**

4 Beauty of Friendship
Acrylic • N/A
400QX3034 • **Value $50**

5 Betsey Clark
Cameo • N/A
650QX3074 • **Value $55**

6 Betsey Clark's Christmas
Handcrafted • N/A
750X1494 • **Value $35**

7 Black Baby's First Christmas
Satin • N/A
400QX2294 • **Value $27**

8 Caroling Bear
Handcrafted • DLEE
750QX1401 • **Value $140**

1980

9 Checking It Twice
(re-issued in 1981)
Handcrafted • BLAC
2000QX1584 • **Value $195**

10 Christmas at Home
Glass • N/A
400QX2101 • **Value $35**

11 Christmas Cardinals
Glass • N/A
400QX2241 • **Value $30**

12 Christmas Choir
Glass • N/A
400QX2281 • **Value $80**

13 Christmas is for Children
(re-issued from 1979)
Handcrafted • N/A
550QX1359 • **Value $89**

14 Christmas Love
Glass • N/A
400QX2074 • **Value $50**

15 Christmas Owl
(re-issued in 1982)
Handcrafted • N/A
400QX1314 • **Value $42**

16 Christmas Teddy
Handcrafted • N/A
250QX1354 • **Value $120**

17 Christmas Time
Satin • N/A
400QX2261 • **Value $28**

18 A Christmas Treat
(re-issued from 1979)
Handcrafted • N/A
550QX1347 • **Value $70**

19 A Christmas Vigil
Handcrafted • DLEE
900QX1441 • **Value $110**

20 Clothespin Soldier
Handcrafted • N/A
350QX1341 • **Value $38**

GENERAL KEEPSAKE

	Price Paid	Value of My Collection
1.		
2.		
3.		
4.		
5.		
6.		
7.		
8.		
9.		
10.		
11.		
12.		
13.		
14.		
15.		
16.		
17.		
18.		
19.		
20.		
PENCIL TOTALS		

VALUE GUIDE — HALLMARK KEEPSAKE ORNAMENTS

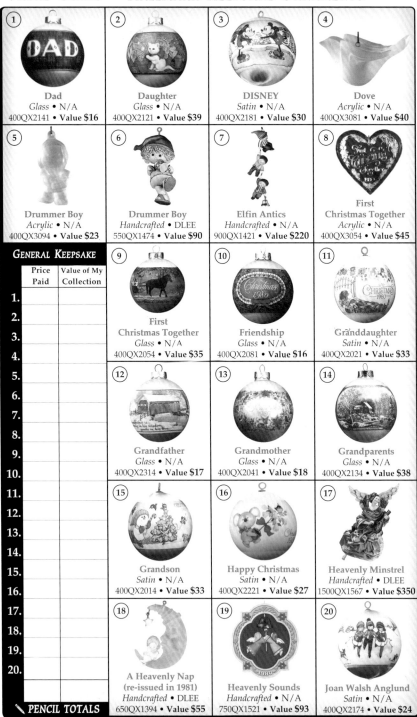

(1)
Dad
Glass • N/A
400QX2141 • **Value $16**

(2)
Daughter
Glass • N/A
400QX2121 • **Value $39**

(3)
DISNEY
Satin • N/A
400QX2181 • **Value $30**

(4)
Dove
Acrylic • N/A
400QX3081 • **Value $40**

(5)
Drummer Boy
Acrylic • N/A
400QX3094 • **Value $23**

(6)
Drummer Boy
Handcrafted • DLEE
550QX1474 • **Value $90**

(7)
Elfin Antics
Handcrafted • N/A
900QX1421 • **Value $220**

(8)
First
Christmas Together
Acrylic • N/A
400QX3054 • **Value $45**

GENERAL KEEPSAKE

	Price Paid	Value of My Collection
1.		
2.		
3.		
4.		
5.		
6.		
7.		
8.		
9.		
10.		
11.		
12.		
13.		
14.		
15.		
16.		
17.		
18.		
19.		
20.		

✎ **PENCIL TOTALS**

(9)
First
Christmas Together
Glass • N/A
400QX2054 • **Value $35**

(10)
Friendship
Glass • N/A
400QX2081 • **Value $16**

(11)
Granddaughter
Satin • N/A
400QX2021 • **Value $33**

(12)
Grandfather
Glass • N/A
400QX2314 • **Value $17**

(13)
Grandmother
Glass • N/A
400QX2041 • **Value $18**

(14)
Grandparents
Glass • N/A
400QX2134 • **Value $38**

(15)
Grandson
Satin • N/A
400QX2014 • **Value $33**

(16)
Happy Christmas
Satin • N/A
400QX2221 • **Value $27**

(17)
Heavenly Minstrel
Handcrafted • DLEE
1500QX1567 • **Value $350**

(18)
A Heavenly Nap
(re-issued in 1981)
Handcrafted • DLEE
650QX1394 • **Value $55**

(19)
Heavenly Sounds
Handcrafted • N/A
750QX1521 • **Value $93**

(20)
Joan Walsh Anglund
Satin • N/A
400QX2174 • **Value $24**

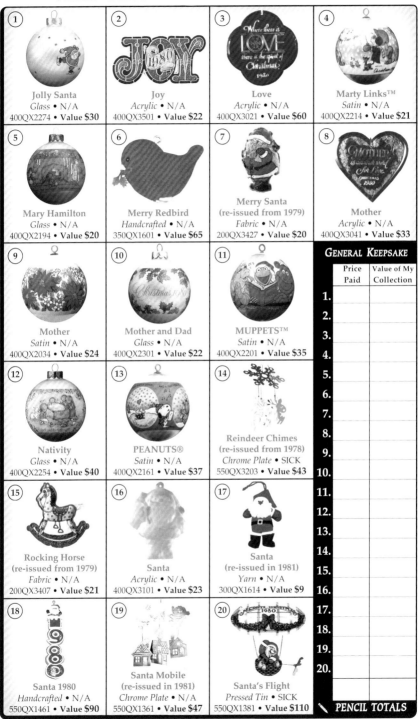

(1) Jolly Santa
Glass • N/A
400QX2274 • **Value $30**

(2) Joy
Acrylic • N/A
400QX3501 • **Value $22**

(3) Love
Acrylic • N/A
400QX3021 • **Value $60**

(4) Marty Links™
Satin • N/A
400QX2214 • **Value $21**

(5) Mary Hamilton
Glass • N/A
400QX2194 • **Value $20**

(6) Merry Redbird
Handcrafted • N/A
350QX1601 • **Value $65**

(7) Merry Santa
(re-issued from 1979)
Fabric • N/A
200QX3427 • **Value $20**

(8) Mother
Acrylic • N/A
400QX3041 • **Value $33**

(9) Mother
Satin • N/A
400QX2034 • **Value $24**

(10) Mother and Dad
Glass • N/A
400QX2301 • **Value $22**

(11) MUPPETS™
Satin • N/A
400QX2201 • **Value $35**

(12) Nativity
Glass • N/A
400QX2254 • **Value $40**

(13) PEANUTS®
Satin • N/A
400QX2161 • **Value $37**

(14) Reindeer Chimes
(re-issued from 1978)
Chrome Plate • SICK
550QX3203 • **Value $43**

(15) Rocking Horse
(re-issued from 1979)
Fabric • N/A
200QX3407 • **Value $21**

(16) Santa
Acrylic • N/A
400QX3101 • **Value $23**

(17) Santa
(re-issued in 1981)
Yarn • N/A
300QX1614 • **Value $9**

(18) Santa 1980
Handcrafted • N/A
550QX1461 • **Value $90**

(19) Santa Mobile
(re-issued in 1981)
Chrome Plate • N/A
550QX1361 • **Value $47**

(20) Santa's Flight
Pressed Tin • SICK
550QX1381 • **Value $110**

GENERAL KEEPSAKE	Price Paid	Value of My Collection
1.		
2.		
3.		
4.		
5.		
6.		
7.		
8.		
9.		
10.		
11.		
12.		
13.		
14.		
15.		
16.		
17.		
18.		
19.		
20.		
PENCIL TOTALS		

1980

Value Guide – Hallmark Keepsake Ornaments

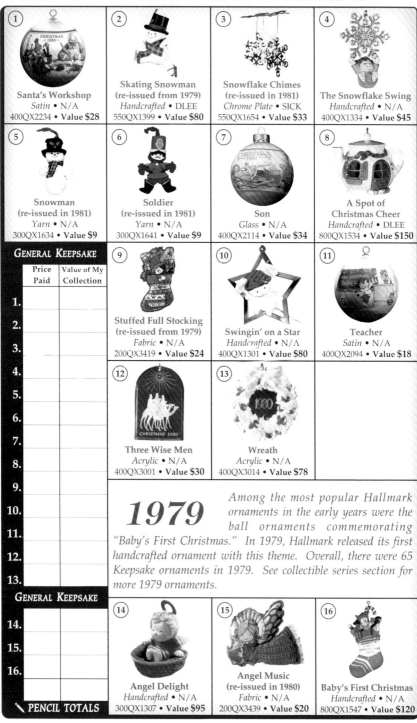

1
Santa's Workshop
Satin • N/A
400QX2234 • **Value $28**

2
Skating Snowman
(re-issued from 1979)
Handcrafted • DLEE
550QX1399 • **Value $80**

3
Snowflake Chimes
(re-issued in 1981)
Chrome Plate • SICK
550QX1654 • **Value $33**

4
The Snowflake Swing
Handcrafted • N/A
400QX1334 • **Value $45**

5
Snowman
(re-issued in 1981)
Yarn • N/A
300QX1634 • **Value $9**

6
Soldier
(re-issued in 1981)
Yarn • N/A
300QX1641 • **Value $9**

7
Son
Glass • N/A
400QX2114 • **Value $34**

8
A Spot of
Christmas Cheer
Handcrafted • DLEE
800QX1534 • **Value $150**

9
Stuffed Full Stocking
(re-issued from 1979)
Fabric • N/A
200QX3419 • **Value $24**

10
Swingin' on a Star
Handcrafted • N/Λ
400QX1301 • **Value $80**

11
Teacher
Satin • N/A
400QX2094 • **Value $18**

12
Three Wise Men
Acrylic • N/A
400QX3001 • **Value $30**

13
Wreath
Acrylic • N/A
400QX3014 • **Value $78**

1979

Among the most popular Hallmark ornaments in the early years were the ball ornaments commemorating "Baby's First Christmas." In 1979, Hallmark released its first handcrafted ornament with this theme. Overall, there were 65 Keepsake ornaments in 1979. See collectible series section for more 1979 ornaments.

14
Angel Delight
Handcrafted • N/A
300QX1307 • **Value $95**

15
Angel Music
(re-issued in 1980)
Fabric • N/A
200QX3439 • **Value $20**

16
Baby's First Christmas
Handcrafted • N/A
800QX1547 • **Value $120**

General Keepsake

	Price Paid	Value of My Collection
1.		
2.		
3.		
4.		
5.		
6.		
7.		
8.		
9.		
10.		
11.		
12.		
13.		

General Keepsake

14.		
15.		
16.		

PENCIL TOTALS

Value Guide — Hallmark Keepsake Ornaments

1. Baby's First Christmas
Satin • N/A
350QX2087 • **Value $30**

2. Behold the Star
Satin • N/A
350QX2559 • **Value $38**

3. Black Angel
Glass • BLAC
350QX2079 • **Value $23**

4. Christmas Angel
Acrylic • N/A
350QX3007 • **Value $90**

5. Christmas Cheer
Acrylic • N/A
350QX3039 • **Value $80**

6. Christmas Chickadees
Glass • N/A
350QX2047 • **Value $30**

7. Christmas Collage
Glass • N/A
350QX2579 • **Value $35**

8. Christmas Eve Surprise
Handcrafted • N/A
650QX1579 • **Value $65**

9. Christmas Heart
Handcrafted • SICK
650QX1407 • **Value $100**

**10. Christmas is
for Children**
(re-issued in 1980)
Handcrafted • N/A
500QX1359 • **Value $89**

11. Christmas Traditions
Glass • SICK
350QX2539 • **Value $35**

12. A Christmas Treat
(re-issued in 1980)
Handcrafted • N/A
500QX1347 • **Value $70**

13. Christmas Tree
Acrylic • N/A
350QX3027 • **Value $70**

14. The Downhill Run
Handcrafted • DLEE
650QX1459 • **Value $165**

15. The Drummer Boy
Handcrafted • N/A
800QX1439 • **Value $120**

16. Friendship
Glass • N/A
350QX2039 • **Value $24**

17. Granddaughter
Satin • N/A
350QX2119 • **Value $33**

18. Grandmother
Glass • N/A
350QX2527 • **Value $22**

19. Grandson
Satin • N/A
350QX2107 • **Value $33**

20. Green Boy
(re-issued from 1978)
Yarn • N/A
200QX1231 • **Value $24**

1979

General Keepsake

	Price Paid	Value of My Collection
1.		
2.		
3.		
4.		
5.		
6.		
7.		
8.		
9.		
10.		
11.		
12.		
13.		
14.		
15.		
16.		
17.		
18.		
19.		
20.		
PENCIL TOTALS		

Value Guide — Hallmark Keepsake Ornaments

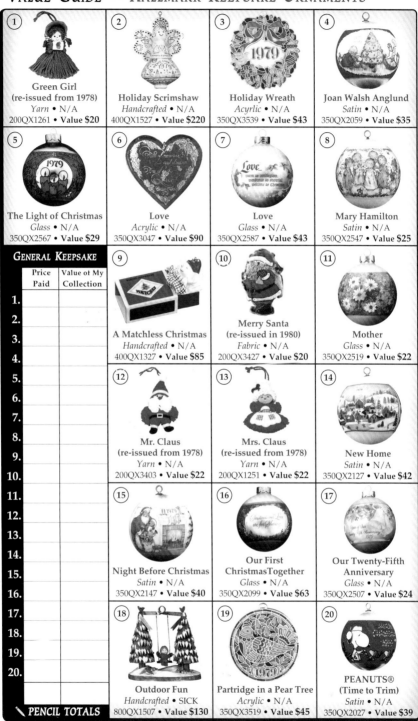

1 Green Girl
(re-issued from 1978)
Yarn • N/A
200QX1261 • **Value $20**

2 Holiday Scrimshaw
Handcrafted • N/A
400QX1527 • **Value $220**

3 Holiday Wreath
Acrylic • N/A
350QX3539 • **Value $43**

4 Joan Walsh Anglund
Satin • N/A
350QX2059 • **Value $35**

5 The Light of Christmas
Glass • N/A
350QX2567 • **Value $29**

6 Love
Acrylic • N/A
350QX3047 • **Value $90**

7 Love
Glass • N/A
350QX2587 • **Value $43**

8 Mary Hamilton
Satin • N/A
350QX2547 • **Value $25**

General Keepsake

	Price Paid	Value of My Collection
1.		
2.		
3.		
4.		
5.		
6.		
7.		
8.		
9.		
10.		
11.		
12.		
13.		
14.		
15.		
16.		
17.		
18.		
19.		
20.		
\ PENCIL TOTALS		

9 A Matchless Christmas
Handcrafted • N/A
400QX1327 • **Value $85**

10 Merry Santa
(re-issued in 1980)
Fabric • N/A
200QX3427 • **Value $20**

11 Mother
Glass • N/A
350QX2519 • **Value $22**

12 Mr. Claus
(re-issued from 1978)
Yarn • N/A
200QX3403 • **Value $22**

13 Mrs. Claus
(re-issued from 1978)
Yarn • N/A
200QX1251 • **Value $22**

14 New Home
Satin • N/A
350QX2127 • **Value $42**

15 Night Before Christmas
Satin • N/A
350QX2147 • **Value $40**

16 Our First
Christmas Together
Glass • N/A
350QX2099 • **Value $63**

17 Our Twenty-Fifth
Anniversary
Glass • N/A
350QX2507 • **Value $24**

18 Outdoor Fun
Handcrafted • SICK
800QX1507 • **Value $130**

19 Partridge in a Pear Tree
Acrylic • N/A
350QX3519 • **Value $45**

20 PEANUTS®
(Time to Trim)
Satin • N/A
350QX2027 • **Value $39**

1 Raccoon
(re-issued from 1978)
Handcrafted • DLEE
650QX1423 • **Value $90**

2 Ready for Christmas
Handcrafted • DLEE
650QX1339 • **Value $140**

3 Reindeer Chimes
(re-issued from 1978)
Chrome Plate • SICK
450QX3203 • **Value $43**

4 Rocking Horse
(re-issued in 1980)
Fabric • N/A
200QX3407 • **Value $21**

5 Santa
(re-issued from 1978)
Handcrafted • N/A
300QX1356 • **Value $60**

6 Santa's Here
Handcrafted • SICK
500QX1387 • **Value $70**

7 The Skating Snowman
(re-issued in 1980)
Handcrafted • DLEE
500QX1399 • **Value $80**

8 Snowflake
Acrylic • N/A
350QX3019 • **Value $38**

9 Spencer® Sparrow, Esq.
Satin • N/A
350QX2007 • **Value $42**

10 Star Chimes
Chrome Plate • SICK
450QX1379 • **Value $68**

11 Star Over Bethlehem
Acrylic • SICK
350QX3527 • **Value $70**

12 Stuffed Full Stocking
(re-issued in 1980)
Fabric • N/A
200QX3419 • **Value $24**

13 Teacher
Satin • N/A
350QX2139 • **Value $15**

14 Winnie-the-Pooh
Satin • N/A
350QX2067 • **Value $48**

15 Words of Christmas
Acrylic • N/A
350QX3507 • **Value $80**

1979

GENERAL KEEPSAKE		
	Price Paid	Value of My Collection
1.		
2.		
3.		
4.		
5.		
6.		
7.		
8.		
9.		
10.		
11.		
12.		
13.		
14.		
15.		
PENCIL TOTALS		

1978

In the 6th year of Hallmark ornaments, several unique handcrafted ornaments proved to be the most popular, including "Angels," "Animal Home," "Calico Mouse," "Red Cardinal" and "Schneeberg Bell." The 1978 collection featured 54 Keepsake ornaments. See collectible series section for more 1978 ornaments.

25th Christmas Together
Glass • N/A
350QX2696 • **Value $30**

Angel
Acrylic • N/A
350QX3543 • **Value $49**

Angel
(re-issued in 1981)
Handcrafted • DLEE
450QX1396 • **Value $85**

Angels
Handcrafted • N/A
800QX1503 • **Value $350**

Animal Home
Handcrafted • DLEE
600QX1496 • **Value $180**

GENERAL KEEPSAKE

	Price Paid	Value of My Collection
1.		
2.		
3.		
4.		
5.		
6.		
7.		
8.		
9.		
10.		
11.		
12.		
13.		
14.		
15.		
16.		
17.		

PENCIL TOTALS

Baby's First Christmas
Satin • N/A
350QX2003 • **Value $80**

Calico Mouse
Handcrafted • N/A
450QX1376 • **Value $175**

Candle
Acrylic • N/A
350QX3576 • **Value $88**

DISNEY
Satin • N/A
350QX2076 • **Value $120**

Dove
Acrylic •PALM
350QX3103 • **Value $125**

Dove
Handcrafted • SICK
450QX1903 • **Value $85**

Drummer Boy
Glass • N/A
350QX2523 • **Value $33**

Drummer Boy
Handcrafted • N/A
250QX1363 • **Value $65**

First Christmas Together
Satin • N/A
350QX2183 • **Value $42**

For Your New Home
Satin • N/A
350QX2176 • **Value $24**

Granddaughter
Satin • N/A
350QX2163 • **Value $44**

Grandmother
Satin • N/A
350QX2676 • **Value $40**

Value Guide — Hallmark Keepsake Ornaments

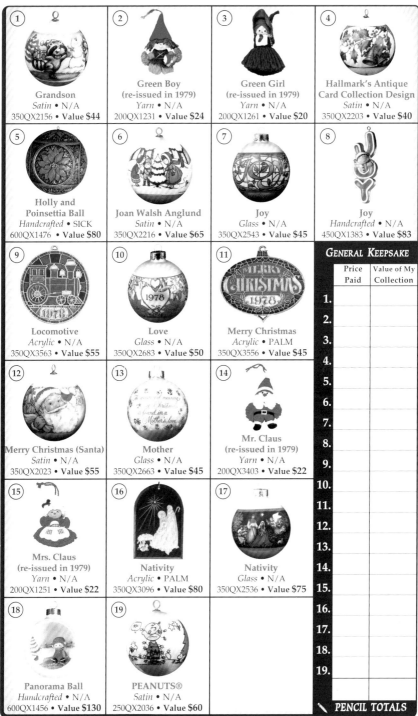

(1) Grandson
Satin • N/A
350QX2156 • **Value $44**

(2) Green Boy
(re-issued in 1979)
Yarn • N/A
200QX1231 • **Value $24**

(3) Green Girl
(re-issued in 1979)
Yarn • N/A
200QX1261 • **Value $20**

(4) Hallmark's Antique Card Collection Design
Satin • N/A
350QX2203 • **Value $40**

(5) Holly and Poinsettia Ball
Handcrafted • SICK
600QX1476 • **Value $80**

(6) Joan Walsh Anglund
Satin • N/A
350QX2216 • **Value $65**

(7) Joy
Glass • N/A
350QX2543 • **Value $45**

(8) Joy
Handcrafted • N/A
450QX1383 • **Value $83**

(9) Locomotive
Acrylic • N/A
350QX3563 • **Value $55**

(10) Love
Glass • N/A
350QX2683 • **Value $50**

(11) Merry Christmas
Acrylic • PALM
350QX3556 • **Value $45**

(12) Merry Christmas (Santa)
Satin • N/A
350QX2023 • **Value $55**

(13) Mother
Glass • N/A
350QX2663 • **Value $45**

(14) Mr. Claus
(re-issued in 1979)
Yarn • N/A
200QX3403 • **Value $22**

(15) Mrs. Claus
(re-issued in 1979)
Yarn • N/A
200QX1251 • **Value $22**

(16) Nativity
Acrylic • PALM
350QX3096 • **Value $80**

(17) Nativity
Glass • N/A
350QX2536 • **Value $75**

(18) Panorama Ball
Handcrafted • N/A
600QX1456 • **Value $130**

(19) PEANUTS®
Satin • N/A
250QX2036 • **Value $60**

1978

GENERAL KEEPSAKE		
	Price Paid	Value of My Collection
1.		
2.		
3.		
4.		
5.		
6.		
7.		
8.		
9.		
10.		
11.		
12.		
13.		
14.		
15.		
16.		
17.		
18.		
19.		
PENCIL TOTALS		

(1) PEANUTS®
Satin • N/A
250QX2043 • **Value $65**

(2) PEANUTS®
Satin • N/A
350QX2056 • **Value $70**

(3) PEANUTS®
Satin • N/A
350QX2063 • **Value $63**

(4) Praying Angel
Handcrafted • DLEE
250QX1343 • **Value $90**

(5) The Quail
Glass • N/A
350QX2516 • **Value $40**

(6) Red Cardinal
Handcrafted • UNRU
450QX1443 • **Value $170**

(7) Reindeer Chimes
(re-issued in 1979 and 1980)
Chrome-Plated Brass • SICK
450QX3203 • **Value $43**

(8) Rocking Horse
Handcrafted • N/A
600QX1483 • **Value $90**

GENERAL KEEPSAKE

	Price Paid	Value of My Collection
1.		
2.		
3.		
4.		
5.		
6.		
7.		
8.		
9.		
10.		
11.		
12.		
13.		
14.		
15.		

PENCIL TOTALS

(9) Santa
Acrylic • PALM
350QX3076 • **Value $75**

(10) Santa
(re-issued in 1979)
Handcrafted • N/A
250QX1356 • **Value $80**

(11) Schneeberg Bell
Handcrafted • N/A
800QX1523 • **Value $175**

(12) Skating Raccoon
(re-issued in 1979)
Handcrafted • DLEE
600QX1423 • **Value $90**

(13) Snowflake
Acrylic • PALM
350QX3083 • **Value $65**

(14) Spencer® Sparrow, Esq.
Satin • N/A
350QX2196 • **Value $50**

(15) Yesterday's Toys
Glass • N/A
350QX2503 • **Value $29**

1977

The 1977 collection was highlighted by a group of handcrafted ornaments designed to have a antique wooden appearance. Called the "Nostalgia Collection," these ornaments were "Angel," "Antique Car," "Nativity," and "Toys." In 1977, there were 53 Keepsake ornaments. See collectible series section for more 1977 ornaments.

1
Angel
Cloth • N/A
175QX2202 • **Value $48**

2
Angel
Handcrafted • DLEE
500QX1822 • **Value $110**

3
Angel
Handcrafted • N/A
600QX1722 • **Value $120**

4
Antique Car
Handcrafted • SICK
500QX1802 • **Value $60**

5
Baby's First Christmas
Satin • N/A
350QX1315 • **Value $80**

6
Bell
Acrylic • SICK
350QX2002 • **Value $50**

7
Bell
Glass • N/A
350QX1542 • **Value $35**

8
Bellringer
Handcrafted • N/A
600QX1922 • **Value $60**

9
Candle
Acrylic • N/A
350QX2035 • **Value $62**

10
Charmers
Glass • N/A
350QX1535 • **Value $58**

11
Christmas Mouse
Satin • N/A
350QX1342 • **Value $55**

12
Currier & Ives
Satin • N/A
350QX1302 • **Value $53**

13
Della Robia Wreath
Handcrafted • DLEE
450QX1935 • **Value $112**

14
Desert
Glass • N/A
250QX1595 • **Value $36**

15
DISNEY
Satin • N/A
350QX1335 • **Value $65**

16
DISNEY (set/2)
Satin • N/A
400QX1375 • **Value $43**

17
Drummer Boy
Acrylic • N/A
350QX3122 • **Value $65**

1977

GENERAL KEEPSAKE

	Price Paid	Value of My Collection
1.		
2.		
3.		
4.		
5.		
6.		
7.		
8.		
9.		
10.		
11.		
12.		
13.		
14.		
15.		
16.		
17.		
PENCIL TOTALS		

VALUE GUIDE – HALLMARK KEEPSAKE ORNAMENTS

(1) First Christmas Together
Satin • N/A
350QX1322 • **Value $68**

(2) For Your New Home
Glass • N/A
350QX2635 • **Value $34**

(3) Granddaughter
Satin • N/A
350QX2082 • **Value $35**

(4) Grandma Moses
Glass • N/A
350QX1502 • **Value $65**

(5) Grandmother
Glass • N/A
350QX2602 • **Value $48**

(6) Grandson
Satin • N/A
350QX2095 • **Value $35**

(7) House
Handcrafted • N/A
600QX1702 • **Value $120**

(8) Jack-in-the-Box
Handcrafted • N/A
600QX1715 • **Value $110**

(9) Joy
Acrylic • N/A
350QX2015 • **Value $54**

(10) Joy
Acrylic • N/A
350QX3102 • **Value $45**

(11) Love
Glass • N/A
350QX2622 • **Value $28**

(12) Mandolin
Glass • N/A
350QX1575 • **Value $38**

(13) Mother
Glass • N/A
350QX2615 • **Value $36**

(14) Mountains
Glass • N/A
250QX1582 • **Value $30**

(15) Nativity
Handcrafted • N/A
500QX1815 • **Value $135**

(16) Norman Rockwell
Glass • N/A
350QX1515 • **Value $77**

(17) Ornaments
Glass • N/A
350QX1555 • **Value $35**

(18) Peace on Earth
Acrylic • N/A
350QX3115 • **Value $57**

(19) PEANUTS®
Glass • N/A
250QX1622 • **Value $75**

(20) PEANUTS® (set/2)
Glass • N/A
400QX1635 • **Value $85**

GENERAL KEEPSAKE

	Price Paid	Value of My Collection
1.		
2.		
3.		
4.		
5.		
6.		
7.		
8.		
9.		
10.		
11.		
12.		
13.		
14.		
15.		
16.		
17.		
18.		
19.		
20.		
PENCIL TOTALS		

1977 Collection

Value Guide — Hallmark Keepsake Ornaments

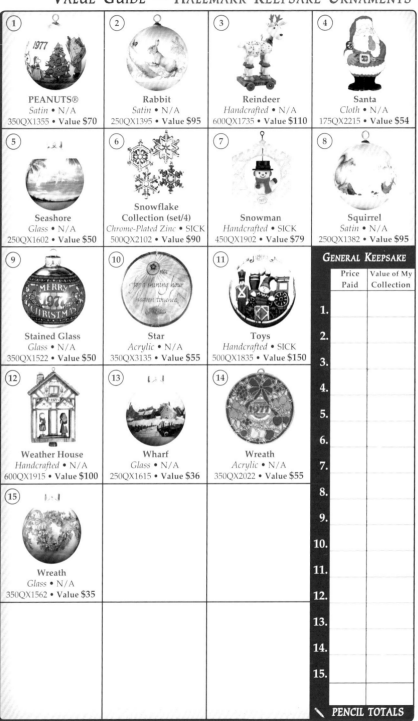

1.
PEANUTS®
Satin • N/A
350QX1355 • **Value $70**

2.
Rabbit
Satin • N/A
250QX1395 • **Value $95**

3.
Reindeer
Handcrafted • N/A
600QX1735 • **Value $110**

4.
Santa
Cloth • N/A
175QX2215 • **Value $54**

5.
Seashore
Glass • N/A
250QX1602 • **Value $50**

6.
Snowflake Collection (set/4)
Chrome-Plated Zinc • SICK
500QX2102 • **Value $90**

7.
Snowman
Handcrafted • SICK
450QX1902 • **Value $79**

8.
Squirrel
Satin • N/A
250QX1382 • **Value $95**

9.
Stained Glass
Glass • N/A
350QX1522 • **Value $50**

10.
Star
Acrylic • N/A
350QX3135 • **Value $55**

11.
Toys
Handcrafted • SICK
500QX1835 • **Value $150**

12.
Weather House
Handcrafted • N/A
600QX1915 • **Value $100**

13.
Wharf
Glass • N/A
250QX1615 • **Value $36**

14.
Wreath
Acrylic • N/A
350QX2022 • **Value $55**

15.
Wreath
Glass • N/A
350QX1562 • **Value $35**

1977

General Keepsake

	Price Paid	Value of My Collection
1.		
2.		
3.		
4.		
5.		
6.		
7.		
8.		
9.		
10.		
11.		
12.		
13.		
14.		
15.		
PENCIL TOTALS		

1976

The 1976 collection of ornaments featured popular themes such as Santa Claus, locomotives, partridges and even little drummer boys in a variety of different handcrafted styles. For the Bicentennial year, Hallmark issued a total of 39 Keepsake ornaments. See collectible series section for more 1976 ornaments.

(1) Angel
Handcrafted • N/A
300QX1761 • **Value $190**

	(2) Angel	(3) Baby's First Christmas	(4) Betsey Clark	(5) Betsey Clark (set/3)
	Handcrafted • SICK	*Satin • N/A*	*Satin • N/A*	*Satin • N/A*
	450QX1711 • **Value $175**	250QX2111 • **Value $140**	250QX2101 • **Value $58**	450QX2181 • **Value $50**

General Keepsake

	Price Paid	Value of My Collection
1.		
2.		
3.		
4.		
5.		
6.		
7.		
8.		
9.		
10.		
11.		
12.		
13.		
14.		
15.		
16.		
17.		

PENCIL TOTALS

(6)
Bicentennial '76 Commemorative
Satin • N/A
250QX2031 • **Value $55**

(7)
Bicentennial Charmers
Glass • N/A
300QX1981 • **Value $65**

(8)
Cardinals
Glass • N/A
225QX2051 • **Value $59**

(9)
Caroler
(re-issued from 1975)
Yarn • N/A
175QX1261 • **Value $20**

(10)
Charmers (set/2)
Satin • N/A
350QX2151 • **Value $80**

(11)
Chickadees
Glass • N/A
225QX2041 • **Value $60**

(12)
Colonial Children (set/2)
Glass • N/A
400QX2081 • **Value $70**

(13)
Currier & Ives
Glass • N/A
300QX1971 • **Value $45**

(14)
Currier & Ives
Satin • N/A
250QX2091 • **Value $48**

(15)
Drummer Boy
(re-issued from 1975)
Handcrafted • SICK
400QX1301 • **Value $170**

(16)
Drummer Boy
Handcrafted • N/A
500QX1841 • **Value $150**

(17)
Drummer Boy
(re-issued from 1975)
Yarn • N/A
175QX1231 • **Value $25**

Value Guide — Hallmark Keepsake Ornaments

1. Happy the Snowman (set/2) — *Satin • N/A* — 350QX2161 • **Value $50**

2. Locomotive (re-issued from 1975) — *Handcrafted • SICK* — 400QX2221 • **Value $210**

3. Marty Links™ (set/2) — *Glass • N/A* — 400QX2071 • **Value $55**

4. Mrs. Santa (re-issued from 1975) — *Yarn • N/A* — 175QX1251 • **Value $23**

5. Norman Rockwell — *Glass • N/A* — 300QX1961 • **Value $68**

6. Partridge — *Handcrafted • SICK* — 450QX1741 • **Value $180**

7. Partridge — *Handcrafted • N/A* — 500QX1831 • **Value $105**

8. Peace on Earth (re-issued from 1975) — *Handcrafted • SICK* — 400QX2231 • **Value $165**

9. Raggedy Andy™ (re-issued from 1975) — *Yarn • N/A* — 175QX1221 • **Value $45**

10. Raggedy Ann™ — *Satin • N/A* — 250X2121 • **Value $60**

11. Raggedy Ann™ (re-issued from 1975) — *Yarn • N/A* — 175QX1211 • **Value $44**

12. Reindeer — *Handcrafted • N/A* — 300QX1781 • **Value $110**

13. Rocking Horse (re-issued from 1975) — *Handcrafted • SICK* — 400QX1281 • **Value $170**

14. Rudolph and Santa — *Satin • N/A* — 250QX2131 • **Value $90**

15. Santa — *Handcrafted • N/A* — 300QX1771 • **Value $215**

16. Santa — *Handcrafted • SICK* — 450QX1721 • **Value $120**

17. Santa — *Handcrafted • N/A* — 500QX1821 • **Value $160**

18. Santa (re-issued from 1975) — *Yarn • N/A* — 175QX1241 • **Value $23**

19. Shepherd — *Handcrafted • N/A* — 300QX1751 • **Value $120**

20. Soldier — *Handcrafted • SICK* — 450QX1731 • **Value $95**

1976

General Keepsake

	Price Paid	Value of My Collection
1.		
2.		
3.		
4.		
5.		
6.		
7.		
8.		
9.		
10.		
11.		
12.		
13.		
14.		
15.		
16.		
17.		
18.		
19.		
20.		
PENCIL TOTALS		

1976 Collection 209

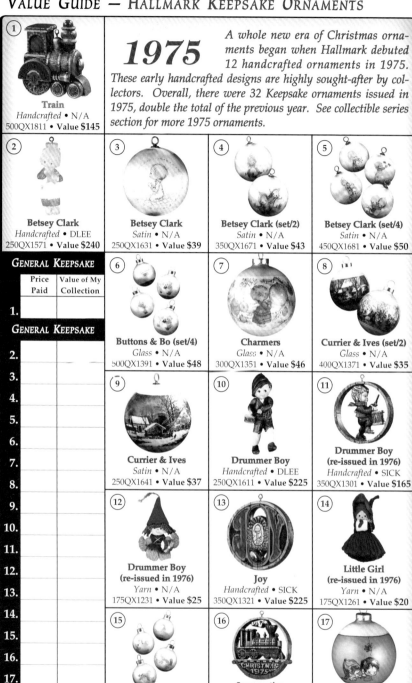

(1)

Train
Handcrafted • N/A
500QX1811 • **Value $145**

1975

A whole new era of Christmas ornaments began when Hallmark debuted 12 handcrafted ornaments in 1975. These early handcrafted designs are highly sought-after by collectors. Overall, there were 32 Keepsake ornaments issued in 1975, double the total of the previous year. See collectible series section for more 1975 ornaments.

(2)
Betsey Clark
Handcrafted • DLEE
250QX1571 • **Value $240**

(3)
Betsey Clark
Satin • N/A
250QX1631 • **Value $39**

(4)
Betsey Clark (set/2)
Satin • N/A
350QX1671 • **Value $43**

(5)
Betsey Clark (set/4)
Satin • N/A
450QX1681 • **Value $50**

(6)
Buttons & Bo (set/4)
Glass • N/A
500QX1391 • **Value $48**

(7)
Charmers
Glass • N/A
300QX1351 • **Value $46**

(8)
Currier & Ives (set/2)
Glass • N/A
400QX1371 • **Value $35**

(9)
Currier & Ives
Satin • N/A
250QX1641 • **Value $37**

(10)
Drummer Boy
Handcrafted • DLEE
250QX1611 • **Value $225**

(11)
Drummer Boy
(re-issued in 1976)
Handcrafted • SICK
350QX1301 • **Value $165**

(12)
Drummer Boy
(re-issued in 1976)
Yarn • N/A
175QX1231 • **Value $25**

(13)
Joy
Handcrafted • SICK
350QX1321 • **Value $225**

(14)
Little Girl
(re-issued in 1976)
Yarn • N/A
175QX1261 • **Value $20**

(15)
Little Miracles (set/4)
Glass • N/A
500QX1401 • **Value $40**

(16)
Locomotive
(re-issued in 1976)
Handcrafted • SICK
350QX1271 • **Value $210**

(17)
Marty Links™
Glass • N/A
300QX1361 • **Value $55**

GENERAL KEEPSAKE

	Price Paid	Value of My Collection
GENERAL KEEPSAKE		
1.		
2.		
3.		
4.		
5.		
6.		
7.		
8.		
9.		
10.		
11.		
12.		
13.		
14.		
15.		
16.		
17.		
PENCIL TOTALS		

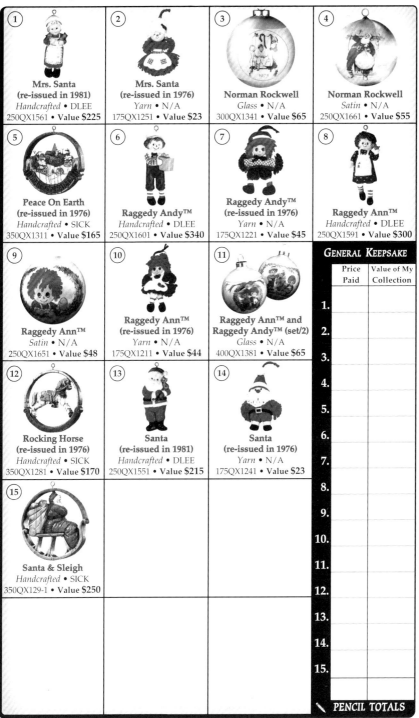

1975

(1) **Mrs. Santa** **(re-issued in 1981)** *Handcrafted* • DLEE 250QX1561 • **Value $225**	**(2)** **Mrs. Santa** **(re-issued in 1976)** *Yarn* • N/A 175QX1251 • **Value $23**	**(3)** **Norman Rockwell** *Glass* • N/A 300QX1341 • **Value $65**	**(4)** **Norman Rockwell** *Satin* • N/A 250QX1661 • **Value $55**
(5) **Peace On Earth** **(re-issued in 1976)** *Handcrafted* • SICK 350QX1311 • **Value $165**	**(6)** **Raggedy Andy™** *Handcrafted* • DLEE 250QX1601 • **Value $340**	**(7)** **Raggedy Andy™** **(re-issued in 1976)** *Yarn* • N/A 175QX1221 • **Value $45**	**(8)** **Raggedy Ann™** *Handcrafted* • DLEE 250QX1591 • **Value $300**
(9) **Raggedy Ann™** *Satin* • N/A 250QX1651 • **Value $48**	**(10)** **Raggedy Ann™** **(re-issued in 1976)** *Yarn* • N/A 175QX1211 • **Value $44**	**(11)** **Raggedy Ann™ and Raggedy Andy™ (set/2)** *Glass* • N/A 400QX1381 • **Value $65**	
(12) **Rocking Horse** **(re-issued in 1976)** *Handcrafted* • SICK 350QX1281 • **Value $170**	**(13)** **Santa** **(re-issued in 1981)** *Handcrafted* • DLEE 250QX1551 • **Value $215**	**(14)** **Santa** **(re-issued in 1976)** *Yarn* • N/A 175QX1241 • **Value $23**	
(15) **Santa & Sleigh** *Handcrafted* • SICK 350QX129-1 • **Value $250**			

GENERAL KEEPSAKE

	Price Paid	Value of My Collection
1.		
2.		
3.		
4.		
5.		
6.		
7.		
8.		
9.		
10.		
11.		
12.		
13.		
14.		
15.		
PENCIL TOTALS		

1974

In the second year of Keepsake ornaments, the collection featured popular Christmas scenes from Norman Rockwell, Betsey Clark and Currier & Ives. Of the 16 Keepsake designs or sets offered in 1974, 10 were ball ornaments and 6 were made from yarn. See collectible series section for more 1974 ornaments.

1
Angel
Glass • N/A
250QX1101 • **Value $75**

2
Angel
Yarn • N/A
150QX1031 • **Value $30**

3
Buttons & Bo (set/2)
Glass • N/A
350QX1131 • **Value $52**

4
Charmers
Glass • N/A
250QX1091 • **Value $48**

5
Currier & Ives (set/2)
Glass • N/A
350QX1121 • **Value $55**

6
Elf
Yarn • N/A
150QX1011 • **Value $25**

7
Little Miracles (set/4)
Glass • N/A
450QX1151 • **Value $55**

8
Mrs. Santa
Yarn • N/A
150QX1001 • **Value $23**

9
Norman Rockwell
Glass • N/A
250QX1061 • **Value $95**

10
Norman Rockwell
Glass • N/A
250QX1111 • **Value $85**

11
Raggedy Ann™ and Raggedy Andy™ (set/4)
Glass • N/A
450QX1141 • **Value $88**

12
Santa
Yarn • N/A
150QX1051 • **Value $25**

13
Snowgoose
Glass • N/A
250QX1071 • **Value $75**

14
Snowman
Yarn • N/A
150QX1041 • **Value $25**

15
Soldier
Yarn • N/A
150QX1021 • **Value $25**

GENERAL KEEPSAKE

	Price Paid	Value of My Collection
1.		
2.		
3.		
4.		
5.		
6.		
7.		
8.		
9.		
10.		
11.		
12.		
13.		
14.		
15.		
PENCIL TOTALS		

1973

The very first year of Hallmark Keepsake Ornaments was 1973. This year's debut offering consisted of 6 ball ornaments and 12 yarn ornaments, making a total of 18 Keepsake designs. The first Keepsake series, "Betsey Clark," began this year. See collectible series section for more 1973 ornaments.

① Angel
Yarn • N/A
125XHD785 • Value $26

② Betsey Clark
Glass • N/A
250XHD1002 • Value $110

③ Blue Girl
Yarn • N/A
125XHD852 • Value $23

④ Boy Caroler
Yarn • N/A
125XHD832 • Value $24

⑤ Choir Boy
Yarn • N/A
125XHD805 • Value $25

⑥ Christmas Is Love
Glass • N/A
250XHD1062 • Value $70

⑦ Elf
Yarn • N/A
125XHD792 • Value $26

⑧ Elves
Glass • N/A
250XHD1035 • Value $75

⑨ Green Girl
Yarn • N/A
125XHD845 • Value $26

⑩ Little Girl
Yarn • N/A
125XHD825 • Value $25

⑪ Manger Scene
Glass • N/A
250XHD1022 • Value $85

⑫ Mr. Santa
Yarn • N/A
125XHD745 • Value $25

⑬ Mrs. Santa
Yarn • N/A
125XHD752 • Value $23

⑭ Mr. Snowman
Yarn • N/A
125XHD765 • Value $25

⑮ Mrs. Snowman
Yarn • N/A
125XHD772 • Value $25

⑯ Santa with Elves
Glass • N/A
250XHD1015 • Value $80

⑰ Soldier
Yarn • N/A
100XHD812 • Value $24

General Keepsake

	Price Paid	Value of My Collection
1.		
2.		
3.		
4.		
5.		
6.		
7.		
8.		
9.		
10.		
11.		
12.		
13.		
14.		
15.		
16.		
17.		
PENCIL TOTALS		

1973

Spring Ornaments

In 1991 Hallmark created a fun new way to collect ornaments with the introduction of Spring Ornaments. Springtime themes and playful animals abound in this collection, while familiar faces like BARBIE™ and PEANUTS® characters are featured prominently There have been a total of 125 Spring Ornaments, including 36 that belong to collectible series.

Collectible Series

1
Apple Blossom Lane
(1st, 1995)
Handcrafted • FRAN
895QEO8207 • **Value $20**

2
Apple Blossom Lane
(2nd, 1996)
Handcrafted • FRAN
895QEO8084 • **Value $15**

3 NEW!
Apple Blossom Lane
(3rd & final, 1997)
Handcrafted • FRAN
895QEO8662 • **Value $8.95**

4 NEW!
BARBIE® as Rapunzel
(1st, 1997)
Handcrafted • RGRS
1495QEO8635 • **Value $14.95**

5
Peter Rabbit™
(1st, 1996)
Handcrafted • VOTR
895QEO8071 • **Value $75**

6 NEW!
Jemima Puddle-duck™
(1st, 1997)
Handcrafted • VOTR
895QEO8645 • **Value $8.95**

7
"Gathering Sunny Memories" (1st, 1994)
Porcelain • VOTR
775QEO8233 • **Value $30**

8
"Catching the Breeze"
(2nd, 1995)
Porcelain • VOTR
795QEO8219 • **Value $19**

9
"Keeping a Secret"
(3rd, 1996)
Porcelain • VOTR
795QEO8221 • **Value $15**

10 NEW!
"Sunny Sunday Best"
(4th & final, 1997)
Porcelain • VOTR
795QEO8675 • **Value $7.95**

11
Locomotive (1st, 1996)
Handcrafted • CROW
895QEO8074 • **Value $32**

12 NEW!
Colorful Coal Car
(2nd, 1997)
Handcrafted • CROW
895QEO8652 • **Value $8.95**

13
Easter Parade (1st, 1992)
Handcrafted • CROW
675QEO9301 • **Value $28**

14
Easter Parade (2nd, 1993)
Handcrafted • JLEE
675QEO8325 • **Value $19**

15
Easter Parade
(3rd & final, 1994)
Handcrafted • RHOD
675QEO8136 • **Value $18**

	Price Paid	Value of My Collection
APPLE BLOSSOM LANE		
1.		
2.		
3.		
BARBIE™ CHILDREN'S COLLECTOR SERIES		
4.		
BEATRIX POTTER™		
5.		
6.		
COLLECTOR'S PLATE		
7.		
8.		
9.		
10.		
COTTONTAIL EXPRESS		
11.		
12.		
EASTER PARADE		
13.		
14.		
15.		
PENCIL TOTALS		

1 Eggs in Sports
(1st, 1992)
Handcrafted • SIED
675QEO9341 • **Value $33**

2 Eggs in Sports
(2nd, 1993)
Handcrafted • SIED
675QEO8332 • **Value $19**

3 Eggs in Sports
(3rd & final, 1994)
Handcrafted • SIED
675QEO8133 • **Value $21**

4 Garden Club
(1st, 1995)
Handcrafted • SICK
795QEO8209 • **Value $19**

5 Garden Club
(2nd, 1996)
Handcrafted • PALM
795QEO8091 • **Value $15**

6 NEW! Garden Club
(3rd, 1997)
Handcrafted • BRIC
795QEO8665 • **Value $7.95**

7 Here Comes Easter
(1st, 1994)
Handcrafted • CROW
775QEO8093 • **Value $30**

8 Here Comes Easter
(2nd, 1995)
Handcrafted • CROW
795QEO8217 • **Value $19**

9 Here Comes Easter
(3rd, 1996)
Handcrafted • CROW
795QEO8094 • **Value $16**

10 NEW! Here Comes Easter
(4th & final, 1997)
Handcrafted • CROW
795QEO8682 • **Value $7.95**

11 Joyful Angels
(1st, 1996)
Handcrafted • LYLE
995QEO8184 • **Value $25**

12 NEW! Joyful Angels
(2nd, 1997)
Handcrafted • LYLE
1095QEO8655 • **Value $10.95**

13 NEW! 1935 Steelcraft
Streamline Velocipede
by Murray® (1st, 1997)
Die-Cast Metal • RHOD
1295QEO8632 • **Value $12.95**

14 Springtime BARBIE™
(1st, 1995)
Handcrafted • ANDR
1295QEO8069 • **Value $35**

15 Springtime BARBIE™
(2nd, 1996)
Handcrafted • ANDR
1295QEO8081 • **Value $27**

16 NEW! Springtime BARBIE™
(3rd & final, 1997)
Handcrafted • ANDR
1295QEO8642 • **Value $12.95**

17 Springtime Bonnets
(1st, 1993)
Handcrafted • DLEE
775QEO8322 • **Value $30**

	Price Paid	Value of My Collection
EGGS IN SPORTS		
1.		
2.		
3.		
GARDEN CLUB		
4.		
5.		
6.		
HERE COMES EASTER		
7.		
8.		
9.		
10.		
JOYFUL ANGELS		
11.		
12.		
SIDEWALK CRUISERS		
13.		
SPRINGTIME BARBIE™		
14.		
15.		
16.		
SPRINGTIME BONNETS		
17.		

\ **PENCIL TOTALS**

SPRING ORNAMENTS

VALUE GUIDE – SPRING ORNAMENTS

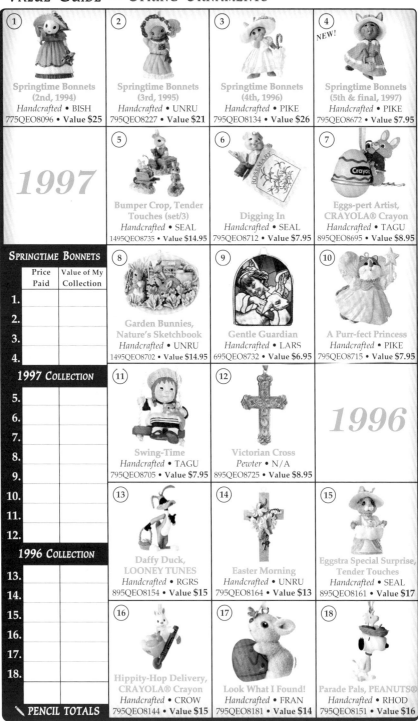

1 Springtime Bonnets
(2nd, 1994)
Handcrafted • BISH
775QEO8096 • **Value $25**

2 Springtime Bonnets
(3rd, 1995)
Handcrafted • UNRU
795QEO8227 • **Value $21**

3 Springtime Bonnets
(4th, 1996)
Handcrafted • PIKE
795QEO8134 • **Value $26**

4 NEW!
Springtime Bonnets
(5th & final, 1997)
Handcrafted • PIKE
795QEO8672 • **Value $7.95**

1997

5 Bumper Crop, Tender
Touches (set/3)
Handcrafted • SEAL
1495QEO8735 • **Value $14.95**

6 Digging In
Handcrafted • SEAL
795QEO8712 • **Value $7.95**

7 Eggs-pert Artist,
CRAYOLA® Crayon
Handcrafted • TAGU
895QEO8695 • **Value $8.95**

8 Garden Bunnies,
Nature's Sketchbook
Handcrafted • UNRU
1495QEO8702 • **Value $14.95**

9 Gentle Guardian
Handcrafted • LARS
695QEO8732 • **Value $6.95**

10 A Purr-fect Princess
Handcrafted • PIKE
795QEO8715 • **Value $7.95**

11 Swing-Time
Handcrafted • TAGU
795QEO8705 • **Value $7.95**

12 Victorian Cross
Pewter • N/A
895QEO8725 • **Value $8.95**

1996

13 Daffy Duck,
LOONEY TUNES
Handcrafted • RGRS
895QEO8154 • **Value $15**

14 Easter Morning
Handcrafted • UNRU
795QEO8164 • **Value $13**

15 Eggstra Special Surprise,
Tender Touches
Handcrafted • SEAL
895QEO8161 • **Value $17**

16 Hippity-Hop Delivery,
CRAYOLA® Crayon
Handcrafted • CROW
795QEO8144 • **Value $15**

17 Look What I Found!
Handcrafted • FRAN
795QEO8181 • **Value $14**

18 Parade Pals, PEANUTS®
Handcrafted • RHOD
795QEO8151 • **Value $16**

SPRINGTIME BONNETS

	Price Paid	Value of My Collection
1.		
2.		
3.		
4.		

1997 COLLECTION

5.		
6.		
7.		
8.		
9.		
10.		
11.		
12.		

1996 COLLECTION

13.		
14.		
15.		
16.		
17.		
18.		
PENCIL TOTALS		

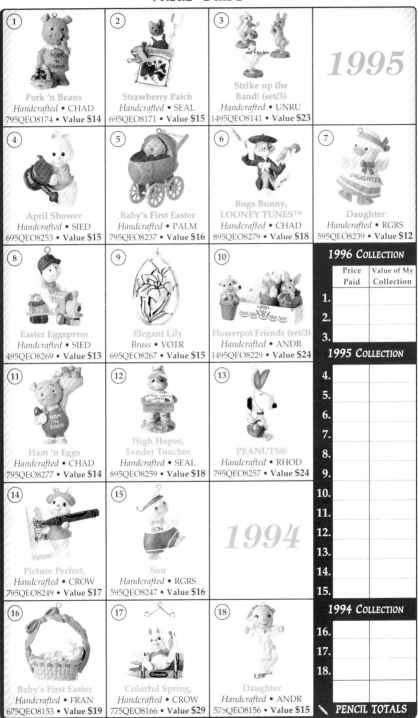

1 Pork 'n Beans
Handcrafted • CHAD
795QEO8174 • **Value $14**

2 Strawberry Patch
Handcrafted • SEAL
695QEO8171 • **Value $15**

3 Strike up the Band! (set/3)
Handcrafted • UNRU
1495QEO8141 • **Value $23**

1995

4 April Shower
Handcrafted • SIED
695QEO8253 • **Value $15**

5 Baby's First Easter
Handcrafted • PALM
795QEO8237 • **Value $16**

6 Bugs Bunny, LOONEY TUNES™
Handcrafted • CHAD
895QEO8279 • **Value $18**

7 Daughter
Handcrafted • RGRS
595QEO8239 • **Value $12**

8 Easter Eggspress
Handcrafted • SIED
495QEO8269 • **Value $13**

9 Elegant Lily
Brass • VOTR
695QEO8267 • **Value $15**

10 Flowerpot Friends (set/3)
Handcrafted • ANDR
1495QEO8229 • **Value $24**

11 Ham 'n Eggs
Handcrafted • CHAD
795QEO8277 • **Value $14**

12 High Hopes, Tender Touches
Handcrafted • SEAL
895QEO8259 • **Value $18**

13 PEANUTS®
Handcrafted • RHOD
795QEO8257 • **Value $24**

14 Picture Perfect,
Handcrafted • CROW
795QEO8249 • **Value $17**

15 Son
Handcrafted • RGRS
595QEO8247 • **Value $16**

1994

16 Baby's First Easter
Handcrafted • FRAN
675QEO8153 • **Value $19**

17 Colorful Spring,
Handcrafted • CROW
775QEO8166 • **Value $29**

18 Daughter
Handcrafted • ANDR
575QEO8156 • **Value $15**

1996 Collection

	Price Paid	Value of My Collection
1.		
2.		
3.		

1995 Collection

4.		
5.		
6.		
7.		
8.		
9.		
10.		
11.		
12.		
13.		
14.		
15.		

1994 Collection

16.		
17.		
18.		
PENCIL TOTALS		

SPRING ORNAMENTS

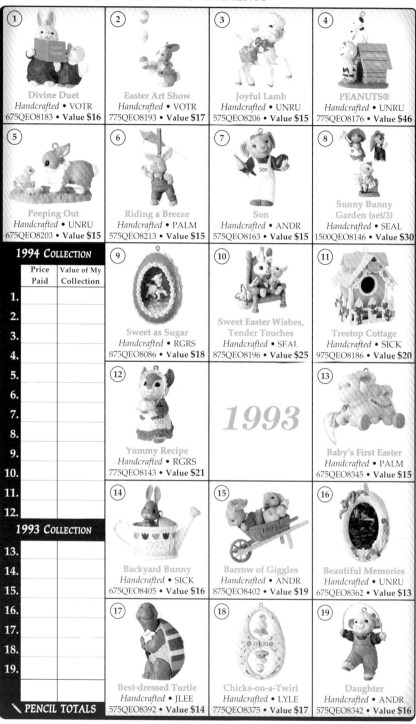

① Divine Duet
Handcrafted • VOTR
675QEO8183 • **Value $16**

② Easter Art Show
Handcrafted • VOTR
775QEO8193 • **Value $17**

③ Joyful Lamb
Handcrafted • UNRU
575QEO8206 • **Value $15**

④ PEANUTS®
Handcrafted • UNRU
775QEO8176 • **Value $46**

⑤ Peeping Out
Handcrafted • UNRU
675QEO8203 • **Value $15**

⑥ Riding a Breeze
Handcrafted • PALM
575QEO8213 • **Value $15**

⑦ Son
Handcrafted • ANDR
575QEO8163 • **Value $15**

⑧ Sunny Bunny Garden (set/3)
Handcrafted • SEAL
1500QEO8146 • **Value $30**

⑨ Sweet as Sugar
Handcrafted • RGRS
875QEO8086 • **Value $18**

⑩ Sweet Easter Wishes, Tender Touches
Handcrafted • SEAL
875QEO8196 • **Value $25**

⑪ Treetop Cottage
Handcrafted • SICK
975QEO8186 • **Value $20**

⑫ Yummy Recipe
Handcrafted • RGRS
775QEO8143 • **Value $21**

1993

⑬ Baby's First Easter
Handcrafted • PALM
675QEO8345 • **Value $15**

⑭ Backyard Bunny
Handcrafted • SICK
675QEO8405 • **Value $16**

⑮ Barrow of Giggles
Handcrafted • ANDR
875QEO8402 • **Value $19**

⑯ Beautiful Memories
Handcrafted • UNRU
675QEO8362 • **Value $13**

⑰ Best-dressed Turtle
Handcrafted • JLEE
575QEO8392 • **Value $14**

⑱ Chicks-on-a-Twirl
Handcrafted • LYLE
775QEO8375 • **Value $17**

⑲ Daughter
Handcrafted • ANDR
575QEO8342 • **Value $16**

1994 Collection

	Price Paid	Value of My Collection
1.		
2.		
3.		
4.		
5.		
6.		
7.		
8.		
9.		
10.		
11.		
12.		

1993 Collection

13.		
14.		
15.		
16.		
17.		
18.		
19.		

PENCIL TOTALS

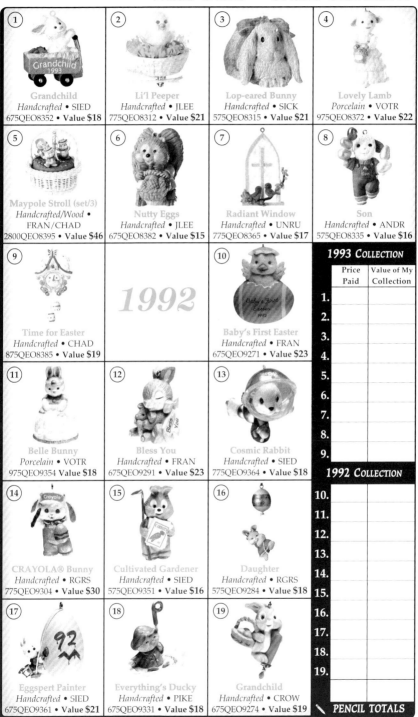

1. Grandchild
Handcrafted • SIED
675QEO8352 • **Value $18**

2. Li'l Peeper
Handcrafted • JLEE
775QEO8312 • **Value $21**

3. Lop-eared Bunny
Handcrafted • SICK
575QEO8315 • **Value $21**

4. Lovely Lamb
Porcelain • VOTR
975QEO8372 • **Value $22**

5. Maypole Stroll (set/3)
Handcrafted/Wood •
FRAN/CHAD
2800QEO8395 • **Value $46**

6. Nutty Eggs
Handcrafted • JLEE
675QEO8382 • **Value $15**

7. Radiant Window
Handcrafted • UNRU
775QEO8365 • **Value $17**

8. Son
Handcrafted • ANDR
575QEO8335 • **Value $16**

9. Time for Easter
Handcrafted • CHAD
875QEO8385 • **Value $19**

1992

10. Baby's First Easter
Handcrafted • FRAN
675QEO9271 • **Value $23**

11. Belle Bunny
Porcelain • VOTR
975QEO9354 **Value $18**

12. Bless You
Handcrafted • FRAN
675QEO9291 • **Value $23**

13. Cosmic Rabbit
Handcrafted • SIED
775QEO9364 • **Value $18**

14. CRAYOLA® Bunny
Handcrafted • RGRS
775QEO9304 • **Value $30**

15. Cultivated Gardener
Handcrafted • SIED
575QEO9351 • **Value $16**

16. Daughter
Handcrafted • RGRS
575QEO9284 • **Value $18**

17. Eggspert Painter
Handcrafted • SIED
675QEO9361 • **Value $21**

18. Everything's Ducky
Handcrafted • PIKE
675QEO9331 • **Value $18**

19. Grandchild
Handcrafted • CROW
675QEO9274 • **Value $19**

	Price Paid	Value of My Collection
1993 COLLECTION		
1.		
2.		
3.		
4.		
5.		
6.		
7.		
8.		
9.		
1992 COLLECTION		
10.		
11.		
12.		
13.		
14.		
15.		
16.		
17.		
18.		
19.		
PENCIL TOTALS		

SPRING ORNAMENTS

1 Joy Bearer
Handcrafted • PALM
875QEO9334 • **Value $25**

2 Promise of Easter
Porcelain • LYLE
875QEO9314 • **Value $17**

3 Rocking Bunny
Porcelain/Nickle-Plated • VOTR
975QEO9324 • **Value $20**

4 Somebunny Loves You
Handcrafted • FRAN
675QEO9294 • **Value $29**

5 Son
Handcrafted • RGRS
575QEO9281 • **Value $17**

6 Springtime Egg
Handcrafted • JLEE
875QEO9321 • **Value $18**

7 Sunny Wisher
Handcrafted • PIKE
575QEO9344 • **Value $15**

8 Warm Memories Photoholder
Fabric • VOTR
775QEO9311 • **Value $15**

1992 COLLECTION

	Price Paid	Value of My Collection
1.		
2.		
3.		
4.		
5.		
6.		
7.		
8.		

1991 COLLECTION

9.		
10.		
11.		
12.		
13.		
14.		
15.		
16.		
17.		
18.		
19.		

PENCIL TOTALS

1991

9 Baby's First Easter
Handcrafted • N/A
875QEO5189 • **Value $25**

10 Daughter
Handcrafted • N/A
575QEO5179 • **Value $31**

11 Easter Memories Photoholder
Fabric • N/A
775QEO5137 • **Value $15**

12 Full of Love
Handcrafted • N/A
775QEO5149 • **Value $44**

13 Gentle Lamb
Handcrafted • N/A
675QEO5159 • **Value $19**

14 Grandchild
Handcrafted • N/A
675QEO5177 • **Value $18**

15 Li'l Dipper
Handcrafted • N/A
675QEO5147 • **Value $23**

16 Lily Egg
Porcelain • UNRU
975QEO5139 • **Value $23**

17 Son
Handcrafted • N/A
575QEO5187 • **Value $24**

18 Spirit of Easter
Handcrafted • N/A
775QEO5169 • **Value $34**

19 Springtime Stroll
Handcrafted • N/A
675QEO5167 • **Value $22**

Merry Miniatures

As the name implies, Merry Miniature figurines have been a delight for collectors since their debut in 1974. Popular features of the collection include collectible series, holiday themes and groupings of recurring characters, like Cameron the cat. Some popular Merry Miniatures are issued for more than one year. There have been over 500 Merry Miniature figurines released to date.

1997

(1)
Apple Harvest – Mary's Bears (set/3)
Handcrafted • HAMI
1295QFM8585 • **Value $12.95**

(2)
Bashful Visitors (set/3)
Handcrafted • AUBE
1295QFM8582 • **Value $12.95**

(3)
Cupid Cameron
Handcrafted • N/A
495QSM8552 • **Value $4.95**

(4)
Easter Parade (set/2)
Handcrafted • TAGU
795QSM8562 • **Value $7.95**

(5)
Getting Ready for Spring (set/3)
Handcrafted • TAGU
1295QSM8575 • **Value $12.95**

(6)
Happy Birthday Clowns (3rd & final, *Happy Birthday Clowns*)
Handcrafted • N/A
495QSM8565 • **Value $4.95**

(7)
HERSHEY'S™ (1st, set/2, *HERSHEY'S™*)
Handcrafted • BRIC
1295QFM8625 • **Value $12.95**

(8)
Holiday Harmony (set/3)
Handcrafted • TAGU
1295QFM8612 • **Value $12.95**

(9)
Making a Wish (set/2)
Handcrafted • TAGU
795QFM8592 • **Value $7.95**

(10)
The Nativity (set/2)
Handcrafted • N/A
795QFM8615 • **Value $7.95**

(11)
Noah's Friends (set/2)
Handcrafted • ESCH
795QSM8572 • **Value $7.95**

(12)
Peter Pan (set/5)
Handcrafted • TAGU
1995QSM8605 • **Value $19.95**

(13)
Santa Cameron
Handcrafted • N/A
495QFM8622 • **Value $4.95**

(14)
Six Dwarfs (set/3)
Handcrafted • ESCH
1295QFM8685 • **Value $12.95**

(15)
Snow White and Dancing Dwarf (set/2)
Handcrafted • ESCH
795QFM8535 • **Value $7.95**

1997 COLLECTION

	Price Paid	Value of My Collection
1.		
2.		
3.		
4.		
5.		
6.		
7.		
8.		
9.		
10.		
11.		
12.		
13.		
14.		
15.		
PENCIL TOTALS		

MERRY MINIATURES

VALUE GUIDE – MERRY MINIATURES

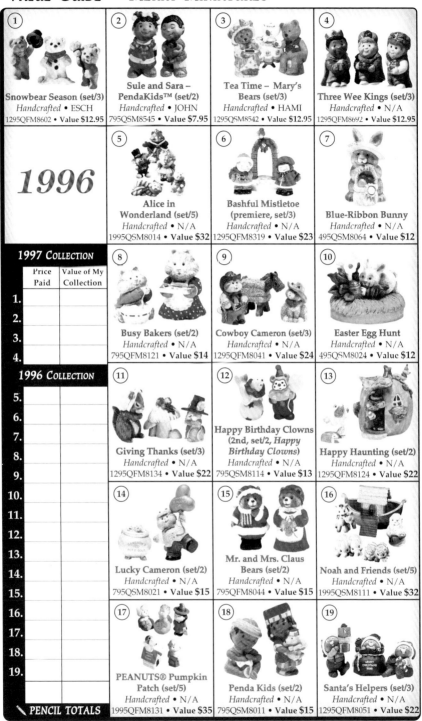

1
Snowbear Season (set/3)
Handcrafted • ESCH
1295QFM8602 • **Value $12.95**

2
Sule and Sara –
PendaKids™ (set/2)
Handcrafted • JOHN
795QSM8545 • **Value $7.95**

3
Tea Time – Mary's
Bears (set/3)
Handcrafted • HAMI
1295QSM8542 • **Value $12.95**

4
Three Wee Kings (set/3)
Handcrafted • N/A
1295QFM8692 • **Value $12.95**

1996

5
Alice in
Wonderland (set/5)
Handcrafted • N/A
1995QSM8014 • **Value $32**

6
Bashful Mistletoe
(premiere, set/3)
Handcrafted • N/A
1295QFM8319 • **Value $23**

7
Blue-Ribbon Bunny
Handcrafted • N/A
495QSM8064 • **Value $12**

1997 COLLECTION

	Price Paid	Value of My Collection
1.		
2.		
3.		
4.		

8
Busy Bakers (set/2)
Handcrafted • N/A
795QFM8121 • **Value $14**

9
Cowboy Cameron (set/3)
Handcrafted • N/A
1295QFM8041 • **Value $24**

10
Easter Egg Hunt
Handcrafted • N/A
495QSM8024 • **Value $12**

1996 COLLECTION

5.		
6.		
7.		
8.		
9.		
10.		
11.		
12.		
13.		
14.		
15.		
16.		
17.		
18.		
19.		

11
Giving Thanks (set/3)
Handcrafted • N/A
1295QFM8134 • **Value $22**

12
Happy Birthday Clowns
(2nd, set/2, *Happy
Birthday Clowns*)
Handcrafted • N/A
795QSM8114 • **Value $13**

13
Happy Haunting (set/2)
Handcrafted • N/A
1295QFM8124 • **Value $22**

14
Lucky Cameron (set/2)
Handcrafted • N/A
795QSM8021 • **Value $15**

15
Mr. and Mrs. Claus
Bears (set/2)
Handcrafted • N/A
795QFM8044 • **Value $15**

16
Noah and Friends (set/5)
Handcrafted • N/A
1995QSM8111 • **Value $32**

17
PEANUTS® Pumpkin
Patch (set/5)
Handcrafted • N/A
1995QFM8131 • **Value $35**

18
Penda Kids (set/2)
Handcrafted • N/A
795QSM8011 • **Value $15**

19
Santa's Helpers (set/3)
Handcrafted • N/A
1295QFM8051 • **Value $22**

PENCIL TOTALS

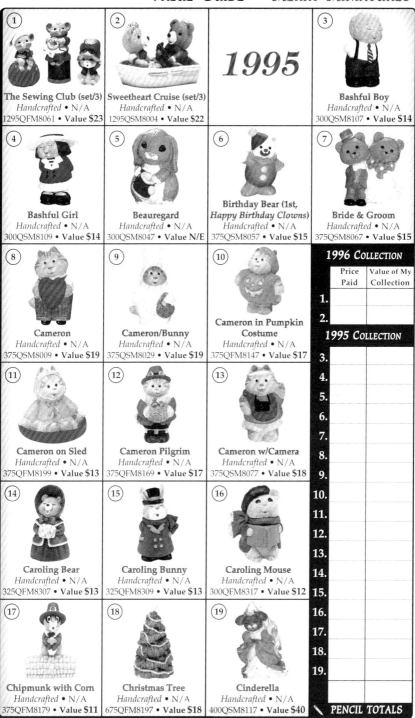

1995

① The Sewing Club (set/3)
Handcrafted • N/A
1295QFM8061 • **Value $23**

② Sweetheart Cruise (set/3)
Handcrafted • N/A
1295QSM8004 • **Value $22**

③ Bashful Boy
Handcrafted • N/A
300QSM8107 • **Value $14**

④ Bashful Girl
Handcrafted • N/A
300QSM8109 • **Value $14**

⑤ Beauregard
Handcrafted • N/A
300QSM8047 • **Value N/E**

⑥ Birthday Bear (1st,
Happy Birthday Clowns)
Handcrafted • N/A
375QSM8057 • **Value $15**

⑦ Bride & Groom
Handcrafted • N/A
375QSM8067 • **Value $15**

⑧ Cameron
Handcrafted • N/A
375QSM8009 • **Value $19**

⑨ Cameron/Bunny
Handcrafted • N/A
375QSM8029 • **Value $19**

⑩ Cameron in Pumpkin
Costume
Handcrafted • N/A
375QFM8147 • **Value $17**

⑪ Cameron on Sled
Handcrafted • N/A
375QFM8199 • **Value $13**

⑫ Cameron Pilgrim
Handcrafted • N/A
375QFM8169 • **Value $17**

⑬ Cameron w/Camera
Handcrafted • N/A
375QSM8077 • **Value $18**

⑭ Caroling Bear
Handcrafted • N/A
325QFM8307 • **Value $13**

⑮ Caroling Bunny
Handcrafted • N/A
325QFM8309 • **Value $13**

⑯ Caroling Mouse
Handcrafted • N/A
300QFM8317 • **Value $12**

⑰ Chipmunk with Corn
Handcrafted • N/A
375QFM8179 • **Value $11**

⑱ Christmas Tree
Handcrafted • N/A
675QFM8197 • **Value $18**

⑲ Cinderella
Handcrafted • N/A
400QSM8117 • **Value $40**

1996 COLLECTION

	Price Paid	Value of My Collection
1.		
2.		

1995 COLLECTION

3.		
4.		
5.		
6.		
7.		
8.		
9.		
10.		
11.		
12.		
13.		
14.		
15.		
16.		
17.		
18.		
19.		
PENCIL TOTALS		

MERRY MINIATURES

Value Guide – Merry Miniatures

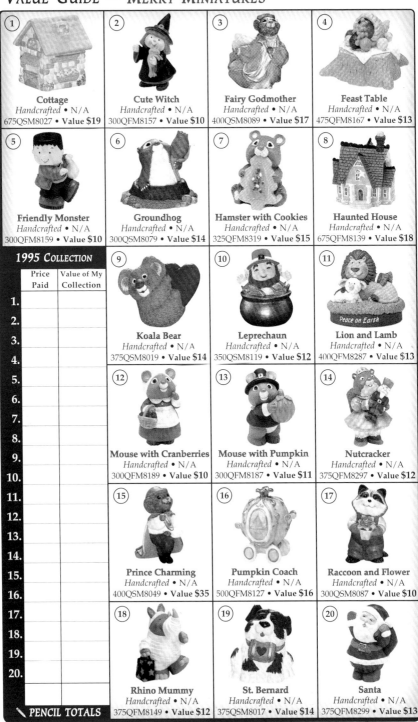

| | 1 Cottage
Handcrafted • N/A
675QSM8027 • **Value $19** | 2 Cute Witch
Handcrafted • N/A
300QFM8157 • **Value $10** | 3 Fairy Godmother
Handcrafted • N/A
400QSM8089 • **Value $17** | 4 Feast Table
Handcrafted • N/A
475QFM8167 • **Value $13** |

5 Friendly Monster — Handcrafted • N/A — 300QFM8159 • **Value $10**
6 Groundhog — Handcrafted • N/A — 300QSM8079 • **Value $14**
7 Hamster with Cookies — Handcrafted • N/A — 325QFM8319 • **Value $15**
8 Haunted House — Handcrafted • N/A — 675QFM8139 • **Value $18**

1995 Collection

	Price Paid	Value of My Collection
1.		
2.		
3.		
4.		
5.		
6.		
7.		
8.		
9.		
10.		
11.		
12.		
13.		
14.		
15.		
16.		
17.		
18.		
19.		
20.		
PENCIL TOTALS		

9 Koala Bear — Handcrafted • N/A — 375QSM8019 • **Value $14**
10 Leprechaun — Handcrafted • N/A — 350QSM8119 • **Value $12**
11 Lion and Lamb — Handcrafted • N/A — 400QFM8287 • **Value $13**

12 Mouse with Cranberries — Handcrafted • N/A — 300QFM8189 • **Value $10**
13 Mouse with Pumpkin — Handcrafted • N/A — 300QFM8187 • **Value $11**
14 Nutcracker — Handcrafted • N/A — 375QFM8297 • **Value $12**

15 Prince Charming — Handcrafted • N/A — 400QSM8049 • **Value $35**
16 Pumpkin Coach — Handcrafted • N/A — 500QFM8127 • **Value $16**
17 Raccoon and Flower — Handcrafted • N/A — 300QSM8087 • **Value $10**

18 Rhino Mummy — Handcrafted • N/A — 375QFM8149 • **Value $12**
19 St. Bernard — Handcrafted • N/A — 375QSM8017 • **Value $14**
20 Santa — Handcrafted • N/A — 375QFM8299 • **Value $13**

VALUE GUIDE — MERRY MINIATURES

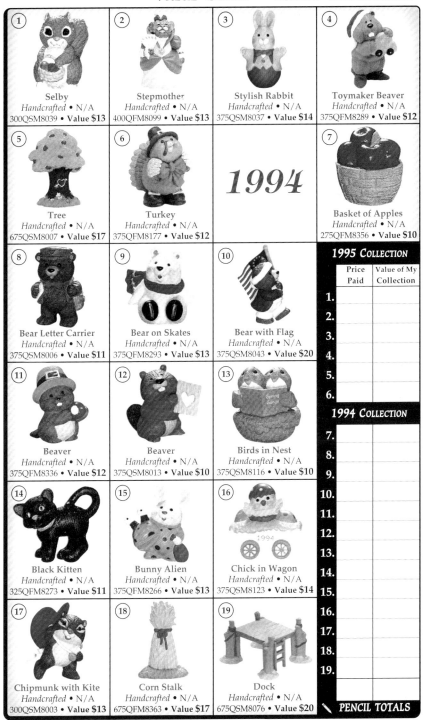

1. Selby
Handcrafted • N/A
300QSM8039 • **Value $13**

2. Stepmother
Handcrafted • N/A
400QFM8099 • **Value $13**

3. Stylish Rabbit
Handcrafted • N/A
375QSM8037 • **Value $14**

4. Toymaker Beaver
Handcrafted • N/A
375QFM8289 • **Value $12**

5. Tree
Handcrafted • N/A
675QSM8007 • **Value $17**

6. Turkey
Handcrafted • N/A
375QFM8177 • **Value $12**

1994

7. Basket of Apples
Handcrafted • N/A
275QFM8356 • **Value $10**

8. Bear Letter Carrier
Handcrafted • N/A
375QSM8006 • **Value $11**

9. Bear on Skates
Handcrafted • N/A
375QFM8293 • **Value $13**

10. Bear with Flag
Handcrafted • N/A
375QSM8043 • **Value $20**

11. Beaver
Handcrafted • N/A
375QFM8336 • **Value $12**

12. Beaver
Handcrafted • N/A
375QSM8013 • **Value $10**

13. Birds in Nest
Handcrafted • N/A
375QSM8116 • **Value $10**

14. Black Kitten
Handcrafted • N/A
325QFM8273 • **Value $11**

15. Bunny Alien
Handcrafted • N/A
375QFM8266 • **Value $13**

16. Chick in Wagon
Handcrafted • N/A
375QSM8123 • **Value $14**

17. Chipmunk with Kite
Handcrafted • N/A
300QSM8003 • **Value $13**

18. Corn Stalk
Handcrafted • N/A
675QFM8363 • **Value $17**

19. Dock
Handcrafted • N/A
675QSM8076 • **Value $20**

	1995 Collection	
	Price Paid	Value of My Collection
1.		
2.		
3.		
4.		
5.		
6.		

	1994 Collection	
7.		
8.		
9.		
10.		
11.		
12.		
13.		
14.		
15.		
16.		
17.		
18.		
19.		
PENCIL TOTALS		

MERRY MINIATURES

VALUE GUIDE – MERRY MINIATURES

(1)
Document
Handcrafted • N/A
275QSM8053 • **Value $13**

(2)
Eagle with Hat
Handcrafted • N/A
375QSM8036 • **Value $13**

(3)
Fence with Lantern
Handcrafted • N/A
675QFM8283 • **Value $16**

(4)
Flag
Handcrafted • N/A
675QSM8056 • **Value $19**

(5)
Fox on Skates
Handcrafted • N/A
375QFM8303 • **Value $12**

(6)
Indian Bunny
Handcrafted • N/A
275QFM8353 • **Value $10**

(7)
Indian Chickadee
Handcrafted • N/A
325QFM8346 • **Value $12**

(8)
Lamb
Handcrafted • N/A
325QSM8132• **Value $11**

1994 Collection

	Price Paid	Value of My Collection
1.		
2.		
3.		
4.		
5.		
6.		
7.		
8.		
9.		
10.		
11.		
12.		
13.		
14.		
15.		
16.		
17.		
18.		
19.		
20.		
╲ PENCIL TOTALS		

(9)
Mailbox
Handcrafted • N/A
675QSM8023 • **Value $14**

(10)
Mouse with Flower
Handcrafted • N/A
275QSM8243 • **Value $11**

(11)
Mrs. Claus
Handcrafted • N/A
375QFM8286 • **Value $15**

(12)
North Pole Sign
Handcrafted • N/A
675QFM8333 • **Value $17**

(13)
Owl in Stump
Handcrafted • N/A
275QSM8243 • **Value $11**

(14)
Pail of Seashells
Handcrafted • N/A
275QSM8052 • **Value $13**

(15)
Penguin
Handcrafted • N/A
275QFM8313 • **Value $16**

(16)
Pilgrim Bunny
Handcrafted • N/A
375QFM8343 • **Value $12**

(17)
Polar Bears
Handcrafted • N/A
325QFM8323 • **Value $13**

(18)
Pumpkin with Hat
Handcrafted • N/A
275QFM8276 • **Value $11**

(19)
Rabbit
Handcrafted • N/A
275QSM8066 • **Value $10**

(20)
Rabbit
Handcrafted • N/A
325QSM8016 • **Value $11**

(1) **Rabbit with Can**
Handcrafted • N/A
325QSM8083 • **Value $11**

(2) **Rabbit with Croquet**
Handcrafted • N/A
375QSM8113 • **Value $9**

(3) **Raccoon**
Handcrafted • N/A
375QSM8063 • **Value $18**

(4) **Sled Dog**
Handcrafted • N/A
325QFM8306 • **Value $13**

(5) **Snowman**
Handcrafted • N/A
275QFM8316 • **Value $10**

(6) **Squirrel as Clown**
Handcrafted • N/A
375QFM8263 • **Value $12**

(7) **Tree**
Handcrafted • N/A
275QFM8326 • **Value $10**

(8) **Wishing Well**
Handcrafted • N/A
675QSM8033 • **Value $16**

1993

(9) **Animated Cauldron**
Handcrafted • N/A
250QFM8425 • **Value $12**

(10) **Arctic Fox**
Handcrafted • N/A
350QFM8242 • **Value $14**

(11) **Arctic Scene Backdrop**
Paper • N/A
175QFM8205 • **Value $7**

(12) **Baby Walrus**
Handcrafted • N/A
300QFM8232 • **Value $11**

(13) **Baby Whale**
Handcrafted • N/A
350QFM8222 • **Value $10**

(14) **Beach Scene Backdrop**
Paper • N/A
175QSM8042 • **Value $8**

(15) **Bear dressed as Bat**
Handcrafted • N/A
300QFM8285 • **Value $9**

(16) **Bear with Surfboard**
Handcrafted • N/A
350QSM8015 • **Value $14**

(17) **Betsey Ross Lamb**
Handcrafted • N/A
350QSM8482 • **Value $13**

(18) **Bobcat Pilgrim**
Handcrafted • N/A
350QFM8172 • **Value $13**

(19) **Box of Candy**
Handcrafted • N/A
250QSM8095 • **Value $17**

1994 Collection

	Price Paid	Value of My Collection
1.		
2.		
3.		
4.		
5.		
6.		
7.		
8.		

1993 Collection

9.		
10.		
11.		
12.		
13.		
14.		
15.		
16.		
17.		
18.		
19.		

PENCIL TOTALS

MERRY MINIATURES

VALUE GUIDE – MERRY MINIATURES

1
Bunny Painting Egg
Handcrafted • N/A
350QSM8115 • **Value $9**

2
Bunny with Basket
Handcrafted • N/A
250QSM8142 • **Value $11**

3
Bunny with Egg
Handcrafted • N/A
300QSM8125 • **Value $10**

4
Bunny with Scarf
Handcrafted • N/A
250QFM8235 • **Value $14**

5
Bunny with Seashell
Handcrafted • N/A
350QSM8005 • **Value $17**

6
Cat & Mouse (3rd &
final, *Hugs and Kisses*)
Handcrafted • N/A
350QSM8102 • **Value $13**

7
Chipmunk
Handcrafted • N/A
350QSM8002 • **Value $13**

8
Display Stand
Handcrafted • N/A
675QFM8055 • **Value $10**

9
Dog with Balloon
Handcrafted • N/A
250QSM8092 • **Value $9**

10
Dragon Dog
Handcrafted • N/A
300QFM8295 • **Value $9**

11
Duck with Egg
Handcrafted • N/A
300QSM8135 • **Value $10**

12
Easter Basket
Handcrafted • N/A
250QSM8145 • **Value $12**

13
Easter Garden Backdrop
Paper • N/A
175QSM8152 • **Value $7**

14
Eskimo Child
Handcrafted • N/A
300QFM8215 • **Value $19**

15
Fox with Heart
Handcrafted • N/A
350QSM8065 • **Value $9**

16
Ghost on Tombstone
Handcrafted • N/A
250QFM8282 • **Value $9**

17
Goat Uncle Sam
Handcrafted • N/A
300QSM8472 • **Value $13**

18
Haunted Halloween
Backdrop
Paper • N/A
175QFM8275 • **Value $7**

19
Heartland Forest
Backdrop
Paper • N/A
175QSM8082 • **Value $7**

20
Hedgehog
Handcrafted • N/A
300QSM8026 • **Value $11**

1993 COLLECTION	Price Paid	Value of My Collection
1.		
2.		
3.		
4.		
5.		
6.		
7.		
8.		
9.		
10.		
11.		
12.		
13.		
14.		
15.		
16.		
17.		
18.		
19.		
20.		
PENCIL TOTALS		

1 Hedgehog Patriot
Handcrafted • N/A
350QSM8492 • **Value $12**

2 Hippo
Handcrafted • N/A
300QSM8032 • **Value $12**

3 Husky Puppy
Handcrafted • N/A
350QFM8245 • **Value $11**

4 Igloo
Handcrafted • N/A
300QFM8252 • **Value $17**

5 Indian Bear
Handcrafted • N/A
350QFM8162 • **Value $13**

6 Indian Squirrel
Handcrafted • N/A
300QFM8182 • **Value $14**

7 Indian Turkey
Handcrafted • N/A
350QFM8165 • **Value $13**

8 Lamb
Handcrafted • N/A
350QSM8112 • **Value $10**

9 Liberty Bell
Handcrafted • N/A
250QSM8465 • **Value $14**

10 Liberty Mouse
Handcrafted • N/A
300QSM8475 • **Value $13**

11 Mouse in Sunglasses
Handcrafted • N/A
250QSM8035 • **Value $13**

12 Mouse Witch
Handcrafted • N/A
300QFM8292 • **Value $11**

13 Owl and Pumpkin
Handcrafted • N/A
300QFM8302 • **Value $14**

14 Panda (3rd & final,
Sweet Valentines)
Handcrafted • N/A
350QSM8105 • **Value $13**

15 Patriotic Backdrop
Paper • N/A
175QSM8495 • **Value $7**

16 Penguin in Hat
Handcrafted • N/A
300QFM8212 • **Value $12**

17 Pig in Blanket
Handcrafted • N/A
300QSM8022 • **Value $15**

18 Pilgrim Chipmunk
Handcrafted • N/A
300QFM8185 • **Value $13**

19 Pilgrim Mouse
Handcrafted • N/A
300QFM8175 • **Value $15**

20 Plymouth Rock
Handcrafted • N/A
250QFM8192 • **Value $16**

1993 COLLECTION

	Price Paid	Value of My Collection
1.		
2.		
3.		
4.		
5.		
6.		
7.		
8.		
9.		
10.		
11.		
12.		
13.		
14.		
15.		
16.		
17.		
18.		
19.		
20.		
PENCIL TOTALS		

MERRY MINIATURES

VALUE GUIDE — MERRY MINIATURES

(1) Polar Bear (3rd & final, *Music Makers*)
Handcrafted • N/A
350QFM8265 • **Value $17**

(2) Prairie Dog
Handcrafted • N/A
350QSM8012 • **Value $14**

(3) Princess Cat
Handcrafted • N/A
350QFM8305 • **Value $17**

(4) Raccoon with Heart
Handcrafted • N/A
350QSM8062 • **Value $9**

(5) Sandcastle
Handcrafted • N/A
300QSM8045 • **Value $13**

(6) Santa Eskimo
Handcrafted • N/A
350QFM8262 • **Value $27**

(7) Seal with Earmuffs
Handcrafted • N/A
250QFM8272 • **Value $12**

(8) Sherlock Duck
Handcrafted • N/A
300QSM8122 • **Value $10**

1993 COLLECTION

	Price Paid	Value of My Collection
1.		
2.		
3.		
4.		
5.		
6.		
7.		
8.		
9.		
10.		
11.		
12.		

1992 COLLECTION

13.		
14.		
15.		
16.		
17.		
18.		

(9) Skunk with Heart
Handcrafted • N/A
300QSM8072 • **Value $9**

(10) Stump & Can
Handcrafted • N/A
300QSM8075 • **Value $11**

(11) Super Hero Bunny
Handcrafted • N/A
300QFM8422 • **Value $11**

(12) Thanksgiving Feast Backdrop
Paper • N/A
175QFM8195 • **Value $7**

1992

(13) Baby's 1st Easter
Handcrafted • N/A
350QSM9777 • **Value $11**

(14) Ballet Pig
Handcrafted • N/A
250QSM9759 • **Value $15**

(15) Bear (2nd, *Sweet Valentines*)
Handcrafted • N/A
350QSM9717 • **Value $20**

(16) Bear With Drum (2nd, *Music Makers*)
Handcrafted • N/A
350QFM9134 • **Value $17**

(17) Bunny & Carrot
Handcrafted • N/A
250QSM9799 • **Value $15**

(18) Cat in P.J.'s
Handcrafted • N/A
350QFM9084 • **Value $12**

\ **PENCIL TOTALS**

Value Guide – Merry Miniatures

1	Chipmunk	Handcrafted • N/A — 250QFM9144 • Value $10
2	Clown (3rd & final, *Birthday Clowns*)	Handcrafted • N/A — 350QSM9819 • Value $14
3	Clown Mouse	Handcrafted • N/A — 250QFM9031 • Value $12
4	Cow	Handcrafted • N/A — 300QFM9034 • Value $16
5	Crab	Handcrafted • N/A — 300QFM9174 • Value $9
6	Dog	Handcrafted • N/A — 300QSM9847 • Value $16
7	Dog in P.J.'s	Handcrafted • N/A — 350QFM9081 • Value $10
8	Ghost with Corn Candy	Handcrafted • N/A — 300QFM9014 • Value $15
9	Giraffe as Tree	Handcrafted • N/A — 300QFM9141 • Value $14
10	Goldfish	Handcrafted • N/A — 300QFM9181 • Value $10
11	Goose in Bonnet	Handcrafted • N/A — 300QSM9789 • Value $13
12	Grad Dog	Handcrafted • N/A — 250QSM9817 • Value $13
13	Haunted House	Handcrafted • N/A — 350QFM9024 • Value $13
14	Hedgehog	Handcrafted • N/A — 250QSM9859 • Value $11
15	Horse	Handcrafted • N/A — 300QFM9051 • Value $17
16	Indian Bunnies	Handcrafted • N/A — 350QFM9004 • Value $12
17	Kitten for Dad	Handcrafted • N/A — 350QSM9839 • Value $13
18	Kitten for Mom	Handcrafted • N/A — 350QSM9837 • Value $13
19	Kitten in Bib	Handcrafted • N/A — 350QSM9829 • Value $11
20	Lamb	Handcrafted • N/A — 250QFM9044 • Value $16

1992 Collection

	Price Paid	Value of My Collection
1.		
2.		
3.		
4.		
5.		
6.		
7.		
8.		
9.		
10.		
11.		
12.		
13.		
14.		
15.		
16.		
17.		
18.		
19.		
20.		
PENCIL TOTALS		

MERRY MINIATURES

Value Guide – Merry Miniatures

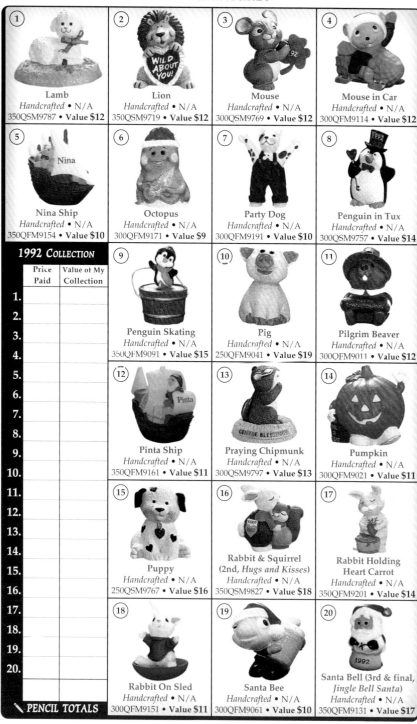

1 Lamb *Handcrafted* • N/A 350QSM9787 • **Value $12**	**2** Lion *Handcrafted* • N/A 350QSM9719 • **Value $12**

1 Lamb
Handcrafted • N/A
350QSM9787 • **Value $12**

2 Lion
Handcrafted • N/A
350QSM9719 • **Value $12**

3 Mouse
Handcrafted • N/A
300QSM9769 • **Value $12**

4 Mouse in Car
Handcrafted • N/A
300QFM9114 • **Value $12**

5 Nina Ship
Handcrafted • N/A
350QFM9154 • **Value $10**

6 Octopus
Handcrafted • N/A
300QFM9171 • **Value $9**

7 Party Dog
Handcrafted • N/A
300QFM9191 • **Value $10**

8 Penguin in Tux
Handcrafted • N/A
300QSM9757 • **Value $14**

1992 Collection

	Price Paid	Value of My Collection
1.		
2.		
3.		
4.		
5.		
6.		
7.		
8.		
9.		
10.		
11.		
12.		
13.		
14.		
15.		
16.		
17.		
18.		
19.		
20.		

PENCIL TOTALS

9 Penguin Skating
Handcrafted • N/A
350QFM9091 • **Value $15**

10 Pig
Handcrafted • N/A
250QFM9041 • **Value $19**

11 Pilgrim Beaver
Handcrafted • N/A
300QFM9011 • **Value $12**

12 Pinta Ship
Handcrafted • N/A
350QFM9161 • **Value $11**

13 Praying Chipmunk
Handcrafted • N/A
300QSM9797 • **Value $13**

14 Pumpkin
Handcrafted • N/A
300QFM9021 • **Value $11**

15 Puppy
Handcrafted • N/A
250QSM9767 • **Value $16**

16 Rabbit & Squirrel
(2nd, *Hugs and Kisses*)
Handcrafted • N/A
350QSM9827 • **Value $18**

17 Rabbit Holding Heart Carrot
Handcrafted • N/A
350QFM9201 • **Value $14**

18 Rabbit On Sled
Handcrafted • N/A
300QFM9151 • **Value $11**

19 Santa Bee
Handcrafted • N/A
300QFM9061 • **Value $10**

20 Santa Bell (3rd & final, *Jingle Bell Santa*)
Handcrafted • N/A
350QFM9131 • **Value $17**

1 Santa Maria Ship
Handcrafted • N/A
350QFM9164 • **Value $11**

2 Seal
Handcrafted • N/A
300QSM9849 • **Value $11**

3 Skunk with Butterfly
Handcrafted • N/A
350QFM9184 • **Value $11**

4 Snow Bunny
Handcrafted • N/A
400QFM9071 • **Value $11**

5 Squirrel Pal (3rd & final, *Gentle Pals*)
Handcrafted • N/A
350QFM9094 • **Value $18**

6 Squirrels in Nutshell
Handcrafted • N/A
350QFM9064 • **Value $11**

7 Sweatshirt Bunny
Handcrafted • N/A
350QSM9779 • **Value $15**

8 Sweet Angel
Handcrafted • N/A
300QFM9124 • **Value $16**

9 Teacher Cat
Handcrafted • N/A
350QFM9074 • **Value $9**

10 Teddy Bear
Handcrafted • N/A
250QFM9194 • **Value $14**

11 Thankful Turkey (3rd & final, *Thankful Turkey*)
Handcrafted • N/A
350QFM9001 • **Value $23**

12 Turtle & Mouse
Handcrafted • N/A
300QSM9857 • **Value $25**

13 Walrus & Bird
Handcrafted • N/A
350QFM9054 • **Value $11**

14 Waving Reindeer
Handcrafted • N/A
300QFM9121 • **Value $15**

1991

15 1st Christmas Together
Handcrafted • N/A
350QFM1799 • **Value $14**

16 Aerobic Bunny
Handcrafted • N/A
250QFM1817 • **Value $16**

17 Artist Mouse
Handcrafted • N/A
250QSM1519 • **Value $15**

18 Baby Bunny
Handcrafted • N/A
350QSM1619 • **Value $12**

19 Baby's 1st Christmas
Handcrafted • N/A
300QFM1797 • **Value $10**

1992 Collection

	Price Paid	Value of My Collection
1.		
2.		
3.		
4.		
5.		
6.		
7.		
8.		
9.		
10.		
11.		
12.		
13.		
14.		

1991 Collection

	Price Paid	Value of My Collection
15.		
16.		
17.		
18.		
19.		
PENCIL TOTALS		

Merry Miniatures

VALUE GUIDE — MERRY MINIATURES

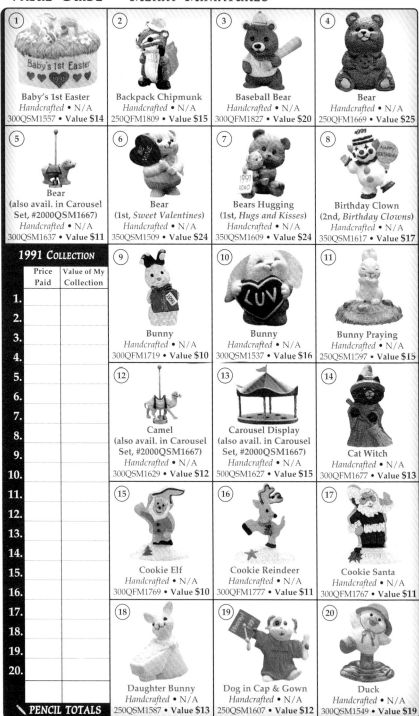

1 Baby's 1st Easter
Handcrafted • N/A
300QSM1557 • **Value $14**

2 Backpack Chipmunk
Handcrafted • N/A
250QFM1809 • **Value $15**

3 Baseball Bear
Handcrafted • N/A
300QFM1827 • **Value $20**

4 Bear
Handcrafted • N/A
250QFM1669 • **Value $25**

5 Bear
(also avail. in Carousel Set, #2000QSM1667)
Handcrafted • N/A
300QSM1637 • **Value $11**

6 Bear
(1st, *Sweet Valentines*)
Handcrafted • N/A
350QSM1509 • **Value $24**

7 Bears Hugging
(1st, *Hugs and Kisses*)
Handcrafted • N/A
350QSM1609 • **Value $24**

8 Birthday Clown
(2nd, *Birthday Clowns*)
Handcrafted • N/A
350QSM1617 • **Value $17**

1991 COLLECTION

	Price Paid	Value of My Collection
1.		
2.		
3.		
4.		
5.		
6.		
7.		
8.		
9.		
10.		
11.		
12.		
13.		
14.		
15.		
16.		
17.		
18.		
19.		
20.		
PENCIL TOTALS		

9 Bunny
Handcrafted • N/A
300QFM1719 • **Value $10**

10 Bunny
Handcrafted • N/A
300QSM1537 • **Value $16**

11 Bunny Praying
Handcrafted • N/A
250QSM1597 • **Value $15**

12 Camel
(also avail. in Carousel Set, #2000QSM1667)
Handcrafted • N/A
300QSM1629 • **Value $12**

13 Carousel Display
(also avail. in Carousel Set, #2000QSM1667)
Handcrafted • N/A
500QSM1627 • **Value $15**

14 Cat Witch
Handcrafted • N/A
300QFM1677 • **Value $13**

15 Cookie Elf
Handcrafted • N/A
300QFM1769 • **Value $10**

16 Cookie Reindeer
Handcrafted • N/A
300QFM1777 • **Value $11**

17 Cookie Santa
Handcrafted • N/A
300QFM1767 • **Value $11**

18 Daughter Bunny
Handcrafted • N/A
250QSM1587 • **Value $13**

19 Dog in Cap & Gown
Handcrafted • N/A
250QSM1607 • **Value $12**

20 Duck
Handcrafted • N/A
300QSM1549 • **Value $19**

VALUE GUIDE – MERRY MINIATURES

1 Elephant
(also avail. in Carousel
Set, #2000QSM1667)
Handcrafted • N/A
300QSM1647 • **Value $12**

2 Football Beaver
Handcrafted • N/A
350QFM1829 • **Value $20**

3 Fox
Handcrafted • N/A
350QFM1689 • **Value $13**

4 Frog
Handcrafted • N/A
300QFM1729 • **Value $10**

5 Gentle Pals Kitten
(2nd, *Gentle Pals*)
Handcrafted • N/A
350QFM1709 • **Value $17**

6 Horse
(also avail. in Carousel
Set, #2000QSM1667)
Handcrafted • N/A
300QSM1649 • **Value $25**

7 I Love Dad
Handcrafted • N/A
250QSM1657 • **Value $9**

8 I Love Mom
Handcrafted • N/A
250QSM1659 • **Value $9**

9 Indian Maiden
Handcrafted • N/A
250QFM1687 • **Value $11**

10 Irish Frog
Handcrafted • N/A
350QSM1539 • **Value $12**

11 Jingle Bell Santa
(2nd, *Jingle Bell Santa*)
Handcrafted • N/A
350QFM1717 • **Value $21**

12 Kitten
Handcrafted • N/A
300QFM1737 • **Value $13**

13 Lamb & Duck
Handcrafted • N/A
350QSM1569 • **Value $12**

14 Lion
(also avail. in Carousel
Set, #2000QSM1667)
Handcrafted • N/A
300QSM1639 • **Value $13**

15 Mother Bunny
Handcrafted • N/A
300QSM1577 • **Value $15**

16 Mouse
Handcrafted • N/A
250QFM1789 • **Value $12**

17 Mummy
Handcrafted • N/A
250QFM1679 • **Value $12**

18 Music Makers Bear
(1st, *Music Makers*)
Handcrafted • N/A
300QFM1779 • **Value $19**

19 Pig
Handcrafted • N/A
300QFM1739 • **Value $13**

20 Puppy
Handcrafted • N/A
300QFM1727 • **Value $12**

1991 COLLECTION

	Price Paid	Value of My Collection
1.		
2.		
3.		
4.		
5.		
6.		
7.		
8.		
9.		
10.		
11.		
12.		
13.		
14.		
15.		
16.		
17.		
18.		
19.		
20.		
PENCIL TOTALS		

MERRY MINIATURES

Merry Miniatures   235

VALUE GUIDE — MERRY MINIATURES

1 Puppy
Handcrafted • N/A
300QFM1787 • **Value $11**

2 Puppy
Handcrafted • N/A
300QSM1529 • **Value $22**

3 Raccoon Thief
Handcrafted • N/A
350QSM1517 • **Value $12**

4 Skating Raccoon
Handcrafted • N/A
350QFM1837 • **Value $20**

5 Snow Bunny
Handcrafted • N/A
250QFM1749 • **Value $11**

6 Snow Lamb
Handcrafted • N/A
250QFM1759 • **Value $10**

7 Snow Mice
Handcrafted • N/A
250QFM1757 • **Value $11**

8 Soccer Skunk
Handcrafted • N/A
300QFM1819 • **Value $18**

9 Teacher Raccoon
Handcrafted • N/A
350QFM1807 • **Value $9**

10 Turkey
(2nd, *Thankful Turkey*)
Handcrafted • N/A
350QFM1697 • **Value $22**

11 Turtle
Handcrafted • N/A
300QFM1747 • **Value $12**

1990

12 1st Christmas Together
Handcrafted • N/A
350QFM1686 • **Value $10**

13 Alligator
Handcrafted • N/A
300QSM1573 • **Value $11**

14 Artist Raccoon
Handcrafted • N/A
350QSM1543 • **Value $15**

15 Baby's 1st Christmas
Handcrafted • N/A
250QFM1683 • **Value $10**

16 Baby's 1st Easter
Handcrafted • N/A
300QSM1536 • **Value $15**

17 Baseball Bunny
Handcrafted • N/A
250QSM1576 • **Value $10**

18 Bear & Balloon
Handcrafted • N/A
300QFM1716 • **Value $11**

19 Birthday Clown
(1st, *Birthday Clowns*)
Handcrafted • N/A
350QFM1706 • **Value $20**

	Price Paid	Value of My Collection
1991 COLLECTION		
1.		
2.		
3.		
4.		
5.		
6.		
7.		
8.		
9.		
10.		
11.		
1990 COLLECTION		
12.		
13.		
14.		
15.		
16.		
17.		
18.		
19.		
PENCIL TOTALS		

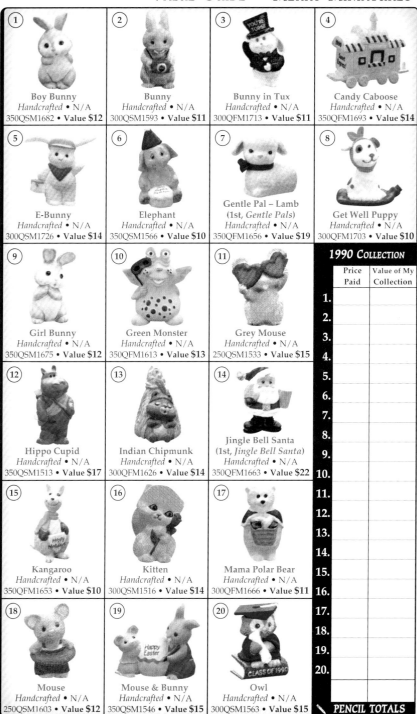

① Boy Bunny
Handcrafted • N/A
350QSM1682 • **Value $12**

② Bunny
Handcrafted • N/A
300QSM1593 • **Value $11**

③ Bunny in Tux
Handcrafted • N/A
300QFM1713 • **Value $11**

④ Candy Caboose
Handcrafted • N/A
350QFM1693 • **Value $14**

⑤ E-Bunny
Handcrafted • N/A
300QSM1726 • **Value $14**

⑥ Elephant
Handcrafted • N/A
350QSM1566 • **Value $10**

⑦ Gentle Pal – Lamb
(1st, *Gentle Pals*)
Handcrafted • N/A
350QFM1656 • **Value $19**

⑧ Get Well Puppy
Handcrafted • N/A
300QFM1703 • **Value $10**

⑨ Girl Bunny
Handcrafted • N/A
350QSM1675 • **Value $12**

⑩ Green Monster
Handcrafted • N/A
350QFM1613 • **Value $13**

⑪ Grey Mouse
Handcrafted • N/A
250QSM1533 • **Value $15**

⑫ Hippo Cupid
Handcrafted • N/A
350QSM1513 • **Value $17**

⑬ Indian Chipmunk
Handcrafted • N/A
300QFM1626 • **Value $14**

⑭ Jingle Bell Santa
(1st, *Jingle Bell Santa*)
Handcrafted • N/A
350QFM1663 • **Value $22**

⑮ Kangaroo
Handcrafted • N/A
350QFM1653 • **Value $10**

⑯ Kitten
Handcrafted • N/A
300QSM1516 • **Value $14**

⑰ Mama Polar Bear
Handcrafted • N/A
300QFM1666 • **Value $11**

⑱ Mouse
Handcrafted • N/A
250QSM1603 • **Value $12**

⑲ Mouse & Bunny
Handcrafted • N/A
350QSM1546 • **Value $15**

⑳ Owl
Handcrafted • N/A
300QSM1563 • **Value $15**

1990 Collection

	Price Paid	Value of My Collection
1.		
2.		
3.		
4.		
5.		
6.		
7.		
8.		
9.		
10.		
11.		
12.		
13.		
14.		
15.		
16.		
17.		
18.		
19.		
20.		
PENCIL TOTALS		

MERRY MINIATURES

VALUE GUIDE — MERRY MINIATURES

1
Papa Polar Bear & Child
Handcrafted • N/A
350QFM1673 • **Value $12**

2
Pig
Handcrafted • N/A
300QSM1526 • **Value $13**

3
Pilgrim Mouse
Handcrafted • N/A
250QFM1636 • **Value $11**

4
Pilgrim Squirrel
Handcrafted • N/A
300QFM1633 • **Value $13**

5
Puppy
Handcrafted • N/A
250QSM1583 • **Value $10**

6
Raccoon
Handcrafted • N/A
350QSM1586 • **Value $13**

7
Scarecrow
Handcrafted • N/A
350QFM1616 • **Value $13**

8
Snowman
Handcrafted • N/A
250QFM1646 • **Value $12**

9
Squirrel
Handcrafted • N/A
250QSM1553 • **Value $18**

10
Squirrel Caroler
Handcrafted • N/A
300QFM1696 • **Value $15**

11
Squirrel Hobo
Handcrafted • N/A
300QFM1606 • **Value $12**

12
Stitched Teddy
Handcrafted • N/A
350QSM1506 • **Value $27**

13
Teacher Mouse
Handcrafted • N/A
300QFM1676 • **Value $10**

14
Thankful Turkey
(1st, *Thankful Turkey*)
Handcrafted • N/A
350QFM1623 • **Value $22**

15
Walrus
Handcrafted • N/A
250QFM1643 • **Value $12**

1989

16
Baby Boy
Handcrafted • N/A
300QFM1585 • **Value $16**

17
Baby Girl
Handcrafted • N/A
300QFM1592 • **Value $16**

18
Baby's 1st Christmas
Handcrafted • N/A
300QFM1615 • **Value $13**

19
Bear
Handcrafted • N/A
250QSM1525 • **Value $15**

1990 COLLECTION

	Price Paid	Value of My Collection
1.		
2.		
3.		
4.		
5.		
6.		
7.		
8.		
9.		
10.		
11.		
12.		
13.		
14.		
15.		

1989 COLLECTION

16.		
17.		
18.		
19.		

PENCIL TOTALS

VALUE GUIDE – MERRY MINIATURES

1. Bear Baker
Handcrafted • N/A
350QSM1522 • **Value $17**

2. Blue King
(also avail. in Nativity
Set, #3550QFM1685)
Handcrafted • N/A
300QFM1632 • **Value $23**

3. Bunny
Handcrafted • N/A
250QSM1512 • **Value $17**

4. Bunny
Handcrafted • N/A
300QFM1565 • **Value $12**

5. Bunny
Handcrafted • N/A
350QSM1552 • **Value $14**

6. Bunny & Skateboard
Handcrafted • N/A
350EBO3092 • **Value $24**

7. Bunny Caroler
Handcrafted • N/A
300QFM1662 • **Value $19**

8. Dog & Kitten
Handcrafted • N/A
350QSM1515 • **Value $25**

9. Elf
Handcrafted • N/A
300QFM1622 • **Value $14**

10. Grey Mouse
Handcrafted • N/A
250QSM1502 • **Value $19**

11. Joy Elf
Handcrafted • N/A
300QFM1605 • **Value $11**

12. Kitten
Handcrafted • N/A
250QSM1505 • **Value $21**

13. Lamb
Handcrafted • N/A
350QSM1545 • **Value $23**

14. Momma Bear
Handcrafted • N/A
350QFM1582 • **Value $16**

15. Mouse
Handcrafted • N/A
250QFM1572 • **Value $19**

16. Mouse Caroler
Handcrafted • N/A
250QFM1655 • **Value $20**

17. Mr. Claus
Handcrafted • N/A
350QFM1595 • **Value $15**

18. Mrs. Claus
Handcrafted • N/A
350QFM1602 • **Value $15**

19. Owl
Handcrafted • N/A
250QSM1555 • **Value $17**

20. Pink King
(also avail. in Nativity
Set, #3550QFM1685)
Handcrafted • N/A
300QFM1642 • **Value $13**

1989 COLLECTION

	Price Paid	Value of My Collection
1.		
2.		
3.		
4.		
5.		
6.		
7.		
8.		
9.		
10.		
11.		
12.		
13.		
14.		
15.		
16.		
17.		
18.		
19.		
20.		
PENCIL TOTALS		

MERRY MINIATURES

Merry Miniatures

239

1 Raccoon
Handcrafted • N/A
350QFM1575 • **Value $14**

2 Raccoon Caroler
Handcrafted • N/A
350QFM1652 • **Value $15**

3 Teacher Elf
Handcrafted • N/A
300QFM1612 • **Value $13**

4 Train Car
Handcrafted • N/A
350QFM1562 • **Value $15**

5 Yellow King
(also avail. in Nativity
Set, #3550QFM1685)
Handcrafted • N/A
300QFM1635 • **Value $12**

1988

6 Dog
Handcrafted • N/A
200GHA3524 • **Value $12**

7 Donkey
(also avail. in Nativity
Set, #3550QFM1685)
Handcrafted • N/A
225QFM1581 • **Value $9**

1989 Collection

	Price Paid	Value of My Collection
1.		
2.		
3.		
4.		
5.		

1988 Collection

6.		
7.		
8.		
9.		
10.		
11.		
12.		
13.		
14.		
15.		
16.		
17.		
18.		
19.		

8 Indian Bear
Handcrafted • N/A
325QFM1511 • **Value $16**

9 Jesus
(also avail. in Nativity
Set, #3550QFM1685)
Handcrafted • N/A
250QFM1564 • **Value $19**

10 Joseph
(also avail. in Nativity
Set, #3550QFM1685)
Handcrafted • N/A
250QFM1561 • **Value $11**

11 Kitten in Slipper
Handcrafted • N/A
250QFM1544 • **Value $16**

12 Koala & Hearts
Handcrafted • N/A
200VHA3531 • **Value $10**

13 Koala & Lollipop
Handcrafted • N/A
200VHA3651 • **Value $23**

14 Koala & Ruffled Heart
Handcrafted • N/A
200VHA3631 • **Value $70**

15 Koala with
Bow & Arrow
Handcrafted • N/A
200VHA3624 • **Value $14**

16 Lamb
(also avail. in Nativity
Set, #3550QFM1685)
Handcrafted • N/A
225QFM1574 • **Value $23**

17 Mary
(also avail. in Nativity
Set, #3550QFM1685)
Handcrafted • N/A
250QFM1554 • **Value $12**

18 Mouse Angel
Handcrafted • N/A
250QFM1551 • **Value $30**

19 Mouse in Cornucopia
Handcrafted • N/A
225QFM1514 • **Value $14**

\ PENCIL TOTALS

Value Guide — Merry Miniatures

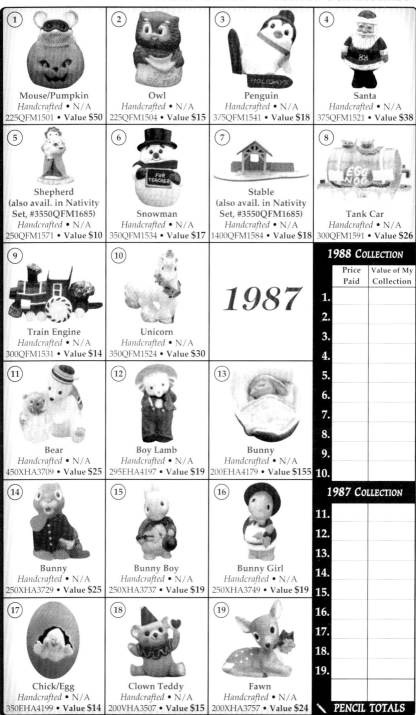

1. Mouse/Pumpkin
Handcrafted • N/A
225QFM1501 • **Value $50**

2. Owl
Handcrafted • N/A
225QFM1504 • **Value $15**

3. Penguin
Handcrafted • N/A
375QFM1541 • **Value $18**

4. Santa
Handcrafted • N/A
375QFM1521 • **Value $38**

5. Shepherd
(also avail. in Nativity
Set, #3550QFM1685)
Handcrafted • N/A
250QFM1571 • **Value $10**

6. Snowman
Handcrafted • N/A
350QFM1534 • **Value $17**

7. Stable
(also avail. in Nativity
Set, #3550QFM1685)
Handcrafted • N/A
1400QFM1584 • **Value $18**

8. Tank Car
Handcrafted • N/A
300QFM1591 • **Value $26**

9. Train Engine
Handcrafted • N/A
300QFM1531 • **Value $14**

10. Unicorn
Handcrafted • N/A
350QFM1524 • **Value $30**

1987

11. Bear
Handcrafted • N/A
450XHA3709 • **Value $25**

12. Boy Lamb
Handcrafted • N/A
295EHA4197 • **Value $19**

13. Bunny
Handcrafted • N/A
200EHA4179 • **Value $155**

14. Bunny
Handcrafted • N/A
250XHA3729 • **Value $25**

15. Bunny Boy
Handcrafted • N/A
250XHA3737 • **Value $19**

16. Bunny Girl
Handcrafted • N/A
250XHA3749 • **Value $19**

17. Chick/Egg
Handcrafted • N/A
350EHA4199 • **Value $14**

18. Clown Teddy
Handcrafted • N/A
200VHA3507 • **Value $15**

19. Fawn
Handcrafted • N/A
200XHA3757 • **Value $24**

1988 Collection

	Price Paid	Value of My Collection
1.		
2.		
3.		
4.		
5.		
6.		
7.		
8.		
9.		
10.		

1987 Collection

11.		
12.		
13.		
14.		
15.		
16.		
17.		
18.		
19.		

PENCIL TOTALS

MERRY MINIATURES

VALUE GUIDE – MERRY MINIATURES

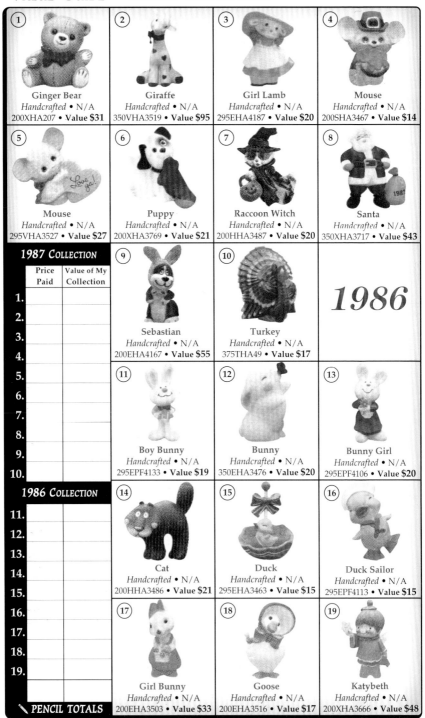

1
Ginger Bear
Handcrafted • N/A
200XHA207 • **Value $31**

2
Giraffe
Handcrafted • N/A
350VHA3519 • **Value $95**

3
Girl Lamb
Handcrafted • N/A
295EHA4187 • **Value $20**

4
Mouse
Handcrafted • N/A
200SHA3467 • **Value $14**

5
Mouse
Handcrafted • N/A
295VHA3527 • **Value $27**

6
Puppy
Handcrafted • N/A
200XHA3769 • **Value $21**

7
Raccoon Witch
Handcrafted • N/A
200HHA3487 • **Value $20**

8
Santa
Handcrafted • N/A
350XHA3717 • **Value $43**

9
Sebastian
Handcrafted • N/A
200EHA4167 • **Value $55**

10
Turkey
Handcrafted • N/A
375THA49 • **Value $17**

1986

11
Boy Bunny
Handcrafted • N/A
295EPF4133 • **Value $19**

12
Bunny
Handcrafted • N/A
350EHA3476 • **Value $20**

13
Bunny Girl
Handcrafted • N/A
295EPF4106 • **Value $20**

14
Cat
Handcrafted • N/A
200HHA3486 • **Value $21**

15
Duck
Handcrafted • N/A
295EHA3463 • **Value $15**

16
Duck Sailor
Handcrafted • N/A
295EPF4113 • **Value $15**

17
Girl Bunny
Handcrafted • N/A
200EHA3503 • **Value $33**

18
Goose
Handcrafted • N/A
200EHA3516 • **Value $17**

19
Katybeth
Handcrafted • N/A
200XHA3666 • **Value $48**

1987 COLLECTION

	Price Paid	Value of My Collection
1.		
2.		
3.		
4.		
5.		
6.		
7.		
8.		
9.		
10.		

1986 COLLECTION

11.		
12.		
13.		
14.		
15.		
16.		
17.		
18.		
19.		

PENCIL TOTALS

242

Merry Miniatures

1 Mouse
Handcrafted • N/A
200XHA3533 • **Value $75**

2 Mr. Mouse
Handcrafted • N/A
200XHA3573 • **Value $30**

3 Mr. Squirrel
Handcrafted • N/A
200THA3403 • **Value $20**

4 Mrs. Mouse
Handcrafted • N/A
200XHA3653 • **Value $30**

5 Mrs. Squirrel
Handcrafted • N/A
200THA3416 • **Value $19**

6 Owl
Handcrafted • N/A
200GHA3456 • **Value $16**

7 Pandas
Handcrafted • N/A
350VHA3523 • **Value $25**

8 Penguin
Handcrafted • N/A
295XHA4413 • **Value $23**

9 Rhonda
Handcrafted • N/A
350XHA3553 • **Value $40**

10 Rodney
Handcrafted • N/A
350XHA3546 • **Value $25**

11 Santa
Handcrafted • N/A
350XHA3673 • **Value $44**

12 Sebastian
Handcrafted • N/A
200VHA3516 • **Value $80**

13 Sebastian
Handcrafted • N/A
200XHA3566 • **Value $90**

14 Sheep & Bell
Handcrafted • N/A
295EPF4126 • **Value $14**

15 Unicorn
Handcrafted • N/A
200VHA3503 • **Value $15**

16 Witch
Handcrafted • N/A
300HHS3473 • **Value $100**

1985

17 Basket
Handcrafted • N/A
200EHA3495 • **Value $45**

18 Bears
Handcrafted • N/A
450XHA3392 • **Value $26**

19 Bunny
Handcrafted • N/A
200EHA3482 • **Value $38**

1986 Collection

	Price Paid	Value of My Collection
1.		
2.		
3.		
4.		
5.		
6.		
7.		
8.		
9.		
10.		
11.		
12.		
13.		
14.		
15.		
16.		

1985 Collection

17.		
18.		
19.		
PENCIL TOTALS		

MERRY MINIATURES

VALUE GUIDE — MERRY MINIATURES

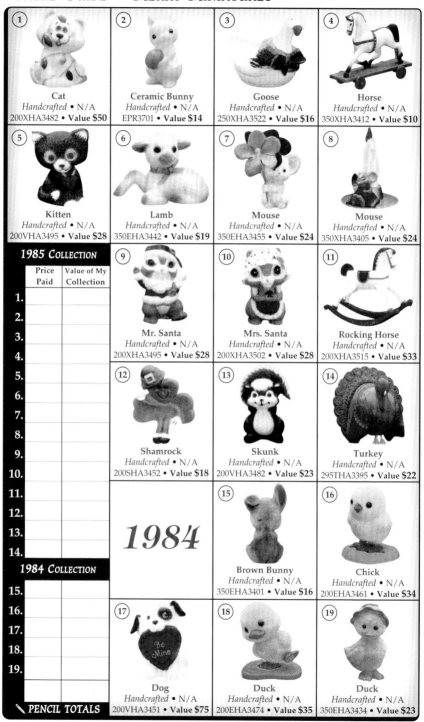

(1) Cat
Handcrafted • N/A
200XHA3482 • **Value $50**

(2) Ceramic Bunny
Handcrafted • N/A
EPR3701 • **Value $14**

(3) Goose
Handcrafted • N/A
250XHA3522 • **Value $16**

(4) Horse
Handcrafted • N/A
350XHA3412 • **Value $10**

(5) Kitten
Handcrafted • N/A
200VHA3495 • **Value $28**

(6) Lamb
Handcrafted • N/A
350EHA3442 • **Value $19**

(7) Mouse
Handcrafted • N/A
350EHA3455 • **Value $24**

(8) Mouse
Handcrafted • N/A
350XHA3405 • **Value $24**

(9) Mr. Santa
Handcrafted • N/A
200XHA3495 • **Value $28**

(10) Mrs. Santa
Handcrafted • N/A
200XHA3502 • **Value $28**

(11) Rocking Horse
Handcrafted • N/A
200XHA3515 • **Value $33**

(12) Shamrock
Handcrafted • N/A
200SHA3452 • **Value $18**

(13) Skunk
Handcrafted • N/A
200VHA3482 • **Value $23**

(14) Turkey
Handcrafted • N/A
295THA3395 • **Value $22**

1984

(15) Brown Bunny
Handcrafted • N/A
350EHA3401 • **Value $16**

(16) Chick
Handcrafted • N/A
200EHA3461 • **Value $34**

(17) Dog
Handcrafted • N/A
200VHA3451 • **Value $75**

(18) Duck
Handcrafted • N/A
200EHA3474 • **Value $35**

(19) Duck
Handcrafted • N/A
350EHA3434 • **Value $23**

1985 COLLECTION

	Price Paid	Value of My Collection
1.		
2.		
3.		
4.		
5.		
6.		
7.		
8.		
9.		
10.		
11.		
12.		
13.		
14.		

1984 COLLECTION

	Price Paid	Value of My Collection
15.		
16.		
17.		
18.		
19.		
PENCIL TOTALS		

VALUE GUIDE – MERRY MINIATURES

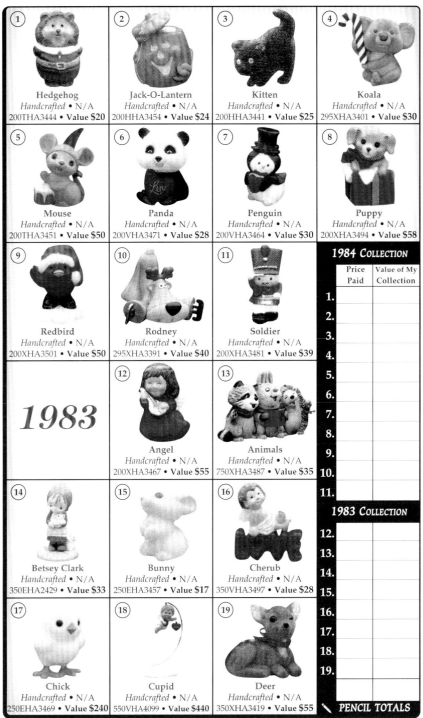

1 Hedgehog
Handcrafted • N/A
200THA3444 • **Value $20**

2 Jack-O-Lantern
Handcrafted • N/A
200HHA3454 • **Value $24**

3 Kitten
Handcrafted • N/A
200HHA3441 • **Value $25**

4 Koala
Handcrafted • N/A
295XHA3401 • **Value $30**

5 Mouse
Handcrafted • N/A
200THA3451 • **Value $50**

6 Panda
Handcrafted • N/A
200VHA3471 • **Value $28**

7 Penguin
Handcrafted • N/A
200VHA3464 • **Value $30**

8 Puppy
Handcrafted • N/A
200XHA3494 • **Value $58**

9 Redbird
Handcrafted • N/A
200XHA3501 • **Value $50**

10 Rodney
Handcrafted • N/A
295XHA3391 • **Value $40**

11 Soldier
Handcrafted • N/A
200XHA3481 • **Value $39**

1983

12 Angel
Handcrafted • N/A
200XHA3467 • **Value $55**

13 Animals
Handcrafted • N/A
750XHA3487 • **Value $35**

14 Betsey Clark
Handcrafted • N/A
350EHA2429 • **Value $33**

15 Bunny
Handcrafted • N/A
250EHA3457 • **Value $17**

16 Cherub
Handcrafted • N/A
350VHA3497 • **Value $28**

17 Chick
Handcrafted • N/A
250EHA3469 • **Value $240**

18 Cupid
Handcrafted • N/A
550VHA4099 • **Value $440**

19 Deer
Handcrafted • N/A
350XHA3419 • **Value $55**

1984 Collection

	Price Paid	Value of My Collection
1.		
2.		
3.		
4.		
5.		
6.		
7.		
8.		
9.		
10.		
11.		

1983 Collection

12.		
13.		
14.		
15.		
16.		
17.		
18.		
19.		
PENCIL TOTALS		

MERRY MINIATURES

VALUE GUIDE — MERRY MINIATURES

(1) Duck
Handcrafted • N/A
250EHA3477 • **Value $240**

(2) Flocked Bunny
Handcrafted • N/A
350EHA3417 • **Value $17**

(3) Kitten
Handcrafted • N/A
200XHA3447 • **Value $45**

(4) Kitten
Handcrafted • N/A
350VHA3489 • **Value $120**

(5) Mouse
Handcrafted • N/A
200XHA3459 • **Value $47**

(6) Mouse
Handcrafted • N/A
350SHA3407 • **Value $20**

(7) Penguin
Handcrafted • N/A
295XHA3439 • **Value $80**

(8) Polar Bear
Handcrafted • N/A
350XHA3407 • **Value $260**

1983 COLLECTION

	Price Paid	Value of My Collection
1.		
2.		
3.		
4.		
5.		
6.		
7.		
8.		
9.		
10.		
11.		
12.		

1982 COLLECTION

13.		
14.		
15.		
16.		
17.		
18.		
19.		

PENCIL TOTALS

(9) Santa
Handcrafted • N/A
295XHA3427 • **Value $45**

(10) Shirt Tales
Handcrafted • N/A
295HHA3437 • **Value $42**

(11) Snowman
Handcrafted • N/A
300XHA3479 • **Value $43**

(12) Turkey
Handcrafted • N/A
295THA207 • **Value $45**

1982

(13) Ceramic Bunny
Handcrafted • N/A
300EPF3702 • **Value $50**

(14) Duck
Handcrafted • N/A
300EHA3403 • **Value $33**

(15) Kermit
Handcrafted • N/A
395VHA3403 • **Value $30**

(16) Kitten
Handcrafted • N/A
395HHA3466 • **Value $55**

(17) Miss Piggy
Handcrafted • N/A
395VHA3416 • **Value $30**

(18) Mouse
Handcrafted • N/A
450XHA5023 • **Value $65**

(19) Pilgrim Mouse
Handcrafted • N/A
295THA3433 • **Value $225**

VALUE GUIDE — MERRY MINIATURES

1
Rocking Horse
Handcrafted • N/A
450XHA5003 • **Value $100**

2
Santa (rigid)
Handcrafted • N/A
450XHA5016 • **Value $180**

3
Tree
Handcrafted • N/A
450XHA5006 • **Value $160**

4
Witch
Handcrafted • N/A
395HHA3456 • **Value $400**

1981

5
Cupid
Handcrafted • N/A
300VPF3465 • **Value $60**

6
Ghost
Handcrafted • N/A
300HHA3402 • **Value $320**

7
Lamb
Handcrafted • N/A
300EPF402 • **Value $30**

8
Leprechaun
Handcrafted • N/A
300SHA3415 • **Value $49**

9
Penguin
Handcrafted • N/A
300XHA3412 • **Value $110**

10
Raccoon Pilgrim
Handcrafted • N/A
300THA3402 • **Value $51**

11
Redbird
Handcrafted • N/A
300XHA3405 • **Value $40**

12
Squirrel Indian
Handcrafted • N/A
300THA3415 • **Value $53**

13
Turkey
Handcrafted • N/A
300THA22 • **Value $55**

1980

14
Angel
Handcrafted • N/A
300XPF3471 • **Value $40**

15
Kitten
Handcrafted • N/A
300XPF3421 • **Value $40**

16
Pipe
Handcrafted • N/A
75SPF1017 • **Value $64**

17
Reindeer
Handcrafted • N/A
300XPF3464 • **Value $110**

18
Santa
Handcrafted • N/A
300XPF39 • **Value $35**

1982 COLLECTION		
	Price Paid	Value of My Collection
1.		
2.		
3.		
4.		
1981 COLLECTION		
5.		
6.		
7.		
8.		
9.		
10.		
11.		
12.		
13.		
1980 COLLECTION		
14.		
15.		
16.		
17.		
18.		
PENCIL TOTALS		

MERRY MINIATURES

Value Guide — Merry Miniatures

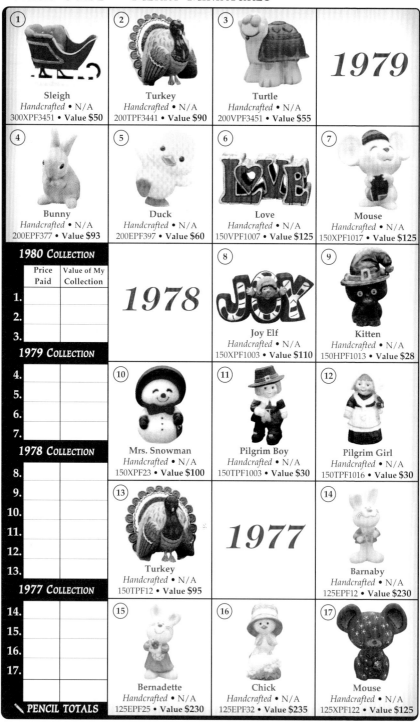

1. Sleigh
Handcrafted • N/A
300XPF3451 • **Value $50**

2. Turkey
Handcrafted • N/A
200TPF3441 • **Value $90**

3. Turtle
Handcrafted • N/A
200VPF3451 • **Value $55**

1979

4. Bunny
Handcrafted • N/A
200EPF377 • **Value $93**

5. Duck
Handcrafted • N/A
200EPF397 • **Value $60**

6. Love
Handcrafted • N/A
150VPF1007 • **Value $125**

7. Mouse
Handcrafted • N/A
150XPF1017 • **Value $125**

1978

8. Joy Elf
Handcrafted • N/A
150XPF1003 • **Value $110**

9. Kitten
Handcrafted • N/A
150HPF1013 • **Value $28**

10. Mrs. Snowman
Handcrafted • N/A
150XPF23 • **Value $100**

11. Pilgrim Boy
Handcrafted • N/A
150TPF1003 • **Value $30**

12. Pilgrim Girl
Handcrafted • N/A
150TPF1016 • **Value $30**

13. Turkey
Handcrafted • N/A
150TPF12 • **Value $95**

1977

14. Barnaby
Handcrafted • N/A
125EPF12 • **Value $230**

15. Bernadette
Handcrafted • N/A
125EPF25 • **Value $230**

16. Chick
Handcrafted • N/A
125EPF32 • **Value $235**

17. Mouse
Handcrafted • N/A
125XPF122 • **Value $125**

1980 Collection

	Price Paid	Value of My Collection
1.		
2.		
3.		

1979 Collection

4.		
5.		
6.		
7.		

1978 Collection

8.		
9.		
10.		
11.		
12.		
13.		

1977 Collection

14.		
15.		
16.		
17.		

PENCIL TOTALS

248

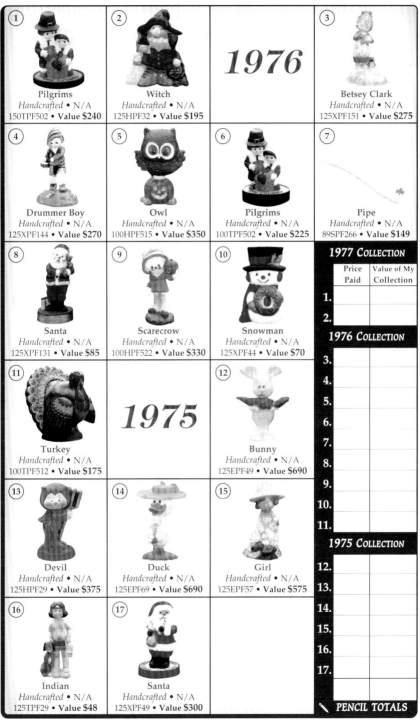

1 Pilgrims
Handcrafted • N/A
150TPF502 • **Value $240**

2 Witch
Handcrafted • N/A
125HPF32 • **Value $195**

1976

3 Betsey Clark
Handcrafted • N/A
125XPF151 • **Value $275**

4 Drummer Boy
Handcrafted • N/A
125XPF144 • **Value $270**

5 Owl
Handcrafted • N/A
100HPF515 • **Value $350**

6 Pilgrims
Handcrafted • N/A
100TPF502 • **Value $225**

7 Pipe
Handcrafted • N/A
89SPF266 • **Value $149**

8 Santa
Handcrafted • N/A
125XPF131 • **Value $85**

9 Scarecrow
Handcrafted • N/A
100HPF522 • **Value $330**

10 Snowman
Handcrafted • N/A
125XPF44 • **Value $70**

11 Turkey
Handcrafted • N/A
100TPF512 • **Value $175**

1975

12 Bunny
Handcrafted • N/A
125EPF49 • **Value $690**

13 Devil
Handcrafted • N/A
125HPF29 • **Value $375**

14 Duck
Handcrafted • N/A
125EPF69 • **Value $690**

15 Girl
Handcrafted • N/A
125EPF57 • **Value $575**

16 Indian
Handcrafted • N/A
125TPF29 • **Value $48**

17 Santa
Handcrafted • N/A
125XPF49 • **Value $300**

1977 Collection	Price Paid	Value of My Collection
1.		
2.		
1976 Collection		
3.		
4.		
5.		
6.		
7.		
8.		
9.		
10.		
11.		
1975 Collection		
12.		
13.		
14.		
15.		
16.		
17.		
PENCIL TOTALS		

Merry Miniatures

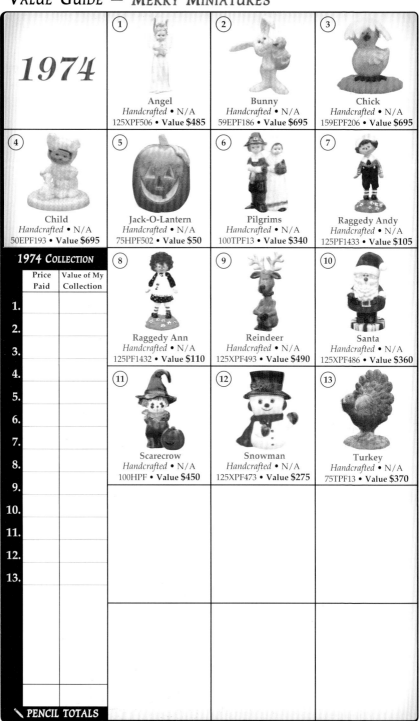

1974

(1) Angel
Handcrafted • N/A
125XPF506 • **Value $485**

(2) Bunny
Handcrafted • N/A
59EPF186 • **Value $695**

(3) Chick
Handcrafted • N/A
159EPF206 • **Value $695**

(4) Child
Handcrafted • N/A
50EPF193 • **Value $695**

(5) Jack-O-Lantern
Handcrafted • N/A
75HPF502 • **Value $50**

(6) Pilgrims
Handcrafted • N/A
100TPF13 • **Value $340**

(7) Raggedy Andy
Handcrafted • N/A
125PF1433 • **Value $105**

(8) Raggedy Ann
Handcrafted • N/A
125PF1432 • **Value $110**

(9) Reindeer
Handcrafted • N/A
125XPF493 • **Value $490**

(10) Santa
Handcrafted • N/A
125XPF486 • **Value $360**

(11) Scarecrow
Handcrafted • N/A
100HPF • **Value $450**

(12) Snowman
Handcrafted • N/A
125XPF473 • **Value $275**

(13) Turkey
Handcrafted • N/A
75TPF13 • **Value $370**

1974 COLLECTION

	Price Paid	Value of My Collection
1.		
2.		
3.		
4.		
5.		
6.		
7.		
8.		
9.		
10.		
11.		
12.		
13.		

PENCIL TOTALS

Kiddie Car Classics

Hallmark's popular collection of Kiddie Car Classics are miniature replicas of old-fashioned pedal cars. Since the collection's introduction in 1992, there have been 39 Kiddie Car Classics released, plus two special editions available only at Artists On Tour events. In addition to the Kiddie Car Classics, there have been 15 releases in the Sidewalk Cruisers collection and 7 introductions to a new collection called Kiddie Car Corner.

1997

1937 GARTON® Ford
(LE-24,500)
Current
6500QHG9035 • **Value $65**

1938 GARTON® Lincoln
Zephyr (LE-24,500)
Current
6500QHG9038 • **Value $65**

1939 GARTON® Ford
Station Wagon
Current
5500QHG9034 • **Value $55**

1940 Gendron "Red
Hot" Roadster
Current
5500QHG9037 • **Value $55**

1941 Steelcraft
Oldsmobile by Murray®
Current
5500QHG9036 • **Value $55**

1956 Murray® Golden
Eagle (LE-29,500)
Current
5000QHG9033 • **Value $50**

1941 Murray® Junior
Service Truck
Current
5500QHG9031 • **Value $55**

KC's Garage (LE-29,500)
Current
7000QHG3601 • **Value $70**

Pedal Petroleum
Gas Pump
Current
2500QHG3602 • **Value $25**

Pedal Power Premium
Lighted Gas Pump
Current
3000QHG3603 • **Value $30**

Sidewalk Sales Signs
Current
1500QHG3605 • **Value $15**

Sidewalk Service Signs
Current
1500QHG3604 • **Value $15**

Welcome Sign (1st in
Bill's Boards Series)
Current
3000QHG3606 • **Value $30**

1937 Scamp Wagon
(LE-29,500)
Current
4800QHG6318 • **Value $48**

1939 American
National Pedal Bike
Current
3800QHG6314 • **Value $38**

KIDDIE CAR CLASSICS		
	Price Paid	Value of My Collection
1.		
2.		
3.		
4.		
5.		
6.		
KIDDIE CAR CORNER		
7.		
8.		
9.		
10.		
11.		
12.		
13.		
SIDEWALK CRUISERS		
14.		
15.		
PENCIL TOTALS		

KIDDIE CAR CLASSICS

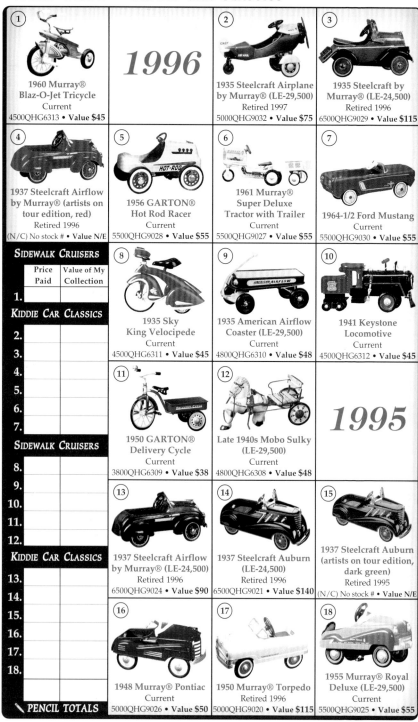

(1) 1960 Murray®
Blaz-O-Jet Tricycle
Current
4500QHG6313 • Value $45

1996

(2) 1935 Steelcraft Airplane
by Murray® (LE-29,500)
Retired 1997
5000QHG9032 • Value $75

(3) 1935 Steelcraft by
Murray® (LE-24,500)
Retired 1996
6500QHG9029 • Value $115

(4) 1937 Steelcraft Airflow
by Murray® (artists on
tour edition, red)
Retired 1996
(N/C) No stock # • Value N/E

(5) 1956 GARTON®
Hot Rod Racer
Current
5500QHG9028 • Value $55

(6) 1961 Murray®
Super Deluxe
Tractor with Trailer
Current
5500QHG9027 • Value $55

(7) 1964-1/2 Ford Mustang
Current
5500QHG9030 • Value $55

Sidewalk Cruisers

	Price Paid	Value of My Collection
Kiddie Car Classics		
1.		
2.		
3.		
4.		
5.		
6.		
7.		
Sidewalk Cruisers		
8.		
9.		
10.		
11.		
12.		
Kiddie Car Classics		
13.		
14.		
15.		
16.		
17.		
18.		
Pencil Totals		

(8) 1935 Sky
King Velocipede
Current
4500QHG6311 • Value $45

(9) 1935 American Airflow
Coaster (LE-29,500)
Current
4800QHG6310 • Value $48

(10) 1941 Keystone
Locomotive
Current
4500QHG6312 • Value $45

(11) 1950 GARTON®
Delivery Cycle
Current
3800QHG6309 • Value $38

(12) Late 1940s Mobo Sulky
(LE-29,500)
Current
4800QHG6308 • Value $48

1995

(13) 1937 Steelcraft Airflow
by Murray® (LE-24,500)
Retired 1996
6500QHG9024 • Value $90

(14) 1937 Steelcraft Auburn
(LE-24,500)
Retired 1996
6500QHG9021 • Value $140

(15) 1937 Steelcraft Auburn
(artists on tour edition,
dark green)
Retired 1995
(N/C) No stock # • Value N/E

(16) 1948 Murray® Pontiac
Current
5000QHG9026 • Value $50

(17) 1950 Murray® Torpedo
Retired 1996
5000QHG9020 • Value $115

(18) 1955 Murray® Royal
Deluxe (LE-29,500)
Current
5500QHG9025 • Value $55

VALUE GUIDE – KIDDIE CAR CLASSICS

1
1959 GARTON® Deluxe Kidillac
Retired 1996
5500QHG9017 • **Value $75**

2
1961 GARTON® Casey Jones Locomotive
Retired 1996
5500QHG9019 • **Value $80**

3
1962 Murray® Super Deluxe Fire Truck
Current
5500QHG9095 • **Value $55**

4
1964 GARTON® Tin Lizzie
Retiring by December 1997
5000QHG9023 • **Value $50**

5
1935 Steelcraft Streamline Velocipede by Murray®
Current
4500QHG6306 • **Value $45**

6
1937 Steelcraft Streamline Scooter by Murray®
Retiring by December 1997
3500QHG6301 • **Value $35**

7
1939 Mobo Horse
Current
4500QHG6304 • **Value $45**

8
1940 GARTON® Aero Flite Wagon (LE-29,500)
Current
4800QHG6305 • **Value $48**

9
1958 Murray® Police Cycle (LE-29,500)
Current
5500QHG6307 • **Value $55**

10
1963 GARTON® Speedster
Current
3800QHG6303 • **Value $38**

11
1966 GARTON® Super-Sonda
Retiring by December 1997
4500QHG6302 • **Value $45**

KIDDIE CAR CLASSICS

	Price Paid	Value of My Collection
1.		
2.		
3.		
4.		

1994

12
1939 Steelcraft Lincoln Zephyr by Murray® (LE-24,500)
Retired 1996
5000QHG9015 • **Value $100**

13
1941 Steelcraft Spitfire Airplane by Murray® (LE-19,500)
Retired 1996
5000QHG9009 • **Value $160**

SIDEWALK CRUISERS

5.		
6.		
7.		
8.		
9.		
10.		
11.		

14
1955 Murray® Dump Truck (LE-19,500)
Retired 1996
4800QHG9011 • **Value $115**

15
1955 Murray® Fire Truck (LE-19,500, white)
Retired 1996
5000QHG9010 • **Value $245**

16
1955 Murray® Ranch Wagon (LE-19,500)
Retired 1996
4800QHG9007 • **Value $95**

KIDDIE CAR CLASSICS

12.		
13.		
14.		
15.		
16.		
17.		
18.		
19.		

17
1955 Murray® Red Champion (LE-19,500)
Retired 1996
4500QHG9002 • **Value $115**

18
1956 GARTON® Dragnet® Police Car (LE-24,500)
Current
5000QHG9016 • **Value $50**

19
1956 GARTON® Kidillac
Retired 1994
5000QHX9094 • **Value $50**

PENCIL TOTALS

KIDDIE CAR CLASSICS

Value Guide – Kiddie Car Classics

①	**②**	**③**	**④**
1956 GARTON® Mark V (LE-24,500) Current 4500QHG9022 • **Value $45**	**1958 Murray® Atomic Missile (LE-24,500)** Retired 1997 5500QHG9018 • **Value $85**	**1961 Murray® Circus Car (LE-24,500)** Current 4800QHG9014 • **Value $48**	**1961 Murray® Speedway Pace Car (LE-24,500)** Current 4500QHG9013 • **Value $45**

1993

⑤
1955 Murray® Fire Chief (LE-19,500)
Retired 1996
4500QHG9006 • **Value $120**

⑥
1968 Murray® Boat Jolly Roger (LE-19,500)
Retired 1996
5000QHG9005 • **Value $90**

1992

Kiddie Car Classics

	Price Paid	Value of My Collection
1.		
2.		
3.		
4.		

⑦
1941 Murray® Airplane (LE-14,500)
Retired 1993
5000QHG9003 • **Value $375**

⑧
1953 Murray® Dump Truck (LE-14,500)
Retired 1993
4800QHG9012 • **Value $280**

⑨
1955 Murray® Champion (LE-14,500)
Retired 1993
4500QHG9008 • **Value $325**

Kiddie Car Classics

5.		
6.		

⑩
1955 Murray® Fire Truck (LE-14,500)
Retired 1993
5000QHG9001 • **Value $340**

⑪
1955 Murray® Tractor and Trailer (LE-14,500)
Retired 1993
5500QHG9004 • **Value $320**

Kiddie Car Classics

7.		
8.		
9.		
10.		
11.		

＼ PENCIL TOTALS

Use these pages to record future Hallmark releases.

HALLMARK ORNAMENTS	Material	Artist	Stock #	Price Paid	Value of My Collection
PENCIL TOTALS				PRICE PAID	MARKET VALUE

HALLMARK ORNAMENTS	Material	Artist	Stock #	Price Paid	Value of My Collection
				PENCIL TOTALS	
				PRICE PAID	MARKET VALUE

VALUE GUIDE — FUTURE RELEASES

Use this page to record future Spring Ornaments, Merry Miniatures or Kiddie Car Classics.

OTHER HALLMARK COLLECTIBLES	Material	Artist	Stock #	Price Paid	Value of My Collection
			PENCIL TOTALS		
				PRICE PAID	MARKET VALUE

Total Value Of My Collection

Record the value of your collection here by adding the pencil totals from the bottom of each value guide page.

HALLMARK ORNAMENTS	Price Paid	Market Value	HALLMARK ORNAMENTS	Price Paid	Market Value
Page 31			Page 55		
Page 32			Page 56		
Page 33			Page 57		
Page 34			Page 58		
Page 35			Page 59		
Page 36			Page 60		
Page 37			Page 61		
Page 38			Page 62		
Page 39			Page 63		
Page 40			Page 64		
Page 41			Page 65		
Page 42			Page 66		
Page 43			Page 67		
Page 44			Page 68		
Page 45			Page 69		
Page 46			Page 70		
Page 47			Page 71		
Page 48			Page 72		
Page 49			Page 73		
Page 50			Page 74		
Page 51			Page 75		
Page 52			Page 76		
Page 53			Page 77		
Page 54			Page 78		
TOTAL			**TOTAL**		

PAGE SUBTOTALS		
	PRICE PAID	MARKET VALUE

Total Value Of My Collection

Record the value of your collection here by adding the pencil totals from the bottom of each value guide page.

HALLMARK ORNAMENTS	Price Paid	Market Value
Page 79		
Page 80		
Page 81		
Page 82		
Page 83		
Page 84		
Page 85		
Page 86		
Page 87		
Page 88		
Page 89		
Page 90		
Page 91		
Page 92		
Page 93		
Page 94		
Page 95		
Page 96		
Page 97		
Page 98		
Page 99		
Page 100		
Page 101		
Page 102		
TOTAL		

HALLMARK ORNAMENTS	Price Paid	Market Value
Page 103		
Page 104		
Page 105		
Page 106		
Page 107		
Page 108		
Page 109		
Page 110		
Page 111		
Page 112		
Page 113		
Page 114		
Page 115		
Page 116		
Page 117		
Page 118		
Page 119		
Page 120		
Page 121		
Page 122		
Page 123		
Page 124		
Page 125		
Page 126		
TOTAL		

PAGE SUBTOTALS	PRICE PAID	MARKET VALUE

Total Value Of My Collection

Record the value of your collection here by adding the pencil totals from the bottom of each value guide page.

HALLMARK ORNAMENTS	Price Paid	Market Value
Page 127		
Page 128		
Page 129		
Page 130		
Page 131		
Page 132		
Page 133		
Page 134		
Page 135		
Page 136		
Page 137		
Page 138		
Page 139		
Page 140		
Page 141		
Page 142		
Page 143		
Page 144		
Page 145		
Page 146		
Page 147		
Page 148		
Page 149		
Page 150		
TOTAL		

HALLMARK ORNAMENTS	Price Paid	Market Value
Page 151		
Page 152		
Page 153		
Page 154		
Page 155		
Page 156		
Page 157		
Page 158		
Page 159		
Page 160		
Page 161		
Page 162		
Page 163		
Page 164		
Page 165		
Page 166		
Page 167		
Page 168		
Page 169		
Page 170		
Page 171		
Page 172		
Page 173		
Page 174		
TOTAL		

PAGE SUBTOTALS		
	PRICE PAID	MARKET VALUE

Total Value Of My Collection

Record the value of your collection here by adding the pencil totals from the bottom of each value guide page.

HALLMARK ORNAMENTS	Price Paid	Market Value
Page 175		
Page 176		
Page 177		
Page 178		
Page 179		
Page 180		
Page 181		
Page 182		
Page 183		
Page 184		
Page 185		
Page 186		
Page 187		
Page 188		
Page 189		
Page 190		
Page 191		
Page 192		
Page 193		
Page 194		
Page 195		
Page 196		
Page 197		
Page 198		
TOTAL		

HALLMARK ORNAMENTS	Price Paid	Market Value
Page 199		
Page 200		
Page 201		
Page 202		
Page 203		
Page 204		
Page 205		
Page 206		
Page 207		
Page 208		
Page 209		
Page 210		
Page 211		
Page 212		
Page 213		
Page 255		
Page 256		
TOTAL		

PAGE SUBTOTALS	PRICE PAID	MARKET VALUE

Total Value Of My Collection

Record the value of your collection here by adding the pencil totals from the bottom of each value guide page.

SPRING ORNAMENTS	Price Paid	Market Value
Page 214		
Page 215		
Page 216		
Page 217		
Page 218		
Page 219		
Page 220		
Page 257		
TOTAL		

MERRY MINIATURES	Price Paid	Market Value
Page 221		
Page 222		
Page 223		
Page 224		
Page 225		
Page 226		
Page 227		
Page 228		
Page 229		
Page 230		
Page 231		
Page 232		
Page 233		
Page 234		
Page 235		
Page 236		
Page 237		
Page 238		
Page 239		
Page 240		
Page 241		
Page 242		
Page 243		
Page 244		
Page 245		
Page 246		
Page 247		
Page 248		
Page 249		
Page 250		
Page 257		
TOTAL		

KIDDIE CAR CLASSICS	Price Paid	Market Value
Page 251		
Page 252		
Page 253		
Page 254		
Page 257		
TOTAL		

GRAND TOTALS	PRICE PAID	MARKET VALUE

Secondary Market Overview

For most collectible lines, secondary market demand is created when pieces are removed from production and are no longer available in retail stores. This results in an increase in their value, based on collector demand for these now hard-to-find pieces. Frequently, there is a range of prices on each piece and not one hard and fast dollar value. Secondary market prices do fluctuate over time; it all depends on what price collectors are selling their pieces for and, more importantly, whether other collectors are willing to pay that price. Hallmark Ornaments follow this general pattern, except for a few important twists.

I. How does the Hallmark Ornaments secondary market work?

First of all, Hallmark Ornaments differs from most collectible lines in that there is an entirely new collection every year. That is, aside from very rare exceptions, the ornaments are produced only for the year and then are never made again. In effect, this makes every Hallmark ornament a one-year limited edition – there are no second chances! Ornament collectors don't have the luxury of waiting a couple of years to buy a piece before it is retired; rather, they must decide in a very short time which ornaments they want, knowing full well that any ones missed are likely to be more expensive additions to their collections if purchased on the secondary market.

Although most ornaments retail from about $8 to $20, some highly sought-after ornaments can reach well into the hundreds of dollars on the secondary market! Two main reasons for this is that Hallmark Ornaments is one of the oldest collectible lines, having started in 1973; and every ornament is severely limited in production. Even though they're technically available for a full calendar year, they do not typically appear in stores until July and then they're gone in December – meaning that collectors have only six months to add the ornaments they're looking for in a given year.

Secondary Market Overview

Ornaments in collectible series generally fetch the highest prices on the secondary market. For example, the first editions in the *Frosty Friends* series ($575), *Here Comes Santa* series ($650) and *Tin Locomotive series* ($560) are today valued anywhere from 4,000 to 8,000% over retail! The first editions of the collectible series generally have the highest value, although there are some cases where a second or third edition, for example, is simply in shorter supply than a first edition and so is more coveted on the secondary market. Several different ornament "themes" have proven to be very popular (and more valuable) over the years, most notably those ornaments featuring BARBIE™.

II. Where is the Hallmark Ornaments secondary market?

There are various ways in which collectors can buy and sell ornaments on the secondary market. The first step is to check with your retailer, as many retailers act as middlemen or have connections with other collectors. One of the easiest ways to reach other collectors is through a **secondary market exchange service**. Collectors list the ornaments they wish to sell or buy with the exchange service, which publishes a list of the pieces and the asking price. The exchange acts as the middleman in the transaction for a commission for each completed sale (usually between 10% and 20%). Most exchange listings are published monthly and may require a subscription or membership fee. A few generate daily listings which collectors can call for and receive by mail.

Most of these secondary market exchanges also list other collectible items as well as Hallmark Ornaments, so these may not be the best route to go if you're looking to do some serious ornament "shopping." Instead, there are a handful of secondary market dealers who specialize in Hallmark Ornaments and are noted ornament authorities. These dealers maintain price listings of their own and many collectors give these dealers more credibility when it comes to buying or selling ornaments. On page 267 is a listing of these dealers and exchanges devoted to Hallmark Ornaments.

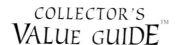

COLLECTOR'S
VALUE GUIDE™

Secondary Market Overview

Many newsletters and magazines feature their own "swap & sell" sections, which operate much the same way as the exchange services. Some collectors place **classified advertisements** in their local newspapers (under Antiques/Collectibles), but it may take longer to sell or find pieces this way because newspapers reach a general readership and not collectors specifically.

The newest and perhaps most exciting secondary market source is the **Internet** via home computer. Here, collectors can find a wealth of information on Hallmark without leaving their homes! Some of the websites and entries will be retail stores that carry Hallmark Ornaments or bulletin boards where collectors can trade, buy and sell pieces. The virtue of these on-line price listings is that they can be updated immediately and can be used for quick sales or trades. The best way to get Hallmark information on the Internet is to use the search functions. Because information is only loosely organized and there can be thousands of entries, it's best to be as specific as possible. You may want to search for specific essential phrases, such as "Hallmark AND secondary" or "Hallmark AND Barbie AND edition." These searches will lead you to retailers, collectors, publishers and secondary market dealers who can help you find what you're looking for. Collectors can also visit the Hallmark web page at *www.hallmark.com* for general information, although Hallmark, like most manufacturers, does not get directly involved with the secondary market.

Some **retailers** are also active on the secondary market, either working as an exchange service or selling directly to collectors. If a collector is looking to sell a large number of ornaments or an entire collection, contacting a retailer may be ideal because of the dollar amounts involved. Other retailers who don't buy and sell secondary market pieces may sponsor **secondary market collector shows** as a service to their customers. Local and regional collector clubs also sponsor secondary market events.

Secondary Market Overview

Whether you're buying or selling on the secondary market, an important factor to consider is the packaging of the ornaments. In the "real world," a box is just a box; but in the world of collectibles, boxes can actually affect the secondary market value of your ornaments. Not only are the boxes perfect for storage and protection of your ornaments, but many collectors will consider an ornament sold without its original packaging to be "incomplete," and these will generally command a lower price on the secondary market.

Many price listings will specify the condition of the box for those pieces listing for sale. "MIB" means the ornament is "mint in box;" some listings won't use this designation, but they will note, for example, that "ornament is MIB unless otherwise noted." Ornaments can also be listed as "NB" (no box), "DB" (damaged box) or even "NT" (no original price tag). All of these conditions will generally reduce the market value of an ornament by 10%, 20% or even up to 40%, especially for "no box."

Secondary Market Overview

EXCHANGES, DEALERS & NEWSLETTERS

Collectible Exchange, Inc.
6621 Columbiana Road
New Middletown, OH 44442
(216) 542-9646

The Baggage Car
Meredith DeGood
3100 Justin Drive, Suite B
Des Moines, IA 50322
(515) 270-9080

Mary Johnson
P.O. Box 1015
Marion, NC 28752-1015
(704) 652-2910

The Ornament Trader Magazine
P.O. Box 469
Lavonia, GA 30553-0469
1-800-441-1551

Ronnie Kesterson
300 Camelot Court
Knoxville, TN 37922
(423) 675-7511

Twelve Months of Christmas
Joan Ketterer
P.O. Box 97172
Pittsburgh, PA 15229
(412) 367-2305

The Xmas Shop
P.O. Box 5221
Cary, NC 27512
(919) 469-5264

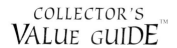

Insuring Your Collection

While the ornaments in your collection hold sentimental value, they also have a dollar value. When you add up each purchase, you may find that you've invested quite a bit putting your collection together. Then, when you look at the secondary market values and figure out what it would cost to replace ornaments in your collection, you might decide you want to insure your collection just as you insure the other valuables in your home. There are three steps to determining whether you should insure your collection; *knowing your current coverage, documenting the contents and value of your collection* and *weighing the risk.*

1. Know your coverage

Collectibles are considered part of the contents of a house and as such, they are typically included in homeowners or renters insurance policies. Ask your agent about the types of loss or damage your policy covers and what it doesn't cover. A standard policy covers household contents for damage or loss from perils such as fire, hurricanes and theft. Common exclusions include earthquakes, floods and breakage through routine handling. In addition to determining the types of loss that are covered, ask your agent about the dollar value that would be paid out in the event that you have to file a claim. The amount paid out will vary based on the type of coverage you have. Today, most insurance policies are written at replacement value which would provide enough money to replace a lost or damaged collection. Replacement value policies pay out the amount needed to actually replace the items which is especially important for collectibles because they appreciate in value.

2. Document the contents and value of your collection

In order to determine how much coverage you need, you must first document your collection to calculate how much it would cost to replace your ornaments. There are many ways to document your collection; from a simple listing to hiring an appraiser, but you should check with your insurance agent first to find out what records the insurance company will accept in the event of a loss. Generally companies want to see proof that you own particular pieces and proof of their value.

COLLECTOR'S
VALUE GUIDE™

Insuring Your Collection

Two of the best forms of documentation are receipts and a "schedule" or listing of each ornament in your collection, including the purchase date, price paid, where you purchased the piece, special markings and secondary market value. Some companies will accept a reputable secondary market guide such as the Collector's Value Guide for pricing.

Two features of the Collector's Value Guide are designed to aid you if you decide to insure your collection. The Value Guide section includes 1997 secondary market prices to help you determine the replacement value of your pieces. Keep in mind that your insurance carrier may want to distinguish between items which are available through normal retail outlets versus pieces which are no longer available. It makes sense to list or "schedule" your valuable pieces on your policy, just as you would for jewelry and other important valuables.

To ensure proper coverage, it is important that your agent understands secondary market values. If you have particularly valuable ornaments or if you have an extensive collection, you should note that the more valuable the item, the more demanding the insurance company will be for industry-accepted valuation. In some cases, the carrier may even want a professional appraisal. For appraisers in your area, contact the American Society of Appraisers at 1-800-ASA-VALU.

Photographs and video footage of your Hallmark ornaments are a good back-up in case of an unforeseen problem claim. Snapshots and video should record closeup views of the piece, including any special markings such as artist signatures. Print two sets of photographs; store one set in your home and give the second set to a friend or put it in a safe deposit box.

Insuring Your Collection

3. *Weigh the risk*

After you calculate the replacement cost of your collection, you can determine if you have adequate insurance to cover any losses. To do this, add the estimated value of your home furnishings to the value of your collectibles (as totaled in this book) and consult your insurance policy for the amount of coverage. Compare the total value of the contents of your home to the dollar amount you would be paid in the event that you had to file a claim.

If you find your policy does not provide enough coverage, you could purchase additional insurance for your collectibles. This can be done by adding a "Personal Articles Floater" (PAF) or a "Fine Arts Floater" or "rider" to your homeowners policy which provides broader coverage and insures your collection for specific dollar amounts. Another option is to purchase a separate policy specifically for collectibles from a specialized insurance provider. One such company is American Collectors Insurance, Inc. in Cherry Hill, New Jersey, which offers coverage for a wide variety of collectibles, from figurines to dolls to memorabilia. A sample application form is shown here. You can reach American Collectors Insurance at: 1-800-257-5758.

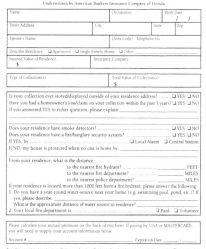

sample application

As with all insurance, you must weigh the risk of loss against the cost of additional coverage.

All About The Artists

From a feeling, from a memory, from an experience . . . an idea is born. For a Hallmark Keepsake artist, new ornaments begin with an idea. Each year, the Hallmark Keepsake artists submit a series of sketches of these concepts to the Creative Product Development Team. The team brainstorms using designers' recommendations to choose the strongest ideas while balancing subject matter and avoiding duplicating previous ornament designs. Final decisions on all ornaments in the Keepsake line are made by the Creative Product Design Team working with the Marketing Division. The real strength of Hallmark Ornaments comes from the creativity and diversity of the Keepsake team and the ability to capture the best from each of the talented artists.

Here are the creative and talented people who bring Hallmark Keepsake Ornaments to life . . .

Patricia Andrews, one of the senior members of the Hallmark staff, began her career at Hallmark in 1976 as an engraver. Since becoming a studio artist in 1987, Andrews – along with husband and fellow Hallmark artist Dill Rhodus – has created some of the more memorable ornaments in the line. Andrews' work with the annual BARBIE™ releases continues in 1997 with four new ornaments celebrating everyone's favorite doll. "Wedding Day 1959-1962," the fourth release in the *BARBIE*™ series, features Barbie as the blushing bride. Andrews also sculpted the BARBIE™ bride in a new two-piece set, "BARBIE™ and KEN™ Wedding Day." "Holiday Barbie™" is the fifth ornament in the series and depicts a dark-haired Barbie in a white ball gown adorned with a velvet ribbon. Andrews has also sculpted the second edition in the Collector's Club Exclusive Series, "1989 Happy Holidays® Barbie® Doll." Among her other offerings are the first editions for two new series ("Scarlett O'Hara™") and ("Marilyn Monroe") the third edition in *A Celebration of Angels* series, and two general ornaments. New Miniature ornaments designed by Andrews are the first edition in the *Snowflake Ballet* series, the third piece in the *Alice in Wonderland* series, and the new three-piece "Casablanca" set.

All About The Artists

Katrina Bricker is one of the newer faces in Hallmark's roster of artists. Although young in years, Bricker is long on talent, as evidenced by her eight new ornament designs. Highlights of her 1997 offerings include the fourth edition in the *Cat Naps* series, the highly-detailed "Yoda™" and several commemorative and photo holders.

Robert Chad, a sculptor, printmaker and animator, has been with Hallmark since 1987. His versatility has resulted in nine new ornaments that range from cartoonish to elegant. Chad taps his sculpting talent for the 10th edition in the *Mary's Angels* series as well as three other Keepsake releases, including the inimitable "Michigan J. Frog" from LOONEY TUNES™. Chad's contributions to the Magic ornaments are another LOONEY TUNES™-based ornament, "Decorator Taz," and a musical ornament, "Santa's Secret Gift." "Santa's Polar Friend," a new general release, depicts Santa happily petting a polar bear pal. Two Miniature ornaments sculpted by Chad are "Ice Cold Coca-Cola®," which features Santa taking a refreshment break, and "Our Lady of Guadalupe," an elegant pewter Precious Edition.

Ken Crow, a former editorial cartoonist and newspaper staff artist, was drawn to Hallmark Ornaments for the chance it gave him to view the world through a child's eyes – something he learned to appreciate from growing up 12 miles from Disneyland. Crow has designed 10 new pieces in 1997 that display the whimsy and creativity his fans have come to expect. In addition to the five adorable bears that make up the Child's Age Collection (for ages one through five), Crow's Keepsake offerings include a Santa-led reindeer bobsled team in "Downhill Run" and the elaborate "The Night Before Christmas," which depicts a scene from the classic tale of holiday magic. Crow makes an elegant statement with his metal and brass "Santa Claus" ornament, while a new Magic ornament, "Santa's Showboat," proves Crow's ability to tackle a complex, detailed design. His Miniature contribution this year is the third and final edition in the *Santa's Little Big Top* series.

John "Collin" Francis has never looked back since he changed his college major from engineering to art. Francis spent his first 17 years at Hallmark working in several departments before landing in the artist studio, where he has created ornaments for 11 years. Francis has designed several memorable ornaments for 1997, including the second edition in the *Madame Alexander*™ series and a fire-fighting panda bear ("Bucket Brigade"). Francis' animated Magic designs are the colorful "Holiday Serenade" and the first edition in the new *Lighthouse Greetings* series. In the whimsical Miniature "Polar Buddies," Francis has a penguin hitching a skating ride with a smiling polar bear.

Tracy Larsen is one of the newest members of the Hallmark family, having joined the staff last year. The multi-talented Larsen captures a variety of styles in his four ornaments. "It's Howdy Doody time" in 1997, as Larsen celebrates the 50th anniversary of the legendary children's TV show in an ornament featuring a happy Mr. Doody waving from an old-style television. A second Keepsake release, "The Spirit of Christmas," depicts an enchanting winter sleighride in an ornament that also doubles as a collector plate. Another heartwarming scene – a cottage nestled in a snowy landscape – is the subject of "The Warmth of Home," a new Magic ornament sculpted by Larsen. Finally, the Miniature collectible series *Old English Village* closes this year with its 10th and final edition, Larsen's "Village Depot."

Joyce Lyle has been a Hallmark Keepsake artist for over 10 years, during which she has produced numerous beautiful ornaments, many of which have been inspired by her family and faith. The creator of the now-retired *Heavenly Angels* series brings an angelic touch to the 1997 Keepsake ornaments with "God's Gift of Love," a porcelain ornament depicting the Holy Family. Other more whimsical Keepsake designs include the eighth edition in the Merry Olde Santa series, a skating beauty ("Elegance on Ice") and the stern "Miss Gulch," the soon-to-be Wicked Witch in *The Wizard of Oz*. Lyle's striking Magic ornament, "Madonna And Child," features Mary and Baby Jesus among the clouds and a softly-lit background.

All About The Artists

Lynn Norton began his career at Hallmark in 1967 and worked as an engraver until 1987, when he joined the artist team. His technical ability and interest in *Star Trek* have made Norton the perennial choice to design the Hallmark ornaments based on the classic television and movie series. Norton's latest Star Trek creation, the "U.S.S. Defiant™," is based on a space cruiser from the *Star Trek: Deep Space Nine* series. Norton returns to earth for more conventional air travel with the first issue in the the *Sky's the Limit* series, which commemorates the Wright brothers' historic first flight at Kitty Hawk.

Don Palmiter has designed Hallmark Keepsake Ornaments for about 10 years, but he's been a member of the Hallmark family for over 25 years. Palmiter began his career as an engraver after joining Hallmark right out of high school. Like many of the Keepsake artists, Palmiter's designs reflect his personal interest, particularly his love of classic automobiles. Among his automobile designs for 1997 are new editions in the *Classic American Cars* series, *Kiddie Car Classics* series, the *All-American Trucks* series, the *Miniature Kiddie Car Classics* series, as well as a new Kiddie Car Classics ornament for the collector's club. Palmiter also has designed Keepsake and miniature versions of the "1997 Corvette." For a change of pace, Palmiter offers the 14th edition in the *Nostalgic Houses and Shops* series and the "Ken" half of "BARBIE™ and KEN™ Wedding Day."

Sharon Pike has been a member of the Hallmark Keepsake Ornaments design team since 1983 and contributes seven Keepsake designs for 1997: two family commemoratives, "Sister to Sister" and "Grandma;" "New Home," for collectors who have changed addresses recently; a mousey card shark in "What A Deal!;" a bell-ringing squirrel in "Jingle Bell Jester;" the heartwarming "Our First Christmas Together," a heart-shaped photoholder with a pair of doves perched on top; and the eighth edition in the *Fabulous Decade* series. Pike also has designed two ornaments in the Miniature line: the first edition in the *Welcome Friends* series and "Future Star," which depicts an adorable ballerina mouse lounging on a pink ballet slipper.

All About The Artists

Dill Rhodus, husband of Keepsake artist Patricia Andrews, has been with Hallmark for almost 30 years as an engraver and designer. Rhodus' contributions to the 1997 ornament collection can be summed up in three words: *sports* and *Star Wars*! Rhodus' "Hank Aaron" ornament is a fine second edition in the *At The Ballpark* series, while "Joe Namath," the third edition in the *Football Legends* series, celebrates the Jets' greatest quarterback. "Jackie Robinson" commemorates the 50th anniversary of the legendary second baseman becoming the first black player in the majors; this ornament also is the final edition in the *Baseball Heroes* series. Rhodus' Star Wars creations include "Luke Skywalker™" (first edition in the *STAR WARS™* series), a "Darth Vader™" Magic ornament and two-piece miniature set, "C-3PO™ and R2-D2™."

Anita Marra Rogers has been with Hallmark since 1984 and a full time artist since 1987. For 1997, Rogers has created a diverse assortment of ornaments that offers something for everyone. Both old and new *Star Trek* fans will love "Commander Data™" and "Dr. Leonard H. McCoy™." Rogers lends an Asian flavor to the *Dolls of the World* series with the second edition, "Chinese BARBIE™," and catches a slipper-chewing puppy in the act in the seventh edition in the *Puppy Love* series. For the Magic collection, Rogers offers "SNOOPY Plays Santa" and for the Miniatures, a four-piece set based on *The Wizard of Oz*.

Ed Seale has been one of the most prolific artists for Hallmark for nearly 30 years. His versatile style has been captured in no less than 17 designs for 1997, which run the range from his signature mice to racing cars to spacecraft! The *Stock Car Champions* series gets the green flag with the first edition, "Jeff Gordon®," while Seale adds a new edition to the popular and long-running *Frosty Friends* series (18th edition). He also contributes a collector's club piece, a special ornament for the fifth annual National Keepsake Ornament Premiere, and four general Keepsake ornaments. For the Magic collection, Seale has created three ornaments, including "Friendship 7," which commemorates the 35th anniversary of the first American manned spaceflight. Among Seale's four Miniature designs are the latest in his annual set of mice and the third edition in the *Christmas Bells* series.

COLLECTOR'S VALUE GUIDE™

All About The Artists

Linda Sickman has created hundreds of ornaments in her 30 years at Hallmark and Sickman adds 15 more for 1997. Her Keepsake offerings include the fourth edition in the *Yuletide Central* series and the simple yet elegant "Praise Him." Sickman's biggest contribution for 1997 is in the Miniature collection, where she introduces the first edition in a new collectible series, *Antique Tractors*. She also is responsible for new editions in the *Nutcracker Guild* series (fourth), the *Miniature Clothespin Soldier* series (third), the *On the Road* series (fifth), the *Noel R.R.* series (ninth) and the Miniature *Rocking Horse* series, which comes to a close with its 10th and final edition. Another Sickman Miniature design, "Gentle Giraffes," complements the "Noah's Ark" special edition set issued in 1994.

Bob Siedler joined Hallmark in 1979 and has been part of the Keepsake Ornament division since 1981. For 1997, Siedler introduces the first edition in *The Clauses on Vacation* series as well as a very happy "Mr. Potato Head®." Other Keepsake releases by Siedler include three family commemoratives ("Mom," "Dad," "Mom and Dad") and the third annual NFL Collection, much to the delight of football fans! For the Magic collection, Siedler has designed the 13th and final edition in the long-running *Chris Mouse* series, "Chris Mouse Luminaria."

Sue Tague is one of the newer faces in the Hallmark artist roster, but she has already solidified herself as a prolific artist with 20 new designs for 1997. Among Tague's Keepsake ornaments are new editions in the *Language of Flowers* series (second edition), *Crayola® Crayon* series (ninth) and the long-running *Here Comes Santa* series (19th edition). Other whimsical new Keepsake releases from Tague's drafting table are "Catch of the Day," "Stealing a Kiss," and – for those special grandchildren – "Grandson" and "Granddaughter." Tague's new Magic ornaments are "Teapot Party" (a diorama set within a teapot, of course) and "Joy to the World," which features a child trumpeting a goodwill message. Finally, the diligent Tague has designed five new Miniature ornaments which range from endearing ("Heavenly Music") to delightfully silly ("Shutterbug").

COLLECTOR'S
VALUE GUIDE™

Duane Unruh has been with Hallmark for 17 years, but arrived there via an unusual route – he coached high school athletics for 24 years and had no formal art training before joining the Hallmark design team. With his background in athletics, it's only natural that Unruh be the creator of the new *Hockey Greats* series, which debuts with a first edition dedicated to "Wayne Gretzky." Other Keepsake releases by Unruh include the highly-detailed "Santa's Magical Sleigh," "Marbles Champion" (based on a Norman Rockwell design) and "Santa's Tree," which was designed by Marjolein Bastin and sculpted by Unruh. Unruh launches a new collectible series for the Miniature collection, *Teddy-Bear Style*, and adds "Victorian Skater" to the general Miniature line.

LaDene Votruba is the senior member of the Hallmark studio artists, having been with the company for 35 years. An appropriate honor belongs to Votruba this year, as she closes two Keepsake series with final editions: "Kolyada," an elegant and ethereal figure, is the third and final edition in the *Christmas Visitors* series; and "Little Boy Blue" draws the curtain on the *Mother Goose* series as the fifth and final edition. Votruba is also the designer of a pair of "Baby's First Christmas" ornaments and the striking new "Classic Cross," an ornate holy symbol. Votruba's contribution to the Magic collection is an angel with a glowing halo and wings holding a bouquet of roses. New to the Showcase Ornaments are a stained-glass style ornament trimmed in gold ("Heavenly Song") and a porcelain Snowman that doubles as a hinged box. For the Miniature collection, Votruba has designed the second edition in *The Nutcracker Ballet* series and a colorful and charming Nativity scene.

Nello Williams, another new arrival to the Hallmark studio, enjoys a special distinction this year as the sole designer of all four Keepsake of Membership ornaments offered to Collector's Club members. The ornaments are based on Clement C. Moore's *The Night Before Christmas*, in honor of the 17th anniversary of the holiday classic. Williams also contributes six ornaments to the general Keepsake line, depicting Santa Claus, various animals and even sports equipment masquerading as snowmen!

COLLECTOR'S
VALUE GUIDE™

Collectors' Corner

Hallmark Cards, Inc. Biography

On January 10, 1910, 18 year old Joyce C. Hall arrived in Kansas City with two shoeboxes of picture postcards and a marketing plan but little money. After a couple of months, Hall had made $200 through his mail-order business. By 1912, his brother Rollie had joined his business and they added greeting cards to their product line. Within three years, they had begun producing some of their own cards. A dozen years after Joyce Hall's arrival, the Hall Brothers firm, which by then also included brother William, had 120 employees and had expanded the line to include gift wrap.

Across the decades, the company continued to grow and expand. In 1954, its name was changed to Hallmark. Joyce Hall turned his chief executive responsibilities over to his son, Donald J. Hall (the current Chairman of the Board), in 1966. In 1967, Hallmark began a series of acquisitions which have included the brand names Springbok and CRAYOLA®. Now a $3 billion enterprise, Hallmark's products haveincluded not only greeting cards, gift wrap and Christmas ornaments but also such items as albums, calendars, candles, mugs, wedding products and writing paper.

Clara Johnson Scroggins Biography

To Clara Johnson Scroggins, ornament collecting is a "healthy sport and a fun exercise for the entire family." As she says, "The Christmas tree is the most traditional part of Christmas to many people around the world. The tree goes up in the beginning of the holiday season, and the season isn't really over until the tree goes down. It's always fun to decorate the tree. It helps you get into the spirit of the holidays and it brings people together." Since she began collecting over 20 years ago, Clara's ornament collection has grown to over 500,000 ornaments of all types and sizes, making Clara the nationally-recognized ornament expert.

COLLECTOR'S
VALUE GUIDE™

Clara Johnson Scroggins was born in Lake Village, Arkansas. She spent her childhood years in Arkansas and later in Illinois. Education was always a big part of her life; her grandfather was the principal of a school, and her brothers and sisters liked to challenge her with quizzes. Clara says she has been curious all her life, and has had a life-long passion for history, particularly reading about the rise and fall of civilizations and stories about royalty. As a young woman, Clara also developed an interest in art, which she studied at the University of Chicago, and at one point she dreamed of being the curator of a museum.

Growing up as part of a big family, it was impossible for Clara to have any "collections" as a child. Anything she possessed for even a short while would eventually be handed down to her younger siblings. Later in life, Clara began to collect rare books, antique sterling pieces (particularly napkin rings), some dolls and original artwork.

Clara began to collect ornaments in earnest in 1972 after buying a silver ornament in memory of her deceased husband. She began collecting Hallmark Keepsake Ornaments from the very first year and the very first ornament in 1973. In 1975, Clara contacted Hallmark in search of information that could help her keep track of her growing collection. Eventually, Clara began compiling information for a book on ornaments. The people at Hallmark were helpful, but Clara recalls they "thought I was a little bit nuts." At the time, the entire Keepsake staff consisted of three artists, an office manager and a department manager (the department was then called "Trim-A-Home") in three little rooms over the parking garage at corporate headquarters and they didn't really believe anyone was collecting Hallmark ornaments.

COLLECTOR'S
VALUE GUIDE™

Collectors' Corner

Clara published her first Hallmark Keepsake Ornament collector's guide in 1983. This comprehensive book profiled the history of Hallmark Keepsake Ornaments since their inception in 1973 and has been cited as a major reason for the rise in popularity of ornament collecting in the United States. It laid the groundwork for a whole new industry of secondary market dealers, ornament shows and publications. In addition to her Hallmark book, which has been printed in six editions, Clara writes a regular column on ornaments in *Collector's mart magazine* and has contributed articles to numerous magazines. The seventh edition of Clara's Hallmark book should be released in 1998 to commemorate the 25th Anniversary of Hallmark Keepsake Ornaments. She also has appeared on several national television and radio talk shows and keeps a busy schedule of personal appearances at collectible shows and Artists On Tour events all over the country.

Production, Packaging And Pricing

Ornaments range in size from 1-3/4" to approximately 5". Miniatures are all smaller than 1-3/4". Prices run from approximately $3 for some of the Miniatures to $40 for some of the Magic ornaments. Most ornaments are marked with the Hallmark copyright and year, and many are dated, although ornaments from the early years of Hallmark Keepsake Ornaments were not marked at all (not even with the Hallmark name). Pieces which are marked with a small pine tree and number are part of a collectible series (although some early series did not include the special marking). Each ornament is packaged in individual boxes with a picture of the ornament on the front, the logo and year, stock number and country of origin. Ornaments are protected by various packings including plastic, bubble wrap, Styrofoam and foam rubber.

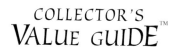

COLLECTOR'S
VALUE GUIDE™

All About The Collector's Club

The Hallmark Keepsake Ornament Collector's Club is the official Hallmark collector's club. Introduced in 1987, it now has a membership of about 300,000.

Hallmark Keepsake Ornament Collector's Club
P.O. Box 419824
Kansas City, MO 64141-6824
1-800-523-5839

For a one-year membership fee of $22.50, 1997 club members will enjoy four gift Keepsake of Membership ornaments based on the holiday classic, *The Night Before Christmas*; four quarterly issues of the *Collector's Courier*, the club's official newsletter; invitations to attend special Hallmark events; a copy of the Dream Book, Hallmark's annual color ornament catalog; and a personalized membership card.

In addition to these free benefits, club members will also have the opportunity to purchase three special Club Edition ornaments that are not available to the general public. "1989 Happy Holidays® BARBIE® Doll" is the second edition in the *Collector's Club Exclusive* series and complements the *Holiday BARBIE*™ series. "1937 Steelcraft Airflow by Murray®" is a die-cast metal pedal car replica that complements the *Kiddie Car Classics* series in the Keepsake collection. The third ornament, "Farmer's Market, Tender Touches" is a delightful design that complements the Tender Touches "Bumper Crop" set in the Easter Ornaments collection.

Club members also will have the opportunity to attend one of ten Artist on Tour events, where club members can participate in workshops, watch demonstrations and, best of all, meet the Hallmark artists. Two special ornaments will be available at these events that have been designed and signed by no less than 19 artists!

COLLECTOR'S
VALUE GUIDE™

Collectors' Corner

Now That's The Way To Display: Twelve Tips

Whether you are new to ornament collecting or your collection numbers in the hundreds, there's always something to learn about creatively displaying your ornament collection. In this section, we've selected twelve tips to help you with your display. While many Hallmark Ornaments are Christmas ornaments, they really can be displayed and enjoyed all year long!

1. Spice up your Christmas tree by creating little vignettes on different sections of your tree. For example, put all your ornaments starring Santa in one section and put ornaments with mice on them in another area.

2. Display your ornaments on wreaths. You can select ornaments by theme (heart ornaments on a heart-shaped wreath) or decor (the rustic-looking Folk Art Americana ornaments on a straw wreath in a "Country" room).

3. Create tabletop displays out of series such as *Nostalgic Houses and Shops*, *Crayola® Crayon* or the new Miniature set "Tiny Home Improvers." Paint a flat piece of cardboard black and add stripes to create a parking lot for *Classic American Cars* or *All-American Trucks* ornaments. You can even edge the cardboard with foam snow drifts.

4. Decorate a miniature tree with special ornaments for someone you love. For example, cover the tree with "Murray Inc.® 'Pursuit' Airplane," "Miniature Clothespin Soldier," "Snowboard Bunny" and "Antique Tractors" for a young boy or "Snowflake Ballet," "Seeds of Joy," "Polar Buddies" and "Victorian Skater" for a young girl.

5. To make a simple but stunning display, select a branch from a deciduous tree after the leaves have fallen off and spray paint it gold. Secure the branch to a base and hang ornaments from it.

6. Use your collection year-round. Try decorating cupcakes with Miniature ornaments, hang ornaments off of cup hooks in the kitchen ("Cat Naps") or hook your favorite Miniature ornaments to a charm bracelet for new ways to enjoy your collection every day!

7. Wear your collection on your sleeve! Attach a different ornament to your lapel to give yourself a new look every day. Or better yet, cover a whole sweatshirt with them. Take a red, green or white sweatshirt and sew strips of ribbon on it (fold the ribbon lengthwise and tack at the center) then tie Miniature ornaments to the ribbon. They can easily be changed or taken off for laundry day.

8. Magic ornaments can be surrounded by holly or evergreens and used as centerpieces. This year's "Lighthouse Greetings," "Chris Mouse Luminaria" and "Teapot Party" would make particularly good table top displays where you can get close and really enjoy them.

9. Combine your ornaments with your other favorite collectibles. For example, you could display the BARBIE™ ornaments with real BARBIE™ dolls or place the *Classic American Cars* on the streets of a lighted village display.

10. For a tabletop display, use polyester quilt batting to create a "heavenly" cloud and arrange various angel ornaments on it.

11. Make a mobile with wooden embroidery hoops (painted red or green) or make a "tree" out of graduated length dowels in a triangle shape and hang ornaments off of them.

12. Mix Hallmark ball ornaments with solid red ball ornaments and intersperse dried flowers (baby's breath or wheat stalks) and simple red ribbons to create a magical old-fashioned Hallmark tree.

Collectors' Notebook

Address Book

Use this space to list your favorite retailers, fellow collectors, collectors clubs, secondary market dealers or anyone who is an important part of your collecting hobby.

Name _____

Address _____

_____

Phone _____

Notes _____

Name _____

Address _____

_____

Phone _____

Notes _____

Name _____

Address _____

_____

Phone _____

Notes _____

Name _____

Address _____

_____

Phone _____

Notes _____

COLLECTOR'S
VALUE GUIDE™

Collectors' Notebook

Name _____

Address _____

_____

Phone _____

Notes _____

Name _____

Address _____

_____

Phone _____

Notes _____

Name _____

Address _____

_____

Phone _____

Notes _____

Name _____

Address _____

_____

Phone _____

Notes _____

Name _____

Address _____

_____

Phone _____

Notes _____

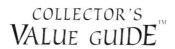

COLLECTOR'S
VALUE GUIDE™

Collectors' Notebook

Monthly Planner

This monthly planner is for your notes about store events, collector shows, club meetings, etc. in your area.

January

February

March

1997 Dream Books are released.

Sneak-A-Peek preview at stores.

April

May

June

COLLECTOR'S
VALUE GUIDE™

Collectors' Notebook

July

1997 Keepsake Ornament Premiere, July 19 & 20.

Artists On Tour event in Cincinnati (7/26).

August

Artists On Tour events in Detroit (8/16) & San Francisco (8/23).

September

Artists On Tour events in Atlanta (9/6),

Kansas City (9/13) and Chicago (9/27).

October

Artists On Tour events in Philadelphia (10/4),

Washington, D.C. (10/11) and Dallas (10/25).

November

Artists On Tour event in Los Angeles (11/1).

1997 Hallmark Holiday Open House, November 15 & 16.

December

Christmas Day, December 25.

COLLECTOR'S
VALUE GUIDE™

Collectors' Notebook

Collection Notes

   This section is designed for you to write down important notes about your Hallmark collection.

Artists on Tour Ornaments—a piece made available *only* at Hallmark artists' appearances. There are two Artists on Tour ornaments for 1997: "Trimming Santa's Tree" (set/2) and "Mrs. Claus's Story." The ornaments are pre-signed by all 19 artists who collaborated on them.

collectibles—anything and everything that is "able to be collected," whether it's figurines, dolls . . . or even *bumper stickers* can be considered a "collectible," but it is generally recognized that a true collectible should be something that increases in value over time.

collectible series—a Hallmark Ornament collectible series consists of annual editions released one per year over several years. Each year, Hallmark introduces several new series and ends several others. Each Hallmark series runs for at least three consecutive years and several have run for longer than ten years.

collection—a grouping of Hallmark Ornaments which have a common theme and are released in the same year (unlike a collectible series, which is spread over several years). Among the 1997 collections are "Classic Movies" and "The Disney Collection."

Collector's Choice—an annual "award" given by Clara Johnson Scroggins to a Hallmark ornament that best exemplifies the spirit of Christmas or is a "can't miss" ornament. "The Night Before Christmas" in the Keepsake collection is the winner for 1997.

commemoratives—ornaments, usually dated with the year, which celebrate special people (grandmother or sister) or special events (anniversaries or baby's first birthday).

DB (damaged box)—a secondary market term used when a collectible item's original box is in poor condition, thus usually diminishing the value of the item.

Dream Book—a color pamphlet issued by Hallmark each year which includes a listing and photographs of the new Keepsake Ornaments for that year.

editions (ed.)—new ornaments released each year which are part of a Hallmark new or ongoing series. For example, "Jackie Robinson" is the 4th and final edition in the *Baseball Heroes* series.

Gold Crown Store—Hallmark stores that meet a certain criteria become classified as "Gold Crown Stores." Selected products are available only through Gold Crown dealers.

handcrafted—the manufacturing process of many Hallmark Ornaments in which the ornaments are hand-assembled and hand-painted.

Glossary

Keepsake Ornaments—the brand name for Hallmark's line of ornaments, which includes miniature, light and motion and regular-size ornaments, although the term "Keepsake" is often used to distinguish the regular ornament line from the Magic and Miniature lines.

limited edition (LE)—a piece scheduled for a predetermined production quantity or time period. All Hallmark Keepsake Ornaments are limited to one year of availability and have varied production runs contingent upon demand.

Magic Ornaments—the Hallmark line of ornaments, first introduced in 1984, which incorporates animated features, such as light and motion.

member only pieces—several ornaments each year are made available only to members of the Hallmark Keepsake Ornament Collector's Club.

MIB (mint in box)—a secondary market term used when a collectible item's original box is in "as good as new" condition, which usually adds to the value of the item.

NB (no box)—a secondary market term used when a collectible item's original box is missing. For most collectibles, having the original box is a factor in the value on the secondary market.

Ornament Premiere—a Hallmark store event featuring the debut of the year's new ornaments. In 1997, the special issue pieces "The Perfect Tree, Tender Touches" and "Snowbear Season" (set/3) are available only at Premiere events.

secondary market—the source for buying and selling collectibles according to basic supply-and-demand principles ("pay what the market will bear"). Popular pieces which have retired or have low production quantities can appreciate in value far above the original retail issue price.

trimmers—holiday tree decorations that are lower in price and are not boxed. They are not part of the Hallmark Keepsake Ornament collection.

"unannounced" series—groups of ornaments that aren't part of official series, but can be connected by theme. For example, The "Superman™" ornaments from 1993 and 1995, the "Batman" ornament from 1994 and the new "The Incredible Hulk®" ornament can be grouped into an unofficial superheroes series.

Alphabetical Index

– Key –

All Hallmark Keepsake Ornaments, Spring Ornaments, Merry Miniatures and Kiddie Car Classics are listed below in alphabetical order. The first number refers to the piece's location within the Value Guide section and the second to the box in which it is pictured on that page.

– A –

Alphabetical Index

Alphabetical Index
– B, cont. –

– C, cont. –

– C, cont. –

Alphabetical Index

– F, cont. –

– F, cont. –

– G –

Alphabetical Index

– G, cont. –

Alphabetical Index

– H, cont. –

– I –

Alphabetical Index

Alphabetical Index
– M, cont. –

– O –

Alphabetical Index

Alphabetical Index
– S, cont. –

Alphabetical Index

Alphabetical Index